The Illustrated Complete Musical Instruments Handbook

Rebecca Berkley, Andrew Cleaton, Alan Charlton,
Andrew Cronshaw, Robin Newton, Jeremy Siepmann

General Editor: Lucien Jenkins

Foreword by Evelyn Glennie

FLAME TREE
PUBLISHING

CONTENTS

SECTION ONE: THE INSTRUMENTS

PERCUSSION

Musical Instruments Handbook

BRASS

WOODWIND

Musical Instruments Handbook

STRINGED INSTRUMENTS

KEYBOARDS

Musical Instruments Handbook

ELECTRIC AND ELECTRONIC

SECTION TWO: REFERENCE

Musical Instruments Handbook

A-Z OF INSTRUMENTS

Musical Instruments Handbook

Musical Instruments Handbook

CASTAGNARI

Musical Instruments Handbook

Musical Instruments Handbook

Musical Instruments Handbook

Musical Instruments Handbook

HOW TO USE THIS BOOK

The *Illustrated Complete Musical Instruments Handbook* is divided into two sections.

Section One contains individual entries on instruments or families of instruments. It is divided into six parts, each one dealing with a particular group of instruments, from Percussion to Electric and Electronic. The entries in each section are subdivided by type of instrument – for example, the entries in the Brass section are divided by non-valved instruments and valved instruments.

Section Two is a reference section, comprising essays on the chronological development, rise and fall of instruments over the centuries, and outlining different types of ensemble. In addition to this, there is a databank of charts explaining decibels and pitches of the most common instruments, as well as an extensive glossary explaining terms that might be unfamiliar.

THERE ARE A NUMBER OF WAYS OF USING THIS BOOK.

You can use the contents listing on **page 4** to direct you to the entry on the instrument or type of instrument you want to find out about.

The complete A-Z listing of instruments on **page 8** contains every instrument that has an entry or a significant reference in this book. It will direct you straight to the entry or reference for the particular instrument you are interested in.

The introductory spreads for each section, found on **pages 20, 92, 124, 188, 258 and 300**, will give you an overview of the history of that instrument family, the construction and playing techniques.

The Chronological Overview on **page 344** offers a timeline of the development of the key instruments, placing them in historical context and allowing you to trace their rise, fall and in some cases, revival, from early times to the twenty-first century.

The Ensembles section on **page 364** will allow you to discover the role of particular instruments in the orchestra or other ensembles, placing the instrument in its musical context in relation to others.

Musical Instruments Handbook

INTRODUCTION

When people look for a book about music and music history, they tend to expect – and find – a book about composers, in the first instance. If their knowledge of music theory is up to it, they may turn to a book of studies in music analysis, looking in detail at the way in which a composer or series of composers built the melodies and harmonies of their pieces.

This is a book that offers to tackle the history and geography of music from a different angle. Here, the focus is on the instruments for which the music was written and on which it was performed and recorded. Nor is the story limited to history, for we look at music's geography as well.

Throughout the book, the authors have looked at the way in which countless musical instruments were first made, how they developed over time, and how they vary in construction and use from country to country.

This is a story of animals' bones and horns, of the timbers of European fruit trees and tropical woods. It is a story of glues and varnishes, or different metal alloys, the different bores and different kinds of reed, and the sounds they give you when blown. The story takes us back to biblical times, around the world and into the modern recording studio. It looks at the way in which, after a long period of instrumental change and development, the late-twentieth century suddenly started investigating medieval, Renaissance and Baroque instruments, previously considered obsolete, and bringing them back into currency after years, sometimes centuries, of neglect and desuetude.

Musical Instruments Handbook

It looks at the inventors and innovators, whose names have never been as well known as the composers and performers, but without whose achievements the music we listen to today would be very different. Who invented the oboe? Who gave Beethoven the piano he was looking for? But equally, what happened to the keyed bugle, the serpent and the ophicleide?

The books also looks at the way in which instruments fit together – after all, music is not purely a story of individuals picking up an instrument and performing alone, it is also about groups forming. What is it about certain combinations that have proved classics, while others have been tried once and then abandoned?

Adopting an international perspective, we have looked for the similarities and differences, so that you will be able to see the way instrument types spread across the world, from the long journeys taken by the shawm to the rise of the bow. This way, a series of links between western music and musics in the furthest parts of the world begins to become clear. Equally, by noticing links, we become more aware of what makes the western world's own varied wealth of music, which is so easy to take for granted, what it is. In this context, we can notice how it is actually an unusually strange and exciting phenomenon, which has roots in many parts of the world, and has, over the last couple of centuries, been adopted and adapted in almost every part of the world.

Lucien Jenkins
2006

Musical Instruments Handbook

FOREWORD

Perhaps the one instrument that is not listed in this fascinating handbook is "Planet Earth"! We all know that if we care to take the time to listen – truly listen – Planet Earth is indeed one giant instrument. From it we experience sounds that the human body can digest without electronic enhancements and then there are infinite sounds that we simply cannot experience except by scientific/electronic means. It is not only an instrument but our very own back-drop to "paint" sound from the myriad sound inventions that man continues to develop.

For me whose profession is a sound creator, living in the twenty-first century is indeed a fascinating time – the ease of travel, the myriad source materials, the explosion of the internet, and the explosion of recorded material means we can all share in the curious world of sound. It can be as private or as social as we want. The time of day, the occasion or event, our mood, and our culture all play a part in the manifold interpretations we each give to sound.

As I write this, I look at my book collection. It ranges from "Bells & Man", "Islamic Musical Instruments" books on the African Balafon, the Musical Saw and Antique Musical Instruments to the development of Electronic Instruments. The list goes on. As a percussion player myself I am rather curious that I cannot put an exact number of how many instruments there are in the percussion family. I own more than 1800 but I know there is easily twice that number. I'm secretly happy of being ignorant to this question for it will allow continual fascination from both professionals and amateurs in years to come to look at the past, present and future of our sound heritage. As we surge forward in our exploration of musical instruments we know it is a subject that builds healthy relationships from all corners of the globe, and even more interesting now that many of the third world territories are opening up to us all due to the internet explosion.

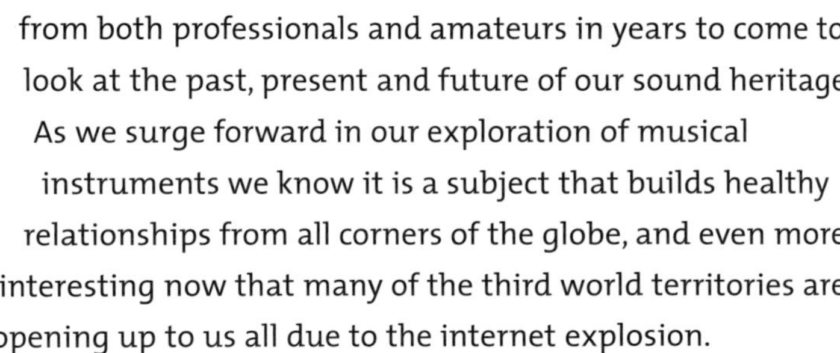

Musical Instruments Handbook

But the terms "professional" and "amateur" don't come into play when dealing with sound creation because we know the importance of sound whilst still in the womb, or the impact sound has when in the final stages of our lives. Look how we embrace sound when feeling happy, or sound at a wedding or a funeral, when studying or going to party – this list goes on and on. It is something we can all choose to participate in whether as sound creators or engaged listeners. At least we can agree that music is our daily medicine and at least once a day we experience some kind of musical instrument.

The *Illustrated Handbook of Musical Instruments* will undoubtedly be a great source to a great number of people from all walks of life – the human race continues, as I write, to push the boundaries in its creativity towards the development of sound especially due to our increasing awareness and importance of sound therapy. The sound world of our everyday changing environment affects our innate listening skills, which in turn affects the instrument development, and the changing ways of teaching music to others. But surely the main musical instrument is our own body and imagination. When we decide to open it up like a resonating chamber we suddenly realise that the body becomes ultra responsive to the mechanics and emotion of sound. All class barriers and categorizations come tumbling down because we are so focused on this wholesome and organic approach to sound.

As we delve into this vast range of listed instruments we are instantly aware that every part of our body will be engaged in experiencing the instruments. They come in all shapes and sizes which is testament to man's continued inventiveness. This new handbook will undoubtedly help stimulate more ideas, experimentation, knowledge, curiosity and most of all fun.

Evelyn Glennie, OBE
June 2006, Cambridgeshire

Musical Instruments Handbook

INTRODUCTION

PERCUSSION

Percussion instruments are a diverse and interesting family. Every human culture plays them, and they are among the oldest instruments known to man. Percussion instruments are indispensable to practically every genre and style of music.

In many cultures, the leader of a musical ensemble plays a percussion instrument to give signals to the other performers, such as when to stop, and to maintain the music's rhythm. Percussion has religious and spiritual significance. Advertisers 'drum up business', an expression that goes back to travelling actors playing drums to attract an audience for their performances.

▲ *Percussion is probably the oldest of the instrumental groups.*

The percussion family incorporates some of the very largest and smallest instruments, from the Japanese *o-daiko* or fat drum, which is a huge 240 cm (96 in) diameter and 240 cm (96 in) long, down to tiny ankle bells worn by dancers. Percussion instruments can be very simple to make, such as a dried bean-pod shaker, or they can require complex and expensive engineering processes like western church bells. Percussionists often train for years to become master performers on their instruments.

◀ *Shaken instruments are thought to predate the drum.*

Musical Instruments Handbook

◀ *Cowbells are often mounted on top of timbales.*

WHAT IS PERCUSSION?

All percussion instruments are struck to make them sound. They can be hit, shaken and scraped, or made to vibrate by friction. They are struck with the hands or with beaters, or struck against one another like a pair of cymbals. Percussion beaters or sticks come in an enormous variety of shapes and sizes. Sometimes the beater may be part of the instrument – like the clapper on a bell – or hidden inside the instrument – like the hammers of a celesta. Percussionists in an orchestra or theatre-pit band may also find themselves playing a host of other instruments and sound effects.

Drums, or membranophones, are struck on the membrane or skin. This is stretched over a hollow body that acts as a resonator and amplifier. Drums are classified according to the shape of their body. All other percussion instruments are idiophones – literally, instruments that sound of themselves. These include instruments like the triangle, which is made of a sonorous material that vibrates when struck. Idiophones can also have resonators to project their sound.

TUNING

Unlike other instruments, both drums and idiophones can be both tuned and untuned. The acoustic construction of the instrument will determine whether or not it can play a specific pitch. Like all instruments, the sound of a percussion instrument is a combination of the fundamental frequency and a series of overtones or harmonics that the ear hears as a homogenous sound. If the overtones are in a harmonic relationship with the fundamental tone, then the ear hears this as a pitched note, as in a tuned percussion instrument like the steel pan or the xylophone. In an untuned percussion instrument like the tambourine, the overtones are not in a harmonic relationship and the ear hears this as noise. Untuned instruments of different sizes may be constructed to make higher or lower sounds, like the tom toms on a drum kit, but they can't be tuned to a pitched note.

▲ *Timbales are played with sticks.*

Section One: The Instruments

QUALITIES OF SOUND

The way the instrument is constructed and the material from which it is made will emphasize certain overtones, and this contributes to its tone colour or timbre. In drums, the shape of the body, the type of skin that the drumhead is made from, how the drumhead is attached to the body of the drum, and what kind of beaters are used are all significant. An African *djembe* is made from goat or calf skin, which is shaved to be very thin on the playing surface. The animal's hair is left around the rim of the drum to muffle the lower frequencies, and both factors contribute to give the drum a bright and ringing sound, clearly distinguishable from the other drums in the ensemble.

▲ *Hands, brushes, beaters, rods, even twigs are used to play drums.*

Where on its playing surface you hit a percussion instrument will also result in different qualities of sound. When an instrument is struck, it produces soundwaves that have 'nodal' and 'antinodal' points. There is no displacement of the soundwave at nodal points, so the instrument will make a limited resonant sound when struck at that spot. The instrument will make a resonant sound when struck at an antinodal point, where there is maximum displacement of the soundwave.

Different musical cultures favour different sounds from percussion instruments. For example, the nodal point on a drum with a bowl-shaped body, like a timpani or kettledrum, is at the centre of the skin. Hitting the drum directly in the middle produces a dull sound. Its antinodes are found at about one-sixth of its diameter in from the rim, and this is the point to hit for maximum resonance. An orchestral timpanist will play the drum only at this point to produce a rich, ringing sound. Indian tabla are also kettledrums, and the tabla player will strike the drum on both nodal and antinodal points on the skin in order to get different sonorities and pitches from the instrument.

Musical Instruments Handbook

▲ *African drums can be made to 'speak' very realistically.*

GLOBAL PERCUSSION

The global map of percussion shows links between instruments in different locations. African concepts of barrel and waisted or goblet drums, shakers, scrapers, bells, and log xylophones travelled to the New World with African slaves and are commonly used in Latin-American music. The orchestral xylophone and marimba also descend from the traditional African instrument. Bells and gongs originated in the Far East and India, and travelled into Western Europe with returning Christian missionaries. Western military drums like the snare drum and timpani, as well as frame drums, derive from Middle Eastern drums. The Turkish cymbal has also been widely used in western music, and is played in the orchestra, and in the drum kit. Percussion instruments have also been developed through local ingenuity – one good example being the Caribbean steel pans.

► *Natural materials are commonly used as instruments, such as the axatse, a hollowed-out gourd.*

Section One: The Instruments

CONGA AND BONGO

Barrel-shaped drums are usually constructed either from a single log, which is carved into a barrel shape like Japanese *byou-daiko* drums, or made like a wine barrel from staves of wood glued together or bound with metal strips, as in conga and bongo drums. Barrel drums can have two heads or a single head, and are played with hands or beaters.

CONGA

The conga, or *tumbadora* (25–30 cm/10–15 in diameter, 50–60 cm/20–24 in long), is a single-headed Latin-American barrel drum used throughout South America, and in pop and jazz fusion music. The conga is the largest hand drum used in Latin America, and may be descended from Congolese *makuta* drums.

▲ *Conga players use all parts of their hand to produce different sounds.*

In modern congas and bongos, the body is made from wooden staves glued and clamped together, or it is moulded from fibreglass, with the calfskin head held in place by a metal ring bolted to the body of the drum with tension rods. The drum is not tuned, but the skin is tightened to give a high ringing sound when played. When played singly, the drummer tilts the conga towards them to allow sound to resonate from the open end. When played in groups of two or three they are placed in a stand.

Conga-playing technique is very similar to the *djembe* (see p. 33). The player produces three tones: by slapping the middle of the drumhead with a cupped hand to get a bass tone; by playing an open slap on the side of the head to produce a medium tone; and by playing a closed slap on the rim of the drum to get a dry, high tone. The side of the drum can also be played with a stick.

BONGO

Bongos are a pair of small, single-headed drums joined together (15 cm/6 in diameter, 20 cm/8 in long; 20 cm/8 in diameter, 30 cm/15 in long). Both the larger (*hembra*) or female drum and the smaller (*macho*) drum are truncated cones. They also have calfskin heads, but these are thinner than conga heads, and tuned to a higher pitch. The bongos are held between the knees or placed on a stand.

▲ *Bongos are unequal in size: the smaller drum is called the 'male', or minor drum, the larger is the 'female' or major drum.*

Both congas and bongos are widely used in Cuban *son*, which originated in the late-nineteenth century. This combined Spanish music with African drumming styles and is the ancestor of salsa. A typical *son* ensemble includes a vocalist, guitars and string bass; and bongos, congas, maracas, guiro and claves. Bongos also are played in salsa, rumba, mambo, and cha-cha music. Within an ensemble, the bongo player leads the other percussion with improvised solos and decorations on the main rhythm. Throughout Latin America, the term 'bongo' is also used for timbales, a pair of single-headed cylindrical drums invented in Cuba in the 1940s, and commonly used in many styles of Afro-Latin music.

Section One: The Instruments

▼ *A medieval kettle drum.*

TIMPANI

Timpani are bowl drums or kettledrums, constructed by stretching a skin across a round metal, wooden or pottery bowl. They are beaten with sticks or leather thongs. Timpani originated in Islamic countries in Africa and the Middle East, where they were used to accompany hunting and for ceremonial and military music.

> **Fact**
>
> **Henry VIII had a mounted ensemble of 12 trumpets and kettledrums, whose main function was to create a noisy spectacle to accompany the king when out in public.**

TUNING

Tuning a large kettledrum or timpani to produce a pitch accurately is an engineering challenge. The drum needs a mechanism to stretch a skin of consistent thickness over a perfect circle and hold it at the appropriate tension. The mechanism also needs to be able to cope with altering the tension of the head if the drum is to be retuned to another note.

▲ *The tuning indicators of a timpani drum.*

The invention of the screw-tensioning tuning mechanism in Germany in the sixteenth century was the first step towards this goal. Instead of lacing the skin to the drum, as in the medieval drum, it was stretched over a metal ring, held in place by metal brackets incorporating tuning screws clamped to the side of the bowl. The tuning screws were adjusted by means of a removable key. This was later replaced by T-shaped taps set around the rim of the drum, which were easier and quieter to use.

EARLY TIMPANI

Timpani first appear in the orchestra in *Thésée* (1675) by Jean-Baptiste Lully (1632–87). Until Carl Maria von Weber (1786–1826) used three timpani in the overture to the opera *The Ruler of the Spirits* in 1811, the orchestra used two hand-tuned timpani with vellum heads of about 60–75 cm (24–30 in) diameter, played with wooden sticks. Like the trumpets, timpani music was scored in C with an indication of the key to which the player should tune the drums:

▲ *Timpani music scored in C.*

The drums almost invariably played the tonic (I) and dominant (V) notes, and rarely retuned during the music. As a result, the timpani only played in the tonic key. In *Messiah* by George Frideric Handel (1685–1759), the timpanist only plays twice in the whole work.

LATER DEVELOPMENTS

In the nineteenth century, instrument makers began to produce machine timpani that could retune more easily, enabling players to play more chromatic parts. A master screw that altered the pitch of all the tuning screws at once was introduced in 1812. However, this model placed much of the tuning mechanism inside the bowl of the drum and impaired the purity of the tone.

A German system invented around 1850 altered the tension of the head by rotating the whole drum. Pedal-tuned drums appeared around 1880, and became the norm in orchestras from the early-twentieth century. Sir Henry Wood (1869–1944) introduced pedal timpani to England in 1905. Plastic timpani heads were introduced around 1960, providing a durable skin far less affected by atmospheric conditions than vellum, which sagged and went flat when the air was humid, and tightened and went sharp when the air was dry – thus altering the pitch of the drum after it had been tuned.

Section One: The Instruments

NINETEENTH-CENTURY COMPOSITIONS

▲ *Older timpani have T-taps around the rim.*

Following the innovations in its construction, composers began to use the timpani as a soloist within the orchestra during the nineteenth century. Ludwig van Beethoven (1770–1827) included a duet between the timpanist and the piano soloist in his Fifth Piano Concerto (1809).

The use of three drums or more became increasingly common from the 1820s onwards and composers explored ways of using the timpani to create orchestral colour. Hector Berlioz (1803–69) was the first composer to specify sticks covered in sponge, wood and leather to achieve different timbres. Richard Wagner (1813–83) used muffled drums in *Parsifal* (1882). In the *Symphonie fantasique* (1830), Berlioz used four timpanists playing overlapping rolls to achieve thunder effects.

TWENTIETH-CENTURY COMPOSITIONS

In the twentieth century, increasing demands were made on the technical competence of the timpanist. These demands included rapid retuning of the drums to play chromatic music on a single drum, as in Béla Bartók's (1881–1945) *Concerto for Orchestra* (1943) and the use of *glissandi* in Carl Nielsen's (1865–1931) Fourth Symphony (1915). There are some works for timpanist as a soloist in its own right, including the *Concerto Fantasy for Two Timpani and Orchestra* (2000) by Philip Glass (b. 1937) and concertos for organ, timpani and strings by Francis Poulenc (1899–1963) and Jean Langlais (1907–91).

THE MODERN TIMPANI

Typically, a modern symphony orchestra will have five timpani, covering a range of *D* to *b*. The timpanist uses a range of different sticks of varying thicknesses, covered in felt, wool, cork, rubber and plastic, to achieve different timbres. Rolls are played as single-stroke rolls. Each drum has a reliable range of a fifth, as tuning becomes inconsistent at the extreme ends of a drum's range.

Although there are differences between manufacturers, generally the modern pedal timpani has a hemispherical or parabolic bowl with a lip turned over and inward. A strengthening collar is placed inside the lip of the bowl. The drumhead

Musical Instruments Handbook

▼ *Pedals enable the drums to be re-tuned in a second or two.*

is mounted on a hoop, which is laid over the open bowl and a counterhoop is laid over the top. The counterhoop is attached to six to eight tension screws, which clamp to the bowl of the drum. Each tension screw is also attached to a rod, which travels vertically down the outside of the drum and is attached to the pedal mechanism. Moving the pedal moves all the rods and tension screws together, which in turn alters the tension of the drumhead. The pedal is also attached to a tuning gauge, which enables the drummer to tune the drum before a performance.

ORCHESTRAL PERCUSSION

The drums must be damped during rests to keep clarity of tone, especially when playing those tuned a perfect fourth or fifth apart, as is very common in orchestral music. The main note heard when the timpani is struck is the nominal, or the first, overtone. The second overtone sounds a perfect fifth above the nominal and will also resonate when another drum plays that note. So playing a drum tuned to a C will make a drum tuned to a G resonate. However, timpanists use this feature as an aid to silent tuning, which can be useful in the middle of an orchestral piece.

The snare drum, xylophone and timpani are the three main instruments that an orchestral percussionist will learn. It takes many years of training and practise to develop co-ordination, dexterity and a good ear for tuning the drums. The timpanist can be one of the stars of the percussion section, capable of producing a wide range of dynamics, and dominating the whole orchestra when played at full volume.

► *Timpani provide dynamism and colour.*

Section One: The Instruments

TABLA

Tabla are a pair of asymmetrical tuned small kettledrums played in northern Indian classical music. The left-hand drum, or *baya* (27 cm/11 in diameter and 30 cm/15 in long), is a hemispherical drum made of copper or brass, and produces a deep sound. The right-hand drum, or *daya* (18 cm/7 in diameter and 30 cm/15 in long), is a tapering wooden cylinder and produces a higher sound.

The tabla are tuned to the tonic note (*sa*) of the *rag* (scale, melody) being played by the vocal or instrumental soloist. The drumhead is laced to the drum with a single long leather strip running in a 'W' formation between the top and bottom of the drum. Short wooden dowels are wedged under the leather strips on the *daya* and hammered down towards the base or loosened to tune the drum. The rim of the *baya* may be hammered to tighten the skin further.

CONSTRUCTION

The head of each drum is constructed to create a range of different sonorities. Each drumhead comprises two goatskin membranes, the upper being cut away in the middle to leave an outer ring about 7 cm (3 in) wide. Striking the skin on the outer ring and exposed lower skin produces different pitches. In the centre of the skin of the *daya*, and slightly off centre on the *baya*, is a circle of hardened black tuning paste (*siyahi* or *gab*). This is made from a combination of iron oxide, ash, glue, flour and copper vitriol, and makes a dry, unpitched sound when struck.

TABLA SOUNDS

Indian musicians use a system of mnemonics to vocalize rhythms, based on seven basic tabla sounds. Sheila Chandra (b. 1966) performs vocalizations of tabla drumming on her album *Weaving My Ancestors' Voices*. On the *baya*, the sound *ghe* describes sliding the heel of the hand to make a *glissando*, and *kat* is

Musical Instruments Handbook

▲ *All parts of the hand are used to play tabla to bring out the expressive quality of the drums.*

a slap. On the *daya*, the sound *ta* or *na* is played on the outer upper skin. *Tin* is played on the exposed lower skin, and *tu* is played on the black spot. Combining *ta* with *ghe* creates the sound *dha*, and combining *tin* with *ghe* creates the sound *dhin*. *Ta*, *tin*, *dha* and *dhin* are the most common strikes in tabla playing.

Indian music organizes rhythm into cycles of stressed and unstressed beats, which provide a framework (*theká*) to the music. In the rhythmic cycle *tintal* (see below), 16 beats are subdivided into a pattern of 4 + 4 + 4 + 4. The tabla player embellishes the *theká* according to the pattern of the stressed beats, and will include increasingly more complex improvisations or *tukrá* immediately before *sam* returns.

count	1	2	3	4	5	6	7	8	9	10	11	12	13	14	15	16
stress	*Sam* (heavy)				*Tali* (medium)				*Khali* (not stressed)				*Tali* (medium)			
thehá	*dha*	*dhin*	*dhin*	*dha*	*dha*	*dhin*	*dhin*	*dha*	*dha*	*tin*	*tin*	*ta*	*ta*	*dhin*	*dhin*	*dha*

▲ Tintal.

Section One: The Instruments

DJEMBE

Goblet and hourglass drums are commonly found in Africa, the Middle East and the Far East. They are not normally tuned to a specific pitch, although the heads may be tightened to create different sonorities. The *djembe* is perhaps the best-known of this type of drum.

GOBLET AND HOURGLASS DRUMS

Goblet drums are single-headed drums shaped like a wineglass, with a hollow bowl tapering to a long, thin body. Hourglass or waisted drums are double-headed drums with a body shaped like two goblet drums attached to each other. Hourglass drums often have floating heads, where the drumhead is stretched across a metal frame that is wider than the drum body. It rests on the drum body but is not attached to it. The heads stay in place by being laced to each other.

In both types of drum, the drum head may be tightened by using tuning pegs, as in the African *kpanlogo* and Middle Eastern *dumbek*, bracing sleeves, as in the Korean *changgo*, or by adjusting the lacing of the drumhead, as in the African sabar drums. Hourglass drums may be tuned so that one head is higher than the other.

CONSTRUCTION

The *djembe* (32–40 cm/13–16 in diameter and 60 cm/24 in long) is played throughout West Africa. It first came to world attention in the 1950s through the European tours of Les Ballets Africains. Latterly, the increased popularity of world music has also helped disseminate its influence.

Musical Instruments Handbook

The *djembe* is normally played with the hands. Traditionally these drums are carved from a single log and have a solid body below the cup of the goblet. The interior of the drum has a series of teardrop-shaped divots that enhance the drum timbre. The head is made from goatskin or calfskin, and is laced to the drum body with cords running vertically down the drum. More cords are woven horizontally through the vertical cords to tighten the head.

Djembes made by western percussion companies may have fibreglass or metal bodies, or wooden bodies made from glued-together slats, skin or plastic heads, with a metal ring holding the drum head in place and metal tuning pegs like a western snare drum.

▲ *Contemporary* djembes *are made from modern materials that pay respect to musical traditions.*

PLAYING TECHNIQUE

Djembe playing technique is similar to that of other goblet and conical drums in West Africa and the Middle East. As with many musical cultures, drum rhythms are vocalized. Playing the centre of the head with the palm and letting it ring produces a bass note, called *goun* (right hand or dominant hand) or *doun* (left hand). An open note played at the rim with fingers only is called *goh* (right hand) or *doh* (left hand). A slap sound has a higher pitch and is played with the cupped hand at the rim. This is called *pa* (right hand) and *ta* (left hand).

◄ *Ivory Coast percussion masters Yelemba D'Abidjan perform on* djembes *at the Womad Festival, UK.*

Section One: The Instruments

DRUMS OF WEST AFRICA

Drumming in West Africa is a rural indigenous art form, and it accompanies dance and singing. Master drummers are members of the *griot* class of professional musical entertainers. These men lead the drumming and promote the tradition by teaching students.

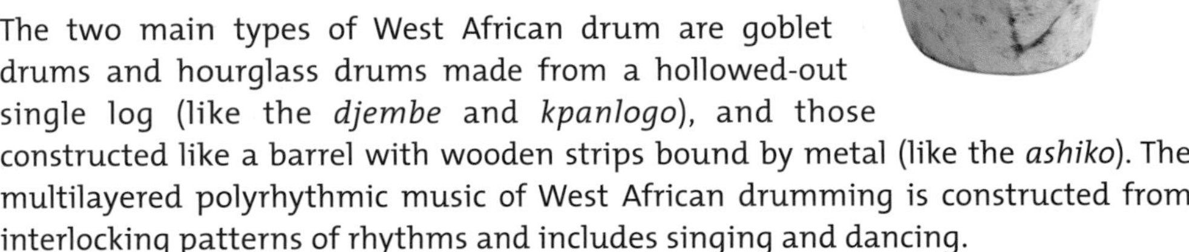

The two main types of West African drum are goblet drums and hourglass drums made from a hollowed-out single log (like the *djembe* and *kpanlogo*), and those constructed like a barrel with wooden strips bound by metal (like the *ashiko*). The multilayered polyrhythmic music of West African drumming is constructed from interlocking patterns of rhythms and includes singing and dancing.

DRUM ENSEMBLES

Drum ensembles utilize a range of different sonorities, and drummers use various playing techniques with sticks and hands to achieve different sounds. Drum ensembles usually also include an *agogo* bell, which leads the ensemble, providing a pulse and starting and stopping signals, and a *calabash* rattle covered with shells or seeds. They are used to accompany singing and dancing at secular and sacred entertainments and ceremonies.

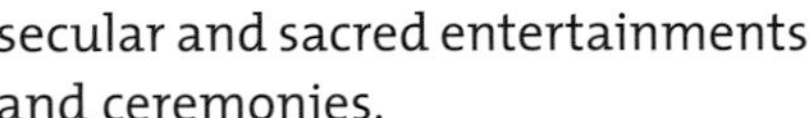

▲ *Talking drum ceremony at the Nmayem harvest festival, Ghana.*

DJUN DJUN

The *djun djun*, *ashiko* and *djembe* form the ubiquitous West African drumming ensemble. The *djun djun* (40 cm/16 in diameter and 53 cm/21 in long) is found throughout West Africa. It is a cylindrical, double-headed bass drum with cowskin or goatskin heads. The fur

Musical Instruments Handbook

▼ A djun djun, *or talking drum.*

is usually left on the skin around the sides of the drum to dampen higher frequencies and thus create a deep, resonant sound. Small, medium and large *djun djuns* are called *sangba, kenkeni* and *dunumba* respectively. The *djun djun* is usually worn in a harness and played with two sticks – one strikes the head and the other plays a bell tied to the side of the drum.

ASHIKO

The *ashiko* (approximately 35 cm/14 in diameter and 53–72 cm/21–29 in long) is played throughout sub-Saharan Africa. It is a low-sounding, cone-shaped drum with a goatskin head. The *ashiko, kpanlogo* and *bougarabou* share the same playing technique as the *djembe* (see p. 33).

KPANLOGO

Kpanlogo is a dance and drumming tradition originating from the Ga tribe of Ghana. The master drummer in the *kpanlogo* ensemble plays the solo drum part, and other percussionists play supporting rhythms on drums, rattles and bells. The *kpanlogo* drum (approximately 22 cm/9 in diameter and 60 cm/24 in long) is often highly decorated and has an antelope skin, laced to tuning pegs that protrude from the body of the drum.

SABAR

Sabar drums are royal drums unique to the Senegambia region. Six basic tones can be produced on each of the drums. Using sticks and hands, it is possible to create a complex musical texture. The *sabar* ensemble also includes *tama* (talking drums). These drums, also called the *dondo* (Ghana) and *dun dun* (Nigeria), are double-headed laced hourglass drums (17 cm/9 in diameter and 48 cm/19 in long) played under the arm and squeezed to alter the tension and pitch of the drumheads. This creates high and low sounds that imitate tonal African languages.

▲ A dun dun *drum from Nigeria.*

Section One: The Instruments

DRUMS OF THE MIDDLE EAST

Drums are an essential part of urban music, classical ensembles, sacred Sufi music, and traditional folk music throughout the Middle East.

▲ *The* dumbek *is said to get its name from the two main sounds of the instrument: the* dum *(its centre) and the* bek *(its rim).*

DUMBEK, *TAR* AND *RIQ*

The *dumbek* is a goblet drum (10–22 cm/4–9 in diameter and 22–40 cm/9–16 in long). It has a hollow pottery, wood or metal body and a goatskin or fish-skin head. There are many regional variations in its name, including *derbocka* (Morocco and Algeria), *darbukkah* and *derbouka* (Iraq), and *zarb* (Iran). The *tar* and *riq* are frame drums. The *tar* (10–20 cm/4–8 in diameter) and the lower-sounding *daf* (18–40 cm/7–16 in diameter) are round or square frames with a goatskin head. The *riq* is a similar size to the *tar* and is a round drum with a double row of jingles like a tambourine.

PLAYING TECHNIQUES

Archeological evidence suggests that the *daf* and *riq* were the chief percussion instruments for much of recorded history in the Middle East, with the *dumbek* becoming popular only in the twentieth century. When playing both the *dumbek* and frame drums, the dominant hand plays most of the rhythm, as the other hand holds the drum and adds in light fills. The *dumbek* is played by holding the drum under the left or non-dominant hand arm with the head facing downwards, and striking the head with the fingers of both hands.

Fact

Frame drums can be highly decorated with mother-of-pearl inlay, and may be adorned with ribbons. They are often played by women, especially for traditional singing and dancing at weddings and family celebrations.

Musical Instruments Handbook

RHYTHM

Rhythms are vocalized on the *dumbek*, *daf* and *riq*. The three main strokes are a right-handed strike in the centre of the drum, which produces a deep tone called *dum*; and a right- and left-handed strike at the edge of the drum, which produces a high tone called *tek* and *ka* respectively. On the *daf* and *riq*, the *tek* and *ka* strokes are played with the ring finger at the edge of the skin and the cupped hand in the middle of the head. The *riq* is also shaken to play the jingles.

TABLAT

Double-headed cylindrical drums called by the generic term *tabl* or *tablat* are commonly played at festivals and in military music throughout the Middle East and northern India. These drums are the ancestors of European military drums. The drumheads are laced together and braced with tension knots, like drums used in marching bands in Western Europe. *Tablat* are suspended from a shoulder strap and played with sticks or bundles of leather thongs. The *tabl baladi* (43 cm/17 in diameter and 30 cm/15 in long) is the ancestor of the snare drum and tenor drum, and the *tabl turki* (55 cm/22 in diameter and 35 cm/14 in long) is the ancestor of the bass drum.

▲ *The Middle Eastern frame drum may seem simple, but is capable of great nuance and sophistication.*

Section One: The Instruments

SNARE DRUM AND TENOR DRUM

The snare drum and tenor drum both originated in the Middle East. Today, cylindrical drums like these are played in western classical music, and in pop, rock and jazz. They appear in marching and military bands, in the orchestra and as part of the drum kit.

CYLINDRICAL DRUMS

The body of a cylindrical drum is usually made from a piece of flat wood, steamed and bent into shape and then lacquered and decorated. Played with sticks, these drums are double-headed and untuned, and come in a range of sizes. Those with calfskin or goatskin heads – like marching snare drums and tenor drums – are laced together with a zigzag of cords running up and down the body of the drum between the two heads, and tightened by leather or cloth 'D'-shaped bracing sleeves. Plastic heads, like those of the orchestral snare drum and bass drum, are held in place by a metal ring and tightened by tension rods that are screwed to the body of the drum.

SNARE DRUM

The snare drum has eight to 20 stretched nylon, wire, silk or cat-gut snares held against the lower or snare head by a screw clamp, which holds the snares taut. The snares respond to the vibrations that occur between the two drumheads as the upper, or batter, head is played. The batter head is kept tight to help the bounced strokes that are essential for playing snare-drum rudiments. It also has an internal damper to keep the resonance of the drum to a minimum. An orchestral snare drum (35 cm/14 in diameter and 8–16 cm/3–6 in long) is lighter in tone than the marching snare drum, which is 25–30 cm (10–12 in) long.

Musical Instruments Handbook

▲ *Jazz legend Buddy Rich displays his formidable technique. Snare drums are an essential part of any jazz drummer's kit.*

The snare drum has been used in the orchestra since the beginning of the eighteenth century, but it was not until the nineteenth century that it began to develop a significant role there. At this time, various composers made use of the snare drum, including Gioacchino Rossini (1792–1868) in *La gazza ladra* (1816) and Maurice Ravel (1875–1937) in *Boléro* (1928), where the snare drum plays an *ostinato* rhythm throughout the work. Carl Nielsen also used it in his Fifth Symphony (1921–22), in which the snare drummer is given the instruction to improvise a solo that will disrupt the rest of the orchestra.

PLAYING TECHNIQUE

The traditional way of playing the snare drum – with the left stick held horizontally and the right stick extending from the thumb and index finger – originates from when it was played when marching, suspended from a harness and hanging over the player's right hip. Many players now use the 'matched grip', where both sticks are held pointing forward. This grip is also commonly used for playing the xylophone and other keyboard percussion, and the timpani.

Section One: The Instruments

SOUND EFFECTS

Snare-drum technique uses single, double and bounced strokes to achieve a range of effects. Single strokes are played with alternate hands (Right Left) and doubles as RR LL. Playing a series of double strokes produces an open roll. If a single-stroke roll is played (R L R L etc.), but each stroke is left to bounce indefinitely and the hands are alternated quickly, it produces a closed or buzzed roll. Other rudiments like paradiddles (RLRR LRLL) promote equal strength in both hands, and ornamental drags and flams are used to decorate rhythms.

▲ *Snares played with wire brushes produce a distinctive sound.*

Normally the drum is played in the centre of the head, where the snares are most responsive. Playing the centre of the head and the rim of the drum simultaneously produces a rimshot (a loud cracking sound) – an effect that can also be achieved by laying one stick across the head and rim, and hitting it with the other stick.

The snare drum can also be played with wire brushes, a technique often used in jazz and Latin-American style drum-kit playing. It can also be played with customized sticks, manufactured by Pro-mark Drumsticks, which are bundles of thin canes bound together to produce a sound somewhere between brushes and sticks.

TENOR DRUM

The tenor drum (38–45 cm/15–18 in diameter and 30 cm/12 in long) is deeper in tone than the snare drum. It originates from the medieval tabor, and normally has two heads and no snares. The tenor drum can be played with wooden sticks or soft mallets. It was used by foot regiments to provide rhythms for marching and drilling from the end of the eighteenth century, and is often played with flourishes of the sticks in marching-drum corps.

Musical Instruments Handbook

BASS DRUM

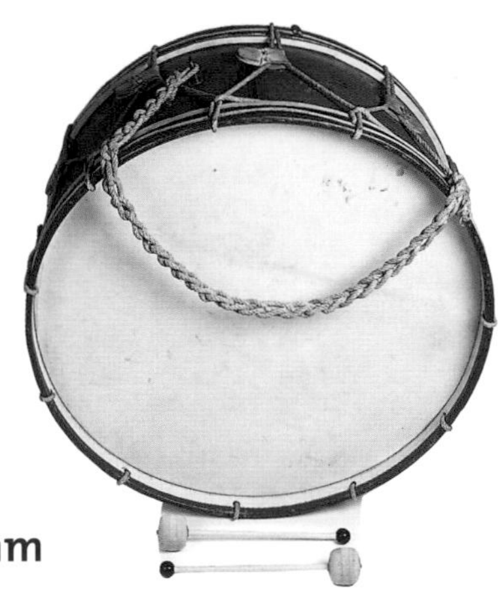

Like the snare drum and tenor drum, the bass drum originated in the Middle East. It is a large instrument with a cylindrical body and two heads, and is the drum used to keep the rhythm in marching bands.

The modern orchestral bass drum (100 cm/70 in diameter and 50 cm/20 in long) is double headed and rod tensioned. Although single-headed orchestral bass drums were popular in the late-nineteenth century, the enclosed cylinder of air in a double-headed drum gives a greater depth of tone and more carrying power at a range of different dynamics. The bass drum is usually played with large soft felt or woollen beaters.

ORCHESTRAL BASS

Orchestral bass drums are mounted on a stand, but in a marching band the bass drum is held in a harness in front of the player. With the snare drum or tenor drum, they start the music with three or five paced rolls to establish the tempo, and give aural cues during the march – such as the double tap played towards the end of the final phrase as a signal that the music is about to end.

▲ *Bass drums provide a powerful sound.*

LAMBEG DRUM

A bass drum can be very loud. The lambeg drums of Northern Ireland (90 cm/36 in diameter and 60 cm/24 in wide) are capable of playing at above 120 dB – the same volume as a pneumatic drill. Like the African *djembe*, the drumheads are tuned almost to breaking point and a fundamental tone like a fizzing or buzzing sound builds up inside the body of the drum, which can be heard a mile or more away. Lambeg drums are played with curved canes, rather than traditional beaters.

Section One: The Instruments

FRAME DRUM

A frame drum is a skin stretched over and nailed to a shallow square or circular frame. It is played with sticks or with the hands.

Frame drums are common to many musical cultures, and the modern tambourine and *bodhrán* are essentially the same instruments that were being played in Arabia and India in pre-Islamic times. They are often played by dancers, and may be painted and decorated with ribbons and pieces of material – like the *timbrels* played by members of the Salvation Army. The drum may also have jingles set into the frame, like the tambourine and *riq*, or have a snare stretched across the drum head, like the *bendir* from the Middle East.

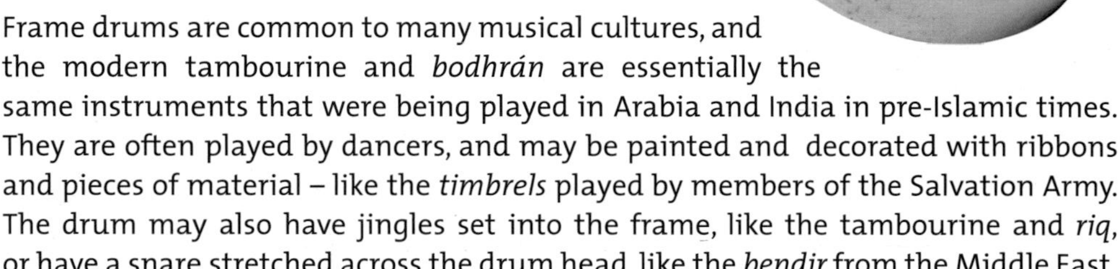

TAMBOURINE

The tambourine (15–25 cm/6–10 in diameter and 5 cm/2 in deep) is a circular wooden hoop with a calfskin or plastic head. Small metal discs like miniature cymbals are mounted singly or in pairs in openings in the hoop, and held in place with pins. The tambourine is commonly used in orchestral and folk music, especially in central and southern Europe. A tambourine without a head – known as a ching ring or jingle ring (*schellenreif*) – is often used in pop and Latin-American music.

The tambourine head can be struck with the flat palm, with a closed fist, or the knuckles. It can be rested on the knee or a soft-topped table and played with fingertips. It can also be shaken to rattle the jingles and create a *tremolo* effect. A thumb roll can be produced by rubbing the head with a moistened thumb tip to make the head shudder and the jingles vibrate.

BODHRÁN

The *bodhrán* (30–45 cm/12–18 in diameter and 10 cm/4 in deep) has a circular wooden frame and a goatskin head. It is played with a double-headed stick, with

Musical Instruments Handbook

▲ *The* bodhrán *is an untuned frame drum consisting of a goatskin head tacked on to a wooden frame.*

brushes or with the knuckles and fingers. The frame is bent from green wood, and is held in shape by crossbars to prevent the drum from warping. It is held vertically, with the left hand (or non-dominant hand) holding the cross bars, and the right hand playing the instrument.

The *bodhrán* has existed in Ireland for centuries, but has only been used in traditional music performance since the 1960s – previously being used in warfare and celebrations as a noisemaker. Contemporary performing techniques focus on producing a range of tones from the drum. These include pressing the left hand or a slide bar against the skin to vary the pitch while playing, dampening the sound with the flat of the left hand, and creating a more ringing sound by pressing with the edge of the left hand while playing the drum with the right hand. The drum can also be played on the rim, and can have shakers and bells attached to the crossbars. The *bodhrán* is played in Irish traditional music and in Celtic folk-rock music. It also appears in Peter Maxwell Davies' (b. 1934) Fifth Symphony.

▲ *Ronan O Snodaigh, of Kila, playing the* bodhrán.

Section One: The Instruments

DRUMS OF THE FAR EAST

Drums are widely used in traditional music in the Far East, along with a diverse range of cymbals, gongs, metallophones and untuned wooden idiophones. In much traditional music of this region, the drum is played by the director of the ensemble, who uses specific signals for the other performers.

CHINESE DRUMS

Most Chinese drums (*gu*) are frame drums or barrel-shaped drums, and are played with sticks. They are often used in folk music and in the Chinese classical orchestra. The director of the Chinese opera orchestra plays the *bangu*, a frame drum with a pigskin head with a small hole in it. The player strikes the edge of the hole with bamboo sticks. The *tanggu* (20–100 cm/8–40 in diameter and 60–80 cm/24–32 in long) is a double-headed barrel drum with cow-, pig- or goatskin heads nailed to the body of the drum. The *tanggu* is used in many types of Chinese music. The drum can be suspended in a frame or worn from a harness in folk music and dancing. A large *tanggu*, or lion drum, is played for the traditional Chinese lion dance performed on the first days of the Chinese New Year.

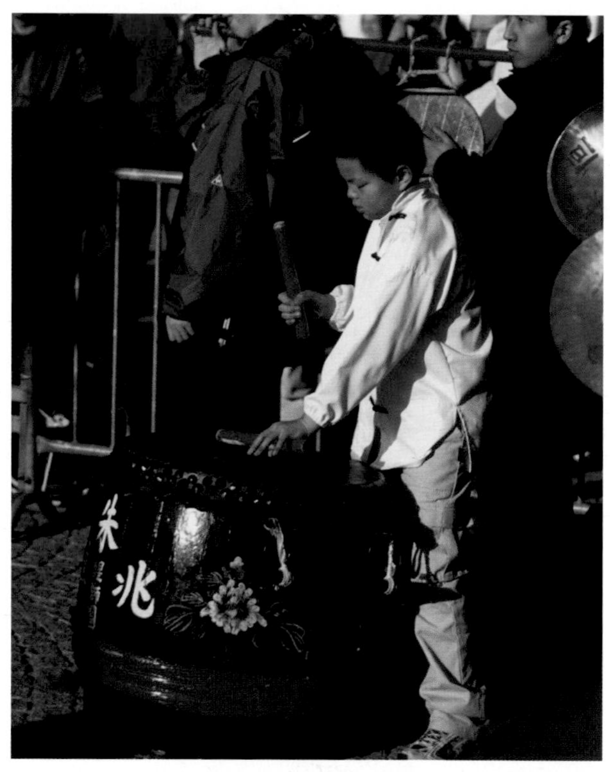

▲ *Chinese drums are integral to the lion-dance tradition.*

Musical Instruments Handbook

JAPANESE DRUMS

Japanese *daiko* or *taiko* drums are a family of barrel-shaped, double-headed drums played with sticks. In feudal Japan, *daiko* were used for military music and to give signals in battles. Today they are used for temple services and for traditional dancing.

Within the family of *daiko* drums, there are drums with heads that are laced on (*shime-daiko*) and those with heads that are nailed on (*byou-daiko*). *Shime-daiko* have floating heads pulled taut by a lace of tension cords and can be tuned. They are slung from the neck and shoulders, allowing the performer to dance while playing. *Kotsuzumi* and *tsuzumi* are hourglass *shime-daiko* made from cherry wood and played in the orchestra of traditional Japanese theatre. They are played with the hands, and – as in the Chinese orchestra – the drummer directs the rest of the ensemble with drum beats, and calls to the other musicians.

Byou-daiko (tack drums) are carved from a single log. Their cowhide heads are nailed on and thus produce only one fixed tone. The *nagado-daiko* is most widely used in Japanese music. It can be played by two performers, one striking the head and one striking the barrel of the drum. *Nagado-daiko* range from small *ko-daiko* (30–45 cm/12–18 in diameter), to the giant *o-daiko* (240 cm/96 in diameter and 240 cm/96 in long), which are among the biggest drums in the world. Some *o-daiko* are so large that they are not often moved and are housed in a temple or shrine. These drums have become popular in the West through touring *taiko* ensembles (*kumi-daiko*) which combine ritualistic displays of martial-arts strength and stamina with drumming expertise.

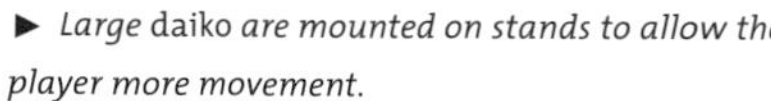

► *Large* daiko *are mounted on stands to allow the player more movement.*

Section One: The Instruments

KOREAN DRUMS

▲ *Drummers playing the Korean* puk.

The *changgo* (30 cm/12 in diameter and 60 cm/24 in long) is a double-headed hourglass drum played in court and folk music, as well as dance and shamanistic music throughout Korea. It usually has a wooden body, often turned from a single log, and floating heads held in place by a single rope laced in a 'W' formation. The drum is either strapped to the body if the performer is dancing, or is placed on the floor. The drum is constructed to make the left-hand head deeper than the right. The left-hand skin is made from cow- or deerskin, which is deep and resonant in tone. It is played with a heavy round-headed beater. The right-hand skin is made from dog- or horse-skin, which gives a light and ringing tone and is played with a light bamboo stick in the right hand. The right-hand skin is also tightened with bracing sleeves.

▲ *Korean drummers performing on the* changgo.

Since the 1980s, the work of *Samulnori* groups (the name means literally 'play four things') have revived an interest in traditional arts among Koreans. *Samulnori* perform a virtuosic concert version of *nongak* (traditional Korean farmers' drumming) using the four traditional instruments of the farmer's band: the *changgo*, the barrel drum called the *puk*, and the two gongs *kkwaenggwari* and *ching*, which has a rising tone when struck. Master drummers working in this style have developed an exacting and complex performance technique for the *changgo* that takes years of careful practice to attain.

FRICTION DRUM

Friction drums are folk instruments of pre-industrialized Central Europe, Africa and Latin America. They are often associated with spiritual music because of their unusual sound.

▲ *The* cuíca *plays an important rhythmic role in samba music.*

CONSTRUCTION

A friction drum comprises a vessel covered in a membrane which is made to vibrate by means of a stick or string rubbed against or pushed through it. In the Brazilian *cuíca*, the end of a stick is attached to the inside of the drum skin. The player rubs the stick with a damp cloth and presses the outer head with the fingers of the other hand to alter the pitch. The closer one presses to the centre of the *cuíca*, the higher the sound.

LION'S ROAR

The drumhead may also be pierced by the stick and played by pushing it up and down, as in the Flemish *rommelpot* (rumblepot). In the Hungarian *köcsögduda* (jughorn) and African lion's roar, a cord is inserted in the drumhead, held taut and rubbed by wet or rosined fingers. The lion's roar may be used as a lure in lion-hunting as it produces a sound similar to that of a female lion. Although not percussion instruments, friction drums are similar to the bullroarers that originated in Australia. There are pieces of flat wood attached to a cord, which are whirled in the air. The sound is produced by the vibrations of the flat object as it rotates. Changes in the speed and angle to the ground will produce different sonorities.

▼ *A Flemish* rommelpot, *with clacker (right).*

Section One: The Instruments

STRING DRUM

String drums are simple string instruments that are struck in a technique similar to playing the violin *col legno* (literally 'with the wood') or *battuta* (measuring time by beating). They are traditional instruments of Hungary and the Balkans.

TTUN TTUN

The *ttun ttun* is a Basque instrument constructed from a tapered hollow wooden case that is 11 cm (4 in) wide at the top, 20 cm (8 in) wide at the bottom, and 80 cm (32 in) long, with six strings stretched the length of the case. The performer holds the case vertically in the crook of the arm, and strikes the strings with a wooden beater. The performer may play *ttun ttun* together with the *txistu*, a three-holed end-blown wooden pipe, holding both the *txistu* and the *ttun ttun* with the left hand, with the stick in the right hand. Two of the strings of the *ttun ttun* are tuned to the same pitch as the main note of the *txistu*, and the other strings are tuned a perfect fifth below.

▼ *The* gardon *is usually made from one piece of beech, maple or willow wood.*

GARDON

The *gardon* or percussive cello (*ütögardon*) is played in Hungary and the Balkans. It is a rough wooden box shaped like a cello with four strings, all tuned to the same pitch. Three of the strings are beaten with a stick and the fourth is plucked vigorously so that it recoils on the finger board. The *gardon* sounds like a deep drum, and accompanies the violin in dance music.

Musical Instruments Handbook

SLIT DRUM

Slit drums, or log drums, are found in many pre-industrialized cultures in Africa, Australasia, Central and South America, and the Far East. They are formed by hollowing a block of wood through a lengthwise slit, and are sounded by the players' stamping feet or by being beaten with sticks.

Slit drums are really idiophones as they have no membrane. The slit may be shaped to leave two or more tongues of wood of different lengths and thicknesses, which play different tones when struck. In central Africa, large slit drums are made from hollowed logs used by chiefs or prominent nobles to transmit messages over long distances. Drums for sending messages may also be suspended from a frame to maximize their resonance and carrying power.

▲ *Some slit drums are made from hollowed-out tree trunks.*

▼ *A woodblock.*

TEMPLE BLOCKS AND WOODBLOCKS

Slit drums are often sited outside temples in the Far East and used to call the faithful to prayer. The temple block is a smaller slit drum, widely used in China, Japan and Korea. It was originally played to accompany Buddhist chants, but is now also used in folk instrumental ensembles. Temple blocks are bulbous in shape and often appear in sets. They can range from 5–50 cm (2–20 in) in width. Smaller slit drums like the woodblock are also used in western music. Modern slit drums, or *gato* drums, were used by the composer Karlheinz Stockhausen (b. 1928) in his piece *Gruppen*, which asked for tuned log drums, and they are also popular instruments in the classroom.

► *A Chinese woodblock.*

Section One: The Instruments

CYMBALS

Cymbals are thin metal discs played by being struck together or placed on a stand (suspended) and hit with sticks or beaters. They are made from beaten metal and so are distinct from *crotales* or antique cymbals, which are tuned cast metal discs.

TURKISH AND CHINESE CYMBALS

Suspended and crash cymbals used in western orchestral music, rock, pop and jazz are developed from Turkish cymbals and have a central boss or bell falling to convex shoulders. They are designed so that only the outside edges touch when they are crashed together, and the fundamental note is difficult to hear when they are played. Cymbals used in traditional Southeast Asian music are generally played as crash cymbals and are developed from the Chinese cymbal (*bo* or *jingbo*), which have either no bell or a squared-off bell, falling to convex shoulders and a wide flat rim. The edge of the cymbal may also be turned up. Turkish cymbals make a smooth, round sound, and Chinese cymbals make a short and abrasive sound.

▲ Chengcheng, *or small Balinese turtle cymbals.*

HISTORY

Cymbals and metal clappers have been played in central Asia and ancient Egypt since around 1200 BC, from where they migrated into India and China. Cymbals appear frequently in the Bible, and are also found in ancient Greek and Roman art and literature. Early cymbals varied in size and were bowl- and funnel-

Musical Instruments Handbook

shaped in cross-section, as well as the flatter cymbals like those found today. They were generally played as crash cymbals, often by dancers. Small brass finger cymbals (6 cm/2½ in diameter) attached to the thumb and first finger – called *zagat* in Arabic and *zills* in Turkish – have been used by dancers across the Middle East, North Africa and India since AD 500.

▲ *Finger cymbals may be plated to give a silvery colour or brighter surface.*

CYMBAL SOUNDS

▲ *Suspended crash cymbals.*

The cymbal is cast from an alloy of copper, silver and tin into a metal disc, which is reheated and passed several times through a rolling mill; and then tempered in water and hammered to straighten it into a circle. The bell of the cymbal is formed and the individual sound of the cymbal is created by hammering the shoulders or bow of the cymbal by hand, and shaving and cutting grooves or tone rings along the edges and underside.

The sound of a cymbal should be brilliant and give a quick response when struck. Although an unpitched instrument, the thickness, weight and diameter of a cymbal and the curvature of the bell and the bow contribute to its timbre. Typically, a symphony orchestra would have four or five suspended cymbals, and pairs of crash cymbals ranging from 30–60 cm (12–24 in) diameter to provide a suitable range of tone colours.

Fact

Smacking cymbals together as if one were clapping one's hands can result in an airlock between the cymbals – an embarrassing mistake to make in the middle of a performance.

Section One: The Instruments

▲ *A skilled player can obtain a large dynamic range from orchestral crash cymbals.*

PLAYING TECHNIQUE

Orchestral crash cymbals are played by passing the face of one cymbal against another at a slight angle with a brushing action, and then damping them against the chest. Different dynamics are achieved by allowing more or less of the face of the cymbals to strike, and by applying more upper-body strength to the velocity at which the cymbals are struck together. Sliding the tip of one cymbal across the other creates a very soft sound without an initial percussive attack. A cymbal *roll a due* is played by rubbing one cymbal in a circular motion against the other.

ORCHESTRAL CYMBALS

The cymbal first appeared in the orchestra in the late-eighteenth century. Some bass-drum and cymbal orchestral parts were written to be played by one player. One crash cymbal would be mounted on the top of the bass drum, so that the player could play the bass drum with one hand and the cymbal with the other.

Christoph Willibald Gluck (1714–87) composed one of the first independent cymbal parts in his opera *Iphigenie en Tauride* (1779). Berlioz was the first composer to specify a cymbal struck with beaters. A suspended cymbal can also be scraped lightly with a metal beater or coin, as in Claude Debussy's (1862–1918) *La Mer* (1905), or played with a cello or double-bass bow, which allows the higher harmonics in the cymbal to sound and give an effect like that of a musical saw. Adding loose rivets to the circumference of a suspended cymbal makes a sizzle cymbal. When struck, the rivets vibrate against the cymbal creating a continuous buzzing or sizzling sound.

Musical Instruments Handbook

GONG AND TAM TAM

Gongs and tam tams are suspended bronze discs played with a beater. In the West, the two names are often confused as the instruments can look similar and both produce a deep, rich sound. However, the tam tam is untuned, and the gong is tuned.

Gongs have been used as melodic instruments throughout Southeast Asia, especially in China, Burma and Java, since 300 BC. They are different shapes. The tam tam is a large, flat, round metal disc (70–100 cm/28–40 in diameter) with a narrow turned-back rim, whereas the gong normally has a raised central boss or bell and a wider rim. Gongs also vary in more in size than tam tams. For example in China gongs range from the *dachaoluo* which is 120 cm (48 in) diameter to the *goujiaoluo* or dog-call gong, 8 cm (3 in) diameter.

TAM TAMS

The tam tam appeared in the orchestra in the late-eighteenth century, and has often been used to create an atmosphere of terror and gloom – such as in Giacomo Meyerbeer's (1791–1864) *Robert le Diable* (1831). The tam tam is struck midway between the centre and the edge. For a very loud single strike, the tam tam may be struck gently a few times in order to start the instrument vibrating, and then hit loudly. Striking the tam tam repeatedly with moderate force will make the higher overtones ring with increasing intensity, and create a menacing shrieking sound.

▼ *Tam tams are usually played with a soft-headed drumstick.*

Section One: The Instruments

GONGS

The timbre of a gong is dependent on the relative dimensions of the raised boss, the bow of the gong and the rim, and the angle at which the lip is turned back. Chinese gongs are hammered into a flat sieve shape and do not always have a raised central boss. The Chinese traditional orchestra includes a set of 10 to 20 *yunlo* (cloud gongs) and the *quing* (tuned bronze bowls).

Javanese and Burmese gongs have a raised boss and are shaped like a curly bracket in cross-section. They also have a wide rim. They are struck with a wooden beater covered in leather or bound with cloth on the central boss, which is the main antinodal point. There are several examples of Southeast Asian gongs that have a rising tone once struck. These include the Chinese *jingluo*, which is used in Chinese opera, and the Korean *ching*.

▲ *Gongs have a clear, resonant tone.*

TEMPLE BELLS

In Japan and Tibet another form of gong is used in Buddhist ceremonies. These are called temple bells (*dobachi*), resting bells or singing bowls. These gongs are a basin of hammered bronze placed on a cushion or held in the hand with the opening upwards. They are struck at the rim, or, in the case of Tibetan singing bowls, played by rubbing the edge with the beater to create a sustained singing effect. These temple bowl gongs have a pure tone and are used as an aid to meditation.

Musical Instruments Handbook

GAMELAN

The gamelan is a percussion ensemble played throughout Indonesia, especially in Bali and Java. A gamelan comprises mainly metallophones, xylophones and gongs. It may also include vocals, the *rebab* (a two-stringed spike fiddle), the *keprak* (a slit drum), and the *kendhang* (a set of three or four double headed, barrel-shaped drums). The *kendhang* sets the tempo and gives starting and stopping signals during the music.

COMPONENTS OF THE GAMELAN

In gamelan music the parts played by all the instruments contribute to the *balungan*, or central melodic thread of the music. The metallophones and xylophones play the main melodic content of the music, and the gongs mark out the structure. In descending order of pitch, the barred instruments span five octaves and include three different sizes of *saron*. Each of these has a single octave of notes, made of thick metal bars mounted over a single trough resonator, played with a wooden or horn mallet. The *saron* family plays the simplest version of the *balungan*. The *gender* and *slenthem* are larger metallophones with thinner, ribbed metal bars held on cords over individual tube resonators. The *gambang* is a xylophone. The *gender* and *gambang* play an elaborated version of the *balungan* in parallel octaves or complex interlocking patterns.

▲ *A gamelan orchestra with* kedhang *in the foreground.*

Fact

Gamelan instruments and their cases are often ornately carved and decorated with animal and floral motifs. The gamelan plays for theatrical performances, shadow-puppet shows and traditional dances.

Section One: The Instruments

▲ *A collection of gongs: gong chimes and hanging gongs.*

GONG TYPES

The gongs include the larger hanging gongs, in which the raised boss points to the side, and the smaller cradled gongs or gong chimes, which rest on rope supports in a wooden frame, with the raised boss pointing upwards. The hanging gongs are shaped like a curly bracket in cross-section with a large lip bent back at about 130 degrees from the face of the gong. They are played with a padded beater or the fleshy part of a clenched fist. Cradled gongs are played in sets of 10 to 12, and each gong is tuned to a different note of the scale. They have a wider lip and more sloping shoulders than the hanging gongs. They are shaped like a lidded saucepan in cross-section and are sometimes called 'pot gongs' in the West. The cradled gongs are played with a wooden beater overwound with string.

ROLE OF THE GONG

The gongs punctuate the cyclical structure of the music, providing aural cues to the other musicians. In ascending order of pitch, starting with the lowest, the hanging gongs include the *gong ageng* (85 cm/34 in diameter), *gong suwukan* (63 cm/25 in), and a set of three to five *kempul* (45 cm/18 in). These gongs mark out keynotes in the *balungan*. The cradled gongs include the *kethuk* and *kempyang* (25 cm/10 in), a set of 10 *kenong* (36 cm/14 in) and two sets of 12 *bonangs* (18 cm/7 in). Between them, the cradled gongs play an elaboration of the hanging-gong pattern, which interweaves with the patterns played by the *gender* and *gambang*.

► *Types of cradled gong:* Ketuk *and* bongang.

Musical Instruments Handbook

DRUM KIT

The drum kit is a collection of drums and cymbals played in all styles of rock, pop, jazz and blues. It is also widely used in urban music across the world, such as Afrobeat and reggae.

DRUM-KIT CONSTRUCTION

A typical drum kit comprises a bass drum and hi-hat cymbal played with foot pedals, a snare drum, two or three tom toms and suspended cymbals. The drummer sits on a stool. A right-handed player will play the bass drum with the right foot, the hi-hat pedal with the left foot, and will place the snare drum immediately in front of them between the knees, with the tom toms arranged from left to right in descending order of pitch. The suspended crash cymbal is placed by the hi-hat and the suspended ride cymbals are placed over the tom toms.

▲ *The modern drum kit was not established until the 1950s.*

DRUMS

The drums are constructed like the orchestral snare drum and bass drum (see p. 38 and p. 41). The bass (or kick) drum (45–60 cm/18–24 in diameter and 35–45 cm/14–18 in deep) is placed on the floor with the playing head vertical. The pedal is clamped to the hoop of the drum. It has a chain or spring action and bounces back after being struck. The outer head of the drum may be decorated with a logo, and the cavity of the drum is often filled with absorbent material to deaden the sound. Two tom toms are mounted on a stand on the bass drum, and the largest tom toms, or floor toms, stand on the floor on legs.

Section One: The Instruments

The tom toms are unpitched (20–45 cm/8–18 in diameter, 18–40 cm/7–16 in long), and are usually tuned to sound lower than the snare drum.

HI-HAT

The hi-hat cymbal comprises two matched cymbals (30–35 cm/12–14 in diameter) on a stand operated by a foot pedal. The lower cymbal is stationary and lies facing upwards. It is not normally struck with the stick. The upper cymbal faces downwards and is clamped to the stand so that it moves as the foot pedal is depressed. The upper cymbal can be played in a closed or open position, notated + and o respectively, making a short or a sustained sizzling sound as the two cymbals vibrate against each other. A typical jazz or swing rhythm exploits this feature of the cymbal (see diagram below).

OTHER CYMBALS

Rhythms are played on the ride or bounce cymbal (45–52 cm/18–21 in diameter), which is designed to have a clean articulation and a dry timbre. Crash cymbals (20–40 cm/8–16 in diameter) are used for single crashes in solos and drum fills, and are built to have a more brilliant ringing sound with a pleasing mix of overtones.

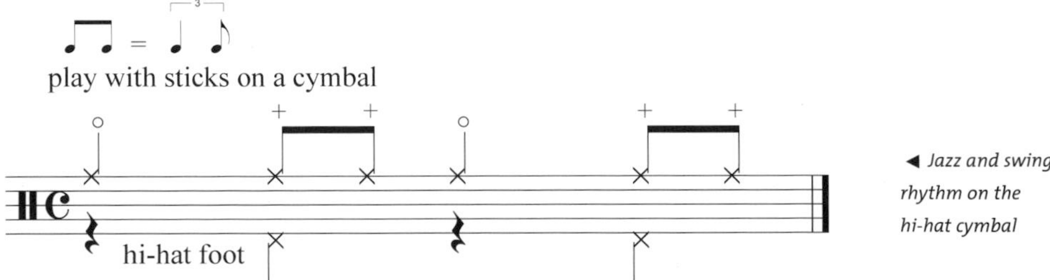

◀ *Jazz and swing rhythm on the hi-hat cymbal*

Musical Instruments Handbook

▲ *The main function of a ride cymbal (on the left) is to maintain rhythm.*

Drummers often customize their kits to include extra drums and cymbals. These might include: the Chinese or *pang* cymbal (35–40 cm/14–16 in diameter), which has an upturned rim and imitates a Chinese gong; the splash cymbal (15 cm/6 in diameter); and the sizzle cymbal. In the late 1970s and the 1980s, drummers of stadium-rock bands like Asia, Kiss, Queen and Styx used very large drum kits that might include 25 to 30 items, among them two bass drums, two hi-hats, extra tom toms, bongos and roto-toms (tuneable tom toms with no shell), multiple cymbals and gongs.

DRUM-KIT HISTORY

The drum kit originated in the multiple drum sets played in theatre and music-hall pits at the end of the nineteenth century. The drummer played the percussion part on a combination of bass drum, snare drum, cymbals and tom toms, and added in special effects on a range of other instruments, including woodblock, triangle, tambourine, castanets, slapstick and whistles.

The modern drum kit came into being with the invention of foot pedals for the bass drum and hi-hat in the jazz bands of the 1920s, in which drums, bass and rhythm guitar, banjo or piano formed the rhythm section. Previously, the bass drum and snare drum were placed side by side and played with sticks, or the bass drum was placed on the floor and kicked (which is why the bass drum is sometimes called a kick drum).

▶ *Asia's customized, super-size drum kit.*

Section One: The Instruments

The original foot-pedal-operated cymbal, or low-boy, rested at floor level, which made playing on this cymbal with sticks awkward. The hi-hat, which places the cymbals at chest height, was developed by Gene Krupa (1909–73) – drummer in the Benny Goodman Orchestra, who played the famous drum solo in 'Sing Sing Sing' – and the Zildjian cymbal company in the late 1930s. The advantages of this new cymbal were quickly recognized by drummers and the hi-hat became a standard part of the kit.

RHYTHM

The pulse played on bass drum and hi-hat with the feet provides the basis of most drum-kit rhythms. The drummer adds the snare-drum part with the left hand and the cymbal part with the right hand, playing either on the hi-hat or the ride cymbal. Improvisation is a key aspect of drum-kit playing, and the drummer may vary the rhythm by adding extra beats on the bass drum and snare drum.

The drummer may also vary a rhythm by altering the snare-drum and cymbal sounds. These include playing a click on the snare drum, by laying the head of the stick across the drum to hit the rim of the drum and the head at the same time, and using brushes or rattan sticks. The bell of the cymbal can be used to imitate a cowbell. In progressive rock, Latin and jazz styles, the drummer often plays more complex rhythms between the bass drum and snare drum.

▼ *The drum kit provides the bedrock of rhythm in any band.*

Musical Instruments Handbook

SOLOS AND FILLS

Short drum fills and longer solos are added to vary the rhythm and mark out the musical structure. In rock, pop, blues and most jazz drumming, fills are played every fourth, eighth or sixteenth measure, and are timed to end on the first beat of the next phrase.

Longer solos can be built up by playing snare-drum rudiments around the kit, developing rhythms already played in the piece and free improvisation. Snare-drum rudiments are developed by splitting them between snare drum, bass drum and tom toms, by adding flams, drags and ruffs, and syncopated accented patterns.

▲ *Keith Moon is a master of the extended drum solo.*

Longer drum solos are found in many styles of music, and became a feature of swing and jazz modelled on the work of Gene Krupa, Buddy Rich (1917–87) and Art Blakey (1919–90), who made full use of the different sonorities available from the kit. Rock drummers in the 1960s and 1970s – including John Bonham (1948–80) of Led Zeppelin, Phil Collins (b. 1951) of Genesis and Keith Moon (1946–78) – developed extensive drum solos, like that in Led Zeppelin's 'Moby Dick', which John Bonham could extend to 30 minutes in live performance.

Section One: The Instruments

KEYBOARD PERCUSSION

Keyboard percussion instruments include the western xylophone, marimba, vibraphone and glockenspiel, the log xylophones and marimbas of Africa and Central America, and the barred instruments played in the Indonesian gamelan.

▲ *Bamboo xylophone, part of a gamelan orchestra.*

The orchestral xylophone, marimba and glockenspiel have thin wooden or metal rectangular bars laid out like a chromatic piano keyboard. The back row of bars – the sharps and flats – are raised above those in front. The bars of the xylophone and marimba are suspended on string held between pegs. Glockenspiel bars are held in place with rubber pins. Keyboard percussion instruments are played with beaters with cane or plastic shafts and small oval or round heads made of plastic, rubber, wood or brass. Marimba beaters are commonly overwound with yarn.

TUNING

The bars of a keyboard percussion instrument are rectangular with a curved underside to ensure that the bar will tune to a true pitch. Tuning the bars is achieved using longer, thinner bars for lower notes, and shorter, thicker bars for higher notes. Fine-tuning is achieved by removing material from the centre underside of the bar to flatten the pitch and filing the underside of the ends of the bars to sharpen the pitch. Any damage to the bar will result in a loss of true pitch and an impaired sonority.

To achieve a resonant sound, the bar is struck either at the very end or in the middle – the points of maximum vibration (antinodes) of the soundwaves produced by the bar. Holes are drilled for supports for the bar at the nodal points, where the bar does not resonate.

Musical Instruments Handbook

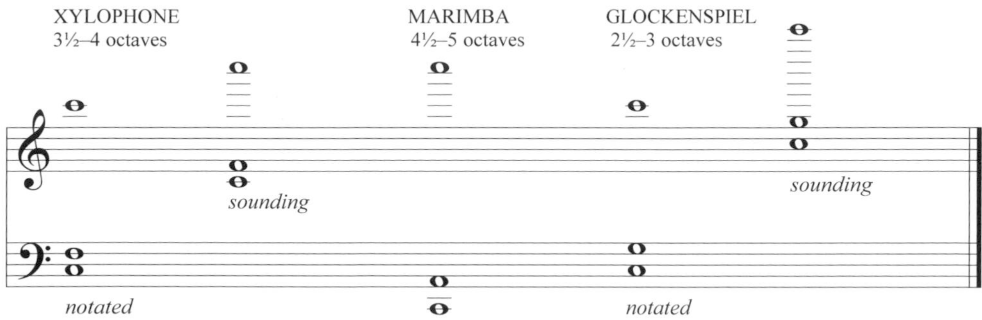

▲ *Typical ranges of the orchestral xylophone, marimba and glockenspiel.*

RESONATORS

Orchestral xylophones, marimbas and some glockenspiels have vertical tube resonators with a stopped lower end, which are placed under each bar. Each resonator is tuned to the same fundamental frequency as the bar, and amplifies the sound. However, the combined vibrations of the bar and the air column in the resonator cause a loud initial attack and a rapid decay. This gives the xylophone and marimba a relatively short sound. The resonators increase in size as the pitch of the bar lowers. On a 4 ⅓-octave marimba they range in size from 6.25 cm (2.5 in) for *c'''* to 71 cm (28.5 in) for *A*. Concert xylophones and marimbas may have a set of dummy resonators on the side of the instrument that faces the audience. These are usually arranged in an arc, with long resonators at the top and bottom of the instrument. These are still tuned in the normal way, but the resonators at the top end are extended below the stopped end.

▲ *A xylophone with resonators to amplify the sound.*

▲ *Percussionist Evelyn Glennie displays her dazzling technique.*

PLAYING TECHNIQUE

Proficiency on keyboard percussion is an important area of competence for the western percussionist. Keyboard percussion instruments are played with a matched grip and the player must develop good memory in order to move around the keyboard fluently. There is a considerable distance between the notes, especially at the lower end of the instrument, and the performers must make sure they hit the correct part of the bar. This is particularly true in fast and furious passages like the xylophone solo in the opening of the overture to *Porgy and Bess* (1934–35) by George Gershwin (1898–1937).

Performers often practise playing a single-stroke roll smoothly and evenly – they need to make an instrument that naturally has a short decay sound smooth and seamless when playing *legato* passages. The marimba and vibraphone can also be played with four beaters – two in each hand – to

▲ *Keyboard percussion is generally played with two or more beaters.*

Musical Instruments Handbook

play chords with up to four notes. These can also be rolled as a single-stroke roll, or played as a *tremolo* with the hands rocking the pair of sticks in each hand to create a shimmering effect. A roll can also be played on a single bar with one hand, by holding the pair of sticks above and below the bar and moving the beaters up and down.

GLOCKENSPIEL

The glockenspiel (65 cm/14 in long, 43 cm/17 in wide at low end and 20 cm/8 in wide at high end) has steel bars laid on felt strips. The bars may rest in a shallow wooden box, or have resonators. Some orchestral glockenspiels also have a pedal damper. As the metal bars ring for a relatively long time, the glockenspiel does not normally play rolls. Before the nineteenth century, the orchestral glockenspiel was often operated by a keyboard. The glockenspiel is often used to represent delicate sounds like small bells, music boxes, fairies and birds – such as in the 'Dance of the Hours' from *La Gioconda* (1876) by Amilcare Ponchielli (1834–86).

XYLOPHONE

The xylophone (140 cm/56 in long, 70 cm/28 in wide at low end, 33 cm/13 in wide at high end) and marimba (200 cm/80 in long, 90 cm/36 in wide at low end, 40 cm/16 in at high end) originated from the African log xylophone variously called the *balafon* (Guinea), *gyil* (Ghana) and *amadinda* (Uganda). The log xylophone has between seven and 21 wooden bars suspended on a bamboo frame over tuned gourd resonators. The gourds may have holes drilled in them, with bat-wing or spiders-egg cases stretched over the holes to make a buzzing sound when the instrument is played.

Log xylophones come in various *tessitura*, roughly equivalent to soprano, alto, tenor and bass versions of the instrument. Log xylophones and marimbas are played by professional musicians or *griots*. Larger instruments may be played by a pair of musicians who sit on either side of the instrument and play interlocking repeated patterns.

Section One: The Instruments

▲ *Log xylophones such as these are prominent in much African music.*

HISTORY

The xylophone first appeared in Europe in early 1500s, and became a popular folk instrument in Eastern Europe. It was suspended from a harness worn by the player, or rested on straw, which gave rise to its alternative name of *strohfiedel* ('straw fiddle'). In illuminated manuscripts it was often played by the dead – a fact exploited by Camille Saint-Saëns (1835–1921) in his representation of the dancing skeletons in *Danse Macabre* (1874). It became an orchestral instrument in the nineteenth century, but was used as a solo instrument in the twentieth-century orchestra – as in Bartók's *Music for Strings, Percussion and Celesta* (1936) and in the music of Stockhausen, Dimitri Shostakovitch (1906–75), Sergei Prokofiev (1891–1953) and Pierre Boulez (b. 1925).

MARIMBA

The marimba appears to have been largely unknown in Europe until the manufacture of orchestral instruments from 1910, but it has become increasingly popular with composers since the Second World War, especially in the music of Olivier Messiaen (1908–92) and Toru Takemitsu (1930–96).

Fact

The marimba is a popular folk instrument in Central America, where it arrived with slaves from western and South Africa. It is the national instrument of Guatemala.

It has a warm and resonant sound, distinct from the drier and more brittle xylophone. Although a relatively new instrument to western classical music, the work of percussionists like Colin Currie (b. 1976), Evelyn Glennie (b. 1965) and Adrian Spillet (b. 1978) – who have commissioned and recorded new works for keyboard percussion – has given it an extensive repertoire of original and arranged music.

Musical Instruments Handbook

CELESTA

The celesta is a type of keyboard glockenspiel, with a range of four octaves upwards from middle C, and a damping pedal like a piano. Inside the body of the instrument is a series of chromatically tuned metal bars, which are struck with felt hammers when the performer plays the keyboard.

CREATION OF THE CELESTA

The celesta was invented in 1886 by Auguste Mustel, a Parisian instrument maker who also manufactured harmoniums and portative organs. It was created at a time when interest in new keyboard instruments was high. Mustel's father, Victor, invented the typophone (1865), a tuning-fork piano that used a piano hammer action to play graduated steel tuning forks or prongs instead of bars.

Auguste took the keyboard-operated glockenspiel of the eighteenth century (used for Papageno's bells in Mozart's *Die Zauberflöte*, 1791), and added a box resonator to each metal bar. He also improved the piano's hammer action so that the celesta could be played like a pianoforte. This gave the instrument a more resonant and sweeter sound than the glockenspiel, as well as a greater capacity to play complex music.

▼ *When played, the celesta sounds an octave higher than written.*

CELESTA MUSIC

The celesta was first used by Piotr Ilyich Tchaikovsky (1840–93) to represent the Sugar Plum Fairy in his ballet *The Nutcracker* (1891–92). It can create a range of ethereal effects, playing runs and arpeggiated chords with great agility. The celesta is used extensively in Bartók's music, in Mahler's Sixth Symphony and in 'Mercury' from *The Planets* (1914–16) by Gustave Holst (1874–1934).

Section One: The Instruments

MBIRA

Like the jew's harp and mechanical music box, the African *mbira* or thumb piano is a lamellaphone, in which the sound is produced by plucking metal tongues or plates.

A *mbira* has between 22 and 52 thin metal tongues, arranged in two or three layers on a hardwood soundboard. The longest tongues are placed in the middle of the instrument, with the higher notes radiating outwards. The soundboard acts as an amplifier and is usually placed inside a large gourd (*deze*), which is the resonator. Bottle caps or snail shells are often attached to the gourd or the resonator to create a buzzing noise as the *mbira* is played. Some *mbira* have the tongues attached to a wooden box, which acts as soundboard and resonator. Each metal tongue is plucked with the thumb and first finger on each hand. Several *mbira* players may play together in an ensemble, and are often accompanied by drums and rattles (*hosho*).

MBIRA MUSIC

The *mbira* is played at religious ceremonies and social gatherings. The Shona people of Zimbabwe traditionally believe that *mbira* music brings the world of the living in contact with the world of the spirits. Skilled *mbira* players, or *vana gwenyambira*, play to persuade the spirits to transform members of the community into mediums, so that the spirits can counsel the living to protect them. *Mbira* music is cyclic and is constructed from several layers of interlocking melodic ideas, which combine to create the mesmeric effect believed to call the spirits.

▲ *The* mbira *has a range of three or more octaves.*

Musical Instruments Handbook

BELLS

Bells are a feature of ceremony and ritual. They are used for meditation and prayer, and to mark significant life events such as funerals and weddings. Bells are used to mark out the timetable of our daily lives – appearing as alarm bells, warning signals and in mechanized chimes in clocks.

In Japan, *bonsho* temple bells are rung 108 times at the end of the old year to banish worldly cares and sin. Public buildings also are decorated with hanging bells like the 13,760-kg (13½-ton) hour bell known as 'Big Ben' in the tower that forms part of the Houses of Parliament in London.

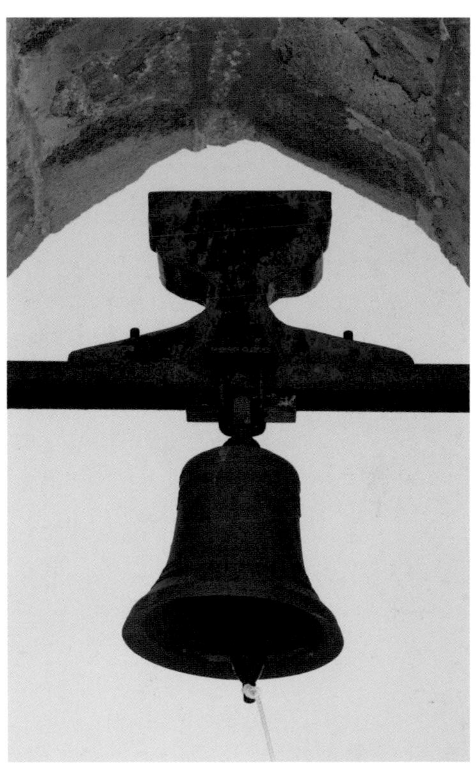

▲ *The sound of a bell such as this can carry for miles.*

CONSTRUCTION

Bells can be made from wood, stone, glass or terracotta, although metal is the most common material. They are usually cast in bronze. In shape they range from spherical or crotal bells, through shallow mushroom shapes, to the classic church bell with a flared lip.

The shape of the bell influences its timbre. Bells that are uniform in cross-section along their body, like Japanese and Chinese temple bells (*bianzhong*), have a slow attack but a long decay, which can make the sound travel a great distance. A cone-shaped bell with an exaggerated lip, like a western church bell, has a very strong attack and a brazen sound. True bells are tuned to a specific pitch.

Section One: The Instruments

▲ *Highly ornate bells in a Chinese temple.*

BELL-CASTING

Bells have been used in Southeast Asia since 2000 BC, and the Chinese are believed to have developed the technique of bell-casting. A metal bell is cast in a mould formed from a cope (the outer skin of the bell) and a core (the inner skin). In pre-industrialized times, bells were made from a wax model, which was coated with layers of clay loam and baked in a bell pit, allowing the wax to melt and drain away, leaving a mould in baked clay into which the heated liquid-bell metal was cast. Once the metal has set cold, the bell is tuned by rotating it on a turntable, mouth upwards, and shaving small amounts of metal off the inside walls of the bell. It is then cleaned and polished.

PITCH AND TUNING

A bell has five principal elements to its sound. The 'hum tone' is the lowest pitched overtone and lasts the longest when the bell is struck. An octave above the hum tone is the prime note, the most prominent pitch heard when the bell is struck. Three further overtones – the tierce, quint and nominal – sound a minor third, a perfect fifth and an octave respectively above the prime. Once tuned at the foundry, a bell needs no further tuning, and provided it is not damaged it will retain its tuning indefinitely.

Different musical cultures prefer bells tuned in different ways. Russian bells, for example, are cast to sound a particular pitch, but they do not have fine adjustments made to their tuning as is common with European bells. Ancient Chinese bells were constructed to play two pitches. Striking the bell at different points would either activate or suppress the hum note, making the bell sound lower or higher.

► Bonsho *are enormous bells found in Buddhist temples.*

Musical Instruments Handbook

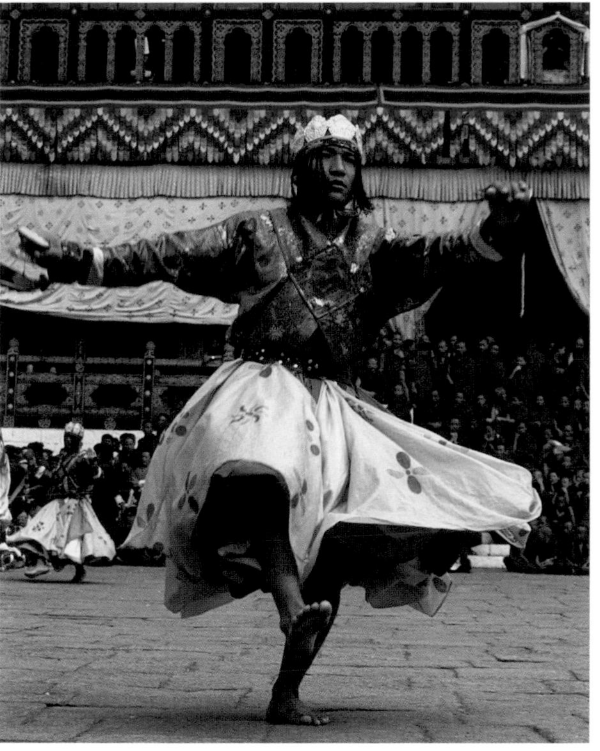

▲ *A Bhutanese monk with handbells dances at a religious festival.*

PLAYING

Bells may be struck by a clapper suspended inside the bell. Those suspended in a tower are either mounted on a wheel, turned by a rope – common in English and American churches – or the bell will remain stationary and be played by the clapper being pulled to one side by an extension cable – as in many Eastern European churches. Bells can also be hit mechanically or manually on the outside with a hammer or ramrod. Large Buddhist temple bells or *bonsho* are played in this way.

HANDBELLS

Handbells are common throughout India, Japan and China, and appear in Indian records as far back as 3000 BC. They reached China in around 1600 BC, Japan from the sixth century AD and then appeared in Europe from the eighth century, probably via Christian missionaries returning from Asia.

Handbells tuned in sets and fitted with leather straps and spring-loaded clappers were introduced in the UK in the late-seventeenth century. Championship competitions in the nineteenth century developed the art further, and after some decline in the twentieth century, handbells now enjoy worldwide popularity. Within a handbell choir, each player will play four or five bells from a chromatic set of bells that could span up to three octaves.

Section One: The Instruments

TUBULAR BELLS

▲ *It can take years to master tubular bells.*

Tubular bells, also known as orchestral or symphonic chimes, are a set of tuned steel tubes with a chrome finish, hanging vertically in a stand with a pedal damper.

The optimum range for a chromatic set of tubular bells is 1½ octaves rising from middle C (*c'–f''*), as notes above or below this range are difficult to tune accurately. Each tube is around 5–6 cm (2 in) diameter, and ranges from 75 cm (*f''*, 30 in) to 155 cm (*c'*, 62 in). The tube is capped at the upper end with a reinforced metal disc. It is also struck at the stopped end with a wooden or rawhide hammer.

COMPOSITIONS FOR TUBULAR BELLS

Tubular bells were invented in the late-nineteenth century as a substitute for church bells in orchestral music, as in Tchaikovsky's overture *The Year 1812* (1880). Although opera houses in Russia and on the European continent housed their own sets of church bells for works like Rossini's *Guillaume Tell* (1829), it was expensive and cumbersome for touring orchestras to travel with these instruments.

In the twentieth century, composers began to write for the tubular bell idiomatically, such as in Messiaen's *Turangalîla Symphony* (1948), and Benjamin Britten's (1913–76) opera *The Turn of the Screw* (1954). Tubular bells are also used occasionally in pop music – most famously in the title song of Mike Oldfield's (b. 1953) album *Tubular Bells* (1973), which was used in the soundtrack for the film *The Exorcist*.

Musical Instruments Handbook

STEEL PANS

Steel pans or steel drums are a Caribbean instrument, originally made from oil drums beaten into shape and tuned. They originate from Port of Spain, Trinidad.

THE ORIGINS OF STEEL PANS

In the late 1930s, local people took to playing discarded metal objects like food tins and engine parts at carnivals and other celebrations, after the British authorities banned the playing of skin drums and other percussion because they had been used by street gangs to incite violence.

Pan folklore states that it was Winston 'Spree' Simon (1930–76) who, in 1942, discovered that dents in the top of the oil drum produced pitches. He created a 14-note ping-pong or melody pan by hammering out the top of an oil drum to produce a diatonic scale, and played this new instrument at the first post-war carnival held on Trinidad in 1946. Other musicians copied his innovation, creating drums of different *tessitura* and bands of tuned steel drums became popular across the island. By 1951, the Trinidad All Percussion Steel Orchestra – which represented Trinidad at the Festival of Britain in London – were playing chromatic pans and bass pans.

Section One: The Instruments

CONSTRUCTION

Modern pans are made from specially constructed steel drums, or use a 45-gallon (204.5-litre) oil drum. First, the head of the oil drum is pounded into a concave shape to stretch the steel. The areas that will be tuned to individual pitches are marked out with a cold chisel – which delineates the borders between notes – in a process known as 'grooving'.

▲ *Steel-pan makers may serve a 10-year apprenticeship.*

TUNING

The metal is tempered, and the drum barrel, or skirt, is cut to the required length, ranging from 14 cm (5 in) for the highest tenor pans, and 85 cm (34 in) for bass pans. The pan is tuned by hammering out hollows where the head was marked. Lower notes require a larger hollow, so bass pans may have only three or four pitches on each drum, whereas tenor or lead pans could have up to 29 notes. Playing the pan may result in a loss of true pitch if the surface is damaged, but a pan may be re-tuned or blended to regain its original tuning. After fine-tuning, the pan is covered with chrome or zinc to prevent rusting.

PLAYING

It is played with rubber-headed sticks, and the smaller drums are suspended on stands. As the sound of the pan has a short decay, it is usually played with a *tremolo* like a xylophone roll or a repeated rhythmic pattern to sustain the sound. The layout of pitches is not consecutive as on a piano or xylophone, Notes are arranged in concentric circles around the pan with adjacent notes a perfect fourth apart (D, G, C, F, etc.) reading clockwise.

◀ *The deeper the drum, the less notes it can play.*

Musical Instruments Handbook

STEEL BANDS

Typically a steel band will have between four and 10 players. Steel-pan music is organized into melody and countermelody, played by tenor, double tenor and double second pans; harmony and chord strums played by cello and guitar pans; and bass parts played on bass pans. Lower pans are played in sets of two or more.

Steel bands commonly include a rhythm section, or 'engine room', which includes a drum kit, congas, and other instruments made from found materials such as a metal scratcher and a percussion iron – a metal disc that was originally the brake drum of a vehicle.

STEEL PANS IN COMPOSITION

In 1992, the steel drum was declared the national musical instrument of Trinidad and Tobago. Many performers and arrangers like Len 'Boogsie' Sharpe (b. 1963) and Ken 'Professor' Philmore (b. 1959) have made adaptations to the tuning and manufacture of the drums, and explored new areas of repertoire.

Steel-pan music has become popular with the spread of Caribbean émigrés across North America and Europe, where it is played in numerous bands and at carnivals such as the Notting Hill Carnival in London. Steel bands were particularly popular in British schools during the 1970s and 1980s, where a growing interest in including pop and world music in the school curriculum resulted in students being given opportunities to learn instruments like the steel drums. Ever since Winston Simon played 'God Save the King' and Franz Schubert's (1797–1828) *Ave Maria* in his inaugural performance in 1946, the steel-band repertoire has always included a combination of popular songs, jazz, hymns, calypsos and extracts from classical pieces.

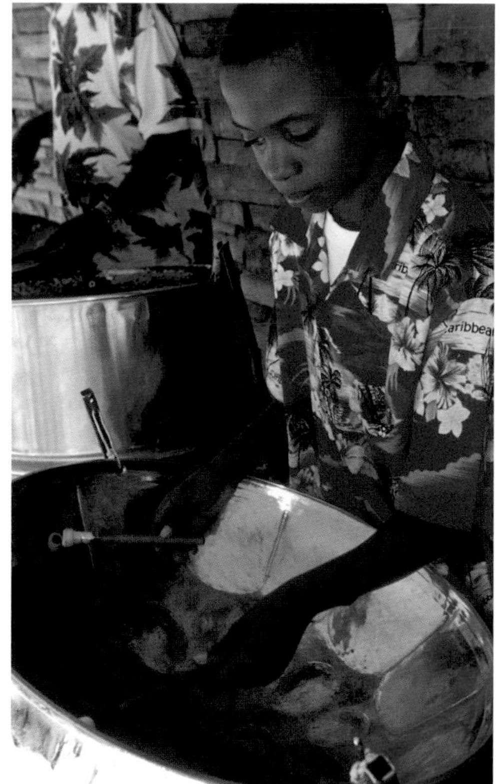

▶ *Steel-pan bands are popular at carnivals.*

Section One: The Instruments

RATTLE AND SHAKER

Rattles and shakers are ubiquitous untuned percussion instruments in all musical cultures. They are used in many forms of music-making, religious ceremonies, dance and other activities. They are often simple in construction and can be made from natural materials.

A rattle comprises a body housing a number of small pellets or beans, which bounce against the internal walls of the instrument when it is shaken or struck, like a maraca. A shaker is played in the same way, but the objects that produce the sound are on the outside of the instrument, like the Latin American *quijada* – the jawbone of a donkey or horse shaken so that the teeth clatter. A shaker may also have jingles made from metal, shell, stone or glass.

Rattles and shakers may have a handle like a baby's rattle, or the whole body of the instrument may be shaken, like the Chilean rain stick. This is a hollowed and dried cactus branch with thorns hammered into it in a spiral pattern. It is then filled with small pebbles, and the ends are capped and sealed. Turning the stick over causes the pebbles to trickle over the thorns, making the sound of gentle rain.

CROTAL BELLS

Rattles are used in a range of extra-musical activities. Crotal or closed bells are worn by dancers throughout Asia and Africa and also added to animals' harnesses. In a crotal bell, the outside of the bell encloses the clapper or pellet. They are usually small, and several can be put together and attached to a strap or handle –

◄ *Untuned percussion instruments: Native American rattle (above);* shekere *(left).*

Musical Instruments Handbook

▲ *Maracas are an integral part of any Latin-American band.*

orchestral sleigh bells comprise 10 to 20 crotal bells. Archeological records indicate that crotal bells have been used since prehistoric times, and were also worn as talismen.

MARACAS

Rattles and shakers like maracas, the *ganzá* and the *cabasa* are widely used in African and Latin-American traditional music, and Latin-influenced pop and jazz. Maracas are a pair of rattles made from wood, metal or coconut shells. They are used to provide a constant pulse in a wide variety of Latin-American dance styles. Although easy to play, the player needs to develop a technique of flicking the pellets in one mass in order to create a tight sound, so the maraca rhythm can be clearly heard.

GANZÁ AND *CABASA*

The *ganzá* (*xique-xique, tubo*) is similar to the maracas – a tube filled with pellets, which is held sideways to ensure an even distribution of the pellets when playing. A *cabasa* (*afuche, xequebum*) is a gourd with beads or small shells strung on the outside, and is a cross between a scraper (see p. 78) and a shaker. *Cabasas* made from natural materials like the Brazilian *xequebum* normally have the beads sewn in a fine net around the gourd, whereas a metal *cabasa* is strung with necklaces of metal beads. It is played by resting the head of the instrument against the hand to make the beads turn one way as the handle is turned the opposite way.

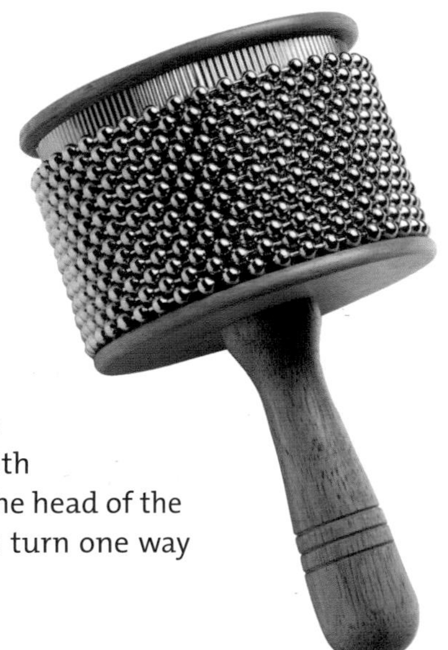

▶ *A Brazilian* cabasa.

Section One: The Instruments

CASTANETS

Castanets are a Gypsy folk instrument and are played with great artistry by Spanish flamenco dancers. They may in fact be a local wooden version of the brass finger cymbals brought into Spain by Muslim conquerors from around AD 700.

Fact

Wooden instruments can be mechanized, like the ratchet, where a cogwheel depresses thin wooden tongues against a set of spokes as its handle is turned. Ratchets have been used as bird-scarers, and were played instead of bells in Roman Catholic churches during Holy Week.

Castanets are a pair of round wooden shells made from ebony or rosewood held together with string. They are held in the palm of the hand and played by looping the string over the thumb and pressing the castanets together with the fingers. Traditionally, a pair of castanets will be played with the lower-sounding male (*macho*) castanet in the right hand and played with four fingers, and the higher-sounding female (*hembra*) castanet in the left hand and played with two fingers. Performers create complex rhythms by alternating beats on the pairs of castanets.

As orchestral percussionists may not be adept at playing the castanets in this way, orchestral castanets used in pieces like Manuel de Falla's (1876–1946) *Three-Cornered Hat* (1919) are usually played against the knee, or a castanet machine is used, in which a pair of castanets are mounted on a wooden block and held open with a spring mechanism. The players drum on the castanets with their fingers.

▶ *In flamenco, castanets are known as* palillos *(little sticks).*

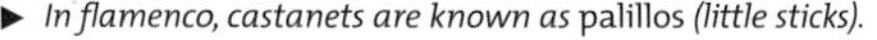

Musical Instruments Handbook

METAL INSTRUMENTS

A range of metal percussion instruments are found in the western orchestra, many of which have ancient and global origins.

TRIANGLE

The triangle comprises a slim steel bar, circular in cross-section, bent into an equilateral triangle (18 cm/7 in each side) with one corner open. It is played with a metal rod, and is suspended from a loop of string. The triangle was originally a sistrum – one of the oldest known percussion instruments. A sistrum is a 'U'-shaped metal frame with a number of bars and prongs attached to it, which hold metal jingles, discs and rings that clatter together as the instrument is shaken. Sistra first appear in the archeological record in ancient Egypt, Sumeria and Babylonia in 2500 BC, and are found in Malaysia and Melanesia. The triangle as we know it today first appeared in Europe in the late-fourteenth century, at which time it was a triangle-shaped sistrum with rings attached.

The orchestral triangle – without rings – appeared in the nineteenth century, and was used to provide a sparkle to orchestrations such as in Franz Liszt's (1811–86) Piano Concerto No. 1 (1853) and in 'Anitra's Dance' from *Peer Gynt* (1876) by Edvard Grieg (1843–1907). Classical composers included the triangle to create Turkish effects, but this may well have been a triangle with jingles attached, which could be shaken and struck (see p. 42).

Fact

Illustrations in illuminated manuscripts indicate that various forms of triangle were used in religious ceremonies, although writers of the time complained that its noise was often a distraction to the worshippers.

Section One: The Instruments

PLAYING THE TRIANGLE

Although it is a simple instrument, the triangle is tricky to play well. It produces a range of tone colours. The purest sound is produced by striking it as close to the top corner as possible, which requires the player to take very good aim to hit a small playing zone. Playing more complex rhythms requires the use of two beaters, and care must be taken to stop the triangle twirling round on its string with each strike of the beater. It can be suspended from the player's outstretched finger and played open and closed (damped), the damping being done by the other fingers in the hand. A roll or *tremolo* is played either by playing a single stroke roll with two beaters, or, more commonly, by moving the end of the beater rapidly side to side inside one corner.

▲ *The triangle's sound cuts through large orchestras'.*

ANVIL

The anvil is a sound effect used in orchestral music to imitate a blacksmith's. It is perhaps most famously heard in Wagner's *Rhinegold* (1876) and in the 'Anvil Chorus' of Giuseppe Verdi's (1813–1901) *Il Trovatore* (1853). It can also be used for dramatic effect, such as in the chorus 'Praise Ye the God of Iron' in William Walton's (1902–83) *Belshazzar's Feast* (1930). It also appears in Edgar Varèse's (1885–1965) *Hyperprism* (1923) and *Ionisation* (1931).

Real anvils can be impractical in the orchestra as they are so heavy. Effective substitutes can be made from sections of scaffold pole or railway track, which provide the same clanging sound. The anvil is played with a heavy metal mallet or hammer.

Musical Instruments Handbook

MUSICAL SAW

The musical saw is a fine-bladed saw without teeth (70–90 cm/28–36 in long), played with a double bass or cello bow. The saw handle is held between the knees and the tip of the saw held in the left (or non-bowing) hand. As the right hand bows the saw, the left hand bends it to create different pitches. Both the bowing pressure and amount of bending must be carefully controlled to make the saw play a true pitch and a sustained musical line. It has a high singing tone, and can play *vibrato* and *glissandi*. Its origins are obscure, but it may have originated from rural North America in the late-nineteenth century. It was a popular musical-hall and vaudeville instrument around the turn of the twentieth century, and Shostakovitch included it in his opera *The Nose* (1927–28).

▲ *A street musician delights his small audience.*

FLEXATONE

The musical saw is similar to the flexatone, which was invented as a jazz instrument in the 1920s. The flexatone is a thin flexible triangular steel plate fixed at the wide end to a frame about 30 cm (12 in) long, with rubber or wooden beaters attached to rods at the lower end of the plate. The player waves the flexatone to make the beaters hit the plate, and at the same time changes their thumb pressure on the plate to change the pitch. It has a limited pitch range, although it plays a melodic part in Aram Khatchaturian's (1903–78) Piano Concerto (1936).

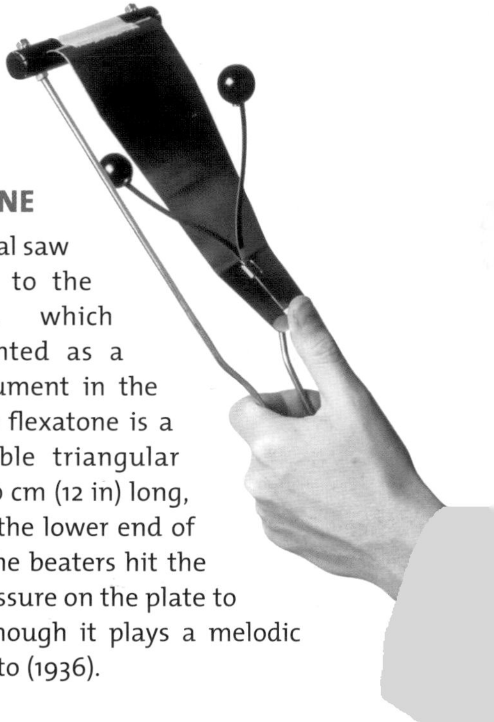

► *The flexatone was patented by the Playatone Company, New York.*

Section One: The Instruments

GLASS INSTRUMENTS

Understanding how to use friction to produce sounds in glass goes back to Galileo Galilei (1564–1642), who discussed the singing effect achieved by running a moistened finger around the rim of a glass.

In 1743, the Irish musician Richard Puckeridge created an angelic organ, or seraphim, from glasses rubbed with wet fingers. The glasses were filled with water to different levels to produce different pitches. The composer Gluck also played a similar instrument.

GLASS ARMONICA

Benjamin Franklin (1706–90) adapted the idea and created an armonica – or glass armonica – in 1761, in which nested bowls of different diameters were mounted on a horizontal spindle turned by a foot-operated treadle. The sound was produced by rubbing the rims of the bowls with moistened fingers. On Franklin's glass armonica, the performer could play up to 10 notes at once, which greatly increased the range and scope of the original instrument, where playing more than two notes at once was almost impossible.

The glass armonica, or musical glasses, enjoyed a brief vogue in the eighteenth and nineteenth centuries. Gaëtano Donizetti (1797–1848) used it in the mad scene in *Lucia di Lammermoor* (1835) and Saint-Saëns used it to represent the underwater world in *Carnival of the Animals* (1886). It became a popular domestic instrument. However, rumours that playing the instrument could send performers and listeners insane – perhaps fuelled by Viennese psychiatrist Franz Mesmer's (1734–1815) use of the instrument in his demonstrations of mesmerism – caused the glass armonica to wane in popularity.

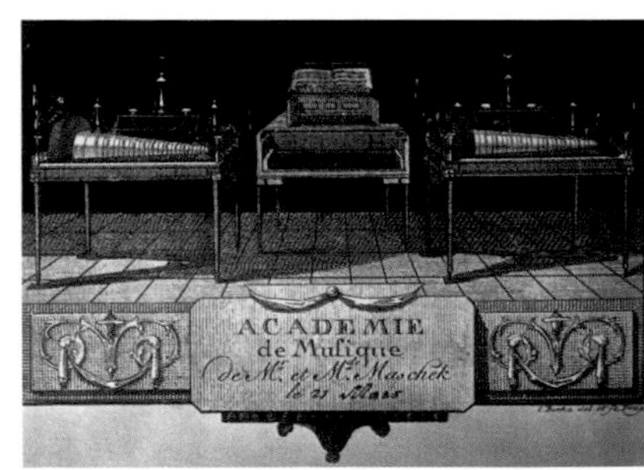

▲ *The glass armonica had its world premiere in January 1762.*

Musical Instruments Handbook

LATIN-AMERICAN PERCUSSION IN THE SAMBA BAND

The music of Latin America combines influences from the traditional music of the African slaves transported between 1450 and the end of the nineteenth century, music from the Spanish and Portuguese colonial powers, and latterly, pop and jazz from North America.

Samba is an umbrella term describing an energetic style of dancing and drumming performed at the annual pre-Lent carnivals in Brazil in February and March, and across Europe and North America. With the abolition of slavery in South America in 1888, many black workers migrated to the cities, and lived in *favelas* (shanty towns) around the edges of the city. Samba developed as a popular style in the *favelas* and by 1917 the first samba record, *On the Telephone*, was released.

▼ *A variety of Latin-American percussion instruments.*

SAMBA STYLE

Depending on the number of performers, samba can vary in style. Typically, its style is two beats in a bar and a medium to fast tempo to encourage the dancers to keep moving. Samba relies on a characteristic *batucada* (rhythmic pattern), which is played by the *bateria* (percussion) in a samba band. There can be between 10 and 50 performers in the *bateria*, who work together to play the *batucada*, which comprises several short repeated rhythms that fit together to create a multilayered, interlocking pattern.

▲ *Samba musician Don Alias performing his rapid-fire technique.*

Section One: The Instruments

A samba piece will be constructed from chorus and verse sections, which use different combinations of the *bateria*, and provide opportunities for other instrumentalists, singers and dancers to perform. Samba music is played without notation and learned aurally. The structure of a piece is likely to vary in performance as performers extemporize solo sections within the basic structure of the music. The ensemble is directed by the *mestre* (master), who will play in the group and give signals to the performers using a whistle (*apito*).

MAKE-UP OF A SAMBA BAND

Typically a samba *bateria* will comprise a group of drums and a shaker (*ganzá*), scraper (*reco-reco*) and the *agogo*, a double- or triple-cone-shaped bell played with a metal or wooden stick. In ascending order of pitch, the drums are the *surdo* (bass drum), *caixa* (snare drum), *cuíca* (friction drum), *tamborin* (frame drum), and *pandiero* (tambourine).

SURDO

The *surdo* is a double-headed cylindrical metal drum (40–50 cm/16–20 in diameter and 60 cm/24 in long) suspended from a harness worn by the player. The player uses a large padded drumstick and muffles the sound with their other hand. The *surdo* plays a pulse and is the heartbeat of the ensemble.

CAIXA

The *caixa* (20–30 cm/8–12 in diameter and 10 cm/4 in long) generally plays a continuous sixteenth-note rhythm with a syncopated accent pattern. The *cuíca* is a popular solo instrument, as it has a wide pitch range and unusual sound.

TAMBORIN AND *PANDEIRO*

The *tamborin* (15–20 cm/6–8 in diameter) and *pandeiro* (20–30 cm/8–12 in diameter) are frame drums. The tamborin does not have jingles and is played with a stick. The *pandeiro* has jingles and is very similar to the European tambourine. When playing these instruments, the forefinger of the non-playing hand is used to muffle the drum head to produce both open and closed sounds. Experienced *tamborin* and *pandiero* players show great flair in performance and perform choreographic routines with the instruments as they play.

Musical Instruments Handbook

INSTRUMENTS TROUVÉS AND SOUND EFFECTS

Sound effects and *instruments trouvés* include found objects and specialist machines for making noises. Composers have made extensive use of both sound effects and found objects in orchestral music, especially in music for theatre, dance and opera.

SOUND EFFECTS

The wind machine was originally a theatrical sound effect, and is a cylinder of wooden slats with a canvas covering. The cylinder is turned by a crank-handle and rubs against the canvas, producing the sound of rushing wind. It is used in the *Sinfonia Antarctica* (1949–52) by Ralph Vaughan Williams (1882–1958). The wind machine may be teamed with the thunder sheet – a large flexible metal sheet suspended from a frame, which gives a rumbling sound when shaken.

Gershwin wrote for four tuned car horns in *An American in Paris* (1928), and Leonard Bernstein (1918–90) instructs the timpanist to blow a police whistle to break up the fight scene in *West Side Story* (1961). There is a starting pistol in Erik Satie's (1866–1925) ballet *Parade* (1917), which also includes a typewriter and a *bouteillophone*, a set of tuned bottles played like a xylophone. Tchaikovsky writes for cannon in his overture *The Year 1812*, but this sound is often produced electronically, as it is a logistical challenge to co-ordinate ballistics with an orchestra in the concert hall.

Section One: The Instruments

FOUND OBJECTS

Found objects can be anything that takes the composer's fancy – such as the table and chairs, rice bowls, chopsticks, two wine bottles, paper napkins, bottle of soft drink, washing-up bowl, tablecloth, wine glasses, apron and rubber gloves played by four percussionists in Stephen Montague's (b. 1943) *Chew Chow Chatterbox* (1998).

Modernist composers in the twentieth century have sought new sonorities for their music, drawing on sounds from the industrial world, electronic music, pop music and world music for inspiration. Instruments previously regarded as novelty items have became integral to the sound world of modern music. Varèse includes hand-cranked sirens and anvil in *Ionisation* (1930), which is written for 13 percussionists. He uses chains dropped into a metal box in *Intégrales* (1920), as did Arnold Schoenberg (1874–1951) in *Gurrelieder* (1910).

▲ *The percussionist has to be able to play a wide variety of instruments.*

COMPOSITIONS FOR FOUND OBJECTS

John Cage (1912–92) challenged the listener to focus on the placement of sounds in his music for prepared piano and music using electronic equipment. *Rocks* (1986) requires radios, television sets, cassette machines and machines emitting fixed sounds like vacuum cleaners, buzzers and alarms. In *Child of Tree* (1975) and *Branches* (1976) cactus spikes are played with toothpicks.

György Ligeti's (b. 1923) opera *Le Grand Macabre* (1978) has a car-horn prelude to each act and a huge range of percussion, including a tray of china that is thrown into a trash can. James Wood combines percussion from around the world with found objects. *Tongues of Fire* (2001) uses a quartet of oil drums played on different parts of their surfaces with different beaters to create a range of sonorities, and using them as resonators for cowbells, gongs and *güiros*.

Musical Instruments Handbook

NEW SOUNDS

The performance group Stomp use an eclectic mix of found objects like trash cans, brushes, sand, boxes of matches and lighters to make dance and percussion performance pieces. Performers like Ensemble Bash and Evelyn Glennie seek to find new and exciting sounds to include in their music. Glennie's improvisations in performance encompass an array of percussion instruments and found objects. Ensemble Bash's repertoire includes pieces that make use of unusual objects, such as Howard Skempton's (b. 1947) *Shiftwork*, which includes thimbles, pottery ramekins and baking beans.

▲ *Water is one of Evelyn Glennie's more unusual creative media.*

Although there are some examples of these new additions to the orchestra being played by other instrumentalists (such as in the percussion concerto *Veni, Veni, Emmanuel* (1992) by James Macmillan (b. 1959), where all the orchestra's members end the work by playing tiny handbells), usually it is the percussionist's job to play *instruments trouvés.*

It is interesting to note that although the musical language of the orchestra has changed radically in the last 100 years, it is largely in the percussion section that new instruments and sonorities have been introduced. Ravel writes for swanee whistle in *L'Enfant et les Sortilèges* (1925) to create the effect of night sounds. The swanee whistle is a pipe with a plunger in the end so that the pitch can be changed in swooping slides as it is blown. In Benedict Mason's (b. 1954) Concerto for Viola Section and Orchestra (1990), the percussionists whirl plastic tubes around their heads. Although both of these are aerophones, and could join the woodwind section, these instruments are always played by the percussionist.

Section One: The Instruments

THE INVENTIONS OF LUIGI RUSSOLO AND HARRY PARTCH

In the twentieth century, some musicians became interested in inventing new acoustic instruments that could take music beyond the tuning systems, scales and harmonic language inherent in the instruments commonly played in western classical music.

Creating new instruments created a revolutionary new sound world. New instruments were often promoted outside the normal scope of the bourgeois concert audience, frequently being used for music theatre and film, and were not commonly included in the orchestra.

▲ *Luigi Russolo with his* intonarumori, *which incorporated environmental sound.*

THE ART OF NOISE

The Italian futurist artist and musician Luigi Russolo (1885–1947) invented a set of *intonarumori*, or noise intoners between 1913 and 1921. He wanted to make it possible for composers to capture 'the infinite variety of noise sounds' in music as he explained in his manifesto *The Art of Noise* (1913). Russolo and his brother Antonio composed music for the new instruments, including incidental music for Futurist films. Russolo's instruments were revolutionary in the way they incorporated noise and environmental sound into modern music. His work was a direct influence on the first generation of composers to work with electro-acoustics, including Varèse, Cage

Musical Instruments Handbook

and Pierre Schaefer (1910–95), the inventor of *musique concrète* and the first composer to work with magnetic tape.

INTONARUMORI

The *intonarumori* created sounds in a similar way to a hurdy-gurdy. Each one comprised a single string inside a box, made to vibrate by a wheel that rubbed against it. The machine had a mechanism to change the tension and pitch of the string, and a diffuser horn to amplify the sound. Using a variety of materials for the different components of the *intonarumori* created different acoustic effects – as illustrated in their descriptive names, including the *scoppiatore* (exploder), *sibilatore* (hisser) and *ululatore* (howler). In 1922, Russolo invented a *rumorarmonio* – a keyboard mechanism that enabled one performer to play several *intonarumori*. Unfortunately, all Russolo's instruments and scores were lost during the Second World War, and there is only one primitive recording of the *intonarumori* available today.

MONOPHONE

The invented instruments of Harry Partch (1901–74) were constructed to play in just intonation – his own system of dividing tones within an octave. Rejecting western music theory, and influenced by the tuning systems of non-western traditional music, Partch created the monophone in 1930. This was basically an adapted viola that could play a 29-tone octave, and was followed in 1933 by a guitar that played a 37-tone octave, and in 1935, by the ptolemy, a bellows-reed organ that played a 43-tone octave.

Partch created mainly bowed and struck chordophones, like the harmonic canon, and idiophones made from wood, glass and metal. Many of his instruments are beautiful sculptural objects in their own right. He used natural materials in boos I and II, large bamboo marimbas with six ranks of tuned bamboo tubes, and found objects such as the mazda marimba, which is 24 tuned light bulbs, and Whang Guns, which are sheets of sprung steel controlled by pedals. Partch composed extensively for his own instruments, often combining them with music drama and singing.

▲ *Harry Partch modified existing instruments and built new ones from scratch so they could use different tuning systems.*

Section One: The Instruments

INTRODUCTION

BRASS

The family of brass instruments includes all those that are sounded by the vibrations of a player's lips. Though not all are actually made of brass, the majority of instruments in the family are made from metal alloys coated with a shiny lacquer.

▲ *The cornet makes use of piston valves.*

Brass instruments differ less in their construction than the woodwind family. Like their cousins, they make use of both conical and cylindrical bores but very often both are used in one instrument. The major revolution in brass-instrument design was the invention of the valve in the early-nineteenth century.

COLUMNS OF AIR

All brass and woodwind instruments employ enclosed columns of air and rely on the properties of the harmonic series (the simultaneous pitches generated by the vibrations of air) combined with methods of altering the length of the air column to sound different pitches.

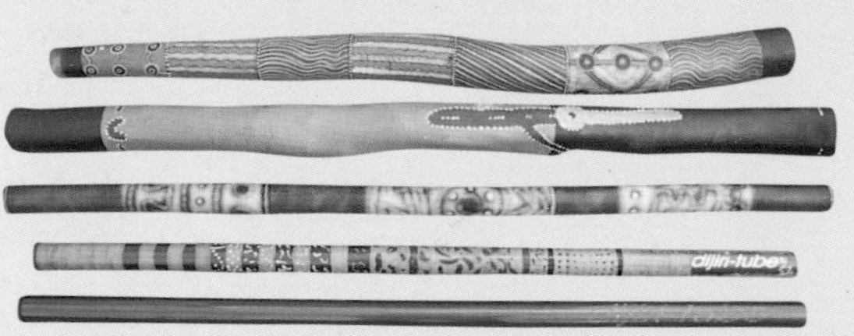

▲ *Didgeridoos are sometimes described as natural wooden trumpets.*

The lowest note a given column of air can sound is known as the 'fundamental'. At the same time as the fundamental, higher notes also sound. These are known as overtones and are precise multiples of the fundamental. The first overtone vibrates twice as fast as the fundamental, the second three times as fast, the third four times as fast, and so on. In musical terms, this translates to the first overtone being an octave higher than the fundamental, the second a perfect fifth higher,

Musical Instruments Handbook

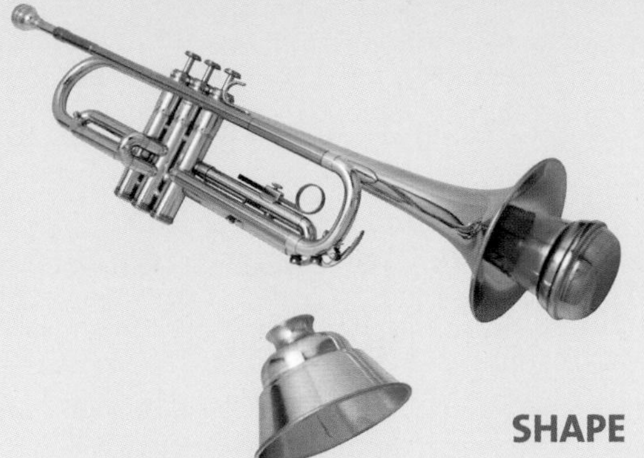

the third a fourth higher, continuing in ever-decreasing steps. Each of these overtones (also known as partials) can be made to sound most prominent by increasing the amount of energy put into the air column, an effect known as overblowing.

▲ *Mutes alter an instrument's tone.*

SHAPE

A significant part of brass-instrument design, therefore, is the creation of a stable column of air that has acoustic properties able to help with sound production. The most useful shapes for brass (and woodwind) instruments are the cylinder and the cone.

In practice, most modern brass instruments are a mixture of the two: it is the extent to which a cone widens and the length of the tube that are largely responsible for the instrument's character. The potential difference can be heard by comparing a trumpet to a flugelhorn. The former – cylindrical except for the mouthpiece shank and the flared-bell section – has a bright, clear sound. The latter – conical except for the tuning shank – has a mellow, dark sound.

EARLY BRASS

The earliest trumpets and horns were simple tubes. They could sound only the pitches common to their fundamental pitch. To play higher, more energy was needed, which was tiring for the player. Gradually the tube's construction improved, making sounding the higher partials easier, until it was possible to play a complete diatonic scale.

Western music since the Renaissance has largely been organized using a system called 'equal temperament', which divides the octave into 12 equal steps called half steps (or semitones). Although based on the properties of the harmonic series, equal temperament in fact irons out inconsistencies that occur with increasing regularity in the higher regions of the series. Consequently, brass instruments using only the harmonic series sounded out of tune on particular pitches. To counter this, instruments were made with different fundamental pitches to match the key of the music being performed. This was a cumbersome system, however, and meant the instruments lacked flexibility.

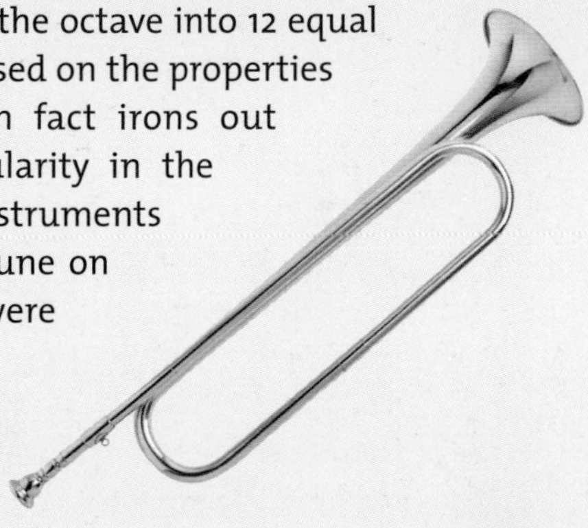

► *The player controls the bugle's pitch as it has no valves.*

Section One: The Instruments

VALVES

The invention of valves in the early-nineteenth century provided a solution, as they allowed access to increasing lengths of tubing. Additional tube lengths of a half step, a whole step and two-and-a-half whole steps could be combined to lower the pitch by a diminished fifth. In instruments of narrow bore, which do not generally sound their fundamental, this was enough to open out the complete chromatic compass. In larger bored instruments, a fourth valve was necessary.

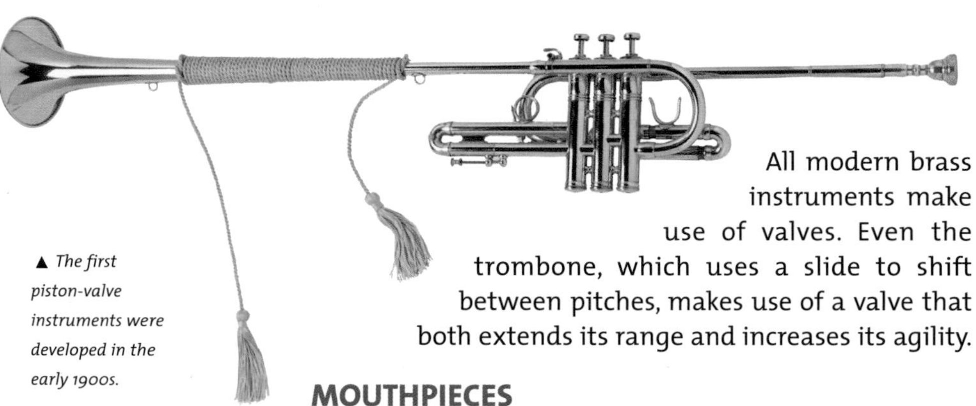

▲ *The first piston-valve instruments were developed in the early 1900s.*

All modern brass instruments make use of valves. Even the trombone, which uses a slide to shift between pitches, makes use of a valve that both extends its range and increases its agility.

MOUTHPIECES

Sound in the brass family is generated from the buzzing of a player's lips. This energy is transferred to the air column in the instrument by the mouthpiece. The design of the mouthpiece is thus crucial in helping the player get the best out of the instrument.

All mouthpieces are funnel-shaped – wide at the point of contact with the lips before narrowing to an aperture, which leads via a short tube to the main body of the instrument. The initial section of the mouthpiece is cup-shaped for trumpets, trombones and tubas, and 'V'-shaped for horns.

Lower-pitched instruments generally have wider mouthpieces to enable a wider lip aperture to generate energy. The horn's mouthpiece, however, is relatively narrow, but enables the sounding of extremely low pitches through its depth. The opposite is true for higher-pitched instruments – the mouthpiece of the piccolo trumpet is very shallow to help with the playing of high pitches.

Musical Instruments Handbook

THE ROLE OF BRASS INSTRUMENTS

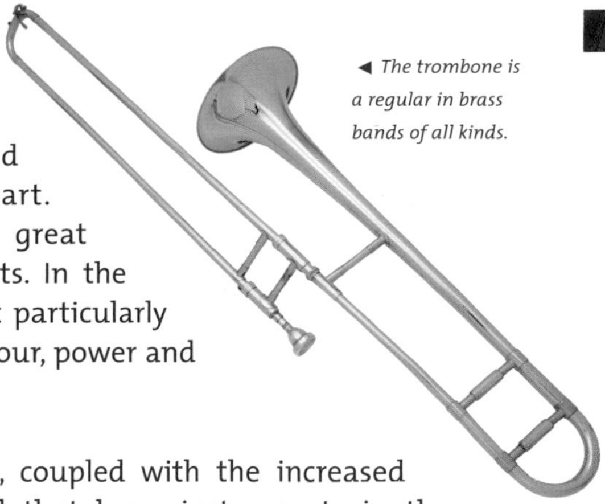

◀ The trombone is a regular in brass bands of all kinds.

The brass family is less expressive and flexible than its stringed counterpart. However, the twentieth century saw great strides in the use of brass instruments. In the orchestra they have become important particularly as a brass choir, able to add weight, colour, power and lustre to the strings or winds.

The growing virtuosity of performers, coupled with the increased demands of composers, have ensured that brass instruments in the orchestra are regarded as the equals of the woodwind and are more than capable of taking important solo lines. Much of this acceptance has come through jazz. The trumpet and trombone in particular have been vital to jazz but equally, jazz has shown how they can be used expressively and flexibly.

As chamber instruments they are less successful. Brass quintets and ensembles are popular, but there is little repertoire of high-enough quality adequate to display their abilities. The brass band, however, has been a central part of music making in England particularly. Since the early-twentieth century, the system of competitions has ensured that almost every town has a brass band; they remain a vital training ground for young musicians.

Section One: The Instruments

SHOFAR

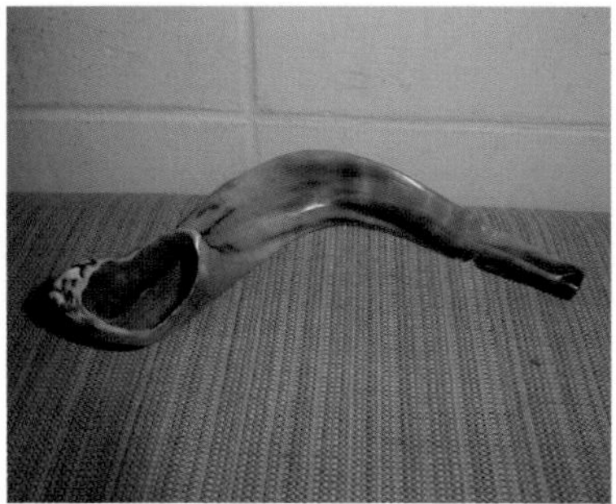

The shofar is a ram's horn used as a musical instrument in Judaism. Broadly speaking, it was sounded at times of ceremony, such as the celebration of the new moon, at times of great significance, such as a drought or famine, and as a signal for war.

Today, its use in secular contexts has largely been abandoned, though it was sounded in celebration of the reunification of Jerusalem in 1967. It retains its religious significance, however, and is particularly associated with Yom Kippur and Rosh Hashanah.

The calls played on the shofar vary greatly according to circumstance, tradition and players. All are essentially made from two notes – the precise pitches being dependent on the specific instrument – and the *tremolo* resulting from fast alternation between them. The shofar player is known as the *Ba'al Tokea* or 'master of the blast'.

CONSTRUCTION

The horn is heated, worked into shape and hollowed out. A hole is made at the tip; some shofars are designed to be played directly through this hole, others use a mouthpiece. All kinds are played with the buzzing lips familiar from trumpets and horns. Due to the irregular nature of the bore, the shofar does not always sound the same intervals.

Given its inconsistent musical nature, the shofar has rarely been used in orchestral music. There is a short part for it in Elgar's *The Apostles*, but this is more usually played by a flugelhorn.

Fact

The shofar is mentioned often in the Hebrew Bible with instructions for its use.

Musical Instruments Handbook

POST HORN

The post horn is a small, valveless brass instrument once used by guards on mail coaches to announce arrivals and departures.

Originally bow shaped, in the seventeenth century post horns were bent in a single loop to play the fundamental pitch *bb'*. Clearly these were small instruments, perhaps only 7 cm (3 in) across; nevertheless they appear in the music of Georg Philipp Telemann (1681–1767), George Frideric Handel (1685–1759) and Johann Sebastian Bach (1685–1750).

DEVELOPMENT

In the eighteenth century, the post horn was extended in length and used by Wolfgang Amadeus Mozart (1756–91) in a number of works. By the nineteenth century, a variety of crooks and tuning slides were in use and the post horn had become a popular instrument in bands across Europe. In Germany there were even experiments with finger holes, designed to change the fundamental pitch from F to B♭.

▲ *An orchestra's horn player usually plays the post horn.*

COACH HORN

In England at this time, the straight post horn was developed that became the standard horn for use on Royal Mail coaches. Keyed in A or A♭, it only sounds up to the fifth partial, but was recognizable enough to be used in Koenig's famous *Post Horn Gallop*. This instrument developed into the coach horn, which was slightly longer, made from copper and had a conical rather than a cylindrical bore. The coach horn was still used by the Royal Mail in the first decades of the twentieth century. There were a remarkable number of tunes composed for so limited an instrument, many of which still survive to this day.

Section One: The Instruments

WORLD HORNS

Virtually any tube, even without any modification as a musical instrument, can be sounded as a horn, producing a series of notes from the harmonic series.

CONCHES

Many of the world's horns are found objects: an animal horn with the tip cut off, or a large spiral-type shell, usually a conch, with the point cut off to give access to the tube within. Separate cup-shaped mouthpieces are often fit. Blown conches aren't particularly suited to playing tunes; their use is usually for signalling and ritual – for example in the ceremonies of Hindu temples in India and in the Buddhist temples of Tibet, Nepal and East Asia.

ANIMAL HORNS

Most of the range of musical animal horns in Africa are blown not at the end but via a hole cut in the side. This approach gives the maker control of the size and shape of embouchure independently of the tube's diameter. Some animal horns, such as the Norwegian *bukkehorn* ('goat-horn', though often a cow's), are drilled with finger holes. Accurate pitching is difficult on such short horns.

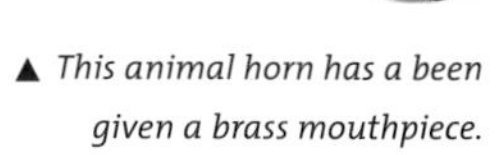

▲ *This animal horn has a been given a brass mouthpiece.*

BARK-BOUND HORNS

Most of the world's many horns are, indeed, made rather than found: at the simplest, a spiral of birch-bark, pegged at the wide end to stop it unravelling, or a branch split, a bore and mouth-cup hollowed out, and then the two halves glued back together and bound with birch-bark. Bark-bound wooden instruments were played, particularly by herders, up to the twentieth century in the Nordic countries, Russia, and in the mountain areas of Europe. Many of these are of great

Musical Instruments Handbook

length; the longer a horn, the more usable are the higher harmonics, which – being closer together in pitch – can produce a more complete scale. The best-known and most engineered of these is the Alpine alphorn, a straight, gradually expanding tube up to 4 m (13 ft) long that curves upwards just before the bell. Modern alphorns usually dismantle for travel, and some are made of carbon-fibre.

DIDGERIDOO

The famous didgeridoo of aboriginal Australians is made from a length of eucalyptus branch hollowed out by termites. Its blowing end is wide, usually smoothed with a beeswax coating, and the player uses a sophisticated technique with slack embouchure producing low drone notes, pulsing his breath, utilizing mouth resonance and adding in vocal yelps and barks that intermodulate with the blown sound, which is maintained continuously by circular breathing.

METAL HORNS

Metal horns are widespread and, being durable, examples have survived from antiquity. Among these are the Bronze Age Scandinavian *lur,* which is 'S'-shaped with a disc bell, and the mouthpiece and animal-headed bell of the otherwise probably wooden *carnyx* of the ancient Celts.

Metal horns played today include ornate straight ceremonial trumpets in Tibet and Benin, which range up to alphorn-length, the *lur*-like 'C'-curved *kombu* and 'S'-curved *narsiga* of India, the short signal horn of English foxhunters, the coiled military signalling bugle, and the whole range of trumpets and other orchestral brass covered elsewhere in this chapter.

◀ *The Tibetan* dung cheng *ranges from 4–20 ft (1.2–6 m) in length.*

Section One: The Instruments

CORNETT

The cornett of European Renaissance art music is a longer finger-hole horn made of wood. A precursor to the modern brass horns, it should not be confused with the valved – and much later developed – cornet.

CONSTRUCTION AND PLAYING TECHNIQUE

The cornett is a long tube, usually around 60 cm (20 in) in length. It is normally curved, like an animal horn, so that the player's hands can reach the finger holes more easily. At the top is the mouthpiece, vibrated by the player's lips. It is this that causes the cornett to be classified as a brass instrument rather than woodwind, despite its other characteristics. This also made it difficult to play. Although the main tube is only of around the same length as a typical woodwind instrument, the player has to use his or her lips to form the sound. Modern brass instruments have much longer tubes, which makes the pitch easier to control.

THE RENAISSANCE CORNETT

In the Renaissance ensemble, the cornett was typically partnered with the sackbut (a sixteenth-century version of the slide trombone). There was an entire family of cornetts, from the bass cornett to the high-pitched cornettino. However, little music composed for the cornett is extant. Christoph Willibald Gluck (1714–87) was among the last to include the cornett in his scoring – for *Orfeo ed Euridice* (1762). Gradually the cornett was replaced by other instruments that provided similar effects more easily in the orchestra, but were simpler to play.

Musical Instruments Handbook

SERPENT

A conically bored baritone instrument, the serpent is supposed to have been invented by Edmé Guillaume in 1590. Like its close relative, the cornett, it is sounded by buzzing the lips into an ivory-, horn- or metal-cup mouthpiece which, in turn, agitates the air column.

Its 213-cm (84-in) length is undulating in appearance, giving it its name. It is normally made out of walnut wood, although it can also be found in brass or silver. The serpent originally had six finger holes, giving the instrument a compass from *C* to *g'*.

ROLE IN THE ORCHESTRA

The serpent was used in bands and orchestras to support bass lines – Handel uses it in his *Music for the Royal Fireworks* (1789) – and was often played by bassoonists, despite the completely different playing technique required. The instrument gradually had keys added, giving a more chromatic range. This, however, did nothing to cure the problems of intonation and poor tone quality; only a skilled player could fully remedy such drawbacks, and even then the serpent received criticism.

Despite this, the serpent continued to be used well into the nineteenth century. It is often unclear which instrument a composer wanted to hear, but there is evidence to suggest that the serpent was often used in Italy by the *bel canto* school of Gaëtano Donizetti (1797–1848) and Saverio Mercadante (1795–1870). Richard Wagner (1813–83) was similarly vague about his intentions; in his case it normally assumed that 'serpent' actually signifies a *cimbasso* or other bass instrument.

TWENTIETH-CENTURY REVIVAL

The serpent enjoyed something of a revival in the twentieth century with the advent of the early-music movement. A number of composers, including Peter Maxwell Davies (b. 1934) and Judith Weir (b. 1954) wrote for the instrument. It has, though, never taken root as permanent orchestral member.

Section One: The Instruments

CORNET

The cornet is very similar to the trumpet in looks and playing technique. It is thought to have been invented by the instrument maker Jean-Louis Antoine in the 1820s.

Antoine, who worked for the Parisian firm Halary, was one of a number of makers experimenting with the new valve technology that was revolutionizing brass instruments at the time. His idea of adding valves to the post horn rapidly caught on, and by 1830 cornet players around Paris were already making names for themselves.

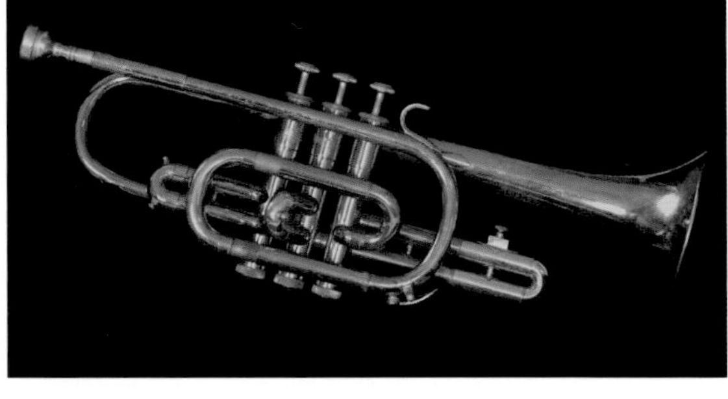

CONSTRUCTION

The cornet looks like a compact version of the trumpet, with three valves located centrally and a flared bell. Like the trumpet, it is keyed in B♭ and has an accepted sounding compass of *e* to *b♭''*, though many players add another third or fourth above that. It uses a cup-shaped mouthpiece that fits snugly into the instrument's end. The particular design of the mouthpiece gives the cornet greater agility than the trumpet, and for that reason it was quickly adopted as an orchestral instrument where it would give a fully chromatic, mobile treble to the brass section.

▲ *Cornets are a staple of wind bands.*

FALL AND RISE

The cornet's sound is mellow and easy, but it lacks brilliance and bite. Consequently a pair of cornets was often used in conjunction with a pair of trumpets. Hector Berlioz (1803–69), César Franck (1822–90) and

Musical Instruments Handbook

Georges Bizet (1838–1875) were early champions of the cornet, and it was also used successfully by Edward Elgar (1857–1934) and Igor Stravinsky (1882–1971).

The trumpet was slower to develop into a suitably flexible instrument, so cornets were often used as substitutes, particularly in the United States and Great Britain. Unfortunately, this proved to be a public-relations disaster, as the brilliance required for classical trumpet parts was entirely lacking from the cornet; it quickly developed a reputation as a feeble, dull instrument. Despite this, the cornet found its true vocation in brass-band music. The British band tradition now uses four separate cornet parts, as well as a high E♭ part.

JAZZ INSTRUMENT

In the United States, the cornet has enjoyed considerable success in jazz. The strong French culture in New Orleans at the beginning of the twentieth century ensured that the instrument was used in the fashionable parade bands. Many well-known jazz performers learned their art on the cornet, including Louis Armstrong and Bix Beiderbecke. It has continued to be a popular instrument in jazz – and has even been heard in bop and free jazz.

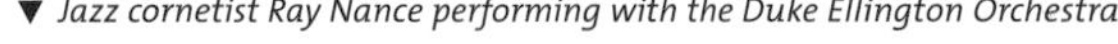

▼ *Jazz cornetist Ray Nance performing with the Duke Ellington Orchestra.*

Section One: The Instruments

FLUGELHORN

The flugelhorn developed from the bugel, a signalling horn used in the Middle Ages and made out of bull or ox horn. This developed into a large, semicircular hunting horn made of brass or silver that was used by the military during the Seven Years' War (1756–63).

HISTORY

Wrapping the horn around itself once, so the bell pointed directly away from the player, enabled keys to be added, and the resulting instrument was known as the *Klappenflügelhorn*. In 1832, Michael Saurle, an instrument manufacturer working in Munich, swapped the keys for valves. The valved flugelhorn quickly gained popularity and was particularly influential on Adolphe Sax (1814–94) in his development of saxhorns. It is considered by some to be a member of the saxhorn family.

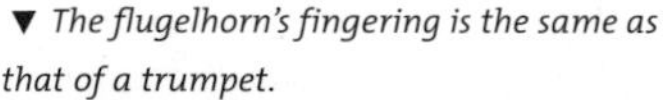

▼ *The flugelhorn's fingering is the same as that of a trumpet.*

CONSTRUCTION

The flugelhorn is conically bored and uses an extended mouthpipe section as a tuning slide so as to not interrupt the bore. It opens out considerably into the bell, which gives it a mellow, smooth timbre, but also contributes to problems in intonation that can only be overcome by the player's skill. Its mouthpiece is cup-shaped but much deeper than that of the cornet or trumpet.

Like the trumpet and cornet, the flugelhorn is pitched in B♭. It extends down to an *e* and can reach *b♭''*. The flugelhorn does not have the same

Musical Instruments Handbook

capacity for playing in high registers as the trumpet and cornet, however, since its wide bore renders the *tessitura* unstable. It uses the same fingering system as the cornet and trumpet. Some modern flugelhorns use a fourth valve to take the pitch down an additional perfect fourth. On most instruments, however, the fourth valve is rather a better-in-tune version of the combination of first and third valves.

THE FLUGELHORN IN PERFORMANCE

The flugelhorn is not commonly used in the orchestral repertoire, but it has found a permanent place in the brass band, where it forms an integral part of the cornet section. It is in jazz that the flugelhorn is heard at its best. It was part of Woody Herman's band in the 1930s, as well as appearing in Duke Ellington's orchestra.

It was in the cool-jazz style epitomized by Miles Davis, however, that the flugelhorn found its natural home. Davis's introspective style, coupled with Gil Evans' colourful orchestrations, made the flugelhorn the perfect vehicle for projects such as *Miles Ahead* and *Sketches of Spain*. Since the 1970s, many players have doubled as both trumpeters and flugel players. It has also been an important part of jazz orchestration, often being used in groups of three or four.

▲ *The flugelhorn has a mellower, darker tone than the cornet.*

Section One: The Instruments

TRUMPET

The trumpet is one of the most ancient instruments still played today. Clear depictions of trumpets survive in Egyptian paintings and two trumpets – one of silver, the other of gold and brass – found in the tomb of Tutankhamun date back to at least 1350 BC. There are many examples of Roman and Greek trumpets which, like the Egyptian instruments, were made from a straight, conical tube flaring to a bell.

II Tromba Romana antica

PITCH

At the beginning of the fifteenth century, makers began to experiment with bending the trumpet. By making it into an 'S' shape, it became more manageable without losing any sound quality. Surprisingly, the first slide trumpet was invented as early as the 1400s. An elongated mouthpiece section slid inside the main length of tubing so the player was able to alter the length of tubing, and thus the pitch.

Fact

The trumpets of the ancient Egyptians, Greeks and Romans were strongly associated with war and shows of strength – a characteristic that remains to this day.

All instruments are reliant on the harmonic series for their ability to play in tune. The brass family relies on it more than most, and at this period, the trumpet was a continuous tube without finger holes or keys. The only pitches available to it were those of the harmonic series. The distance between pitches is large at the lower end of the harmonic series and it is only when the eighth partial is reached that movement

Musical Instruments Handbook

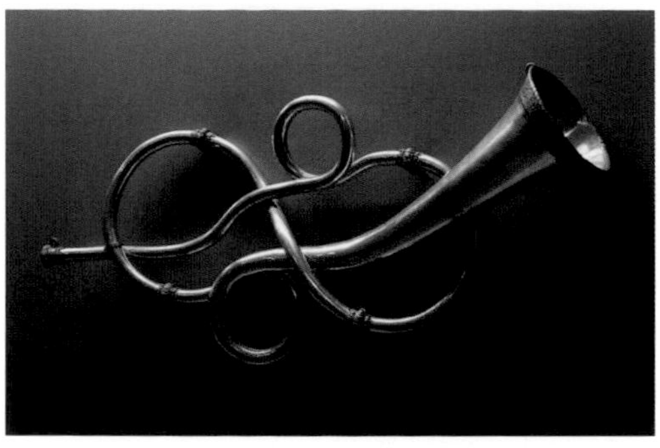

▲ *One of many styles of sixteenth-century German trumpet.*

by step can be achieved. By the mid-sixteenth century, the trumpet was able to play up to the thirteenth partial, so a half scale of *c''*, *d''*, *e''*, *f'* and *g''* was available. This high register became known as the 'clarion', after the small, high trumpet of the same name.

DESIGN DEVELOPMENT

During the sixteenth century, the trumpet came to be revered above all other instruments. Royal courts often employed up to 20 trumpeters, and in 1548 Emperor Charles V declared that trumpeters were to come under his direct jurisdiction. Not surprisingly, given its royal status, the trumpet's aesthetics received considerable attention during this period. The mouthpiece section of the 'S'-shaped design was brought alongside the bell section so the familiar elongated spiral was achieved. The parallel lengths of tube were bound together for strength, and coloured tassels or other ornaments were often added.

From the long mouthpieces of the slide trumpet developed the idea of separate mouthpieces for natural trumpets. The basic design of mouthpiece during the sixteenth and seventeenth centuries was a cup shape with a flat rim and fairly sharp edge, where the shank left the mouthpiece to join with the trumpet's main body. By this time different mouthpiece designs were being used for different purposes: a shallower cup for the higher registers and a deeper cup for the lower registers.

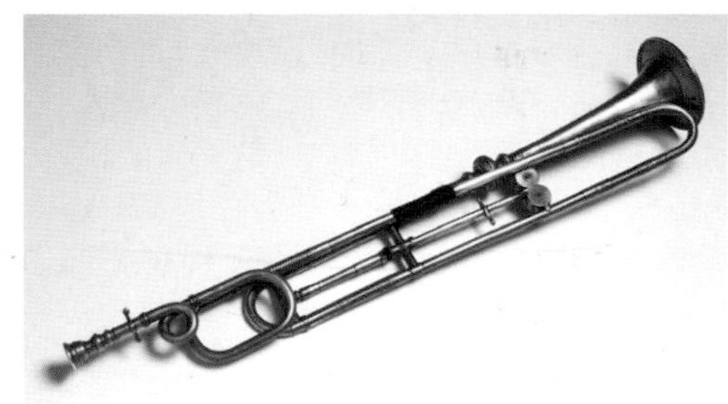

▲ *Slide trumpets have a slide instead of valves.*

By the first half of the seventeenth century, it was common for trumpeters to play up to the twentieth partial, and many were capable of ascending to the twenty-fourth or even higher. This gave composers a diatonic scale of an octave and a half to use – more than adequate for using the trumpet as a melodic instrument. The second *Brandenburg Concerto* by Bach includes a famously virtuosic trumpet part written in this register playing a solo part alongside recorder, violin and oboe.

Section One: The Instruments

GOLDEN AGE

The mid-eighteenth century was a golden period for trumpet playing. All the great composers wrote concertos for it and its ringing tones became forever associated with glorification and opulence. As the Baroque moved into the Classical, however, the trumpet took on a less glamorous role; it was used mainly as a *tutti* instrument, to add weight to important moments and often in combination with its old partner the timpani to add rhythmic strength.

Up to this point, the trumpet had only been capable of playing in the key of its fundamental and those closely related to it. Consequently players had to constantly change trumpets, or use crooks, additional lengths of tubing that could be placed in to alter the trumpet's length. Towards the end of the eighteenth century, designs for a keyed trumpet appeared. Operated with one hand, leaving the other free to hold the instrument, there were between four and six keys on a keyed trumpet, which opened up the entire chromatic range. In spite of concerti by such eminent composers as Joseph Haydn (1732–1809), however, the keyed trumpet failed to catch on.

▲ The modern trumpet, complete with piston valves and cup-shaped mouthpiece.

THE ADDITION OF VALVES

The real revolution in trumpet-making came in the 1820s, when valves were added. Development in valve mechanisms during the 1810s had opened up the possibility of genuinely chromatic brass instruments that retained control of tone colour over the entire range. In the late 1820s, the first valve trumpets appeared and were soon taken up by composers: by 1830 valve trumpets were present in works by Berlioz, Gioacchino Rossini (1792–1868) and Giacomo Meyerbeer (1791–1864).

Initially, the valve trumpet was pitched in F. The length of this instrument meant that works requiring agility were incredibly demanding technically. Alongside the trumpet had developed the cornet, which was pitched a fourth higher in B♭, and was much more able to cope with tricky music. Even so, it wasn't until the 1850s that the first B♭ trumpets appeared – and not until the 1870s that they were accepted as standard.

Musical Instruments Handbook

THE TWENTIETH-CENTURY TRUMPET

By the beginning of the twentieth century, the trumpet had reached the form we know today. Most instruments are in B♭, with three valves and a tuning slide. The bore begins cylindrically, but quickly becomes conical – and finally flares out to a bell. The cup-shaped mouthpiece sits snugly inside the opening of the trumpet and comes in many different forms. Broadly speaking, the shallower the cup, the more easily the high registers can be played.

▲ *The piccolo trumpet has rotary valves.*

E♭ AND B♭ TRUMPETS

There are two additional trumpets in common use. The trumpet in E♭, a fourth above the standard instrument, has a narrower bore and more penetrating tone. It is often used to play Baroque parts but has also been specifically written for by composers including Maurice Ravel (1875–1937), Benjamin Britten (1913–76) and Stravinsky.

The piccolo trumpet in B♭ sounds an octave above the standard trumpet. This was originally developed by Adolphe Sax in the 1840s and revived by Goeyens in 1906 for the performance of Bach's second *Brandenburg Concerto*. There is also a bass trumpet, which is normally in B♭ and sounds an octave lower than the standard trumpet. As a result of its size, the bass trumpet requires a large mouthpiece, placing it in the domain of the trombonist. Numerous composers including Wagner and Leos Janácek (1854–1928) have used it successfully.

▲ *The trumpet is popular in all genres of music – a good all-rounder.*

Central to the development of the trumpet in the twentieth century has been its use in jazz. It has been a key instrument since the style's inception and players such as Louis Armstrong, Dizzy Gillespie and Miles Davis have taken the trumpet to new expressive levels. Their influence is now finding its way back to the orchestral arena with composers such as Mark-Anthony Turnage (b. 1960) finding a new melodic character in the trumpet.

Section One: The Instruments

TROMBONE

A trombone is a brass instrument sounded by buzzing the lips into a mouthpiece. It is peculiar amongst brass instruments in using a double 'U'-shaped slide to alter its pitch. The early history of the trombone is confused, mostly due to a lack of clarity in naming instruments.

▲ *A sackbut was derived from the medieval slide trumpet.*

It is generally accepted that the immediate precursor to the trombone was the sackbut. This term was used from the fifteenth to eighteenth centuries to refer to any brass instrument using a slide – it could equally be applied to a trumpet with a single slide as an instrument with a double slide. The issue is further complicated by the terms 'trombone' and 'posaune': both these words were regularly used to refer to large trumpets without a slide.

HISTORY

The earliest surviving depictions of the trombone as we know it today date from the final decades of the fifteenth century. The earliest extant instrument is dated 1551 and is almost identical to those in use today. In fact, early trombones were more like contemporary trumpets than modern trombones. Their bores were narrow, the bells flared only gently and the sound they produced was brassy but not powerful. Played quietly, however, it could be a serene and elegant instrument. Early trombonists were virtuosic performers, often embellishing music with an agility that belied the difficulty of the instrument.

Fact

Calling the Renaissance and Baroque instrument a sackbut is really a modern convention to distinguish it from the trombone. The differences are slight and mostly affect the shape of the bill and mouthpiece.

Musical Instruments Handbook

Although it never gained the social distinction of the trumpet, the trombone became a vital part of both sacred and courtly music. During the seventeenth century – perhaps due to its burnished and melancholy timbre – the trombone developed an association with death and the underworld, a link that Claudio Monteverdi (1567–1643) put to good use in *Orfeo* (1607). Interest in the instrument declined, however, and by the eighteenth century it had almost disappeared.

THE EIGHTEENTH CENTURY

It was in the Classical era that the trombone recovered lost ground. Retaining its darker associations, Mozart famously used it in the 'Tuba mirum' of his *Requiem* as well as in his opera *Don Giovanni* (1787). Military bands also began to employ the trombone as a means of strengthening the bass line.

Up to 1750, the trombone had been used as a diatonic instrument. The tenor instrument was in A and had four slide positions. Trombones came in many sizes but it was normal to use three – alto, tenor and bass – in ensemble. By the late-eighteenth century, a new design was accepted as normal: a trombone in B♭ with seven slide positions, allowing access to the full chromatic range. The bass instruments, which previously had been in E♭ or D, were now made in F or G, also with seven slide positions.

THE NINETEENTH CENTURY

◀ *The trombone has undergone myriad changes to become what we know today.*

In the early-nineteenth century, the bore was enlarged by as much as 20 or 30 per cent and the bell was widened. These changes are often credited to the needs of Wagner and combined to significantly increase the trombone's power. Even before this, though, the trombone had acquired a reputation for being too loud – Berlioz declared it the perfect instrument for characterizing the 'wild clamours of the orgy' – which led at least one conductor to use instruments with bells pointing back over the player's shoulders.

Section One: The Instruments

Nevertheless, the trombone continued to grow in popularity and by the middle of the nineteenth century, a trio of trombones (two tenor and one bass) was standard in the orchestra. By the early-twentieth century, the trombone had also became a standard instrument in jazz and swing bands.

THE JAZZ TROMBONE

Jazz trombonists probably did more to exploit and develop the trombone's capabilities than anyone else. In the early-twentieth century, Kid Ory brought 'tailgate' trombone to the rhythm section. In the middle of the century, Louis Armstrong's favourite trombonist, Jack Teagarden, with his tender, long-breathed phrases, became the first to make it a lead instrument. Its capacity for a brash, hard-edged sound became an important part of bop in the hands of players such as J. J. Johnson later in the century.

TENOR TROMBONE

The modern tenor trombone is cylindrically bored for half its length – more when the slide is extended – and then widens to a flared bell. It has a compass from E to *f''* and exists in a variety of bore sizes, the choice of which to use is for the player to decide depending on the repertoire. The slide has seven positions: root position (not extended) plus six more, each dropping the pitch by a half step.

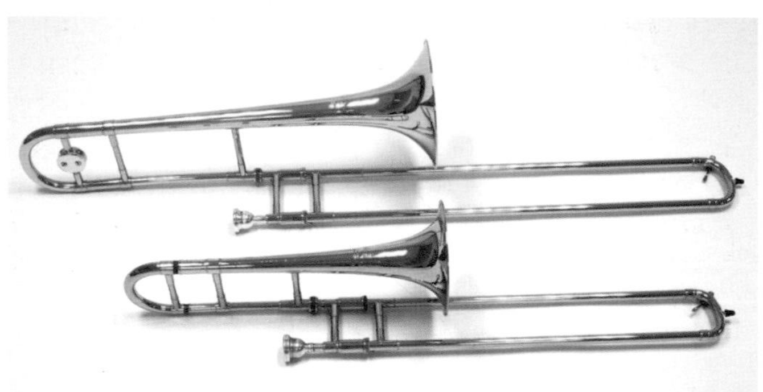

▲ *Tenor (top) and alto trombones.*

Most trombones today employ an additional length of tubing above the bell section which, when accessed via a valve, drops the fundamental pitch by a perfect fourth to F. This makes some notes accessible in more than one slide position, reducing the need for excessive movement at high speed. In spite of the trombone's fundamental pitch being B♭, it is notated as a non-transposing instrument in C.

BASS TROMBONE

The modern bass trombone is actually the same as the tenor in its basic set-up. Keyed in B♭, it has two additional lengths of tubing, which allow it to play potentially as low as *C'*. Bass trombones also have wider bores than their tenor counterparts, giving them a deeper tone.

Until the 1950s in Britain the bass trombone in G – a minor third below the tenor – was in common use. This was an instrument without valve-accessed tube extensions, however, and its length meant that a handle was needed on the slide in order to utilize the bottom positions.

CONTRABASS TROMBONE

The true contrabass trombone is an extraordinary instrument, measuring some 5.5 m (18 ft) in total length. Its fundamental note of *B♭''* necessitated the use of a double-slide – two slides joined together, which meant that any extension was effectively doubled in length. This allowed for a total of nine positions instead of the more normal seven.

The contrabass trombone was a regular member of nineteenth-century opera houses and it was scored in works including Wagner's *Ring* cycle (1848), Richard Strauss's (1864–1949) *Elektra* (1909) and Arnold Schoenberg's (1874–1951) *Gurrelieder* (1901). An instrument designed by G. C. Pelitti in 1881 at Giuseppe Verdi's (1813–1901) request and subsequently known – incorrectly – as a 'cimbasso' was in fact just such a contrabass trombone. The instrument Verdi refers to as a cimbasso in his operas prior to this point was more likely a valved ophicleide than a bass trombone.

ALTO TROMBONE

The alto trombone in E♭ or F, a perfect fourth or fifth above the tenor, was in common use between the sixteenth and eighteenth centuries. As the tenor became better able to perform at altitude, the alto's value declined. Many still prefer its brighter tone, however, and it has been specifically scored for by Alban Berg (1885–1935) and Britten.

Section One: The Instruments

HORN FAMILY

The term 'horn' is generally used to refer to the orchestral horn, also known as the French horn. Although it is used in jazz slang to indicate any wind instrument played by a soloist, the name here refers to the orchestral horn.

HISTORY

▲ *A hunting horn: the modern horn's ancestor.*

The early history of the horn is bound intimately to that of the trumpet. Both instruments were made of brass, both were sounded by buzzing lips, both were used to give signals during the hunt. The first clear distinction was made in France in the late-seventeenth century. Jean-Baptiste Lully's (1632–87) ballet *La princesse d'Elide*, performed at Versailles in 1664, is unequivocally scored for *cors de chasse* (hunting horns). An engraving of a scene from the work clearly shows circularly coiled horns as opposed to the more rectangular trumpets.

Two horns from this period survive – one by Starck from 1667 and one by Crétien from 1680. They clearly show the key characteristics of the modern horn: the circular spiral coil and conical bore (the trumpet at this time was cylindrically bored). French makers were vital in the development of the horn, and its 'French horn' title is an accurate reflection of the instrument's origins.

CONSTRUCTION

Having no valves or keys, the horn could only play notes in the harmonic series of its fundamental pitch. Instruments were initially made with different fundamentals for use in music of different keys. Early-eighteenth-century Vienna, however, saw the first use of crooks (see p. 107). In conjunction with the development of crooks, a new playing technique appeared. During the early eighteenth century, players discovered that the tuning of a note was affected by

Musical Instruments Handbook

▲ *The addition of valves meant all the notes reachable in the horn's range could be played.*

inserting the hand into the bell. Partially closing the bell lowered the pitch by around a half step, and fully closing the bell raised it by a half step. While both actions altered the instrument's timbre, it was possible to disguise the change created by a partial closure almost completely.

HAND HORN

The technique of hand-stopping, as it became known, made the whole chromatic scale available to the horn, revolutionizing the instrument. By the middle of the eighteenth century, hand horn playing was the standard in orchestras across Europe. The horn concerti of Haydn and Mozart, along with Beethoven's horn sonata all use this technique. In fact, it became so popular that players, conductors and composers were reluctant to leave it behind. All of Johannes Brahms' (1833–97) orchestral parts are written for the hand horn, even though the horn was by then fully equipped with valves; hand-horn techniques were still taught in the 1920s.

Despite this popularity, though, instrument technology continued to move forwards and by the early 1800s there was a growing demand for instruments that produced an even colour across their entire compass. The first attempt at this was the curiously named 'omnitonic' horn, first constructed by J. B. Dupont in Paris around 1815.

▼ *The hand-horn technique made the horn a true melodic instrument.*

Section One: The Instruments

OMNITONIC HORN

In truth, the omnitonic horn was not an attempt to achieve a fully chromatic instrument. The development of hand-horn technique had not done away with the need for crooks; players still needed the fundamental pitch of the horn to be closely related to that of the music being performed. The omnitonic horn was devised to eliminate the need to change crooks. It did this by combining all the different crook lengths together on the horn's main body. The player could select a particular crook by turning a dial, and play the horn in that key using hand-stopping techniques. It was a cumbersome and heavy instrument, though, and despite the attentions of some distinguished makers, it never caught on.

NINETEENTH-CENTURY DEVELOPMENTS

The early-nineteenth century was a time of great change in the brass world. The invention of the valve had provided an efficient way to access the full chromatic range, and many new instruments flooded the market. Two makers, Stölzel and Blühmel, both devised valved horns between 1811 and 1814. The former used a tubular piston valve and the latter a box-shaped piston valve. Not long after, in 1822, Luigi Pini invented the first horn to use rotary valves.

Band players and soloists quickly took up this new horn, but there was reticence among orchestral musicians. The obvious advantages of the valved horn – consistent tone colour, ease of execution, a fully chromatic lower register – proved too great to resist, however, and by the late 1800s it had become the standard.

THE MODERN HORN

The modern horn is made in five parts: body, bell, valve system, mouthpipe and mouthpiece. It is conically bored except for the central valve system and made of brass alloy. The mouthpiece differs significantly from most other brass instruments in being 'V'-shaped; the player places his lips at the widest part, and the shank leaves at the point to join the mouthpipe. This shape of mouthpiece produces a softer, mellower sound than the bright cup-shaped mouthpieces of the other brass.

Musical Instruments Handbook

There is a variety of horns in use today, but the most common is known as the F/B♭ horn, and uses four valves. Taking a leaf from the omnitonic horn, this has two sets of tubing, one pitched in F, the other in B♭. The fourth valve, operated with the thumb, switches between the two. The reason for this combination is twofold: some notes on the B♭ tubing are out of tune and are better played on the F tubing; and the B♭ tubing misses some notes in the lower register, which are provided on the F tubing.

COMPOSITIONS FOR THE HORN

The horn has been well catered for musically ever since its introduction in the eighteenth century. Aside from the famous concertos by Mozart, there are works by Carl Maria von Weber (1786–1826), Beethoven, Haydn, Strauss, Oliver Knussen (b. 1952), György Ligeti (b. 1923) and Britten. One of the horn's most striking characteristics is its timbral variety. It is a great partner for the voice, as well as being able to partner woodwinds and brass with equal ease. Indeed, one of the horn's most vital roles in the orchestra is to act as a bridge between the brass and woodwind sections, enabling the colours of the two sections to blend well.

▲ *Horns are notoriously difficult to play, although several works exist for the instrument*

Section One: The Instruments

SAXHORN

The early part of the nineteenth century was a rich period for the development of instruments; many designs dating from this period are now established as the standard forms. The brass world was no exception.

ADOLPHE SAX

A man with business acumen and a fascination with design, Adolphe Sax was quick to seize on these developments. Having found major success with his patented saxophone family in the early 1840s (see p. 156), Sax had moved from Brussels to Paris, where he rapidly established himself as an instrument maker to be reckoned with.

His next move was to create a family of brass instruments based around the valve system, and in 1845 he applied for a patent for his new designs. Ever keen to seize an opportunity, Sax saw his instruments as a means of reinvigorating the wilting tradition of French military music. He organized a public contest between an established military band and a group of his new instruments in the presence of the Minister of War, as a result of which the saxhorns were officially adopted.

THE DISTIN FAMILY

This was not quite the coup Sax had hoped for, however, since a number of well-established manufacturers contested his claim to originality. Their concerns were well founded since the essential components of the saxhorn – the mouthpiece, bore and valve system – were already in use elsewhere. Sax played another trump card in persuading the Distin family quintet, the leading British brass quintet of the time, to adopt his instruments. The backing of the Distin

Musical Instruments Handbook

family inevitably led to the saxhorn taking off in Britain; in 1853, the first major brass-band competition was won by a group all playing saxhorns.

There is considerable confusion about the term 'saxhorn'. Adolphe Sax himself used it only once and it is claimed that Henry Distin was the term's source. Distin also contributed to the confusion, since he held the franchise for Sax's instruments from the 1840s until the late 1850s. When he lost the franchise, however, he continued to sell instruments that bore a strong resemblance to Sax's, but were referred to as 'flugel horns', 'euphonions' and 'tubas'.

THE SAXHORN FAMILY

Sax's instruments were made of brass, with conical bores finished off by a flared bell; the tubing sections directly linked to the valves were cylindrically bored. In general the main tubing section looks like large trumpets except that the bell always points upwards. Like all brass instruments, the mouthpiece is cup-shaped and sound is created from the player buzzing his lips together.

There are seven instruments in the family – although at one point 10 were posited – keyed alternately in E♭ and B♭, in the same way as saxophones. The E♭ soprano is today seen as the E♭ cornet, the B♭ contralto has disappeared, the E♭ alto is better known today as the tenor horn, the E♭ baryton is the modern baritone, the B♭ bass is the euphonium and below that are the E♭ and B♭ contrebasse saxhorns.

► *The sound of the saxhorn is characteristically mellow.*

Section One: The Instruments

TUBA

The tuba is essentially a large, valved bugle, designed to take the bass part in an orchestra or band. Like the trumpet, it is sounded by buzzing the lips into a mouthpiece. It is conically bored, like the horn, and consequently has a smooth, velvety sound.

HISTORY

The tuba is a youngster among brass instruments; it is one of a number of instruments developed in the furiously inventive atmosphere of the early-nineteenth century. The invention of the piston valve around 1815 breathed new life into brass-instrument design. Ten years later an entirely new range of tenor and soprano instruments had appeared, but the valves were too long to work adequately at the scale required for a lower-pitched instrument. In 1827, however, the self-proclaimed inventor of the valve, Heinrich Stölzel, devised a shorter piston valve that was suited to bass instruments.

▲ *A staple of brass bands, the tuba is also becoming popular as a solo instrument.*

By 1835, the first tuba had been created. Prussian bandmaster Wilhelm Wieprecht and instrument-maker J. G. Moritz, worked together on a design for a bass tuba in F (playing a fundamental of *F'*) with five valves. Their instrument soon caught on and by the mid-1840s there were tubas of all shapes and sizes, including a version using the rotary-valve system developed by J. F. Riedl in Vienna. The saxhorn family designed by Adolphe Sax in the 1850s clearly shows the influence of the tuba.

Musical Instruments Handbook

THE TUBA IN THE ORCHESTRA

Up to the early-nineteenth century, the bass instrument in the brass section of the orchestra had been the keyed ophicleide. While this had proved successful, it had significant drawbacks – including loss of tone quality on some notes and a lack of power compared to the higher brass in use by this time. It also had an effective compass that only reached as low as *C* – already regarded as inadequate by many musicians.

The tuba solved all these issues and quickly became a regular orchestral member in Germany. In the rest of Europe, however, it was slower to catch on, despite the advocacy of the ever-adventurous Berlioz. In France and England, the change from ophicleide to tuba only took place after the 1870s; players in some orchestras were required to be skilled on both instruments right up to the turn of the century.

▼ *Tubas have been used in jazz since the music's beginning.*

TYPES OF TUBAS

One of the difficulties associated with the tuba is the lack of standardization of instrument choice. The original tuba in F (with a fundamental of *F'*) was the standard instrument in most European orchestras until the mid-twentieth century, when it was replaced by an E♭ tuba (often known as EE♭, or double E♭, to make clear its low fundamental of *E♭'*), which remains the most common orchestral tuba today.

In the United States, an even lower tuba in double C (with a fundamental of *C'*) is used. This is particularly useful for playing in the sharp keys that form the majority of the orchestral repertoire. There is also a double B♭ tuba which is normally seen only in bands.

Section One: The Instruments

In France, a completely different instrument is used. Pitched in C (with a fundamental of *C*), it is an octave higher than the standard US model. It uses a system of six valves – three for each hand – to reach the lowest notes and, because it is relatively slight, it is able to play significantly higher than its deeper cousins. The famous solo in Ravel's orchestration of Modest Mussorgsky's (1839–81) *Pictures at an Exhibition* (1874) was written for just this instrument.

BODY SHAPE

In all sizes, however, the tuba's conical bore is coiled in an elliptical shape, with the flared bell pointing upwards and the mouthpipe turning in to the player. There have been experiments with bells pointing forwards, away from the player, but these have all adversely affected the tuba's timbre and have only been adopted in marching bands. Smaller tubas can be held in the arms, but larger models are normally supported on the player's lap. The mouthpiece is cup-shaped, wide and deep. Both piston and rotary valves are used; the latter are essential in the widest-bored tubas since the pistons cannot operate quickly enough to allow necessary agility.

Although there are a number of effective concerti for the tuba, most notably by Ralph Vaughan Williams, the full extent of the tuba's capabilities are rarely displayed. Skilfully played, it is a surprisingly flexible instrument, able to produce long, singing phrases.

EUPHONIUM

The euphonium is a tenor tuba in B♭ with a fundamental note of *B'*. It was designed in 1843, shortly after the invention of the original tuba. Its name has its roots in the Greek *euphonos*, meaning 'sweet-voiced'. Generally made with four valves, the euphonium has a compass extending from *F'* to *b♭'* – potentially higher.

▼ *The euphonium is not often used orchestrally.*

The euphonium's introduction to the orchestra came by accident. Richard Strauss's tone poem *Ein Heldenleben* was scored for Wagner tuba (see opposite), but the conductor at the premiere swapped the Wagner tuba

Musical Instruments Handbook

for a euphonium with great success. The euphonium has subsequently become a regular visitor to orchestral repertoire, where it is normally played by a trombonist.

The euphonium's most important role has been in bands, where it takes the top line of the bass section and fulfils a vital melodic role.

▲ *The original sousaphones had upright bells and were nicknamed 'rain catchers'.*

SOUSAPHONE

The sousaphone is a bass tuba in E♭ or B♭ (with fundamentals of *E♭'* and *B♭''* respectively). Its unique feature is being coiled in such a way that it encircles the player, resting on the left shoulder and passing under the right arm with the bell pointing forwards above the head. It was derived from the earlier helicon by the bandmaster John Philip Sousa, composer of *The Stars and Stripes Forever*, and first made in the 1890s.

WAGNER TUBA

Especially designed for Wagner's operatic *Ring* cycle, the Wagner tuba is an elliptically coiled instrument from which the bell emerges at the top at a slight angle. It is conically bored, like the tuba, and has four rotary valves. The Wagner tuba's mouthpiece, however, is more like that of a French horn and in the orchestra it is performed by horn players. Intended to play a role in the texture by lying between the horn and trombone lines, it has never caught on as an orchestral instrument, mainly due to its slightly dull attack and wayward intonation. Nevertheless, it was also used by Strauss and Stravinsky, and a number of film composers.

◀ *The Wagner tuba has a more mellow sound than the French horn.*

Section One: The Instruments

INTRODUCTION

WOODWIND

The term 'woodwind' refers collectively to the orchestral instruments whose sound is generated by reeds or by passing air across (as opposed to directly into) a mouthpiece: this covers the flute, oboe, clarinet and bassoon.

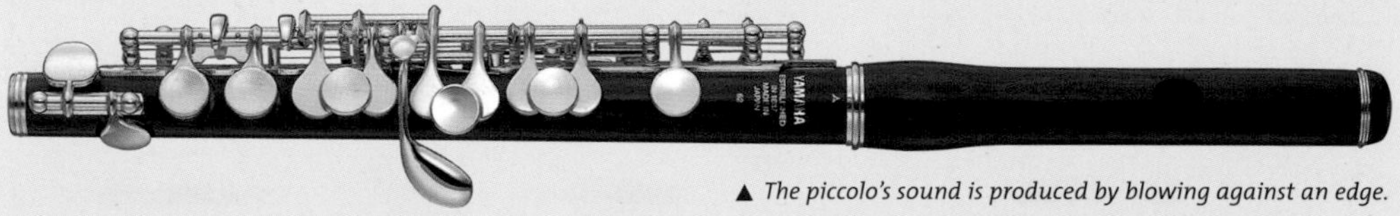

▲ *The piccolo's sound is produced by blowing against an edge.*

All woodwind instruments sound different pitches in the same way as brass instruments – using enclosed columns of air, based on the principles of fundamentals and overtones (see p. 92). The woodwind section now includes a regular visitor that is made of brass. The saxophone, however, uses a reed to generate sound and is in all respects except the material of its construction, a woodwind instrument.

BODY SHAPE

The prime concern in the development of the woodwind family was creating bodies to encase columns of air that were stable and whose overtones were in tune. Different shapes of air columns have different acoustic properties; only with a suitable shape can a good sound quality be generated. Conical tubes with a tiny aperture at the thin end produce the best results, and this form can be seen in most woodwind instruments, including the oboe, bassoon and saxophone.

Second to the conical tube is the cylinder. These can be open at both ends, such as the flute. A cylinder open at one end but closed at the other has unusual acoustic properties, the most audible of which is a predominance of low harmonics. The clarinet is constructed in this way.

▲ *A mouth organ, or harmonica, is a free-reed instrument.*

Musical Instruments Handbook

▲ *Saxophones' upturned bells were developed from those of the bass clarinet.*

The sound of a woodwind instrument is projected mainly from the finger holes around the lowest depressed key. The function of the bell is mainly to reflect soundwaves back into the instrument rather than to distribute them into the air. This is a vital function, however, and considerably influences the sound.

FINGER HOLES

A tube open only at the mouthpiece and bell ends can only sound pitches from the harmonic series. In order to sound additional notes, it is necessary to alter the tube's length. This was first achieved by adding finger holes. With all the holes covered, the tube's fundamental pitch was sounded; uncovering the lowest hole effectively shortened the tube, making the pitch higher. By gradually uncovering the holes from the bell towards the mouthpiece it was possible to play a range of pitches – a system still used with some instruments.

The positioning of the finger holes was vital to their success and it was quickly discovered that some combinations of open and closed holes were more effective than others. The positions and number of holes were limited, however, by the size of player's hands and the number of fingers.

► *Members of the shawm family, all with double reeds.*

Section One: The Instruments

KEYS

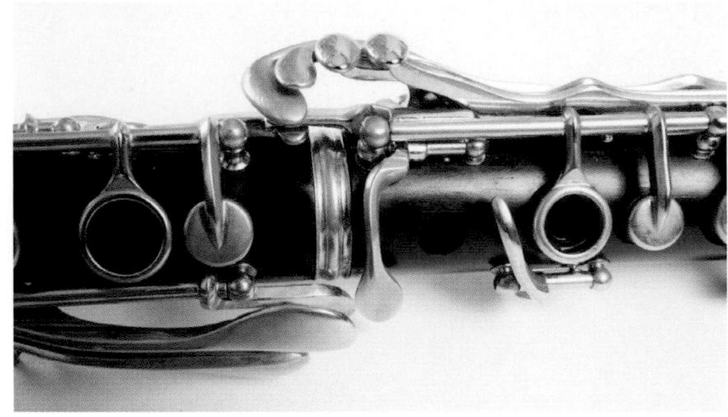

▲ *Mechanical keys allow every note of the chromatic scale to be reproduced.*

The development of mechanical keys to help close the finger holes in the seventeenth century marked the initial steps towards modern woodwind instruments. Originally just used for hard-to-reach notes, it wasn't until the work of Theobald Boehm (1794–1881) in the mid-1800s, however, that systems of keys reached their full potential. His developments brought together the work of his predecessors, and produced the proportions and fingering system that are the basis of the modern flute. His innovations were influential in varying degrees in the modernization of all woodwind instruments.

OVERBLOWING

Even with sophisticated keywork, the basic compass of a woodwind instrument might seem to be limited, since the tube cannot be continually shortened and still produce a sound of any significant quality. This situation is overcome by using the overtones naturally present in the instrument's fundamental pitch.

By increasing the energy put into the air column, a player can cause the first overtone to sound. This is an octave higher in all instruments except the clarinet, which overblows at the twelfth interval. Releasing the keys from this point gives access to a higher register using a largely unchanged fingering.

Sounding overtones can make the instrument unstable and for this reason a 'speaker' or 'octave' key is used in modern woodwind. This key opens a small hole near the mouthpiece, which slightly alters the behaviour of the air column and allows the overblown notes to sound more easily.

MOUTHPIECES

Perhaps the clearest distinguishing factor between the different woodwind instruments is the means by which the sound is generated. Clarinets and saxophones use a single reed, oboes and bassoons use a double reed, and flutes and whistles use an edge.

▲ *The bassoon's reed is made from a single piece of cane doubled over.*

Musical Instruments Handbook

▲ *Dvojnice: a Balkan double flute.*

The single reed is attached to a hollowed-out mouthpiece that leads directly to the instrument's bore. The double reed is actually two individual reeds bound together and inserted into a thin piece of cork, which is in turn inserted into the bore. The edge is simply a tapered or rounded edge that divides the air stream partly into the instrument's bore and partly away from the instrument.

The method of sound production has a clearly audible effect on the instrument's timbre. It also affects articulation. The double reed, for instance, requires considerable energy to make an initial attack; quick repeated articulation is therefore arduous and runs the risk of spoiling the sound. The edge-blown instrument, however, requires very little energy initially and is ideally suited to fast passages of music.

ORCHESTRAL WOODWIND

Modern woodwind instruments are individually less colourful and less flexible than their string colleagues. Their predecessors were generally raucous, and were most closely associated with outdoor celebrations and military bands.

Nevertheless, through continued refinements, this family of instruments has come to form a major part of western musical culture. Their presence in the orchestra is now essential for the provision of melodic colour and textural variation. These instruments reached maturity in the twentieth century, and increasing demands have been made on them over the past 100 years.

As solo instruments and in wind ensembles woodwind has had some success. In military bands they have remained central components, and in jazz some instruments – notably the saxophone and the clarinet – have played critical roles.

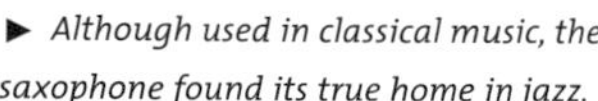

► *Although used in classical music, the saxophone found its true home in jazz.*

Section One: The Instruments

FLUTE

The flute most familiar to us from its use in orchestral and solo music is more properly known as a 'transverse' or 'side-blown' flute.

The flute family is distinct from the other woodwind instruments in that it does not use a reed to generate sound. Instead, a stream of air striking the edge of an opening in the side of a tube agitates the enclosed air column. The pitch of the note is dependent on the length of the air column; therefore, by covering or uncovering holes in the tube, the pitch can be altered.

ORIGINS OF THE FLUTE

There are examples of flutes dating back thousands of years. A Paleolithic flute made from a swan's bone discovered in Geissenklosterle, Germany, is thought to be the most ancient surviving example of any musical instrument, at around 36,000 years old. More direct relations of the modern concert flute are known to have existed in the tenth and eleventh centuries, and by the sixteenth century it had become immensely popular.

Fact

European court inventories from the period show that Henry VIII had 74 flutes and the Stuttgart court had 220, compared with just 48 recorders.

TECHNICAL DEVELOPMENTS

The invention of keys in the seventeenth century began the slow transformation of the flute. Prior to this, the flute was able to produce only a limited number of pitches and could not accurately sound every chromatic degree of the scale. In order to overcome this problem, flutes of different lengths (and therefore capable of sounding different pitches) were used by the same player.

The use of keys, however, enabled the player to cover holes beyond the normal reach of his fingers. At a stroke, the instrument's compass was extended, its intonation improved, and access to the full chromatic range of pitches was granted.

▲ *A one-key Baroque flute, which would have had a limited range.*

Musical Instruments Handbook

In spite of this development, there remained a great variety of flute designs – and therefore of performing techniques – divided largely along national lines. It was not until the mid-nineteenth century that a design was developed which was good enough to consign all others to a chapter in the history books.

BOEHM'S FLUTE

Theobald Boehm was a goldsmith, flautist and flute maker. His particular revolution was the use of ring keys, in which a ring surrounding a finger hole also operated a second hole, allowing one finger to cover two or more holes simultaneously. Boehm also developed a clear relationship between the size and diameter of the flute and the size and placement of the finger holes, as well as changing from a conically bored to a cylindrically bored instrument. He arrived at his final design in 1847, after many years of experimentation.

Boehm's developments were not universally accepted. Although many enjoyed the tonal power, secure intonation and agility afforded by the German's design, others felt that it lacked the subtleties of colour found in older models and were unwilling to learn the new fingering patterns Boehm's model demanded. Only since the early-twentieth century has the flute conformed to a standard Boehm design. Even now it remains one of the most individual of instruments.

▲ *The flute has a sweet, sensual sound, popular in many genres of music.*

Section One: The Instruments

THE MODERN FLUTE

The basic design of the modern flute is tripartite: a head joint (containing the hole into which the player blows), the middle joint (containing the main keywork) and the foot joint (containing the keys for the right little finger). The basic scale of a flute begins on a *d'* and extends upwards for three octaves. The keys on the foot joint extend the compass downwards to a *c'* and sometimes a *b*.

The flute's timbre is greatly affected by the material of construction. Normally, flutes are made of nickel-silver or sterling silver, which gives a flexible, well-projected tone. Wooden flutes are much richer, with a very strong lower register, while gold flutes produce a beautifully mellow sound. Many players mix materials – for example using a wooden head joint and silver middle and foot joints.

PICCOLO

The flute has larger and smaller siblings, of which the most frequently used is the piccolo. Sounding an octave higher than the flute, the piccolo is fingered in the same way as its larger relative, except that it has no foot joint, which means that its lowest note is *d''*.

▲ *The piccolo's full name,* flauto piccolo, *is Italian for 'small flute'.*

There are also larger flutes such as the alto flute – whose range is a perfect fourth below the standard flute, and the bass flute – which sounds an octave below a standard flute. There are even sub-bass flutes, sounding a twelfth lower, and double-bass flutes, sounding two octaves lower.

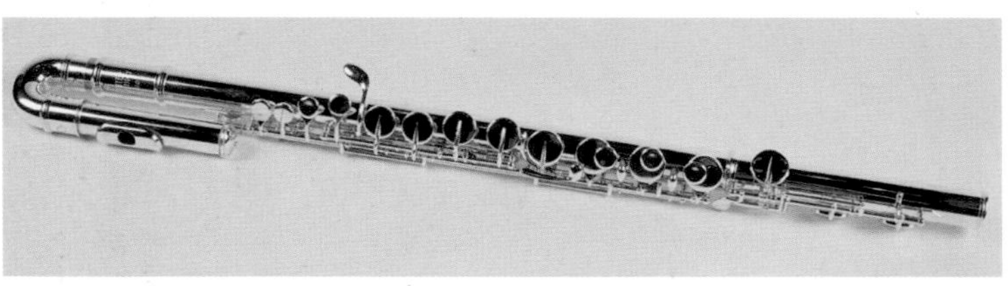

▲ *The alto flute has a distinctive shaped body.*

Of these instruments, only the alto flute and piccolo are in regular concert use. Since Beethoven's time, the piccolo has been an integral part of the orchestral woodwind section. The alto flute, created by Boehm around 1854, has been particularly attractive to twentieth-century composers. Igor Stravinsky (1882–1971) used it to great effect in the *Rite of Spring* and Toru Takemitsu (1930–96) was a particular fan.

Musical Instruments Handbook

FLAGEOLET

Another member of the flute family, the flageolet is an end-blown flute that encompasses a wide range of instruments. It is most similar in design to the recorder, consisting of a mouthpiece and a main body, with finger and thumb holes, made of ebony, ivory or boxwood.

It was popular in England during the seventeenth century and was particularly associated with the pastoral character. Both George Frideric Handel (1685–1759) and Jean-Philippe Rameau (1683–1764) used the flageolet and Wolfgang Amadeus Mozart (1756–91) wrote for it in his opera *Die Entführung aus dem Serail* (1782).

In addition to the standard flageolet, there existed a double flageolet, which had two bodies joined to a single mouthpiece – one operated by the left hand, the other by the right. This allowed simple melodies to be played in thirds and also gave access to a wider range of pitches than the single flageolet.

In 1843, Robert Clarke invented a cheap flageolet that became known as the tin whistle or pennywhistle. The instrument was immensely popular in Ireland, where it remains a favourite in performances of folk music.

▲ *The tin whistle can also be described as an end-blown fipple flute, as can many other traditional woodwind instruments.*

Section One: The Instruments

TRANSVERSE FLUTES AROUND THE WORLD

Transverse flutes worldwide, though they vary cosmetically and in size, have few variations on a common design: a parallel-bored tube with blowing aperture and a row of finger holes on the front (and occasionally a thumb hole). Most are made from locally available tubular materials, particularly bamboo.

End-blowing means that, in a bamboo or reed flute, the size of aperture across which the player blows tends to vary with the bore of the particular piece of raw material. Stopping up the end and making a new blowing hole in the side of the flute allows the maker to control the aperture's size and shape.

INDIAN FLUTES

In north India the name bansuri, derived from the word *bas*, meaning 'bamboo', applies to both transverse and duct flutes. The transverse flute, usually eight-holed, used in the Carnatic music of southern India is called a *venu*.

CHINESE FLUTES

In China, most transverse flutes, named *dizi*, have an extra hole between the blowing aperture and the equal-sized finger holes (usually six); this is covered with a piece of thin paper-like membrane peeled from the inner surface of bamboo. Carefully adjusted, this *dimo* resonates with the blown note to create a mirliton effect similar to that of a kazoo or comb and tissue paper. The Japanese *shinteki*, Okinawan *fanso* and Korean *taegum* have a similar device. These days many *dizis* are fitted with a metal tuning slide, but they are made so accurately, and bamboo is so temperature-stable, that it is rarely necessary to adjust it.

▶ *The tone of the Chinese* dizi *has a hard edge.*

Musical Instruments Handbook

END-BLOWN FLUTES

Cut a clean end to a length of bamboo, reed or other tube, place it near the mouth and direct a narrow stream of breath at its edge, and with a little practice, a pitched note can be produced.

Blow a little harder and that note will jump to a series of ascending harmonics. It is not even necessary to mouth-blow – the corrugated plastic whirly-tubes sold as toys are whirled through the air to produce a harmonic series, ascending through five notes the faster the tube is whirled.

PANPIPES

If the tube is closed at the non-blown end, the note produced will be an octave lower than it will if the end is open. Panpipes are a series of closed-ended tubes arranged to make a scale. Each creates a single note or, if blown harder, an additional – sometimes usable – higher harmonic.

▲ *Andean* siku *(double-row panpipe, right) with Chinese and Philippine panpipes.*

In Europe, the most famous and highly skilled players come from Romania, where the instrument is called a *nai* or by its Greek name of *syrinx*. Here it usually takes the form of a curved row of tubes set into a wooden frame. In another centre of excellence, the Andean countries of South America (where it is known by the Spanish names *zampoña* or *rondador*), the tubes range up to a metre or more in length, and may be in double or triple rows. To play the largest versions, these rows are separated and a pair of players takes one each.

The Lithuanian *skuduciai* and Filipino *saggeypo* are sets of panpipes played by a group, each player with just one or two tubes, while each player of the Russian *kugikly* or *kuvikly* has up to five.

Section One: The Instruments

FINGER HOLES

It is not necessary for a flute to have a separate tube for each note. It is possible to have a single tube and change the length of its air column. The usual method is to make finger holes in the tube; in an open-ended tube, closing them all gives the lowest note, opening them progressively from the bottom gives an ascending scale. Blowing harder while repeating or modifying the fingering extends that scale to a second and at least partial third octave. Part-covering holes, or leaving a hole open while closing some or all below it, gives intermediate notes producing varying degrees of chromaticism as well as allowing pitch-bending. (Unlike the western orchestral flute, virtually none of the other flutes in the world are equipped with keys; chromaticism and the playing of microtones is in the fingering and breath control, not a mechanism).

▲ *End-blown flutes are difficult to master, but once learned a player can play the simplest tube.*

End-blown flutes with finger holes can be found all over the world, and go under many names, including in the Middle East *ney* and in parts of Eastern Europe *kaval*, but apart from their length, material of construction and number and arrangement of finger holes they differ little from one another. Regions that grow suitably robust tubular plants such as bamboo or reed cane have a head start in flute-making and playing, and their musicians have highly developed flute skills on instruments that are still made from the original plant-tubes.

Musical Instruments Handbook

NEY

Ney, nai or *nay* is an old Persian word for reed, and that – or other members of the grass family such as bamboo – is what most of the Middle Eastern, Turkish and North African end-blown flutes of that name are made from. Unlike the panpipes, where the breath-stream is aimed at the far edge of the rim, with a similar embouchure (mouthpiece) to a transverse flute, to play an end-blown, open-ended flute one puts the end in the corner of the mouth, holding the flute at an angle of about 30 degrees to the body's vertical axis, and blows at the side of the rim, which entails an embouchure more like whistling. The rim is sharpened to make it thinner. Sometimes, on the longer *neys* where the playing position is awkward, it is surrounded by a lip-disc.

The main exception to this method of embouchure is the Iranian *ney*, for which the rim is placed inside the mouth, hooked into the gap between the front teeth, and air directed by the teeth and tongue. This can be tricky, but gives a particularly wonderful, expressive breathy tone.

Neys commonly have between five and seven finger holes in the front and a thumb hole at the back. In North Africa the same instrument also goes under names including *nira, talawat, gasba, qsbah* or *qasaba*, although the latter three can also refer to a short *ney* with six finger holes and no thumb hole, known in Egypt as a *salameyya*.

KAVAL

In the Balkans, instruments using effectively the same technique as the non-Iranian *neys*, but made of turned wood rather than cane or bamboo, are generally called *kaval*. Bulgaria in particular is home to some brilliant *kaval* players, and their instrument is made in three pieces, usually with the rim made of some more robust material than wood, such as horn or fibreglass, and decorated reinforcing ferrules at the joints. Macedonian *kavals* are very thin-walled, turned from a single piece of wood (usually ash), and typically kept in matched pairs on sticks inserted up the bores to prevent bending and damage.

▶ Neys *have been played continuously for almost 5,000 years.*

Section One: The Instruments

▼ *Macedonian* kavals *are so thin and light they are kept on a stick to protect them (shown here on the left).*

The norm for a Macedonian or Bulgarian *kaval* is seven finger holes on the front and one on the back, all the same size and equally spaced. This might suggest a scale far from equal temperament or even just intonation, but in fact these instruments are capable of almost total chromaticism in their middle and high range, and cover a wide compass of three octaves – with a soaring high end and a multiphonic ability that gives a fine split-tone breathiness to the low notes.

Fact

The Madagascan end-blown flute is known as a *sodina*. Its best-known player, Rakoto Frah, favoured lengths of old metal ski-pole as a material for making his instruments.

▼ *The Madagascan* sodina, *like the* kaval, *is an end-blown flute.*

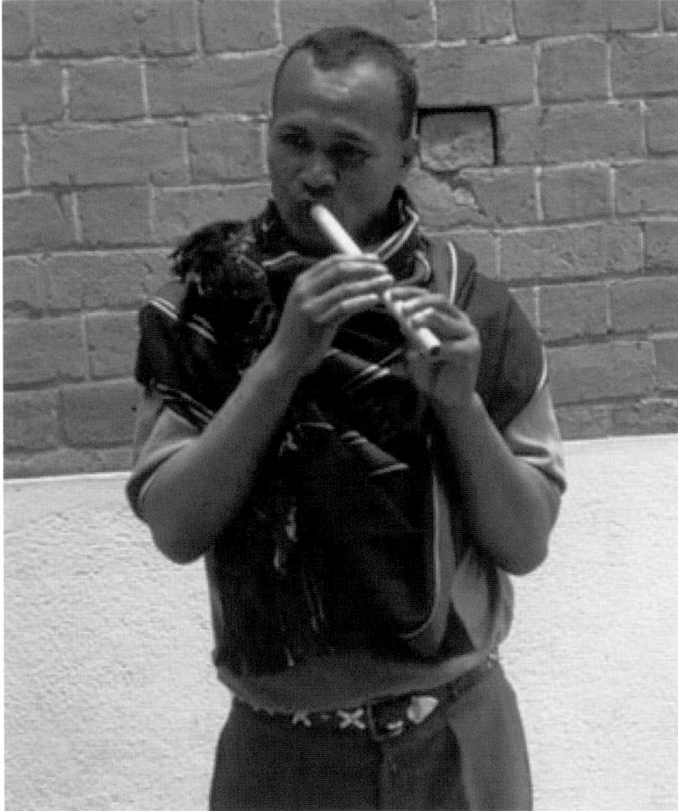

Musical Instruments Handbook

NOTCH FLUTES

In East Asia and South America, some end-blown flutes have a feature that requires a different embouchure from *neys* and *kavals*.

A 'U'-shaped notch is cut in the rim on the opposite side to the player. It is bevelled on the inside or the outside of the tube to make a thin edge at which the breath is directed. The rest of the tube's diameter is sealed by the outside of the player's lower lip. The flute is held vertically.

SHAKUHACHI

▶ *The Chinese notch flute,* Xiao.

The best known of these notch flutes is the Japanese *shakuhachi*, an instrument of lumpy appearance but refined technique. The name derives from the Japanese for 'one foot eight (tenths)', the traditional length for the instrument – though many are longer. Made from the bamboo cut near the root where the nodes are close together, the flute is almost club-like, with the lower end extremely thick-walled, slimming towards the blowing end. The blowing edge (*utaguchi*) is often made more robust by an insert of hardwood, horn, acrylic or other durable material. There are four finger holes on the front and one on the back.

XIAO

The notch flute is said to have arrived in Japan, in antiquity, from China, via Korea, where a similar instrument is called a *tanso*. The Chinese notch flute is called a *xiao* or *dongxiao* and is somewhat different. It is a long, narrow bamboo tube, usually with five holes on the front and one on the back, which produce a diatonic scale. The notch is cut at a node, and most of the node septum is left intact, so it performs a similar role to the player's lower lip on a *shakuhachi* (though players tend to cut away more of the septum to make a better embouchure). Its sound is quiet and reflective.

▲ *The Japanese* shakuhachi *is a notch flute made from the base of a bamboo stem.*

Section One: The Instruments

WHISTLES

Whistles, or duct flutes, have a device to channel the player's breath, so a narrow air stream hits a sharpened edge, causing the necessary turbulence to vibrate the air column without the player using any special embouchure.

Usually this duct is created by inserting a block, known as a fipple, into the end of the tube, with one side shaved. This allows a narrow air stream that emerges into a usually rectangular or 'D'-shaped window cut in the tube to hit the sharpened tone-producing edge on its far side.

NO-HOLED WHISTLES

It is possible to make a whistle by sliding the bark off a sappy willow stick, cutting a notch in the bark tube, and reinserting a short length of the stick with one side shaved as a fipple to direct air at the notch. Blowing progressively harder produces an ascending series of harmonics. Alternately opening and partially closing the lower end with a finger allows the gaps between those harmonics to be bridged by intermediate whole steps and half steps.

No-holed whistles like this, and less ephemeral ones of wood or other more robust material, have been made for millennia, often as a pastime by animal herders. In Norway, for example, this type of whistle is known as a *seljefløyte*, in Sweden a *sälgpipa* (both meaning 'sallow flute'), elsewhere *vilepill* (Estonia), *svilpas* (Lithuania), *koncovka* (Slovakia), *tilinca* (Romania), and among the Hutsuls of the Carpathians, *tylynka* or *telenka*.

◄ *Whistle and recorder, two of the best-known duct flutes.*

INSTRUMENT SIZES

Drilling finger holes in the tube produces an instrument that can play in a range of modes and keys.

Musical Instruments Handbook

Generally no attempt is made to make a single instrument cope with all possible key signatures (though it is possible – the recorder is one such). A six-hole whistle, for example, copes easily with complete diatonic scales in two keys, plus their related minors; for others, the player simply swaps to a different-sized whistle. Thus the well-known European tin whistle (not necessarily made of tin) much used in 'Celtic' music comes in a range of sizes down to the *C* or *D* of the low whistle.

EXTERNAL DUCTS

While tin whistles and recorders have a beak-shaped mouthpiece, many of the world's duct flutes are flat-ended. In some, such as the Javanese *suling*, rather than the breath passing inside the tube to the tone-edge, it is channelled via a short external duct formed by tying a loop of palm-leaf, bamboo or other material around the tube just above the rectangular edge-aperture.

In another external-duct flute, the Native American courting flute, the air passes out of a hole into an external duct formed by a small piece of wood tied to the flute body, which directs it against the edge of a second aperture.

▼ *The* suling, *from Java, has an external duct that channels the player's breath.*

Section One: The Instruments

Many duct flutes have the edge-window on the back. If it is sufficiently near the top, this makes it possible to affect the air stream with the lower lip or chin. This creates a breathier tone, emphasizing the low octave and lowering the pitch slightly. A further timbral change can be wrought by vocalizing while playing; the voice and blown tone intermodulate to produce a grainy multiphonic effect.

FUJARA

Slovakia is particularly rich in duct flutes, and the home of one of the largest, the *fujara*, a pastoral flute normally about 180 cm (71 in) long. A blowing tube, tied parallel to the main pipe, conducts the breath to the fipple, which is some distance above the player's head. A similar air-tube arrangement is found in the Andean *moxeño*.

A *fujara* has just three finger holes, but it can play a full diatonic scale by overblowing into higher octaves. The same method is used on smaller whistles, such as the three-holed Basque *txistu*, smaller *txirula* and larger *silbote*, old English tabor-pipe, Portuguese *pifaro* and the Provençal *galoubet*. These are played with one hand while the other beats a drum. The Catalan *flabiol* uses keys to allow control of up to eight holes with one hand.

WHISTLE PAIRS

In the Balkans and surrounding regions, pairs of whistles bound together or bored from the same piece of wood are common. One bore has enough finger holes – usually six – to make a diatonic scale of at least two octaves, while the other either has three or more finger holes for playing in harmony or has none and provides drones. Names include *dvojnice* (Croatia, Serbia, Montenegro), *dvojnica* (Poland), *dvojacka* (Slovakia, Czech Republic), *dvodentsivka* (Ukraine), *dvoyanka* (Bulgaria), and further afield *xeremia bessona* (Balearics), *satara* (Rajasthan) and the Kurdish *doozela*.

OCARINA

Some duct flutes are not in fact tubes, but rather closed vessels. *Ocarina* means 'little goose' in Italian, and is a vessel – usually ceramic – of varying globular shapes that produces a rounded, plummy flute tone. It is known throughout Europe, and there are similar instruments with a long history in South America, and among the Maoris of New Zealand (where it is called a *nguru*). The Maoris also

▲ *A Balkan* dvojnice.

Musical Instruments Handbook

▲ *A collection of South American* ocarinas, *and (right) a North American sweet potato.*

have an end-blown version, the *koauau*. The *xun*, an egg-shaped, end-blown ceramic vessel flute with five or more finger holes and a delicate, hollow sound has existed in China for at least 2,000 years.

The player's mouth serves as the vessel, and the nose as the air supply, for the plastic 'humanotone' nose-whistle, which sounds like a plummier version of ordinary mouth-whistling. The sports whistle is a closed-vessel duct flute with a ball that, as it is blown into a circular path inside, causes regular fluctuations in the air stream. The Brazilian samba whistle is similar, but with the addition of two finger holes that give it a three-note capability. The police whistle emits two notes differing slightly in pitch that interact to create a third, lower, difference tone. Water whistles, in which the air-stream bubbles through water, emit bird-song-like warbling.

Section One: The Instruments

RECORDER

The first known examples of the recorder date from the Middle Ages. It became hugely popular in the Renaissance and Baroque periods and then, surpassed by the concert flute, it largely fell out of use in the professional arena. At the beginning of the twentieth century, however, it was redesigned by Arnold Dolmetsch and subsequently enjoyed a remarkable revival, which continues today.

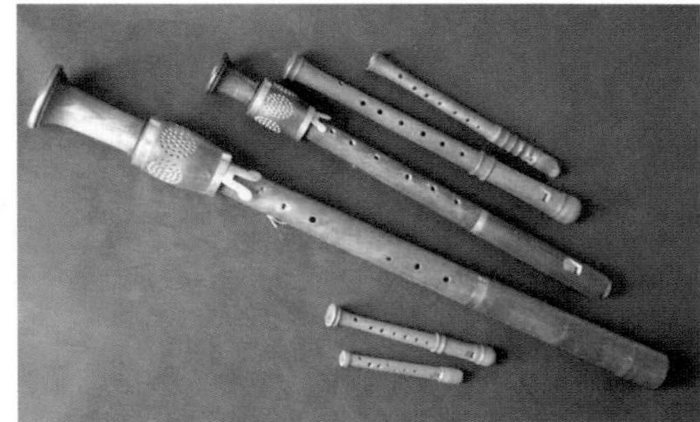

▲ *A consort of recorders (top to bottom): soprano, alto, tenor, bass, sopranino, garklein.*

PLAYING AND PITCH

All recorders are end-blown duct flutes. The main body of the instrument contains a column of air, open at the bottom. The head joint of the instrument is partially blocked, leading the player's breath to a sharp edge, which splits the air in two, to induce sound vibrations. One part continues into the instrument's air column, agitating it into vibrating; the other part is forced out through a window in the head joint and away from the instrument.

Like all aerophones, the recorder's pitch is dependent on the length of the air column. In order to alter the pitch, finger holes can be covered (to create a longer air column and lower pitch) or uncovered (to create a shorter air column and a lower pitch). By increasing the breath velocity, a player can make a fingering sound an octave higher (overblowing).

EARLY RECORDER MUSIC

By the sixteenth century, the recorder was one of the most popular instruments in Europe. It was used in instrumental and vocal music by Claudio Monteverdi (1567–1643), Jean-Baptiste Lully (1632–87), Marc-Antoine Charpentier (1645–1704), Henry Purcell (1659–95), George Frideric Handel (1685–1759) and Johann Sebastian

Musical Instruments Handbook

▲ *The soprano, or descant, is the most common recorder learned by children.*

Bach (1685–1750). Perhaps more significant, though, was its use among amateurs.

The ease with which the recorder could be played made it a perfect instrument for household use. In times where there was no recording and no broadcasting, it was a good medium through which to disseminate new music. Transcriptions of songs, arias and even whole operas were made well into the nineteenth century.

THE MODERN RECORDER

The revival of professional interest in the recorder began in the early-twentieth century when Arnold Dolmetsch (1858–1940) created a new design in the 1920s. Together with his son Carl, Dolmetsch altered the instrument's bore, redesigned the finger holes and rescaled the size and positioning of the finger holes for modern pitch and equal temperament. Much of the renewed popularity of the recorder is due to the surge in demand for historically informed performance, in which performances take place on exact replicas of instruments used in the time that the music was written.

The modern recorder has a range of just over two octaves. This means that instruments of different sizes must be used to access the full pitch compass, particularly in an ensemble. Recorders are most often tuned in C or F (referring to their lowest pitch, available when all the finger holes are covered). The standard instrument is a descant, with a lowest note of *c'*. Above that is the sopranino, with a lowest note of *f'*. Below the descant are the alto, lowest note *f*, the tenor, *c*, and the bass, *F*. The relative simplicity of the instrument has made it enduringly popular, and it is still the first instrument that many children learn.

Section One: The Instruments

CLARINET

Unusually among musical instruments, a specific date has been posited for the invention of the clarinet. Johann Christoph Denner of Nuremberg has been claimed as the man who, in 1700, devised and built the first of these instruments.

Like all the best stories, however, the history of the clarinet is shrouded in mystery. The instrument attributed to Denner, which now resides in the National Museum in Bayern, Germany, is in fact a chalumeau. The chalumeau is the clarinet's direct ancestor and the defining difference between the two lies in the invention of the 'speaker key'. Nobody, though, is certain who the inventor of the speaker key was.

CHALUMEAU

By the middle of the seventeenth century, the recorder had become an immensely popular instrument but it had many drawbacks, not least of which was a lack of volume. Attempting to overcome this flaw led directly to the creation of the chalumeau. Instead of splitting a stream of air on a sharp edge to induce sound vibrations, the chalumeau used a single reed attached to a tapered mouthpiece. Passing a stream of air over the reed agitated it, which in turn caused the column of air contained in the instrument's body to vibrate.

In spite of the improvement in volume, the chalumeau was only able to produce accurately a limited range of pitches at the lower end of its compass. The 'speaker key', operated by the thumb, was invented around 1700 specifically to allow access to the higher pitches. The close link between the chalumeau and the clarinet is retained in terminology: the low end of the clarinet's compass is still referred to as the 'chalumeau' register.

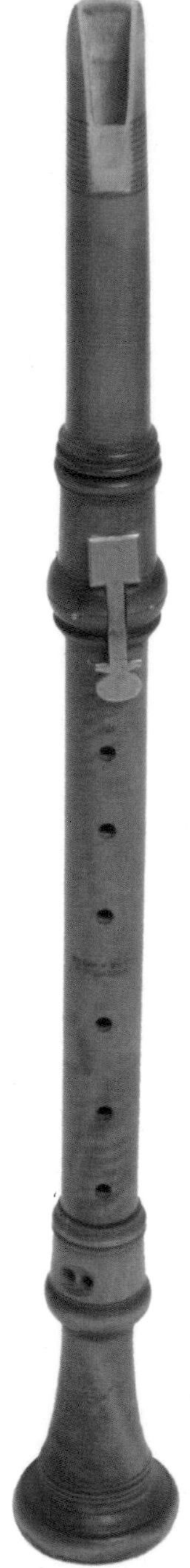

▶ *The chalumeau had eight finger holes, and usually one or two keys for extra notes.*

Musical Instruments Handbook

▼ *The modern clarinet, complete with speaker key and Boehm key system.*

PITCH

Like all wind instruments, the clarinet's pitch is a function of the length of the vibrating air column; covering or uncovering finger holes therefore alters the pitch. The use of keys to facilitate this began with the chalumeau and continued with the clarinet. The clarinet as we know it today came about as a result of a collaboration in the early 1840s between clarinettist Hyacinthe Eléonore Klosé and maker L.-A. Buffet. Buffet used the mechanical principles of Theobald Boehm – the man responsible for revolutionizing flute design – to create a system of keys that is the standard today. (Unfortunately for Buffet, the design carries Boehm's name in spite of the fact that the latter had nothing to do with it.)

CONSTRUCTION

The modern soprano clarinet consists of five sections: mouthpiece, barrel, upper or left-hand joint, lower or right-hand joint and bell. These sections are joined by tenon and socket joints lined with cork to ensure a snug, airtight fit. The upper and lower joints together constitute the body. The mouthpiece is tapered on the upper side. On the lower side is a slot, over which is fitted a single reed attached by a metal ring. The chamber inside the mouthpiece makes a smooth transition to the main body of the clarinet, which is bored cylindrically.

◀ *The clarinet's reed is usually made of cane, but can also be plastic.*

Section One: The Instruments

Curiously, there appears to be no purpose to the barrel joint that separates the main body from the mouthpiece. The most persuasive reasons for its existence are purely aesthetic since in all practical senses it could be dispensed with. The main body carries the keywork and the bell opens out the cylindrical bore to a funnel. The bell is only of use in projecting the lowest notes in the clarinet's compass – the majority of notes are projected almost entirely through the side holes. Most modern clarinets are made of African blackwood; although there are plastic and metal alternatives, no material has yet matched the blackwood for beauty of sound.

REGISTER

Uniquely among wind instruments, the clarinet behaves as though it was a stopped cylindrical pipe – even though it is open at the bell end. Acoustically this means that there is a predominance of low vibrations in the clarinet's sound: its lower register sounds an octave below that of a flute or oboe using the same length of pipe. This gives the lower chalumeau register a particularly rich, dark sound.

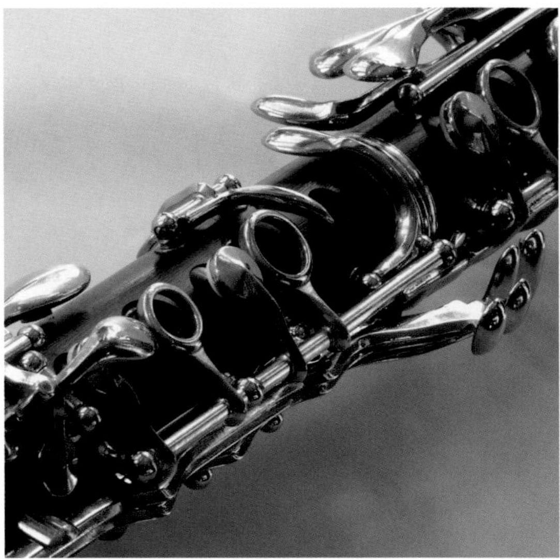

▼ *The speaker key enables the player to move between registers.*

The sound-wave formation of the clarinet means that it overblows at the twelfth instead of the usual octave. It is this peculiarity that gave rise to the 'speaker key', which is designed to help the overblown notes – known as the clarinet register – to speak.

COMPASS

The standard Boehm-system clarinet has a lowest note of *d*. Some models, known as Full Boehms, have an extension of 5 cm (2.5 in) that allows access to an additional half step below that. The upper limits are largely dependent on the player. Most would put a cap of *g'''* but it is possible to achieve a *c''''* or even an *e''''*. The difficulty of the highest register is that the intonation is largely dependent on breath and embouchure control – at such extreme pitch almost any fingering combination will work.

Musical Instruments Handbook

The compass of the clarinet is divided into four categories, each of which is distinct in timbre from the others. The already-discussed chalumeau is from *d* to around *g'*. The register achieved by overblowing the chalumeau is known as the 'clarinet register'. The awkward few pitches that bridge the chalumeau and clarinet registers are collectively known as the 'throat register' and are difficult to play with beauty and character. The uppermost pitches are known as the 'extreme register'.

▲ *In wind bands, clarinets are central to the instrumentation.*

THE CLARINET IN PERFORMANCE

Composers used the clarinet as early as 1716 in Antonio Vivaldi's (1678–1741) *Juditha triumpans* but it was the Mannheim Orchestra that most boosted the instrument's popularity, causing Mozart to rue the lack of them in his orchestra. He wrote a number of pieces especially for versions of the instrument, including the Clarinet Concerto (K622) and the Clarinet Quartet (K581). By the nineteenth century, the clarinet had become a regular feature of the orchestra and had developed a reasonable body of solo and chamber music.

In the twentieth century, the clarinet came into its own as an orchestral instrument. It was vitally important to composers such as Arnold Schoenberg (1874–1951), Stravinsky, Béla Bartók (1881–1945) and George Gershwin (1898–1937). New playing techniques and extreme expressive demands were also ideally suited to the clarinet's wide pitch range and variety of tonal colours. In the first half of the twentieth century, the clarinet was also a central part of the jazz movement, with players such as Benny Goodman, Artie Shaw and Woody Herman placing instrument in the heart of popular culture.

◄ *Clarinets are particularly suited to jazz music.*

Section One: The Instruments

A CLARINET

The clarinet is a transposing instrument – that is, the music is not notated at the same pitch as the resulting sound. Transposition is calculated in relation to the pitch *C*; an instrument in *F*, for example, sounds F when playing a written C. This is to maintain a relationship between fingerings where several instruments exist of the same basic design but of different sizes (and therefore different total pitch compasses). The music is written in the same way for each instrument, so switching between them is as simple as possible.

▼ *The clarinet in A is the most common type after the B♭ soprano.*

The standard clarinet is in B♭, so sounds a whole step lower than written. Most clarinettists also use a clarinet in A, which sounds a minor third lower than written. Although both instruments sound almost identical, music composed in sharp keys (i.e., G major, D major, A major etc. and their relative minors) used to be impossible to finger on a B♭ instrument. Developments in key mechanics have made it much easier, but there is still an audible sense that a clarinet is better in keys closely related to its own.

E♭ CLARINET

The E♭, or piccolo, clarinet sounds a minor third higher than written. It is a constant member of military and concert bands, often used in the orchestra and hardly ever in solo or chamber music. It has a shrill, penetrating tone that can

Musical Instruments Handbook

▼ *Big-band jazz saw clarinets take a central role.*

easily carry over a full orchestra. For this reason, it is usually used in moments of extreme tension. It does have a more playful side, however, that Richard Strauss expertly deployed to reflect the crafty hero in his tone poem *Till Eulenspiegels lustige Streicher* (1894–95). Strauss actually wrote the part for a clarinet in D which, although still available, is largely obsolete.

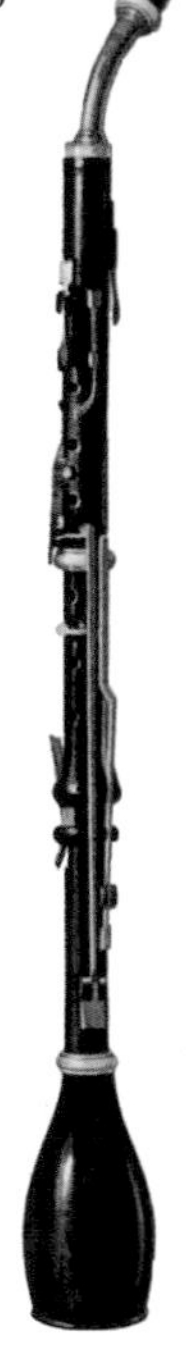

▶ *An early twentieth-century basset horn.*

BASSET HORN

The basset horn is a member of the clarinet family, though not a clarinet itself. It is pitched in F and has a compass that extends down to a sounding *F*. Its dark, slightly veiled timbre is more like that of a chalumeau than a clarinet. While resembling the main body of the clarinet, the upper section bends towards the player, but the bell bends away and is generally made of metal.

The instrument is thought to have been devised in the 1760s, but it is unclear whether it was developed from a clarinet or a chalumeau. Mozart had a fondness for the instrument, using it particularly in his masonic pieces. The basset horn never really caught on, in spite of Beethoven using it in the overture to *Prometheus* (1801) and Richard Strauss in his opera *Daphne* (1936–37), and it slowly died out.

Section One: The Instruments

BASSET CLARINET

Not to be confused with the basset horn, the basset clarinet is a soprano clarinet in B♭ or A whose range has been extended downwards to a written *c* (thus sounding *B♭* or *A*). The instrument is believed to have been created by the clarinettist Anton Stadler, a colleague of Mozart's, in the eighteenth century. Several of Mozart's compositions, including the famous concerto and quintet, were written for the basset clarinet. Like the basset horn, the instrument fell out of use, but was revived in the mid-twentieth century specifically to perform Mozart's works as intended.

BASS CLARINET

Generally pitched in B♭, the bass clarinet sounds an octave below its standard soprano counterpart, with a lowest pitch of *D♭* or *C*. It looks very similar to a basset horn but usually has a full crook at both the mouthpiece and bell end, with the instrument doubling back on itself before angling out. A spike is normally attached to the lower end of the main body so that the bass clarinet can be rested on the floor during playing.

There are examples of bass clarinets from the late-eighteenth century, but it only came into its own after the developments of Adolphe Sax (1814–94) in the early-nineteenth century. There are a number of examples of music written for instruments similar to the bass clarinet.

Musical Instruments Handbook

It was Giacomo Meyerbeer's (1791–1864) opera *Les Huguenots* (1836) that marked the musical starting point for the bass clarinet, however. Since then, the bass clarinet has been an ever-present member of the orchestral wind section, and has been used to great effect by composers such as Gustav Mahler (1860–1911), Schoenberg, Stravinsky and Leos Janácek (1854–1928).

The bass clarinet's size necessitates changes to the keywork of its smaller siblings. Not only do the keys have to reach further, the holes they cover must be larger – too large, in fact, for any to be covered by the fingers alone. Fortunately, the instrument's size allows for the additional key mechanisms that compensate for these issues.

ALTO CLARINET

The alto clarinet occupies a similar compass to the basset horn but has a much fuller, brighter tone, enabling it to blend more effectively with other instruments. It is normally pitched in E♭, and fingered similarly to the standard soprano clarinet.

The alto clarinet was first used in the early-nineteenth century for use in military bands. It has never established itself as an orchestral instrument, however, and today mostly appears in American concert bands.

◀ *Bass (left) and alto clarinets.*

▶ *The bass clarinet is a popular solo jazz instrument.*

Section One: The Instruments

SINGLE-REED INSTRUMENTS AROUND THE WORLD

At its simplest, a reed-pipe is made by slicing a flap out of a length of hollow reed or cane near the closed end, so that the cut piece springs slightly outwards, still joined to the rest of the reed at one end.

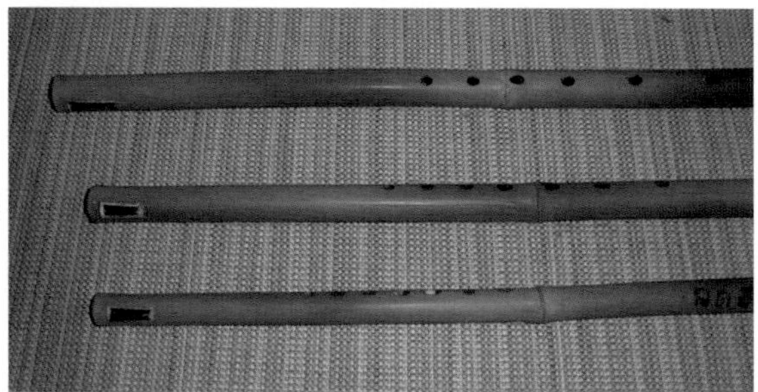

▲ *Thai free-reed pipes.*

HOW REEDS WORK

The reed, including the blocked end and section with the flap, is placed in the mouth and blown. This breath pressure causes the flap first to bend inward towards the aperture left by its cutting, and then spring back. It does this repeatedly, hundreds of times per second. The regular pressure fluctuations caused by this reed vibration cause the air in the tube to vibrate, and a note is produced whose pitch is determined by the length of the tube; the presence of the air column forces the reed-flap to vibrate at the resonant frequencies of the column, not the flap's natural pitch. The effective tube length can be varied, usually by making finger holes.

Though it is possible to make the whole instrument out of one reed or similar material, usually the vibrating section – known as the reed – and the tube are made of different materials and fitted together. The reed can thus be replaced when it wears out or breaks without disposing of the whole instrument.

REED PIPES

An example of a simple two-part reed pipe is the instrument known in Croatia as a *diplica*. It is made from two pieces of reed: a section of reed tube with

Musical Instruments Handbook

vibrating cut flap fits inside a section with five finger holes, and can be slid in or out for tuning. This is a delicate instrument, of limited life, but the sound is similar to that of a single-reed bagpipe chanter.

In most reed-pipes, the fingered tube is made of a more robust material – be it an existing tube such as bamboo or other cane, or wood, which requires some tool to make it hollow, or modern commercial tubing. Such are the Turkish *sipsi* and Serbian *klanet*.

HORN PIPES

Often a feature known in English as a bell is added to the bottom end of the pipe, intended to project or direct the sound, which on reed instruments emerges from the end and from the finger holes. This can be a cone made from the apex of a cow or other animal horn; such a horn-equipped reed-pipe is sometimes known as a horn pipe. Examples with wooden tube include the Armenian *pku* and Russian *zhaleika*.

Sometimes the blowing end also has a cow-horn cone surrounding the reed; the player presses the wide end against his mouth, thus avoiding the need to get the reed wet by putting it in his mouth. An example is the Welsh pibgorn – an instrument that virtually disappeared but is now undergoing a slight revival.

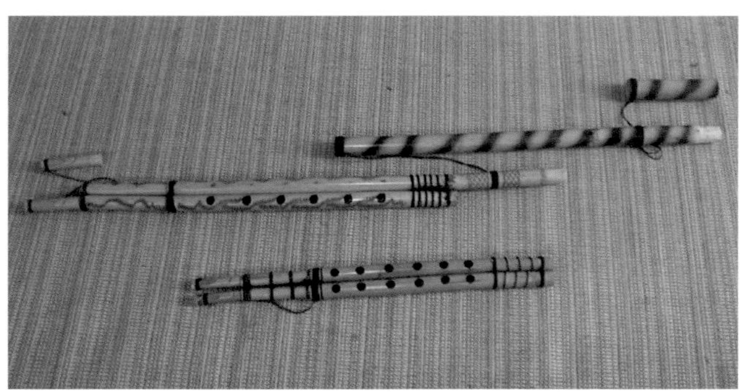

▲ *The* zummara *has two parallel pipes, each with a single reed.*

SINGLE-REED VARIATIONS

Pipes sounded by single reeds are found worldwide. In the Mediterranean and the Middle East especially, it is common to find them joined together, to sound two notes at the same time. Sometimes, as on the *miswij* (common in Egypt and nearby countries), both cane tubes have finger holes. Even more commonly, one tube has finger holes for the melody, while the other has none, or very few, and acts as a drone. An instrument of this type widely played in Arabic countries is the *arghul* (the name and spelling varies), in which the drone tube can be the same length as the melody pipe or extended for a lower drone.

Section One: The Instruments

DOUBLE-PIPE VARIATIONS

Double horn pipes are also common, either with one horn bell for each tube or a common one for both. A further occasional addition, as with the single horn pipe in the case of the Welsh pibgorn, is a horn reed chamber. One example is the *alboka*, played in the Basque country, in which two short cane reed-pipes – one with five holes and the other with three – are supported on a wooden 'D'-shaped frame, with a small cow-horn reed chamber to blow into and a larger one forming the bell.

Some double-reed pipes, such as the Indian *murali, murli* or *pungi* – the latter the instrument used by snake-charmers – have a reed chamber made out of a spherical or pear-shaped gourd.

▲ *The Welsh pibgorn is a single-reed horn-pipe.*

LAUNÉDDAS

The *launéddas* has been played on the island of Sardinia for around 2,000 years. It consists of two cane reed pipes, a short melody pipe and a longer drone, tied together, plus a second separate melody pipe. As in some other reed-pipes, the attached end of the reed, rather than the vibrating end, is at the top. The player inserts the reed ends of all of them into his mouth to make a fat, polyphonic sound.

▲ *The* launéddas *is played using circular breathing.*

As with the majority of double-reed pipes, the *launéddas* player uses circular breathing – the skill of taking in air through the nose while keeping a continuous sound going on the pipes. This involves expansion and contraction of the

Musical Instruments Handbook

player's cheeks to provide a steady airflow. It is then only a short design step to provide reed-pipes with a built-in variable air reservoir.

TYPES OF REED

Some reed-pipes are made not with what is termed an 'idioglot reed' – one sliced from the reed or cane material of the tube itself – but from a 'heteroglot reed', in which the vibrating reed is a separate sliver of reed or other suitable material, these days including plastic, tied over an aperture in a reed-bearing mouthpiece.

The most widespread of this type of single-reed instrument are the familiar clarinet and saxophone families, which were developed in Western European classical music, but have their origins in less-engineered instruments. Simple, unkeyed clarinets include the rough-hewn Finnish *mänkeri*. Made of wood, often with a birch-bark bell, this has a cylindrical bore like an idioglot reed-pipe, but its close relative the Finnish *liru* has a conical bore, a frequent feature among heteroglot clarinets. Norway's *tungehorn* has a conical bore, since its juniper reed is tied to a goat or cow horn.

HETEROGLOT REED PIPES

The Lithuanian *birbyne* is basically a horn pipe, and still exists in that form, but it has also been developed for ensemble playing into a larger, fatter wooden tube with relatively small finger holes, a cow-horn bell and a heteroglot reed assembly similar to that of an orchestral clarinet. Like many of the clarinet-type instruments, it has a much softer, more controllable tone than reed pipes – largely because the player can control the vibration of the reed with lips and tongue.

Even closer to the orchestral clarinet, but with a wider conical bore and consequent honkier tone, is the *taragot*, invented in the mid-nineteenth century by instrument maker J. Schunda in Budapest and nowadays played by traditional musicians in Romania.

▶ *The* tarogoto *is a wider-bored form of clarinet, with a fat tone.*

Section One: The Instruments

SAXOPHONE

The saxophone occupies an unusual position in that it is a bespoke instrument that has barely changed since its creation. Although it does not occupy the position in the orchestra its creator had envisaged, Adolphe Sax's invention has played a central part in music ever since it burst on to the scene in the 1840s.

Sax's father, Charles, was a successful instrument maker and Adolphe himself had been involved in a number of instrument refinements and inventions – most notably the bass clarinet – prior to the creation of the saxophone. Sax seems to have been particularly interested in bass instruments, since the first saxophone stemmed from an attempt to improve on the ophicleide.

OPHICLEIDE

The ophicleide was a keyed brass instrument, developed in the early 1800s, which used a trombone-style mouthpiece. Through the advocacy of composers including Hector Berlioz (1803–69), Giuseppe Verdi (1813–1901) and Richard Wagner (1813–83), it had quickly established itself as the standard bass wind instrument of the orchestra. Its obvious advantages of power and tone quality, however, were offset by erratic intonation and inconsistency of execution.

Sax attempted to solve these problems by combining various elements in one instrument. To a body resembling the ophicleide's he added new keywork and substituted the trombone-like mouthpiece for one much closer to that of the bass clarinet. The new instrument was

◀ *The ophicleide was eventually succeeded by the tuba.*

Musical Instruments Handbook

paraded at the second Brussels Industrial Exhibition in August 1841 as a *saxophone basse en cuivre* ('bass saxophone made from brass').

THE SAXOPHONE FAMILY

Berlioz heard Sax's creation and responded enthusiastically, reporting that 'there is not a bass instrument to compare it with' and cementing the term 'saxophone' in the public consciousness. Buoyed by this success, Sax went on to create a family of saxophones and in 1846 applied for a patent for the design of 14 different instruments. By 1850, the standard family of six sizes – sopranino, soprano, tenor, alto, baritone and bass – was established, with the contrabass as a rarely used extra.

CONSTRUCTION

The saxophone is a conically bored instrument with a flared bell. It widens considerably from mouthpiece to bell and consequently is capable of great power. It has between 22 and 24 note-holes, all of which are closed with keypads via a system of keys derived from the flute and clarinet systems. Like most wind instruments, the saxophone overblows at the octave; it uses two 'speaker keys' to facilitate the playing of higher notes. All saxophones have the same basic compass – from a written *bb* to a written *f'''* – but are transposing instruments.

With the exception of the sopranino saxophone, all the instruments require bending to make them a manageable length. This is done to a greater extent at the bell: the baritone saxophone almost doubles back on itself. The mouthpiece is detachable, as is the upper section of the body. The upper section is bent at right angles on the alto and tenor instruments to create an easy playing position. On the baritone and lower instruments, the upper section folds over itself to further reduce height.

Section One: The Instruments

REED AND MOUTHPIECE

All saxophones produce sound with a single reed. The mouthpiece, made of ebonite, wood, metal, plastic or glass, slopes down to meet the reed. Hollowed out, it is the shape of the mouthpiece chamber and the inlet that affect the sound. Saxophone mouthpieces are generally designed to fit over the neck of the instrument; an airtight fit is achieved with a thin cork sheet wrapped around the tip of the neck.

Sax retained the sole rights to the saxophone until 1866, at which point other manufacturers began developing their own models. Although some alterations in fingering and design took hold, the design of the saxophone has remained similar to Sax's original.

THE SAX IN PERFORMANCE

The saxophone was taken into military bands almost immediately after Sax introduced it to the public. In 1845, French bands had two as standard, rising to eight by 1854 and dropping back to four by 1894. By the second half of the nineteenth century, the saxophone was in use in military bands in Russia, the Netherlands, Belgium, Spain, Italy and Japan. It was slower to win acceptance in Germany and Austria, and only became a regular member there in the 1930s.

The powerful tone and flexibility of the saxophone made it an ideal band instrument, particularly for performing outdoors. It was its presence in bands that took the instrument to the United States, where it rapidly grew in popularity. By the 1920s, bands made up solely of saxophones were commonplace, sometimes with up to 100 players. From this point on, the saxophone became a vital component in jazz and has since taken an equally strong position in many other branches of popular music, its dexterity and range of tones offering something for many different genres.

Unfortunately for Adolphe Sax, his creation has never taken root where he wanted it to – in the orchestra.

Musical Instruments Handbook

Many commentators have suggested that this was due to Sax's arrogant and irascible nature. He was certainly effective in making enemies, which resulted in considerable prejudice against his designs.

A HYBRID INSTRUMENT

Perhaps more pertinent, however, is the saxophone's occupation of a no-man's land in instrumental terms. By the time Sax created his saxophone, the form of the orchestra was firmly established: the main body of strings, the soloists of the woodwind section, the brass chorus and finally the percussion.

The saxophone was in many senses a hybrid instrument. Made of brass and obviously related to the ophicleide, it was sounded like a clarinet and had a woodwind instrument's flexibility. Although possessing an impressively variable tone that allowed it to blend well, the saxophone did not sit comfortably with either the woodwind or the brass – and the vital role of bridging between the woodwind and brass was already brilliantly served by the French horns.

THE SAX IN COMPOSITION

Despite this, composers often used the saxophone. As early as 1844, the French theorist Jean-Georges Kastner (1810–67), a big fan of Sax's, used it in his opera *Le Dernier roi de Juda*. The original score for Gaëtano Donizetti's (1797–1848) opera *Dom Sébastien* is said to have included saxophones. On discovering the composer's intentions, the orchestral musicians revolted and refused to play the new instruments. When Sax himself was engaged to play, the orchestra threatened to boycott the performance, eventually forcing Donizetti's retreat.

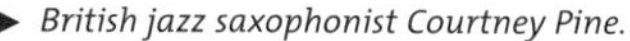
▶ *British jazz saxophonist Courtney Pine.*

Section One: The Instruments

A similar story surrounds Georges Bizet's (1838–1875) use of the saxophone in the incidental music to *L'Arlésienne*, with a clarinet often taking the saxophone part. However, Bizet retained the saxophone's designation in the score and it has become one of the most celebrated examples of successful use of the instrument. Other examples include Maurice Ravel's (1875–1937) *Boléro*, Darius Milhaud's (1892–1974) *La Création du monde* and Strauss's *Symphonia domestica*. The late-twentieth century saw a resurgence in the orchestral saxophone's popularity; it has been used by composers such as Harrison Birtwistle (b. 1934), Mark-Anthony Turnage (b. 1960) and John Adams (b. 1947) to great effect.

◄ *Saxes of different sizes play in different registers.*

A VERSATILE INSTRUMENT

The saxophone is perhaps one of the most flexible of instruments in terms of its variety of colour and articulation. This has made it particularly suited to ensemble work, and the saxophone quartet has established itself as a rich medium. At the same time, its ability to generate a strong, edgy colour means it is ideally suited to solo situations. The great advantage of the saxophone is that such variety is largely in the hands of the player. The choice of reed and mouthpiece has some impact, but as with any instrument, two players can make the same body sound completely different.

All saxophones play in a similar way – the fingering system is carried between instruments – and it is common for saxophonists to also play the clarinet.

◄ *The sopranino sax, one of the smallest members of the family.*

Musical Instruments Handbook

In addition, the saxophone is capable of a wide variety of avant-garde techniques, such as multiphonics, multiple tonguing and *glissandi*.

◀ *Soprano saxes are little used in bands and orchestras.*

SOPRANINO SAXOPHONE

With a sounding range of *d♭'* to *a♭'''*, the E♭ sopranino is the highest-pitched of the family. It is not generally used except in wind groups for creating special effects. The part in Ravel's *Boléro* is written for a sopranino, but this is more because the composer was unsure of the soprano's range.

SOPRANO SAXOPHONE

A fourth lower than the sopranino, the B♭ soprano's compass extends from *a♭* to *e♭'''*. Originally the soprano – like the sopranino – had a straight body. Equally common today is the soprano with an outward curve at the bell. This change in design creates a noticeably softer sound, but both are difficult to play in tune. The soprano saxophone really made its mark in the hands of jazz saxophonist Sidney Bechet in the 1920s to 1950s.

ALTO SAXOPHONE

Sounding an octave below the sopranino with a range of *d♭* to *a♭''*, the E♭ alto and tenor saxophones are the most ubiquitous of the saxophone family. It was the alto that took the first orchestral parts and for which were written the two best-known concertos: by Alexander Glazunov (1865–1936) and Jacques Ibert (1890–1952).

The alto saxophone is probably best known for the part it played in jazz. By the mid-1920s it was an established solo instrument and was brought to the forefront of this nascent musical form by players such as Johnny Hodges in Duke Ellington's band. The instrument's capacity to play everything from smooth, lyrical music to hard-edged bop fit perfectly with the idiosyncratic style of jazz musicians.

▶ *The alto sax is the size most commonly composed for by classical composers.*

Section One: The Instruments

OBOE

Of the woodwind instruments, the oboe has experienced perhaps the most organic development. There is no single, revolutionary moment at which the oboe became a modern instrument, and it retains strong links with the past both in sound and design.

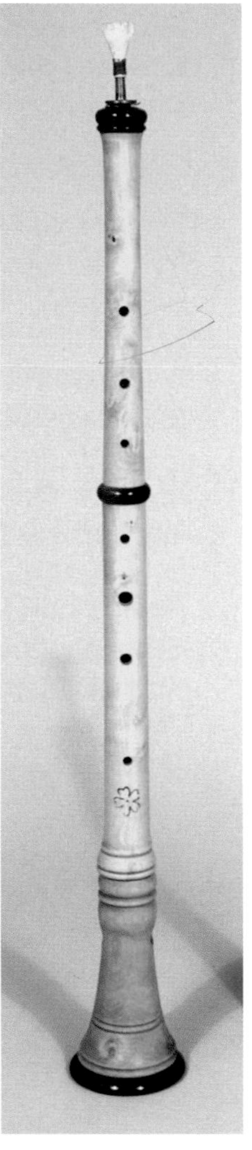

▲ *The oboe's Renaissance ancestor, the shawm.*

SHAWM

The modern oboe is a direct descendant of the shawm and the hautboy. The shawm was a conically bored, straight wooden instrument with a flared bell, popular throughout Europe from as early as the twelfth century. The shawm used finger holes to alter the pitch. It generated sound from a double reed held in a pirouette – a small, upturned wooden cup attached to the top of the instrument, which covered the lower half of the reed. The player could either rest his lips on the top of the pirouette, supporting his embouchure and allowing the reed to vibrate unimpeded in his mouth, or control the reed directly with his lips for greater variety of tone colour.

The shawm created a powerful, even raucous, noise; it was consequently associated with loud outdoor music, particularly ceremonial music and processionals. There were quiet shawms, but its

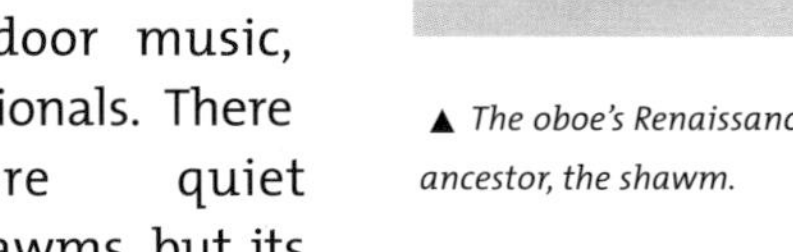

strong association with trumpets and drums, as well as sackbuts and cornetts, remains to this day. The early-music movement has created a shawm revival, and the instrument can be heard in performances of Renaissance music.

Fact

It is thought that the shawm arrived in Europe from the Middle East. The instrument itself doubtless has ancient roots, but sources are both scarce and unclear until the thirteenth century.

Musical Instruments Handbook

EVOLUTION OF THE SHAWM

Terminology has always been a contentious issue when discussing the evolution of the shawm into the oboe. For many commentators the term 'shawm' can be used interchangeably with hautbois or hautboy. Others argue that each is a distinct instrument. Whichever school one subscribes to, it is clear that changes to the shawm's design had, by the mid-seventeenth century, given rise to a new instrument, which will be referred to here as the hautboy.

HAUTBOY

The hautboy used eight finger holes, two of which were operated via keys; the shawm normally had six finger holes and no keys. The hautboy was made from three separate joints – two for the main body and one for the flared bell; the shawm was normally constructed from a single piece of wood.

The most significant difference between the shawm and the hautboy, however, was the jettisoning of the pirouette in favour of a completely exposed reed. This afforded the player greater control and softened the instrument's timbre, but simultaneously made it far more difficult to play.

▲ Hautbois *(hautboy) means 'high (or loud) wood'.*

EVOLUTION OF THE HAUTBOY

Between the seventeenth and nineteenth centuries many subtle changes occurred to the hautboy's design. The bore became narrower and the walls thinner; at the same time the finger holes became smaller. This focused, softened and quietened the instrument's tone as well as increasing its agility, so that by the late-eighteenth century, the hautboy had become an instrument of genuine virtuosity with celebrated soloists working all over Europe. It had also found a regular position in the orchestra, where its particular timbre made it an excellent partner for violins.

Section One: The Instruments

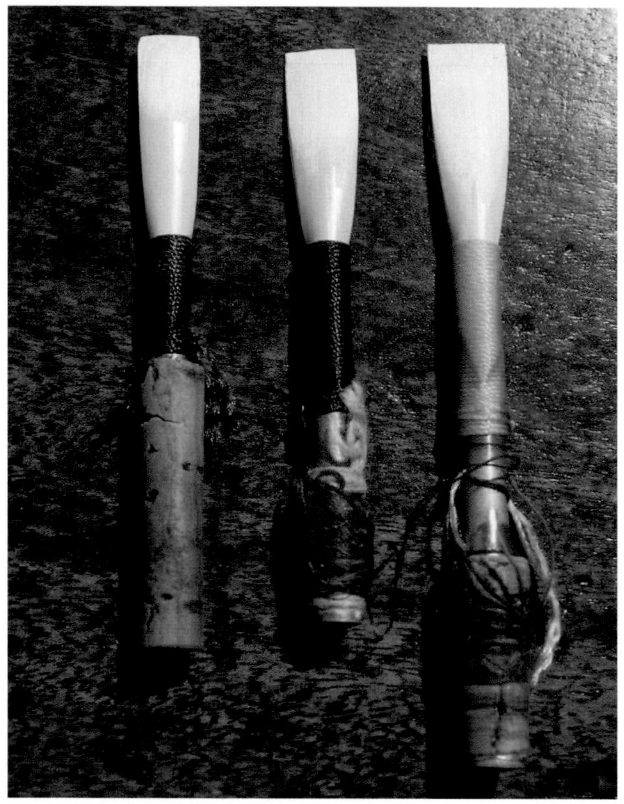

▲ *Three eras of oboe reed: Baroque, Classical and modern.*

Up to this point, the hautboy relied on two keys – even the 'speaker key' that facilitated the playing of overblown pitches was not generally used. As a consequence, some pitches sounded markedly different to others. Notes that were distant from the hautboy's fundamental pitch (i.e., the pitch of the tube with all finger holes covered) could only be achieved through a complicated system of fingering. This often entailed half covering holes so some pitches sounded veiled while others – closer to the instrument's fundamental pitch – were much brighter.

PITCH AND TIMBRE

The hautboy's lack of keys also meant that some pitches were completely inaccessible and many others could only be played using a complex system of fingering. This limited the instrument's use at a time when its siblings, the flute and clarinet, were developing rapidly and gaining in popularity.

The peculiarities of the hautboy's timbre were highly prized up to the beginning of nineteenth century. The very design features that gave it this quality, however, also caused problems – poor intonation, a timbre that did not blend well with other wind instruments, a compass that did not cover the entire chromatic range, and inconsistent execution. The hautboy's double reed gave players the flexibility to counter some of these problems, but it was lagging behind other wind instruments by the early 1800s, and change was needed.

Musical Instruments Handbook

There remained great attachment to the hautboy's unique colours, and developments came only slowly. Bit by bit, though, keys were added to the hautboy that extended its range, made intonation more certain, allowed trills to be played more easily, and opened up the complete chromatic range of pitches. Around 1800 a 'speaker key' was added to facilitate attacking high, overblown notes. Even so, many works were still written for a two-key hautboy.

THE OBOE ARRIVES

By the mid-nineteenth century, the hautboy had become very close to what we would now recognize as an oboe. Most orchestral players used models with only 10 to 13 keys, but work by various makers – particularly in France – continued making the instrument more agile and better in tune.

The most revolutionary figures on oboe development were Frédéric Triébert and A. M. R. Barret who, in 1862, announced a new design and fingering system for the oboe. This design gave a lowest pitch of $b\flat$, more than a tone lower than some previous models. The upper limits remained the same – around g'''.

▼ *The oboe had become a staple of chamber ensembles by the nineteenth century.*

Section One: The Instruments

CHANGES IN DESIGN

In spite of the loss of tone quality and pitch stability that this new design entailed, it became established as the oboe standard and was known as the *Conservatoire* system. Alongside this operated a similar fingering system, in which a thumb-plate was used to access the notes *b♭'* and *c''* instead of the first finger on the right hand. This was known as the thumb-plate system and has remained popular, especially in Britain.

At the same time as Triébert and Barret were developing the Conservatoire system, a number of other oboe makers were experimenting with radical new designs based on the theories of Theobald Boehm, the man who revolutionized the clarinet. None of these were particularly successful, though, exaggerating as they did the oboe's rougher qualities, and Boehm-system oboes were largely consigned to military bands.

Another vital change in oboe construction was the move away from boxwood. This had been preferred since the eighteenth century, but was soft and liable to warp. Experiments were made with rosewood, grenadilla and ebony; of which grenadilla, or African blackwood, has proved the most successful.

With numerous refinements, the Conservatoire-system oboe has remained pre-eminent around the world since the 1870s, with one vital exception: Vienna. To this day the Austrian city has held out against the French model. The Vienna Philharmonic Orchestra still uses a design that necessitates complex fingerings and a reliance on lip control, and which produces a warm, smooth tone.

◀ *The treble or soprano oboe is the principal member of the oboe family.*

Musical Instruments Handbook

▶ *The modern oboe has more than 20 keys.*

THE MODERN OBOE

The modern oboe is just under 60 cm (24 in) long and made of three parts: the upper joint, including the reed slot, the lower joint and the bell, which is just slightly flared. It is conically bored and requires very little air to play – with the result that players must learn to exhale stale air before breathing in again. It is a non-transposing instrument, and music is written for it in the treble clef at sounding pitch.

The double reed has changed far less than the body of the instrument. It is made from the stem of a large semi-tropical grass known as *Arundo donax*. Two separate leaves are bound together and inserted in a piece of cork that in turn nestles in the neck of the oboe. Air pressure causes the two leaves to vibrate, which in turn agitates the air in the instrument into motion. The reed is cushioned between lips curled inwards over teeth, so that it is gripped by the teeth rather than bitten by them. Controlling the reeds requires a high degree of skill.

PERFORMANCE

While not as flexible as the clarinet, a wide range of performing techniques are available to the oboist, including *glissandi*, double-, triple-, and flutter-tonguing, as well as multiphonics. To a large extent, though, the oboe retains its links with the past. It is often called upon for nostalgic effect, or to create the sense of an ancient court or of a more pastoral scene. Because of its evolutionary development, the oboe carries with it vestiges of the shawm and, despite the softening of timbre and increase in agility, it still has the capacity for raucous, rough celebrations.

▶ *An experienced oboist can produce a rich, warm, beautiful tone.*

Section One: The Instruments

OBOE D'AMORE

The oboe's double reed afforded a high degree of flexibility in terms of bending pitches. As a result, even early two-keyed instruments had access to most pitches. This meant that there was no pressing need to produce instruments with different fundamental pitches to perform music in different keys. It was more the desire for instruments of a different colour that led to the development of the oboe d'amore and oboe da caccia.

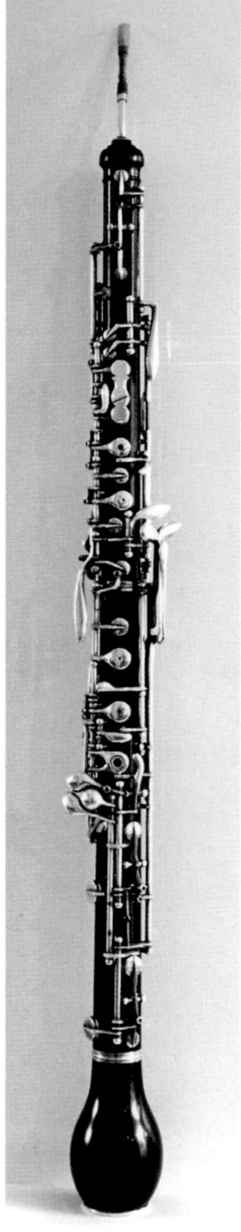

▲ *The oboe d'amore is a mezzo-soprano oboe.*

The early eighteenth century oboe d'amore was a mezzo-soprano oboe in A with a bulb bell. Its tone, slightly darker than the oboe's, made it popular with Bach and Georg Philipp Telemann (1681–1767) in particular. The greatest concentration of oboe d'amore makers seems to have been in Leipzig, which would explain its enduring popularity in Germany.

Its appeal had diminished significantly by the 1760s, but it experienced a revival in the later nineteenth century, when a new key mechanism enabled its use by Strauss, Mahler, Debussy and even Ligeti.

OBOE DA CACCIA

The oboe da caccia was developed around the same time as the oboe d'amore. A tenor oboe, keyed in F and sounding a perfect fifth below the standard soprano instrument, the oboe da caccia was made in one piece and was strongly curved, often in a complete semi-circle, with a flared bell. Such a horn-like appearance provided its name, which translates from Italian as 'hunting oboe'.

COR ANGLAIS

The cor anglais, or English horn, is a tenor oboe in F – like the oboe da caccia – that sounds a perfect fifth below the soprano oboe. The only significant difference between the two instruments at first was that the cor anglais employed a bulb bell instead of a flared one. The similarity of the cor anglais to medieval depictions of angel's horns led to the instrument being referred to as 'engellisch' which in Middle German means 'angelic'. The same word means 'English' and the two meanings were conflated and the 'English' tag stuck.

Musical Instruments Handbook

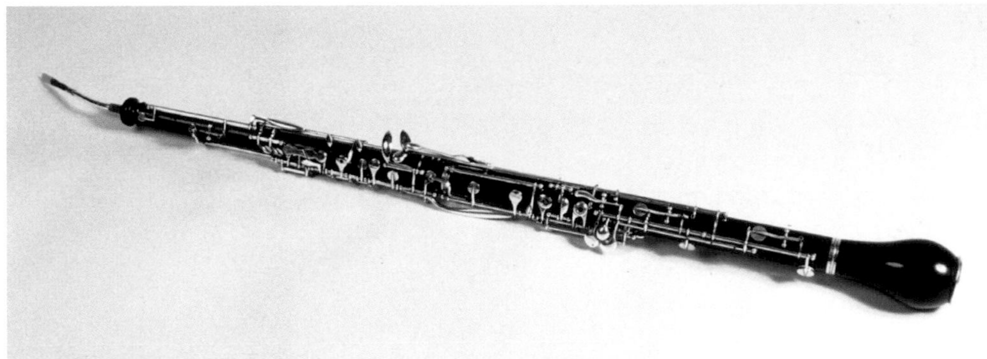

▲ *The cor anglais has a richer, throatier tone than the oboe.*

Although the oboe da caccia faded away, the cor anglais remained popular. Its first significant outing was in Christoph Willibald Gluck's (1714–87) opera *Orfeo ed Euridice*. It became particularly associated with Italian opera during the late-eighteenth century and the major cor anglais makers were all in cities with thriving operatic lives.

DEVELOPMENTS TO THE COR ANGLAIS

Like the oboe, the cor anglais remained two-keyed for many years. Triébert, the man whose work so influenced the oboe, also made significant developments to the cor anglais, adding new keys, and partially straightening the body. He was helped by virtuoso player Gustave Vogt. Vogt was greatly admired by Berlioz, and together they did much to cement the instrument's reputation. By incorporating it into their works.

▲ *There are many famous cor anglais solos in the orchestral repertoire.*

It was another performer, Henri Brod, who took the cor anglais to the form we know today. Brod also collaborated with Triébert and a senior craftsman in his workshop, François Lorée. It was Lorée who in the 1880s completely straightened the cor anglais and redesigned the keywork to match the oboe. Before this, bassoonists played the cor anglais as often as oboists.

By the twentieth century, the cor anglais had become a mainstay of the orchestra. Although it can be played by oboists, the cor anglais requires skilful handling and is played by a specialist, who also plays the oboe when required to.

Section One: The Instruments

DOUBLE-REED INSTRUMENTS AROUND THE WORLD

At its simplest, to make a double reed the end of a piece of reed or similar plant tube is flattened so its sides nearly touch. Putting this flattened end into the mouth and blowing causes the two sides to briefly close against each other then spring back, hundreds of times a second. This causes a regular stream of air puffs – a squeak.

When this squeaking reed is inserted in the top of a tube, the reed is forced to vibrate at a pitch determined by the length of the tube – the longer the air column, the lower the note – and this is effectively varied by making a series of finger holes.

▼ *Tibetan monks playing their distinctive shawms.*

Musical Instruments Handbook

Squashed-tube reeds are used in some instruments, but more often the reed is made by binding the narrow ends of two thin wedge-shaped pieces of reed, cane or similar material to a small metal tube (known in English as the staple), which is then inserted into the top of the playing tube.

THE GLOBAL SHAWM

Members of the shawm family are by far the most numerous and widely played of the double-reed instruments across the globe. Details vary worldwide, but the prime features of a shawm are a double reed fitted into conical bored tube that usually ends in a flared bell. A strident sound is also characteristic. The western classical oboe and its orchestral relatives have key systems and a tamed tone, but are nevertheless types of shawm (see p. 164).

Turkey and the surrounding area are shawm heartland, and many other shawms of the world have their origins in the Ottoman Empire. The English name 'shawm' – that of a Renaissance instrument developed from the oriental form – could derive from the Latin *calamus*, meaning a reed or stalk, or (perhaps more likely since shawms seem to have arrived in Western Europe during the Crusades) from an old Arabic name for a reed instrument, *salamiya* or *salameya*, to which the Latin word also appears to be related. Some other instrument appellations are similar, such as the Italian *ciaramella*, which is characteristically played in duet with a *zampogna* (bagpipe) and *chirimia*, a historical instrument in Spain, and a folk shawm still played in Guatemala.

EASTERN DOUBLE-REED INSTRUMENTS

The Ukrainian shawm, introduced from Turkey or the Caucasus and once played by Cossack armies, is called a *surma*. The word suggests a link between the *salamiya* name-line and another name family tree – the shawm of Turkey and Armenia is called *zurna*, which is believed to be a modification of the Persian name for the instrument, *shahnai* (from the Persian words *shah* and *nai*, meaning 'king' and 'reed' respectively).

Many other shawms – most of them very similar in design – share that derivation, with spelling or transliteration differences even within the same region: the Indian *shehnai*, Afghan, Iranian, central Asian and north African shawms variously spelt *sornai*, *surnai*, *sorna* and *surnay*, Greek Thracian *zournas*, Macedonian *zurla*, and probably also the Tunisian *zokra*.

▲ ► *Turkish* zurna *(top) and North Indian* shahnai.

Section One: The Instruments

◀ *Chinese* suona, *a double-reed instrument of the worldwide shawn family.*

The name of the Chinese shawm, *suona*, which usually has a metal bell, is in keeping with its Middle Eastern origins. Among the numerous other shawms of East and Southeast Asia are the Vietnamese *ken*, Korean *p'iri*, Thai *pi*, and Tibetan *rgyaling*. The sound of Egypt's *mizmar*, whose name derives from *mzr*, meaning 'to play', is ubiquitous in Egyptian music, although in today's Arabic pop it is usually synthesized on a keyboard.

EUROPEAN AND AFRICAN DOUBLE-REED INSTRUMENTS

The Moorish invasion of Iberia resulted in the spread of instruments like the shawm. In much of central Spain it is known as the *dulzaina*, in Valencia a *dolçaina*, in Catalunya a *gralla* and across the French border in Languedoc a *graille*. In the Basque country in the north, despite that region being less affected by Moorish culture than the rest of Iberia, it is called a *gaita* – a name that more usually across Europe refers to a bagpipe, but in the Moorish homelands of North Africa *ghaita*, *ghaïta*, *ghaida*, *rhaita*, *rhita* or *ghayta* means a shawm, and it is a common instrument. Close relatives in Niger, Mali, Chad, Cameroon and Nigeria – on which the wooden playing tube is sometimes covered in leather (rather like a cornett) – incorporate the Arabic definite article 'al' as *algaita*, *alghaita*, etc.

▲ *An ornate shawm from Burma.*

SUPPORTING INSTRUMENTS

A common accompanying instrument for shawms, particularly among itinerant and Roma musicians, is drums. Also typical is support from another shawm, either in unison or providing a drone, as for example in the Karnatic tradition of the south Indian *nadaswaram*. The other member of the pair is sometimes a bagpipe, as in the Breton pairing of the very shrill *bombarde* with the bagpipe *biniou*, in which the bagpipe sustains the tune as the *bombarde* player takes a breath.

Some of the more oboe-like shawms are played in ensembles of different sizes. The *sopila* of Istria and the nearby island of Krk on the Adriatic exists in two sizes, both unkeyed, that play intertwining lines. Crucial to the sound of a *cobla*, the brass and woodwind band playing for *sardana* dancing in Catalunya, is a pair of oboe-like keyed *tibles* plus two lower *tenoras*.

Musical Instruments Handbook

▲ *The* ghaita *is a double-reed instrument from North Africa.*

DUDUKS AND RELATED INSTRUMENTS

There is a distinct group of double-reed instruments that, unlike the shawms, have a very seductive mellow, voice-like tone. In appearance they are all quite similar: a cylindrical playing tube with no bell, into which is fitted a very large reed of the squashed-tube variety, fitting directly into the top of the tube with no staple. Slipped over the reed is usually a tuning bridle of rattan.

The best-known of these today – largely through the playing of Djivan Gasparyan – is the Armenian *duduk*. Made of apricot-wood, the body has nine finger holes on the front, of which seven are fingered, and a thumb hole at the back. Normally a second player provides a continuous drone, using circular breathing. Close kin of the *duduk* are the Georgian *diduku*, Turkish *mey*, Mongolian *guan*, Chinese *kuan* or *guanzi*, and a characteristic instrument of *gagaku* (Japanese court music), the bamboo *hichiriki*.

► *The* duduk *being played by Armenian music legend Djivan Gasparyan.*

Section One: The Instruments

BASSOON

As ensemble music became more popular during the sixteenth century there was increased demand for wind instruments that could elegantly negotiate the lower ranges.

Large versions of wind instruments intended for the higher registers lacked volume and agility and were often difficult to play. Various elements of existing instruments – the bass recorder's crook and the shawm's double reed, for instance – were combined to create the bassoon's predecessor: the dulcian.

DULCIAN

Meaning 'sweet' (presumably in comparison with the raucous shawm), the dulcian, standing at nearly 1 m (3 ft) high, was constructed from a single piece of wood, into which were cut two conical bores that were connected at the base. With eight finger holes and two keys the dulcian, overblowing at the octave, had a range of *C* to *g'*. At the same time, versions of the dulcian were made out of separate pieces of wood, which were then bound together, giving rise to the term 'fagot' because of its resemblance to a bundle of wood.

DEVELOPMENT OF THE BASSOON

The dulcian was gradually developed over the ensuing centuries. Keys were added, the distribution and size of finger holes was experimented with, the wood altered, the range extended, and crook and bell redesigned. During this period, it acquired the name bassoon, probably derived from the term 'basson', which was often applied to bass-register instruments.

During the nineteenth century, versions of the bassoon were created by Adolphe Sax and Theobold Boehm, though neither were ultimately successful. It was Carl Almenraeder's (1786–1846) innovations between 1817 and 1843 that led to the creation of the modern bassoon. His work was continued by J. A. Heckel and the Heckel bassoon – as it came to be known – has been adopted as the standard design.

Musical Instruments Handbook

WOODWIND

HECKEL BASSOON

At 134 cm (53 in), the Heckel bassoon, made of maplewood, is constructed of four joints, which combine for a total tube length of 275 cm (108 in). The bassoon is held at an angle with a crook enabling the double reed to sit comfortably in the player's embouchure. With 21 keys on the standard design, the Heckel bassoon has a compass extending from *B♭'* to at least *a'* and possibly up to *e''*. Some composers, notably Wagner, have written for a bassoon that can play a low *A'*, but this requires an extra-long bell and an additional key that most players believe destabilizes the instrument too much to become a standard feature.

Although the Heckel system is generally accepted as standard, it has competition from a French design. The Buffet bassoon was created in the 1830s and has a much softer, more singing tone. This is principally due to a different wood – dark rosewood – and a different key and fingering system. It remains in use in France and Spain, and was the instrument many composers had in mind when writing orchestral music, including Giacomo Puccini (1858–1924), Claude Debussy (1862–1918) and Edward Elgar (1857–1934).

▲ *The bassoon sounds smoother and less reedy than the oboe.*

CONTRABASSOON

Sounding an octave below the bassoon, the contra- or double bassoon is a conical tube 550 cm (217 in) long. Doubling back on itself five times, it stands at around 120 cm (47 in) high and rests on a steel spike. Like the bassoon, it was Heckel who developed the contrabassoon as we know it today. Capable of sounding a *B♭''* or even an *A''*, it requires a much longer and wider double reed than its smaller sibling. Heckel's version was completed in 1877, and one of the first examples of its use occurs in Johannes Brahms's (1833–97) Symphony No. 1. There were earlier versions of the contrabassoon, however, which can be heard in Handel's *Music for the Royal Fireworks* (1749) and Ludwig van Beethoven's (1770–1827) *Fidelio* (1805).

Section One: The Instruments

CRUMHORN

The crumhorn is a double-reed wind-cap instrument. This means that the two reeds are enclosed in a rigid cap. The player blows through a hole in one end of the cap, which makes the reed vibrate unimpeded, since there is no direct contact with the lips. The crumhorn is a cylindrically bored instrument, normally made of maple with a curved lower section.

PITCH AND COMPASS

Since the crumhorn uses a wind-cap, it cannot overblow. The instrument's compass, therefore, is limited to about a ninth unless keys are provided to extend it downwards. It is possible to use a technique called underblowing, which can extend the range downwards by a perfect fifth.

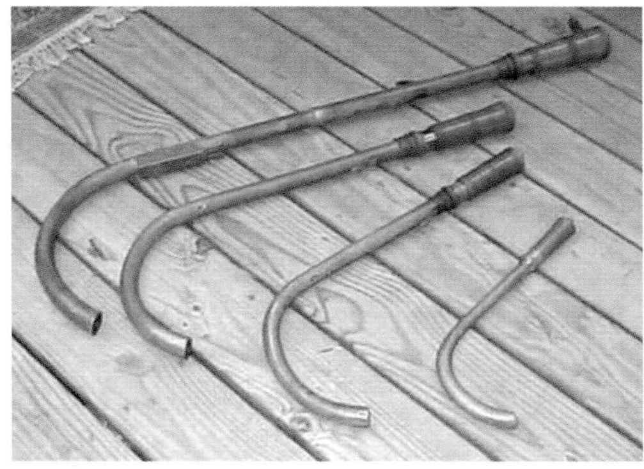

▲ *A consort of cumhorns: soprano, alto, tenor and bass.*

Because it could not be overblown, a number of different crumhorns were necessary to cover a useful range of pitches. From the soprano to the extended great bass, every pitch from *G'* to *d"* was covered. The narrow range of the crumhorn meant that a set of instruments was needed to play even simple music, and its manner of construction, which involved bending while damp to achieve the hockey-stick curve, made it a relatively expensive instrument, so it was largely restricted to professional court musicians.

RISE AND FALL

The earliest evidence of the crumhorn is in a painting from 1488, but descriptions of the instrument began to appear as early as 1300. Most popular during the Renaissance period, the crumhorn was still in use in the seventeenth century. Its inflexibility as a musical instrument contributed significantly to its downfall, however, and by the eighteenth century it was largely obsolete.

Musical Instruments Handbook

BAGPIPES

The bagpipe principle is simple: instead of the player blowing directly on a reed pipe, the air is supplied from a reservoir, usually made of animal skin, which is inflated either by mouth or by bellows. The result is the ability to produce a continuous tone, and the possibility of adding extra reed-pipes to enable a single player to make homophonic music.

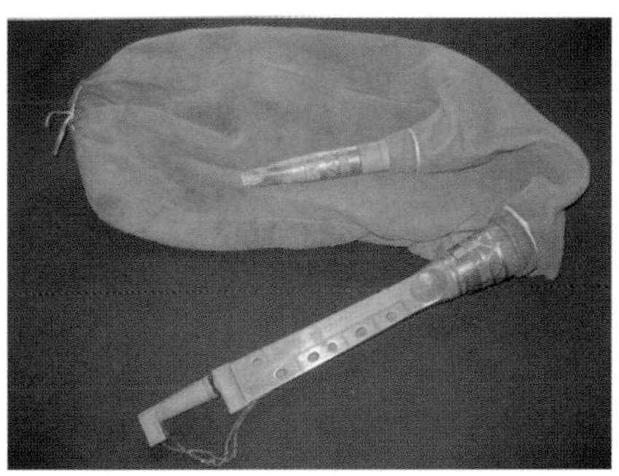

▲ *The* bouhe, *traditional to Gascony.*

HISTORY

The early history of bagpipes is unclear. Because they were made of perishable organic materials, no early examples survive, and as they have been regarded in recent years as something of a peasant instrument they have not been much documented (except for the Scottish Great Highland bagpipe, which is just one of the wide range and by no means the earliest).

However, playing a melody against a drone, and achieving a continuous tone by circular breathing, have been common among reed-pipe players for millennia; plugging the reed-pipes into a bag is a logical development. Bagpipes can be seen in the art of the Middle Ages, and there is evidence that they were in use at least 1,000 years before that.

CONSTRUCTION

The basic components of a bagpipe are:

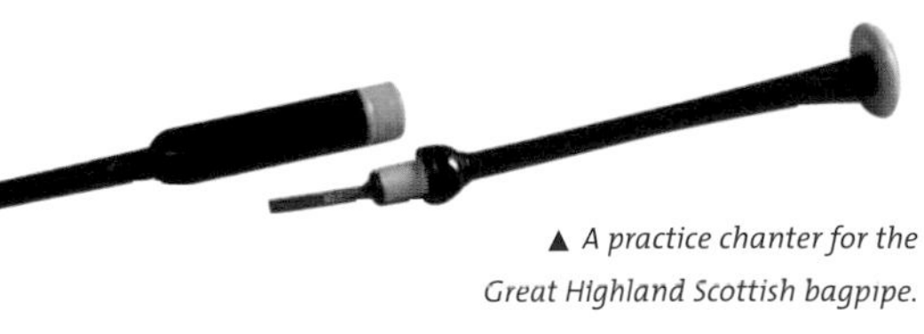

▲ *A practice chanter for the Great Highland Scottish bagpipe.*

1 The bag, usually made of a whole or partial animal skin.
2 A blow-pipe, with a non-return valve, to inflate the bag. Some bagpipes are inflated by a bellows tucked under the player's arm.
3 The chanter – the melody pipe, equipped with finger holes. It may have a single bore, with a single or double-bladed reed, or have additional bores with

Section One: The Instruments

or without finger holes, each with a reed. The chanter is normally fitted into the bag via a tied-in wooden tube known as a 'stock'.

4 Most bagpipes have one or more drone pipes, usually with single-blade reeds, plugged into the bag via one or more extra stocks. Each usually gives a continuous single note that accompanies the melody.

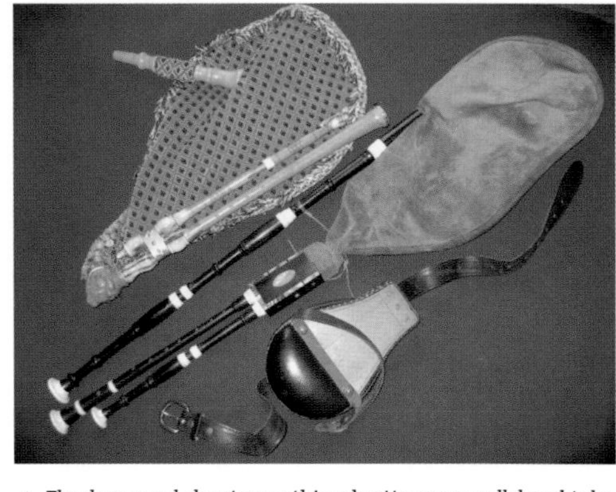

▲ *The drone and chanter on this* cabrette *are parallel and take air from a common stock.*

GREAT HIGHLAND BAGPIPE

The world's best-known bagpipe – largely because of its use in the British army and the former Empire – is Scotland's Great Highland Bagpipe. In fact, this is just about the only bagpipe to have had substantial military use. Quite similar to the *gaitas* of Spain's Galicia and Asturias and northern Portugal, it is mouth-blown with a single nine-holed, conical-bored chanter. Today's standardized version has three separate drone pipes: two tenors an octave below the chanter's keynote, and a bass an octave below them.

PITCH

The exact pitch of that keynote varies; while called A, it is generally between B♭ and B. Until recently, Highland pipes were not played with other instruments with a defined scale, so, as with many bagpipes, their overall pitching and the tempering of the notes within the scale depended on the ear and satisfaction of the maker and player. Nowadays pipes made for playing alone or in pipe bands still use the exciting non-equal-temperament intervals, but there now exist pipes with their pitch and scale modified to blend better with the wider instrumentation of the Scottish folk-music revival.

Musical Instruments Handbook

HIGHLAND PIPE MUSIC

It is a convention that Highland pipe tunes are written down as if the keynote was A, but with no key signature shown; F and C are read as sharps. The chanter's total range is an octave, plus one tone below the keynote made by closing the bottom hole with the little finger. No overblowing to the next octave is possible.

The music of the Highland pipe falls into two categories: the solo music called in Gaelic *ceòl mór* ('big music'), also known as *piobaireachd* ('pipbrock') consisting of a theme and variations, and the more familiar dance and other music, called in Gaelic *ceòl beag* ('small music'). As with other upstopped chanters, notes are separated and tunes given style and impetus by rapid finger-flicking grace notes.

BAGPIPES OF THE BRITISH ISLES

Scotland has other bagpipes, including the bellows-blown small-pipes, reel-pipes and lowland or border pipes, but south of the border, most of England's bagpipes (and also the Welsh *pibacwd*) had died out until recent revivals.

The exception to this is in Northumberland, where there have long been skilled players of the quiet, reedy-sounding Northumbrian small-pipes. These are bellows-blown, and their chanter – usually equipped with keys and so able to play chromatically – has a stopped end, so that by closing all the finger holes it can be silenced between notes, producing a characteristic *staccato* style.

The end of the chanter of the Irish uilleann pipes, also bellows-blown, can be pressed on the player's thigh to close it, and it can be overblown into the second octave. The uilleann pipes are extremely highly developed; the bunch of drones that lies across the player's knees includes some closed-ended ones known as regulators, fit with keys that allow them to be switched on and off during play to give a chordal accompaniment.

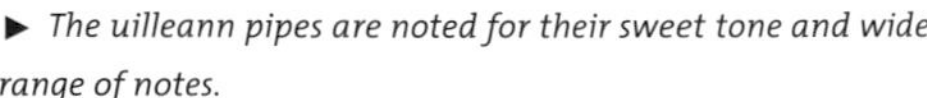

▶ *The uilleann pipes are noted for their sweet tone and wide range of notes.*

Section One: The Instruments

IBERIAN BAGPIPES

Most countries of Europe and some beyond have at least one distinctive type of bagpipe. The *gaitas* of Spain's Galicia and Asturias have recently experienced a renaissance. Iberia has other pipes, too, including the *gaita de foles* of Portugal's Trás-os-Montes, the *sac de gemecs* of Catalunya, Mallorcan *xeremies* and the *gaitas* of Aragon and Zamora.

FRENCH AND ITALIAN BAGPIPES

France has an array of regional pipes, including the high-pitched Breton *biniou*, the *chabrettes* of Limousin, Berry and Bourbonnais, Auvergne *cabrette*, Gascon *boha*, the *Grande Cornemuse Bourbonnais* (often played with hurdy-gurdy), and the *musette*, a small bellows-blown pipe with four drones, whose bores are all folded into a single stubby cylinder.

Italy has even more, among them the *gran zampogna*, one of the world's largest, the widespread *zampogna di Scapoli* which is often played together with the *shawm piffero*, and in Calabria about five forms of *ciaramedda*.

For Western European pipes the double-bladed reed is the norm, in a chanter with usually a single, often conical bore, but most of the other bagpipes of the world have single-bladed chanter reeds, and often have two or more usually parallel bores in the chanter, like the bagless reed-pipes from which it is likely they are derived.

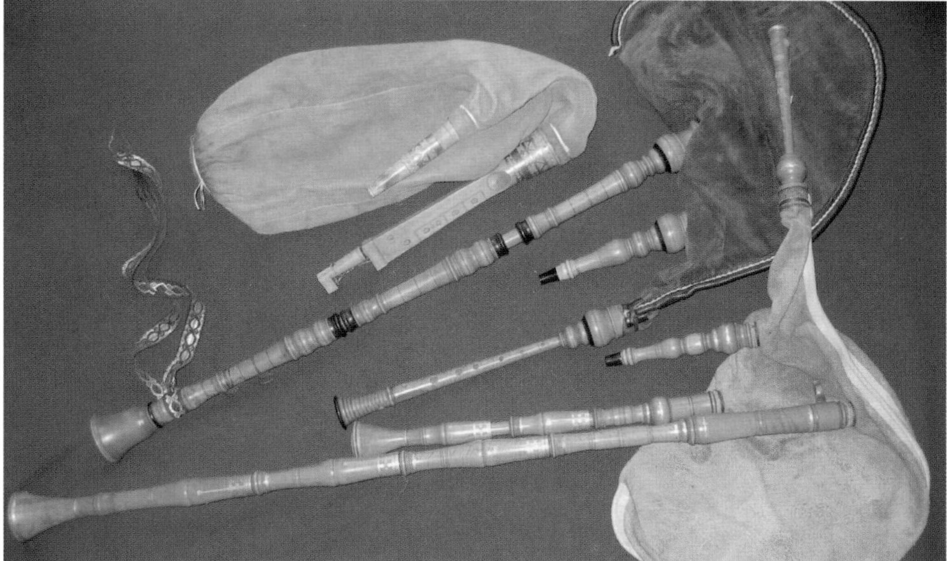

▲ *French bagpipes: Limousin* bouhe, *Breton* veuze *and Breton* biniou.

Musical Instruments Handbook

BALKAN BAGPIPES

The Balkans and surrounding countries are rich with bagpipes. Bulgaria has two main forms – the *gaida* and *kaba* ('big') *gaida*, both with a single-blade reed in a single-bore chanter – which are central to the sound of the country's highly sophisticated traditional music. Romania's *cimpoi* is similar in design. In neighbouring Macedonia there is a saying: 'without the *gajda* there is no wedding'.

Serbia, Montenegro, Bosnia- Herzegovina and Croatia have a wide range, including the double-chantered *diple* (which also exists without a bag), the droneless, double-chantered *mih* (whose bag in the Herzegovinian form features claws at the skin's leg-apertures), the robust *gajde* with its curved, bell-ended double chanter, and the *dude*, which can have triple or even quadruple chanter bores.

▲ *Bulgarian bagpipe being played in a Balkan bagpipe workshop.*

Greek pipes include the Thracian *gaïda* and double-chantered Dodecanese *tsambouna*. To the north can be found the double-chantered Hungarian *duda* and Slovak *gajdy*, on into Belarus for the *duda*, Russia for the *volynka*, then Lithuania's *minu ragelis*, Latvian *dudas*, Estonian *torupill* and Swedish *säckpipa*.

A WORLD OF PIPES

Names such as the *bock* of Bohemia (a complex form with a folded bass drone like the Polish duda), the *koza duda* of Ukraine and *koziol* and triple-chantered koza of Poland refer to the goat, which often supplies the skin. In eastern and central European pipes, an effigy of its horned head is commonly carved at the top of the chanter, whose stock is tied into the goatskin's neck opening while the blow-pipe and drone stocks occupy its leg apertures.

To the east and south, the Laz people of the Turkish shore of the Black Sea have the *tulum*, whose double chanter consists of canes set into a wooden yoke, showing very clearly the reed-pipe connection, as does the Tunisian *mezoued*, which has two, five-holed unison-tuned hornpipes tied into a droneless bag with claws like the Herzegovinian *mih*. The Berbers have the *ghaita*, Azerbaijan has the *balaban*, Iran the *ney-anbhan*. India's *shruti* has been largely supplanted by Scottish Highland bagpipes, many of them made in neighbouring Pakistan.

Section One: The Instruments

JEW'S HARP

The pocket-sized instruments known in English as jew's harps (or in some periods of history trumps, and in French *guimbardes*), have no connection with Judaism – nor are they harps.

A strip of bamboo or metal, in a frame of the same material, is twanged, and the oral cavity acts as an amplifying soundbox whose capacity can be changed, selecting particular harmonics to emphasize. Thus, individual pitches from the harmonic series can be selected and tunes played. The rhythm of the twang can be augmented with extra beats by breathing in and out.

WORLD JEW'S HARPS

Southeast Asian jew's harps are generally made of either bamboo or metal. In the bamboo version, a narrow tongue is cut out of a thin strip of bamboo; placed against the lips, the bamboo frame, not the tongue, is twanged, either with a finger or a thread, and this causes the tongue to vibrate. The Filipino *kubing* is one such. The delicate Vietnamese *dan moi* and Chinese *kou xiang* are of similar construction but made of springy brass.

▲ *Jew's harps are known by at least 40 different names.*

Elsewhere, in the world, a springy metal tongue is attached inside a keyhole-shaped frame of thick, stiff metal, the latter pressed against the player's partially open teeth, and the tongue twanged with a finger. Such instruments are made and played across Asia and Europe. Notable centres include Siberia (where it is known as a *khomus*), Rajasthan in north India (*morchang*), Hungary (*doromb*), Norway (*munnharpe*) and Austria (*maultrommel*). Those sold in Britain are mainly made in Austria; many millions have been exported by makers in the town of Molln since the seventeenth century.

Musical Instruments Handbook

FREE-REED INSTRUMENTS AROUND THE WORLD

The birthplace of free reeds seems to have been eastern Asia. There, it is typical to place a small free reed, made of metal or bamboo, into a bamboo tube cut to the appropriate length so that its air column resonates at the reed's frequency, increasing the volume and allowing the player to allow it to sound, or to stop it, by opening or closing the airway.

WHAT IS A FREE-REED INSTRUMENT?

If the tongue of a Vietnamese *dan moi* (jew's harp) is bent slightly so that its rest position is no longer in the plane of the frame, it is possible to activate it without plucking, simply by blowing or sucking (depending which way it is sprung), to produce a steady, non-decaying note. The instrument has thus been transformed from 'plucked idiophone' to a free reed. Unlike the single and double reeds, a free reed doesn't produce its sound by opening and closing an airstream – it produces it by its own vibration.

SHENG

Bunches of such reed-pipes, tuned to chords or a scale, are attached to a single mouthpiece; each tube has a hole that the players keep covered with their fingers unless they wants that particular note to sound.

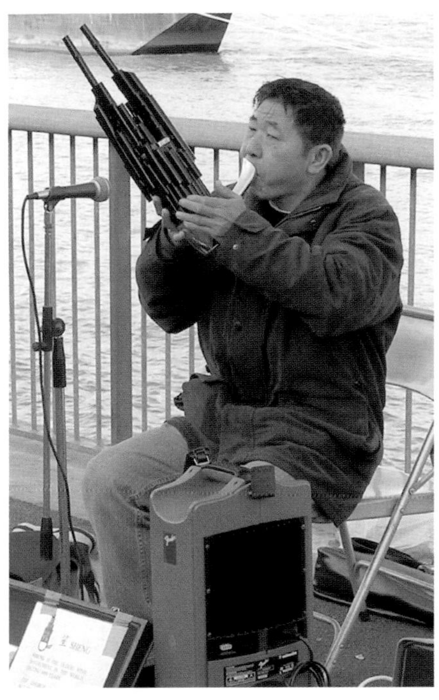

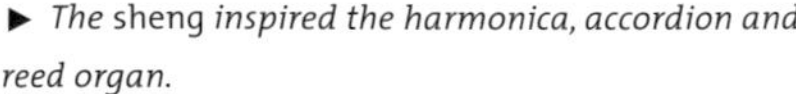

▶ *The* sheng *inspired the harmonica, accordion and reed organ.*

Section One: The Instruments

The best-known of these 'mouth-organs' is the Chinese *sheng*, which looks a little like a metal teapot with a thicket of 17 or more thin bamboo pipes emerging from its lid, with the spout to blow or suck down. Instruments working on the same principle can be found in the neighbouring countries of Korea, Laos, Thailand, Borneo, Vietnam and Japan.

The Japanese *sho* is descended from a version of *sheng* introduced from China in the eighth century. The Lao and Thai *khaen* has two rows of bamboo pipes, each with a tuned reed, that extend both above and below the wind-chest; the pipes can be very long, up to a couple of metres, as can those of the almost bow-and-arrow shaped Laot and Thai *gaeng*, and the similar south Chinese *lusheng*, both of which have a long tubular wind-chest and fewer pipes.

▲ *The Thai* khaen *(centre) can have up to 18 pipes in two parallel rows.* Sheng *is shown right.*

CHINESE PIPES

The pipes of the Chinese *hulusheng* ('gourd sheng'), an older but still played form of which the modern *sheng* is a development, have lower openings flush with the bottom of the gourd wind-chest; the player can bend notes by closing these with his thumb.

This principle is taken further in the small range of single-pipe free-reed instruments, of which the best known is the *ba-wu* of China's Yunnan region. It looks like a bamboo transverse flute, but a 'V'-shaped brass free reed is set into it where a flute's blowing hole would be. By blowing through the reed and fingering as one would a flute, the reed is forced above its fundamental into a scale of just over an octave, with an alluring dark, clarinet-like tone. There are kindred single-tube free-reed instruments in Laos, Thailand and Vietnam. The Vietnamese *ala* and *ding tac ta* are sucked rather than blown.

Musical Instruments Handbook

THE SPREAD OF FREE-REED INSTRUMENTS

There are few details, but it seems likely that it was from the *sheng* or similar that all western free-reed instruments have been developed. Organ-builders were early on the scene in the eighteenth century, but soon there were the first mouth-blown instruments such as the *aeolian* or *aeolina*, which was a simple set of free reeds mounted side by side. Like most western reeds, their vibrating tongues were bolted on to a plate rather than cut from it.

HARMONICA

Soon the modern harmonica or mouth organ began to appear – essentially a row of reeds mounted side by side on a reed plate to make a diatonic or chromatic scale, with a slotted 'comb' to direct the breath to them. The scale is usually achieved by alternate blowing and sucking as one moves from channel to channel. This means that if one blows several at once, a chord is produced, with a different chord on the suck.

▲ *The harmonica is also known as a mouth organ.*

The chromatic harmonica, in its standard form (there are many refinements and variations of both diatonic and chromatic harmonicas) has a hand-operated slider that opens and closes holes to direct the breath to one of two reed-banks tuned a half step apart. On tremolo harmonicas, pairs of reeds are slightly detuned to give a beating effect. Sophisticated playing techniques have developed, including bending notes (a style evolved by blues players) and manufacturers, early on in Germany and other parts of Western Europe, but now also back in the birthplace of the free reed, East Asia, are constantly creating new models to suit, and to add to the huge and ingenious range which exists, including the splendidly chugging bass harmonica.

Section One: The Instruments

INTRODUCTION

STRINGED INSTRUMENTS

Stringed instruments, or chordophones, are those in which sound is generated from a vibrating string held in tension. They form the backbone of almost every substantial musical culture, probably because of the ease with which they can be tuned, their clarity of pitch and their great adaptability. There are three types of stringed instrument, defined by the method of sound production: bowed, plucked and struck.

STRINGS

Gut strings have been used for making music for thousands of years. Examples have been discovered in excavations of ancient Egyptian sites dating from 1500 BC, and there is plentiful evidence of their use in Greek and Roman culture.

Typically, gut strings were made from the small intestines of a young sheep. Washed, scoured and sliced into strips, they were then twisted into threads before being bleached and polished. The *e''* string on a violin was normally made from between five and seven threads; the lower strings on the double bass, though, needed 85 or more.

STRING TENSION

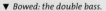

Marin Mersenne (1588–1648), a great French thinker, proved that the pitch a string sounds is not only related to its length. It is also a function of its tension, its diameter and its density. A long, thin string at high tension will sound higher than a short, fat string at low tension. It is easy enough to see this by plucking an elastic band: held flaccidly its pitch is low; stretched out it becomes much thinner and vibrates quicker so the pitch is higher.

▼ *Bowed: the double bass.*

▲ *Plucked: the sitar.*

Musical Instruments Handbook

From Mersenne's work came the discovery in Italy that winding wire around the string would increase its mass per unit length, thus enabling strings to sound lower pitches while remaining a workable length – a crucial development for the design of bass instruments.

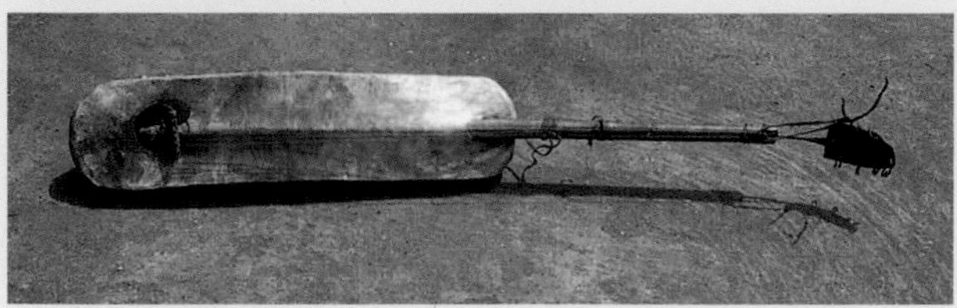

▲ *The* ngoni *may be the African ancestor of the banjo.*

The invention of nylon in 1938 promised to be a similarly vital moment in string technology, combining great strength with a durability way beyond that of gut. The particular acoustic qualities of gut strings, however, have ensured that they remain in widespread use, most often overspun with aluminium or silver – sometimes even gold.

BODY

On its own, the string is not an adequate sound-producer; it requires amplification. The body of all stringed instruments is just such an amplification system, designed to accept the string's vibrations, increase their power and project them towards the listener.

The bodies of the bowed and plucked stringed instruments are all similarly constructed: the strings run over the top of body and are brought into contact with it via the bridge. The prime function of the bridge is to transfer vibrations from the strings to the thin, resonating sheet that forms the top of the body.

SOUNDBOARD

This sheet, known as the soundboard, is designed to vibrate in sympathy with the strings. Although it cannot literally amplify the sound, it rapidly passes the strings' energy through itself and into the rest of the instrument. This spread of sound, which includes the air contained within the instrument's body, is what makes the string audible. From this it is easy to see that every part of the instrument's body affects the final quality of sound.

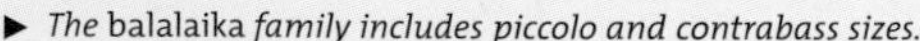

► *The* balalaika *family includes piccolo and contrabass sizes.*

Section One: The Instruments

SOUNDHOLES

Some stringed instruments make use of soundholes in the soundboard: in the violin family they are 'f'-shaped; in lutes 'C'- or flame-shaped. Other instruments, including the sitar, have none. Where they are used, the function of soundholes is twofold. Firstly, they influence the vibration patterns of the soundboard. Secondly, in bowed instruments, they allow flexibility in the soundboard so the bridge can rock slightly without splitting it.

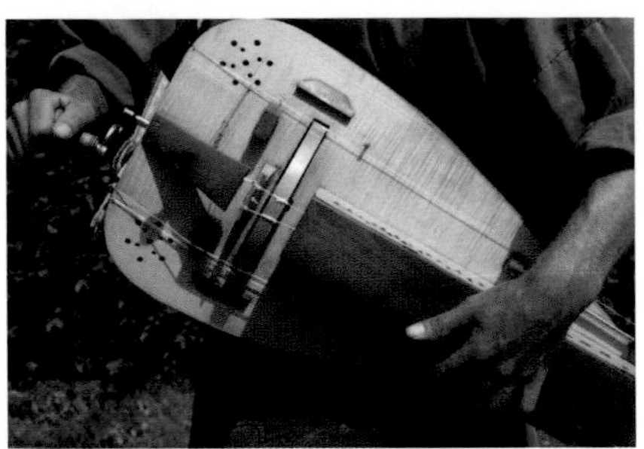

▲ *The hurdy gurdy is essentially a mechanical violin.*

The function of directing the sound is carried out by the back of the body. Thicker than the soundboard, it acts as a reflector, bouncing the sound back into the body then out of the instrument. The back also supports the forces generated by the string tension.

BOWING

The use of a bow to sound a string was discovered in the Byzantine Empire in the tenth century. The bow is made of horsehair stretched taut, which is drawn across the string. Horsehair is covered in tiny hooks that grab and release the string as the bow moves over it, keeping it in constant motion. Rosin, a substance made from distilling oil of turpentine, is rubbed on to the hair to help its grip.

The action of the bow means that energy is constantly transferred to the string; in the hands of a skilled player the sound quality is seamless even as the bow changes direction. There are four variables under the player's control: bow speed, bow pressure, where the bow is placed on the string, and the angle at which the bow is tilted. These four factors offer the player an almost limitless variety in timbre.

PLUCKING

The plucked string is less flexible than the bowed, most obviously in its lack of sustain: new energy can only be put into the string by re-plucking it, which

▲ *Violinists use rosin to make their bows grip the strings better.*

Musical Instruments Handbook

necessarily creates a new attack. Despite this, plucked stringed instruments are equally capable of variety in timbre depending on where the string is struck, at what velocity, with what angle of the fingernail or plectrum, and so on.

Striking the string offers the least variability in timbre; in essence all that is achieved is the string being shocked into vibrating and subsequently left to its own devices before being damped. Nevertheless, the material of the striking hammer, the makeup of the strings, the quality of the soundbox, and the way a player's touch affects the striking mechanism all have a significant effect on the sound.

▲ *Harps are plucked with the fingers.*

A DIVERSE MUSICAL FAMILY

The adaptability of stringed instruments and their incredible expressiveness have placed them at the centre of every major musical culture. The vibrating string is uniquely flexible: it is equally at home in solo instruments, in ensembles large and small, in domestic music-making, in large-scale music making, in acoustic and electronic instruments.

▲ *The electric guitar was the defining sound of the twentieth century.*

The bowed stringed instruments are pre-eminent among their peers in western culture, rivalled only by the piano. Violins and viols have been the most vital part of music for the past 400 years. They are the backbone of the orchestra, which stands alongside the string quartet as one of the more extraordinary examples of human creativity. Of all these instruments it is perhaps the violin that stands out as the paradigm. Barely changed since the seventeenth century, it remains the pre-eminent instrument, second only in expressive power to the human voice.

Section One: The Instruments

LYRE

The lyre has a distinguished history. It was the instrument used by the Greeks to accompany plays and recitations. Greek mythology tells us that the lyre was created by Hermes, the son of Zeus, from a tortoise shell. Singing to the accompaniment of the lyre was thought to promote a sense of justice.

Fact

In ancient Greece, the lyre was associated with the Apollonian virtues of moderation and balance, and is often mentioned in connection with education.

CONSTRUCTION

The lyre is formed of a soundbox, to which are attached two arms that run parallel to its surface. At their outer ends, the arms are joined by a crossbar, often called a 'yoke'. The lyre's strings are attached to the crossbar and the part of the soundbox furthest from the crossbar.

The defining feature of the lyre is that the strings run in the same plane as the soundbox, whereas the strings of a harp run perpendicular to the soundbox. Most lyres are plucked with a plectrum and normally the strings only sound at their fundamental pitch (i.e., they are not stopped as on a violin).

AN ANCIENT INSTRUMENT

Examples of the lyre have been found dating from as far back as the third millennium BC. These were made from tortoiseshell, with animal hide pulled over the underside to create a soundbox. The arms are thought to have been made from antelope horns and the strings from sheep gut, plucked with a horn plectrum.

▶ *The lyre may have four, seven or ten strings.*

Musical Instruments Handbook

The lyre remained a popular instrument during the Roman Empire but it subsequently declined in Europe. In Africa, though, it remains important, particularly in the eastern and north-eastern regions, its use following the path of the Nile from Egypt to Lake Victoria.

AFRICAN LYRES

The African lyres differ widely in their construction. The soundbox is made from gourd, wood, clay and even still tortoiseshell, with an animal or reptile skin pulled over the main opening. The strings are even more varied: some are still made from gut but many are made from wire or nylon from any number of sources, including fishing nets and tennis rackets. They are plucked with either the fingers or a plectrum.

The number of strings on African lyres can range from five to 17, and they are primarily used to accompany a singing voice by playing in unison with it. It is rarely used as a solo instrument, but often features in ensembles.

▲ *It is possible the lyre was introduced into Greece in pre-classical times.*

THE MODERN LYRE

The twentieth century has seen the development of a number of new lyres in Europe. Many of these are chromatic lyres, which use multiple strings arranged in rows. In spite of the use of modern materials in the strings, the lyre remains a quiet, though clear and beautiful, instrument. It has never strongly attracted the attention of art composers and is only used in reconstructions of ancient music.

Section One: The Instruments

HARP

The harp is clearly recognizable from its triangular shape, consisting of the resonator and neck. The strings in all harps run perpendicular to the resonator. In many cases a supporting arm, known as a forepillar, runs from the end of the neck to the resonator to help sustain the strings' tension.

EARLY HARPS

Although the earliest known use of the term 'harp' was in AD 600 by the Bishop of Poitiers, Venantius Fortunatus, pictorial examples of the design have been found as early as 3000 BC in the Middle East and Egypt. Images of harp-like instruments have even been found in rock paintings in France dating from 15,000 BC. It is often suggested that the harp's origins lie in the plucking of a hunter's bowstring, although there is no evidence to give credence to this.

MEDIEVAL HARPS

The oldest examples of European harps date from the fourteenth century, but the distinctive medieval design, in which the resonator is carved out of a single piece of wood, is thought to date as far back as the eighth century. These harps could have been strung with a variety of materials, often what was most readily available, including gut, horsehair, brass or bronze and even silk.

Medieval harps were small, with a range around that of the human voice, and were limited to playing one diatonic scale. By the early 1500s, the harp's compass had been extended to over three octaves. Techniques of stopping the strings to obtain chromatic notes were developed in Spain during the sixteenth century as well as experiments with harps using more than one rank of strings.

◄ *All harps today are tuned to C-♭ major.*

Musical Instruments Handbook

Harps with multiple ranks were cumbersome to play, however, and in the seventeenth century, a technique was developed of stopping the string by turning a small metal hook next to the string on the fingerboard to increase its tension. Such a system was too slow to be of any value but it led to the creation of the pedal harp, in which every note in all octaves (for instance, all the Cs) could be sharpened by using a pedal.

SINGLE-ACTION PEDAL HARP

By using seven pedals, one for each note of the scale, the entire chromatic compass became available. This system, known as the single-action pedal harp, is generally credited to Jakob Hockbrucker, though other makers have also been closely linked to its invention.

Despite modifications, the single-action pedal harp was limited since it could only play in eight major and five minor keys. The chromatic style of music popular by the nineteenth century meant that the harp was too inflexible to play a major role.

THE ERARD HARP

A solution was found by a man named Erard, who designed a system that increased the tension at both ends of the string allowing not one but two changes to be made to each string. The harp has 14 pedals each of which has two positions. Depressed once, the strings are raised by a half step; depressed again they are raised by a further half step, giving a tone altogether. This double-action system, patented in 1810, gave access to the complete chromatic range from E' to e'''' and remained in use almost unchanged until 1996 when the French firm Camac Production made a number of improvements.

▲ *A harpist can play up to eight notes at once.*

The only other harp design of significance was by Gustave Lyon, of the French firm Pleyel, Wolff et Cie who, in the late nineteenth century came up with an ingenious design using two interlocking ranks of strings, offering the full chromatic range with no pedals. This proved immensely popular with nearly 1,000 instruments being made over 30 years. By the middle of the twentieth century, however, it had fallen out of favour in spite of its capacity to play not only harp but also piano repertoire.

Section One: The Instruments

LUTE

The word 'lute' is the collective term for a category of instruments defined as 'any chordophone having a neck that serves as string bearer, with the plane of the strings running parallel to that of the soundboard'. In other words, the lute is a soundbox with a neck sticking out. The strings of some are plucked, some are bowed.

THE WESTERN LUTE

The lute family consists of a large group of stringed instruments in which the mechanism for holding the strings and the resonating body are joined, and in which the strings run parallel with the resonating body (i.e., guitar-like rather than harp-like).

The western lute evolved from the Arabian *oud* (see opposite). It is recognizable by its characteristic pear-shaped vaulted body, from which stems the neck. The gut strings are usually in pairs, passing over an ornately decorated sound-hole, along the neck and into the tuning pegs, which are generally set at a right angle to the neck.

EARLY WESTERN DESIGNS

From pictorial evidence it is clear that a standardized design of the *oud* existed as early as the ninth century. The earliest design for a lute is thought to be that recorded by Henri Arnaut de Zwolle in 1440. He described the instrument's geometrical proportions, implying that it would be made in different sizes.

Until the fifteenth century, lutes had five courses (pairs of strings), generally tuned in fourths around a central third (e.g. *G-c-e-a-d'*). By the sixteenth century, six courses had become standard, with the third in the middle. This Renaissance-style lute tuning is the most familiar to us today, however there was never a truly

Musical Instruments Handbook

standardized system. Instruments with 10 courses were not uncommon, usually to give extra bass pitches.

The lute was played at first with a plectrum and occupied a more rhythmic than melodic role. However, from the mid-fifteenth century it became standard to use the fingers – this meant that it could perform melody and harmony, making it the perfect instrument for accompanying song.

OUD

There is a huge number and variety of lutes in use worldwide, and they have a history going back thousands of years. Most similar to, and ancestors of, the lutes of European art music are the *ud* or *oud* family. Much played in classical, popular and traditional music throughout the Middle East, Turkey, Greece, the Mediterranean coastal countries of North Africa, and also in Malaysia, they have a large but light body, shaped something like a bisected pear, a medium-length neck bearing a flat, fairly wide, tapering fingerboard, the peghead bent back at an angle approaching 90 degrees.

▲ *The* oud *has a fretless fingerboard.*

Arabic music, like much of the traditional and classical music of non-European cultures, is not chordal so, unlike the European lutes, with their tied or fixed frets, *ouds* have fretless fingerboards, giving the player the freedom to slide notes and to achieve the microtones of Arabic maqam scales. They generally have six courses of nylon or wound-nylon strings – five double and a single – plucked with a long flexible strip plectrum. The Romanian *cobza*, a staple of Gypsy *lautari* bands until displaced by the guitar in the 1970s, is a shorter-necked, wider-bridged variant.

EUROPEAN WAISTED LUTES

It was the Moors who brought lutes to Iberia, where they evolved into the waisted, flat-backed, fretted Spanish guitar and Portugal's regional range of violas (also guitar-like but usually with five or six pairs of steel strings). One of these, the *viola beiroa*, has a further pair of shorter higher-pitched strings that run to machine heads attached where the neck meets the body.

Section One: The Instruments

Waisted guitar-type lutes spread to Spain's South and Central American colonies, as did smaller variants that are now a range of *tiples* and *cuatros* (the latter name deriving from their four pairs of strings, as the larger Cuban *trés* does from its three pairs and Mexico's *bajo sexto* from its six pairs). Portugal's little four-stringed *cavaquinho* travelled to the Portuguese colonies of Madeira (there known as a *braguinha*), the Azores and Cape Verde, and onward to Hawaii to become the ukulele, and to South America to become the armadillo-backed *charango*.

▲ *The back of a* charango *was made from armadillo shell.*

In Iberia, however, there are also lutes with bodies of pear or teardrop shape. In Spain there is the *laúd* and smaller, higher-pitched *bandúrria*, and in Portugal the fluid-toned *guitarra*. All three have six pairs of strings. The tuning pegs of the guitarra are in the form of a fan of screw-operated string-tensioners; the same sort of mechanism was used in the eighteenth-century English guitar, from which the Portuguese *guitarra* is descended.

SPIKE-LUTES

Though the *oud* is popular in the Arabic music of North Africa, in both North and West Africa an extensive family of long-necked lutes is played, all of them with the soundboard made of animal skin stretched over a circular or oblong body, usually made from a gourd or wood.

Known by classifiers as spike-lutes, these have no fingerboard, and the neck, usually cylindrical, is essentially a stick that passes right through the soundbox, emerging as a spike at the other end. Spike-lutes are not restricted to Africa; they and spike-fiddles are also found across Asia. A design more specific to Africa is the semi-spike lute, in which the stick does not go right across the soundbox, but emerges through a hole in the skin soundboard.

SEMI-SPIKE LUTES

In both forms the strings are attached to the ends of the spike; in effect, though the stick is not curved, spike-lutes are musical bows with a soundbox. At the top, each string is tied to a tuner, either a plaited skin noose that grips the neck but can be slid up or down it to tune, or a wooden tuning peg or geared metal machine-head.

Musical Instruments Handbook

▲ *The* ngoni *is a West African spike-lute.*

The archetypal semi-spike lute widespread in West Africa, particularly among the *griots* (a French word signifying musician castes), has many names but is best known as *ngoni*, in Wolof *xalam*, or among the Gnawas of North Africa *gimbri* (which sometimes has attached to the top of its spike a metal plate bearing rattling rings). The Saharawi of Mauritania have the *tidinit*, the Tuareg the *tehardent*. Designs vary a little, but these instruments generally have a long soundbox and three or four strings, some of which may stop short part way up the neck.

The neck has no fingerboard nor frets; the melody string is stopped by the player's fingers, with the other strings mainly acting as drones. Sometimes the uppermost string is a short chanterelle string played on the off-beat in the same way as the fifth string on the American five-string banjo – a descendant of the West African spike-lutes.

Some spike-lutes have a soundbox that is circular because it's made from a gourd (or occasionally a tin can). This type have the spike running right through the gourd, and the bridge resting on the skin, as it does on a banjo vellum.

► *Gnawas play the traditional* gimbri, *accompanied by* qaraqib *(crotal bells).*

Section One: The Instruments

HARP-LUTES

▼ *The* kora *is the best-known harp-lute.*

The name *ngoni* is also used for some types of harp-lutes. These are spike-lutes with a larger number of strings, picked harp-style, one note each, rather than having one string producing several notes by being finger-stopped. The bridge is made taller to accommodate the extra strings, which then run parallel to different tuning nooses on the neck.

The *donzo ngoni* of the Wassoulou people has a large circular gourd soundbox and six or seven strings, and is specific to hunters and songs about hunting. The *kamele ngoni*, which can be played even by non-hunters, has been taken up and developed for stage use – with tuning pegs or metal machine heads – by some internationally touring Wassoulou musicians.

KORA

The best-known harp-lute, in West Africa and internationally with many virtuoso *griot* players, is the one with the most strings, the *kora*. Its soundbox is a very large hemisphere made from a calabash – half a gourd – over which is stretched a cowhide soundboard. Penetrating this skin are two wooden rods that protrude for a distance upward, parallel to the neck. These serve as hand-holds for the player, who plucks with his thumbs and forefingers the two rows of strings (nowadays made of nylon fishing line) that stretch from the neck to the sides of a tall bridge and onward to their anchoring point at the bottom of the spike. The spike emerges from the gourd having passed right through it. *Kora* music, an intricate weaving of melody and rhythm, has many fine practitioners, and some have achieved wide international acclaim.

▲ *Mory Kante, the singer and virtuoso* kora *player.*

ASIAN LUTES

There have been lutes in Asia for at least four millennia, and today many indigenous forms are played across the continent and in Eastern Europe. Most have a long, usually narrow neck bearing a fingerboard with or without frets, joined to a soundbox with a soundboard of wood or stretched skin. They are so numerous that it is only possible to describe a few here.

The Iranian *tanbur* is of a form found throughout central Asia. It has a teardrop-shaped mulberry-wood body, with wooden soundboard flowing gracefully into a long neck bearing tied frets and three strings. Some other *tanburs* have more strings; for example, the Turkish *tambur*, whose body is more hemispherical, typically has seven. In Turkish music this is a keyed instrument but it can also be bowed.

▼ *(L to R): A Turkish* baglama *and Iranian* tanbur *and* yayli tanbur.

The teardrop-bodied *dotar* or *dutar*, which archetypically has two strings is found right across central Asia, including Uzbekistan, Tajikistan, Turkmenistan, Afghanistan and among the Uighur people of western China. *Setar* means 'three strings', but today's Iranian setars tend to have four: two of steel and two brass.

The Turkish *saz* or *baglama* family closely resemble the *tanbur* in structure. They have three or four courses of double or triple strings. Bosnia's *sargija* and Albania's *çifteli* are similar, but the latter has just two strings.

Section One: The Instruments

GREEK *TANBURA*

▲ *The* bouzouki *is played with a plectrum and has a sharp metallic sound.*

Greece has a *baglamas*, but this is a very small version of the country's well-known member of the *tanbura* family, the *bouzouki*. This has a soundbox similar to but smaller than that of the *oud*, and a long neck body bearing eight steel strings in four courses, running to a guitar-type head of geared metal tuners.

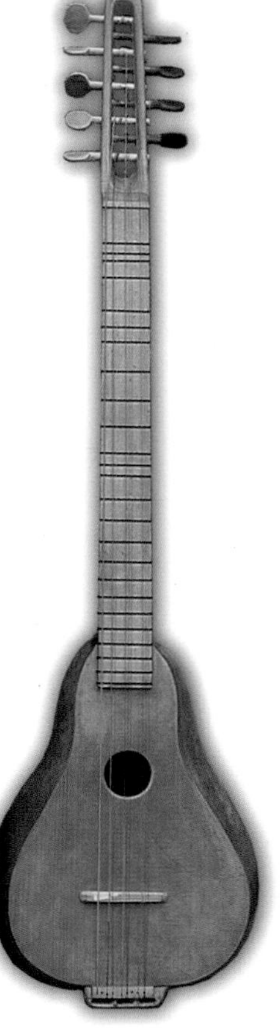

In the 1960s, the Greek *bouzouki* was introduced into Irish traditional music, and has now become transformed in today's Irish and Scottish traditional music to a flat-backed instrument similar in appearance to the mandolas and citterns now also used in that context. It has recently been further developed in Swedish traditional music with the addition of microtone frets, stud-capos that click into the fingerboard to shorten individual pairs of strings, and extended bass strings.

EUROPEAN *TANBURA*

The Kyrgyz national instrument is the *komuz*, a small three-stringed fretless lute with a pear-shaped body of apricot-wood. Kazakhstan's prime lute is the fretted, two-stringed *dombra*. The bodies of the three-stringed fretted Georgian *panduri* and unfretted *chonguri* are more rounded-diamond than teardrop; the chonguri has a short fourth string that runs to a peg part way up the neck.

Serbia, Montenegro, Macedonia, Bosnia-Herzegovina, Croatia, Bulgaria and Romania all have variants of *tambura*, which has a teardrop or spoon-shaped body with a shallower bowl-back than the *tanbur*. They come in a range of sizes, particularly among the *tambura* ensembles of the former Yugoslav states, where most

◀ Tambura *orchestras have a whole range of instrument sizes.*

Musical Instruments Handbook

have escalated from two strings to five. The series of Croatian *tamburas*, apart from the smallest, are guitar-shaped – a change that occurred in the early-twentieth century.

DOMRA

The early Russian *domra*, a three-stringed lute said to have arrived with the Tartars in the thirteenth century, became largely obsolete, but a revival version, with three metal strings, oval shallow body, metal fretted fingerboard and guitar-type machine heads, was instigated in the late-nineteenth century, and developed into an orchestral series by band-leader Vassily Andreev. He did the same with the three-stringed *balalaika*; the huge triangular body of the bass *balalaika* makes it possibly the world's most awkward-shaped instrument.

BANDURA

The Ukrainian *bandura*, whose neck and body-shell is traditionally carved from a single piece of wood, looks like a fretless lute whose body has swelled to accommodate up to 30 steel strings (there can be around 60 on some models of the chromatic *bandura*). A few of these run up the neck while the rest – the melody strings – fan from the tailpiece across the long bridge to tuning pins on the top curve of the body.

Although it evolved from the much longer-established Ukrainian *kobza*, a true lute, with a fairly short, fretted neck and no body strings, the *bandura*'s kinship is much closer to the Baltic zithers than to lutes. None of its strings' sounding-length is altered by fingering – those running up the scroll-headed neck are bass strings, plucked on the neck by the left hand while the right hand plucks the body-mounted melody strings. The Soviet-era Chernihiv factory produced very heavy instruments, some with lever mechanisms to shift the pitches of pairs of treble strings by a half step. However, craftsmen are now making less clumsy models, some of them the simpler, so-called 'classical' form.

▼ *The* bandura *is a plucked stringed instrument from the Ukraine.*

Section One: The Instruments

SITAR

The dominant lutes of India are a very distinctive family, with wide necks and often numbers of sympathetic resonating strings. The best-known is the sitar of northern India.

The sitar's main soundbox, made from gourd with a wooden soundboard, flows into a wide teak neck bearing about 20 movable brass-bar frets that curve away from the hollowed neck, which often has an extra gourd resonator attached near the top. The three or four playing strings can be pressed deeply between the frets and slid sideways across them to bend notes. Running alongside them are three or four drone strings. These are all attached to large tuning pegs, and the main playing strings have fine tuners – beads that slide across the soundboard near their anchor point on the soundbox. Nine to thirteen thin sympathetic strings of different lengths run across their own bridge under the frets to tuning pegs along the neck. Instead of the bridges being a clean edge as is usual on many lutes, the strings pass over a wide and nearly flat bone surface (actually very slightly and critically curved, and slightly angled), producing the characteristic sitar sound.

▲ *World-renowned* sitar *player, Ravi Shankar performs with a* tabla *player.*

The *surbahar* is a larger, lower-pitched form of sitar, with long, rich sustain and strings slack enough for a note to be bent as much as an octave at a single fret. The *tampura* or *tanpura* is like a stripped-down sitar – just four strings, no sympathetic strings, no frets – that provides a steady drone behind the sitar or other Indian solo instruments.

SARASWATI VINA

The sitar began to develop in the eighteenth century; the *surbahar* was invented in the nineteenth. An instrument with a longer history than either is the *saraswati vina*, the leading stringed instrument of Carnatic (south Indian)

Musical Instruments Handbook

▲ The tampura's strings are plucked to make a drone sound.

music. Like the sitar, it has a broad neck, flowing from a soundbox, with a buzz-inducing bridge, but it has no sympathetic strings, and thus has much less sustain than the sitar. The frets are not adjustable, but are attached at the peaks of scallops on the fingerboard. Four melody strings run over them, and another three shorter rhythm-drone strings run from the side of the bridge and part-way along the side of the neck to tuning pegs. There is a top gourd, but this – probably a remnant from the twin-gourd-resonated zithers – has no acoustic purpose; it serves as a support for the instrument, resting on the cross-legged player's left thigh. The *chitra vina* is an unfretted version, played with a slide like a Hawaiian or steel guitar, and unlike the *saraswati vina* it has sympathetic strings.

OTHER INDIAN LUTES

The *rudra vina* or *bin* of northern India is actually closer to a stick zither than a lute, having a hollow soundboard with a large gourd resonator near each end. But in playing terms it fits with the other Indian lutes, having four melody strings, passing over 24 tall fixed frets, plus three or four drone strings running alongside, all with buzz-inducing bridges. The *vichitra veena* is its unfretted version, played with a slide, and like the southern *chitra vina* it has sympathetic strings. Several Indian virtuosi have recently added sympathetic strings to the steel-strung western guitar and play it with a slide in a new and impressive tradition.

◀ As the vichitra veena is fretless, it is able to emulate the subtle nuance and fluidity of the human voice.

Section One: The Instruments

▲ A pipa *player uses plastic or tortoiseshell fingerpicks to get the desired tone.*

PIPA

Southeast Asia has many lutes among its myriad instruments. One of the best known is China's *pipa*, which has a short neck blending smoothly into the shallow body, making the whole instrument appear teardrop-shaped. The neck is zigzagged with deep wooden frets, and more are glued to the body, which has no soundholes. The picking technique is very highly developed, involving all the fingers and the thumb of the right hand, to which picks are taped. Its forerunners are said to have arrived from central Asia. The Japanese *biwa*, descended from the *pipa*, is similar but with fewer, higher, broader frets. The Vietnamese equivalent is the *dan ty ba*.

OTHER ASIAN LUTES

China's *yue qin* is a lute with a short neck, two, three or four strings and a circular, flat-backed soundbox. It has also evolved into the four-stringed *ruan*, or 'moon-guitar', which has a similar shape but is more heavily built. Similar to the *yue qin* are Japan's silk-stringed *gekkin* and Vietnam's more oval *dan nhat* or *dan doan* 'sun-lutes'. The circular-bodied Vietnamese *dan nguyet* or *dan kim* 'moon lute' and

Fact

Thailand's lutes include the three-string *phin*, which has a teardrop-shaped soundbox, fretted fingerboard and a peg-box that flowers into expansive, elegantly flowing carved ornamentation – even on the electric versions.

Musical Instruments Handbook

▲ *Chinese lutes:* zhong ruan *(medium lute) and* yueqin *(moon lute).*

Cambodian *chapey deng veng* have a more slender neck and higher frets spaced for a pentatonic scale.

INDONESIAN LUTES

The two-stringed Indonesian *kachapi* (the name is also used for a type of zither), Filipino *kudyapi* or *hegalong* and Thai *krajappi* show a variety of soundbox-shapes, from very slim to lozenge- or boat-shaped. The outline of the three or four-stringed *sape* of Sarawak and Borneo is broadly paddle-shaped, beautifully decorated with swirling tattoo-like patterns; most of its frets are not positioned on the short neck, but rather on the unusually long wide soundbox, so the player must stretch across several inches of soundboard to reach them. The Indonesian *sambe* is a less extreme example of the paddle shape.

The present population of Madagascar is largely descended from seafarers from Indonesia, and their instrumental ideas came with them. It is likely that this is the origin of the Malagasy *kabosy*, a lute of variable but usually box-like body-shape that often has partial frets to facilitate the moving of chord shapes up and down the neck.

BOWED WORLD LUTES

Apart from the African spike- and semi-spike lutes, all the lutes here have wooden soundboards. In most of the same regions, however, there are lutes with soundboards of stretched skin, which give them a sound with relatively strong attack but short sustain. Bowing the strings is a way of producing and controlling long notes, and many of these plucked lutes with a skin soundboard have close kin that are bowed.

Section One: The Instruments

TAR

Just as various forms of *dotar* are widespread throughout central Asia, so are instruments named *tar* (from Persian for 'string'). Most of these have a skin soundboard. The *tar* found in Iran, Azerbaijan, Armenia and several other central Asian countries has the soundbox so deeply waisted that its skin-covered front looks like a figure-of-eight. The six strings are in three pairs, and they run over a long neck with about 26 tied frets that can be adjusted to the tones and microtones of the scale being used.

▲ *The* rubab *is used in ensembles as well as for solos.*

RUBAB AND *SAROD*

Afghanistan's dominant lute is the *rubab* or *rabab*. Its short thick neck and body, with deep 'C'-shaped cutaways on both sides, are carved out of a single piece of mulberry wood. It has three nylon melody strings and two steel drone strings, plus, running under the bridge to tuning pegs along the edge of the body, 11 steel sympathetic strings. The Indian *sarod*, a descendant of the Afghan *rubab*, shares its goatskin soundboard and sympathetic strings, but all its strings are metal and it has a shiny metal-clad tapering fingerboard that allows extreme sliding of notes.

◄ Dotar *literally means 'two strings'.*

The *rubab*, *rabab* or *rawap* of Uzbekistan and the *uighurs* of western China are long-necked fretted lutes with snakeskin soundboards on a circular soundbox, often with wooden arches curving from the lower end of the neck towards the body. The *sgra-snyan* of Tibet and Nepal is similar, but in the place of arches there are just swellings at the base of the

Musical Instruments Handbook

neck. Bhutan's long-necked lute is the *dranyen*. Bangladesh's versions of the *dotar*, which have two to six strings, have a skin soundboard, as do some forms of Mongolia's fretless two-stringed, horsehair strung *tobshuur*.

ASIAN BOWED LUTES

The skin-soundboard lutes of Southeast Asia are generally delicate, long-necked spike-lutes with snakeskin or lizard-skin soundboards stretched over the front of circular, curved-rectangular or polygonal soundboxes. The Chinese *san hsien* or *sanxian* has three strings and a round or rounded-rectangular soundbox. The similar Okinawan *sanshin* and Japanese *shamisen*, played with a surprisingly large, stiff pick the size and shape of a car ice-scraper, are its descendants. Their Vietnamese cousin is the *dan day*.

A very different instrument in sound and appearance is the Turkish *cümbüs*, in which the idea of a skin soundboard has bounced back from the American banjo to the old world. Invented in the 1920s by Zeynel Abidin in Istanbul, and named by the country's president, Kemal Atatürk, whose desire for a new, innovative Turkey inspired Abidin to launch it, the *cümbüs* has a banjo skin on a deep, saucepan-like spun aluminium body, a fretless fingerboard veneered with plastic, and six pairs of steel strings. With a range of neck options it takes the role of a *saz*, *oud* or *tambur* in situations such as wedding bands where extra power and volume is necessary.

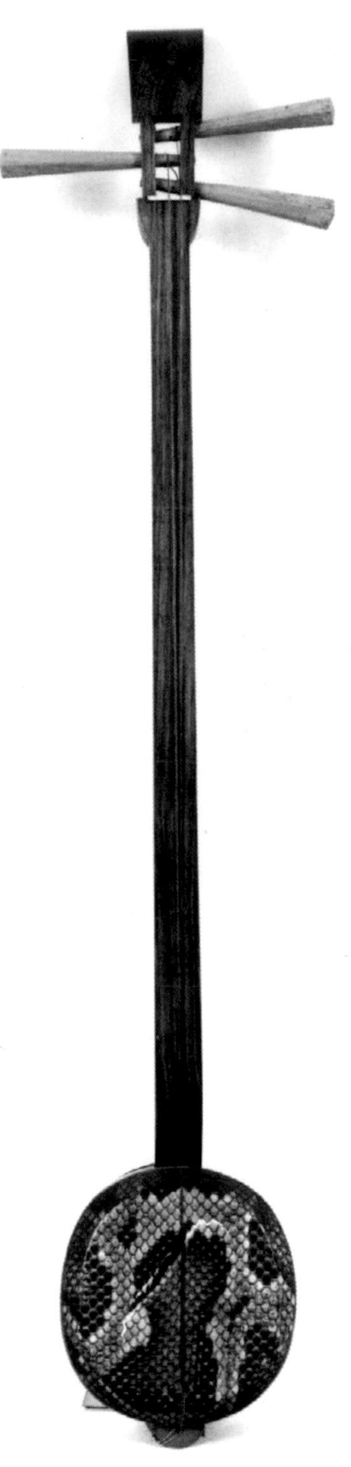

▶ *The* sanxian *has a dry, somewhat percussive tone.*

Section One: The Instruments

MANDOLIN

The mandolin is a small, teardrop shaped, plucked stringed instrument. Its most famous form is the Neopolitan mandolin, beloved of all romantics for its use on Venetian gondolas. It is descended from the lute and, since its rejuvenation in the nineteenth century, has remained a popular and versatile instrument.

MANDOLA

The mandolin developed from the Italian *mandola*. The *mandola* and its French equivalent, the *mandore* (not to be confused with the *mandora*: a bass lute commonly used for continuo accompaniments in eighteenth-century Germany), was a small lute used in the sixteenth century. Lutes, however, used six courses, each made up of a pair of strings tuned to a characteristic pattern of fourths and thirds. By contrast, the *mandola* had only four courses and was tuned in patterns of perfect fourths and fifths.

Fact

The term'mandolino', used as a diminutive for mandola, appears to have been employed from the mid-1600s. It seems likely that it was meant more as an indication of affection than a technical description of size, since 'mandolino' and 'mandolo' occur interchangeably in writings and music from the time.

DEVELOPMENT OF THE *MANDOLINO*

The *mandolino* retained its popularity through the seventeenth and eighteenth centuries and hardly altered its form. Like the lute, its body had a rounded back and flat front with a rosette inserted into the soundhole, to which was attached a fingerboard with eight or nine gut frets tied around the fingerboard to stop the strings.

Musical Instruments Handbook

▲ *A seventeenth-century mandolin.*

The *mandolino* received its first major reworking in the mid-1800s at the hands of the Monzino family in Milan. The body was increased in size and the overall instrument strengthened. The frets were changed from gut ties to inlaid metal or bone rods and increased in number to about 20. This instrument became known as the Milanese mandolin.

Standard performance technique on the lute was to use the fingers to pluck the strings, and it is clear that the *mandolino* was initially played in the same manner. During the eighteenth century, though, players began to use a plectrum to sound the strings. This characteristic performance technique was first carried out using quills, either attached to the index finger or held between thumb and index finger. By the beginning of the twentieth century this style of playing had become the norm and it remains one of the mandolin's distinctive features.

NEOPOLITAN MANDOLIN

The Monzino family's development of the Milanese mandolin in the 1800s was complemented by Pasquale Vinaccia of Naples who, in 1835, built a mandolin that has remained the standard to this day.

The Vinaccia family had been active in instrument-making for several years and in 1740 its members built a four-course mandolin tuned in perfect fifths, as opposed to the mixture of perfect fourths and fifths common to the *mandolino*. The particular selling point of the Vinaccia mandolin was that it was tuned in exactly the same way as a violin: *g–d'–a'–e"*. This meant it was immediately accessible to musicians who were not specialist lutenists, and the Vinaccia model quickly spread through Europe.

► *Great dexterity is required to play the mandolin due to its close frets.*

Section One: The Instruments

NEOPOLITAN MANDOLIN IN PERFORMANCE

The small size of the mandolin meant that it had little resonance, so notes decayed very quickly. The polyphonic style of music played by lutes meant this had never previously caused problems, but the immense popularity of the mandolin among less-skilled performers increased the demand for simple music. To combat this, performers repeatedly rearticulated single notes to give the impression of sustaining them. The *tremolo* technique, as it was known, was immensely popular among Italian street musicians, though it was frowned upon by the more highbrow classical mandolinists.

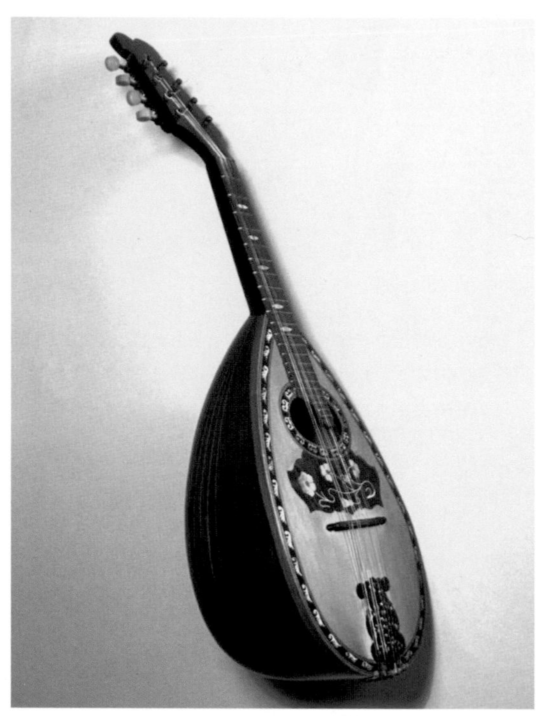

▲ *The mandolin is often made from rosewood inlaid with tortoiseshell.*

The Neopolitan mandolin's success is reflected in its frequent appearances in art music. Giovanni Paisiello (1740–1816), Antonio Salieri (1750–1825) and, most famously in *Don Giovanni* (1787), Wolfgang Amadeus Mozart (1756–91) all used it in operas; Ludwig van Beethoven (1770–1827) and Johann Nepomuk Hummel (1778–1837) composed solo works for it. In spite of a lull during the early nineteenth century, the mandolin soon regained popularity. Giuseppe Verdi (1813–1901) used it in *Otello* (1884–86), Ruggero Leoncavallo (1857–1919) in *I Pagliacci* (1892) and Gustav Mahler (1860–1911) used it his seventh and eighth symphonies and in *Das Lied von der Erde* (1907).

THE MODERN MANDOLIN

By the beginning of the twentieth century, the mandolin's popularity had spread to the US where it was famously taken up by Bill Monroe, one of the earliest exponents of the country-bluegrass style, and it became part of the characteristic bluegrass sound. As jazz developed, the mandolin went with it and was used with success by musicians such as Sammy Rimington and Dave Grisman.

Musical Instruments Handbook

The mandolin became increasingly common in folk music during the twentieth century. In Ireland it is often a partner or substitute for the violin, where its characteristically bright sound is ideally suited to the jigs and reels central to the repertoire. The mandolin is also popular in Brazil, where it is most often heard in a small ensemble playing a style of music called *choro*. Similar to the tango, the choro was especially popular during the early to mid-1990s.

▲ *A family of modern mandolins, with their flat-back style.*

The mandolin has proved immensely popular in Japan. It was often heard in the early-twentieth century performing characteristically Italian music, but a number of composers grew fond of the instrument and began to incorporate it into their own style. The 1940s saw a strong growth in its popularity and by the 1990s the Japan Mandolin Union boasted over 10,000 members.

Despite its popularity in folk music, particularly in bluegrass, the mandolin has yet to develop a serious body of solo work. Its particular timbral qualities – high pitch, little sustain, limited variety of colour – suggest that it is unlikely to gain acceptance as a heavyweight. Nevertheless, its flexibility and clarity of articulation ensure that in the right context it remains a hugely enjoyable instrument to listen to.

► *American band the Magnetic Fields made use of a mandolin on their 1999 album* 69 Love Songs.

Section One: The Instruments

UKULELE

The ukulele is a fretted stringed instrument that looks like a four-stringed guitar. It is most commonly associated with Hawaii, where its name translates as 'leaping flea', but there are no other string instruments native to Hawaii and the ukulele in fact has its roots in Portugal.

ORIGINS OF THE UKULELE

Three Portuguese instrument makers arrived in Hawaii in 1879, bringing with them native instruments including the *cavaquinho*, on which the ukulele is based. They opened shops selling their new instrument and it quickly caught on among the local population. It was often used at times of celebration and even made an appearance at the jubilee of King Kalakaua. Very soon the ukulele took off in other states, as the craze for Hawaiian music swept across the United States in the early-twentieth century.

▲ *Ukelele-playing pop group Petty Bouka.*

TYPES OF UKULELE

There are four sizes of ukulele: the soprano, the concert, the tenor and the baritone. Each has four strings and a varying number of frets, from around 14 on the soprano to at least 22 on the baritone. All the instruments have four strings based on the intervals fourth–major third–fourth. There are not set pitches for each instrument, however, and players raise or lower their strings in order to play in a key that best accommodates their music.

In the 1930s and 1940s the ukulele's success spread to Europe. It became particularly successful as part of the British music-hall tradition, or variety acts that performed during the Second World War.

Musical Instruments Handbook

BANJO

The banjo is a plucked stringed instrument with a circular body and fretted neck. Its roots lie in the French and British colonies of Africa, where instruments made from a hollowed-out gourd covered with animal skin, bamboo neck and catgut strings were popular.

Particularly associated with celebrations and dancing, these instruments went by various names including *banza* and *banjer*. Similar instruments also existed in South Africa which were possibly adaptations of the *cavaquinho*.

THE TRAVELLING BANJO

The journey from Africa to America was made during the slave trade. There are paintings from South Carolina in the late 1700s showing slaves dancing to the music of gourd banjos. The transition from the gourd-body to the instrument we know today is generally believed to have been due to the innovations of Joel Walker Sweeney (1810–60) in the 1830s. Some doubt has been cast on the extent of his role in the banjo's modernization, but he certainly had a strong influence.

Sweeney's use of the banjo was in his minstrel group the Sweeney Minstrels, a band who blackened their faces as a comedy gimmick. This rapidly caught on and by the 1850s the banjo and its minstrel musicians were popular throughout the southern states of America. During the American Civil War (1860–65), minstrel shows were a popular entertainment among soldiers, who took back home with them their appreciation of the banjo.

PLAYING STYLES

The banjo's big break came with the growth of parlour music. This association lifted the instrument from its links with the lower classes and brought it to almost universal attention. By this time, two distinct styles of playing had developed. The traditional, or stroke, style is today known as 'clawhammer' or 'frailing', in which the player strikes the string using a downward motion of the

Section One: The Instruments

▲ *The earliest banjos were unfretted, like the African instruments that inspired them.*

finger and making contact with the upper portion of the nail. In contrast, the 'fingerpicking' style is more akin to guitar technique, using the underside of the nail and the finger in an upward motion.

USE IN RAGTIME

The banjo's staccato sound made it ideally suited to the ragtime style that developed around the turn of the century. The jagged, syncopated character of ragtime increased the banjo's appeal and by the 1920s it had begun to play a part in the birth of jazz, appearing in the Dixieland bands of New Orleans. Surprisingly, the banjo was also used in blues, where its role was much more like that of a guitar.

Ragtime used the banjo mainly as a rhythm instrument, working together with the drum section, and its qualities as a solo voice were increasingly overlooked. It soon began to give way to the guitar, and the electric guitar in particular. The 1940s, however, saw a revival in the banjo's fortunes with the development of bluegrass in the southern USA. A combination of dance and religious music, bluegrass showed off the best of the banjo's attributes: strong rhythm, clear articulation and agility.

Few names other than Sweeney's have endured from the banjo's early history, but the bluegrass style has made many more recent players household names, most notably the American performer Earl Scruggs. The banjo has regained some ground in jazz, but it remains less well regarded in art-music circles. Its occasional appearances have been in the lighter side of the repertoire, in works such as Kurt Weill's (1900–50) *Mahogany* (1927).

Musical Instruments Handbook

THE MODERN BANJO

The modern banjo is generally made with five steel-wire strings attached to a ring of laminated wood some 28 cm (11 in) in diameter. A plastic skin is stretched over the ring immediately beneath the strings, and very often a wooden resonator is attached to the ring's underside.

▲ 'Sing', one of British band Travis's greatest hits, featured the banjo.

A unique feature of the five-string banjo is its short thumb-string. The four full-length strings are tuned to *d–g–b–d'* while the fifth thumb string is tuned to *g'*: the highest note of the five. The fifth string is attached to the side of the neck at the fifth fret position and is used like a drone note, always sounding the same note in passages of figuration, whatever the underlying chord is.

Equally common is the four-string banjo, though this does not normally use the thumb-string. The most common method of performing on a banjo today is the fingerpicking technique. Many players today use plectrums; one for the thumb and one each for the first and second fingers. Partly this is for ease of playing, but is also because it creates a particularly crisp sound that is not easily replicated with the fingers alone. Four-string banjo players usually prefer the flat-pick.

Section One: The Instruments

GUITAR

The guitar is a plucked stringed instrument played resting on the lap. Although it has a long history – thought by many to reach as far back as the ancient Greek lyre known as the *kithara* – it is best-known today in the design of the Spanish guitar-maker Antonio de Torres Jurado (1817–92).

The modern or classical guitar developed from the short-necked lutes that appeared in central Asia during the fourth and third centuries BC. Many pictures from the ensuing millennium depict instruments exhibiting guitar-like characteristics. However, the guitar as we know it today has its roots in the Renaissance period.

VIHUELA

One of the most significant precursors of the guitar is the *vihuela*, a plucked stringed instrument with six or seven courses popular in the fifteenth and sixteenth centuries. The *vihuela* is closely associated with Spain and areas under Spanish influence, although it was also used in Italy and Portugal.

In looks, the *vihuela* is very close to the modern guitar. It has the characteristic figure-of-eight body shape, a long neck and a head set back at a slight angle. Rose patterns were often set into the body, functioning as sound holes. The *vihuela* was a fretted instrument, using 10 lengths of gut tied around the neck to stop the string. Like the lute, the six courses followed the tuning pattern of fourth–fourth–major third–fourth–fourth.

It is not clear why the *vihuela* gained such popularity in Renaissance Spain at a time when the rest of Europe used the lute for the same purposes. Nevertheless, the guitar's strong association with Spain began at this time, and the Spanish passion for the *vihuela* was responsible for its introduction to Latin America during the colonization of that part of the world.

Musical Instruments Handbook

BAROQUE GUITAR

The guitars of sixteenth-century Europe were considerably smaller than the modern instrument. Initially they had four courses tuned fourth–major third–fourth. Baroque guitars often had a single, central rose as a soundhole and between eight and ten gut frets. The courses' pitches were by no means set in stone, a characteristic shared with the *vihuela*: they were often changed to suit the music being performed.

▲ *A flat-backed, five-course Portuguese* guitarra *c. 1590.*

By the end of the fifteenth century, five-, six- and even seven-course guitars were being used. In Italy the six- and seven-course guitars were often referred to as *viola da mano* or 'hand viola', as opposed to the *viola da arco* or 'bowed viola'.

PLAYING TECHNIQUES

One of the most common uses of the guitar was as a strumming accompaniment to songs. The *rasgueado* technique, in spite of its close association with Spanish flamenco repertoire, in fact developed in the sixteenth century when it was more commonly known as *battuto*. The strum could be executed in either direction, indicated by an arrow pointing up or down immediately preceding the chord affected.

The English guitar and Portuguese *guitarra* date from this period. Generally six-course instruments, they tended to be closer to the lute in design and were designed to be used domestically as drawing-room instruments. Their function was mainly to accompany voices or play simple tunes, and they were therefore normally tuned to C major in order to best facilitate the playing of chords.

Section One: The Instruments

EIGHTEENTH-CENTURY GUITARS

The earliest guitars with six single strings began to appear in the second half of the eighteenth century. The gut frets gave way to specially created fingerboards with ivory or metal frets built in; the central rose became an open sound hole; the neck narrowed; and the proportions were altered.

There was still no standard technique at this point – performers were even divided about how best to strike the strings: with the nail or not. Nevertheless, it is at this point that the first lasting guitar music was written. The work of Fernando Sor (1778–1839) and Mauro Giuliani (1781–1829), while slight, is often charming and elegant; it is easy to see how they helped increase the guitar's popularity.

◀ *A classical, or Spanish, guitar with six, generally nylon, strings.*

THE SPANISH INFLUENCE

The work of Spanish instrument maker Antonio de Torres Jurado was central to the development of the modern guitar. He set the vibrating string length at 65 cm (26 in), increased the overall dimensions, used 19 frets, altered the construction of the soundbox and set the standard string tuning of *E–A–d–g–b–e'*. These alterations were so successful that Torres's model became the standard to which every other maker aspired – and which is known today as the classical guitar.

▲ *Acoustic guitars have steel rather than nylon strings.*

The undoubted brilliance of Torres was not enough on its own to launch the guitar to new heights, and for some time it remained confined to Spain. Support from composer performers such as Francisco Tárrega (1852–1909) and Emilio Pujol (1886–1980) won more admirers, but it was the advocacy of Andrés Segovia (1893–1987) that finally launched the modern guitar.

Musical Instruments Handbook

ANDRÉS SEGOVIA

Up to the beginning of the twentieth century, most guitar music was written by composers who played the guitar themselves. Segovia's great legacy was to raise the guitar's status to that of respected concert-hall instrument. His influence was naturally focused on Spain and South America, encouraging composers including Joaquín Rodrigo (1901–99), Manuel de Falla (1876–1946), Mario Castelnuovo-Tedesco (1895–1968) and Heitor Villa-Lobos (1887–1959) to write for the guitar.

Fact

Despite his success with the guitar, Anonio de Torres was forced to take on other work, and became a glassware merchant, because guitar making was not lucrative enough to support his large family.

By the time of his death in 1987, there existed a strong body of music that continues to grow. The guitar repertoire has been enlarged by works from some of the composing heavyweights of the twentieth century, including Francis Poulenc (1899–1963), Benjamin Britten (1913–76), Michael Tippett (1905–98), Hans Werner Henze (b. 1926), William Walton (1902–83) and Rodney Bennett (b. 1936). Segovia's zeal for encouraging new work has been taken up by a number of guitarists, including Julian Bream (b. 1933) and David Starobin (b. 1951).

ELECTRIC GUITAR

The guitar has developed slowly since Torres's revolutionary changes, with one notable exception – amplification. It was the guitar's involvement with popular music, most notably jazz, that fuelled the desire for greater volume. As early as the 1920s, experiments were carried out using pickups that carried the guitar's sound to an amplifier. The first commercially manufactured electric guitar was sold by Fender in 1948, quickly followed by Gibson in 1952, thus establishing a commercial rivalry that drove development forward.

As well as creating guitars that were purely electronic – i.e. that made negligible sound without amplification – the pickup technology was applied to the classical guitar. Gradually, hybrid instruments developed that combined qualities of both and the guitar began to take a more prominent place in jazz and pop music.

Section One: The Instruments

DOBRO

During the 1830s, Mexican cattle-herders introduced the guitar to Hawaiians, who quickly incorporated it into their own music-making, typically tuning all the strings to the notes of a major triad. Joseph Kekuku is credited with developing a technique of using a comb to slide up and down the neck to create *glissandi*. Clearly this was difficult to achieve holding the guitar in a conventional manner, so instead it was laid across the lap.

LAP STEEL GUITAR

As the Hawaiian style of playing increased in popularity, the guitars were increasingly made in rectangular form and the comb was replaced with a steel rod. When they began to be commercially manufactured in the 1930s they acquired the name 'lap steel guitar'.

Since the playing style of the lap steel limits the performer to a few keys, players began using instruments with more than one neck in order to increase the number of pitches available without having to retune. Having multiple sets of strings soon became cumbersome, however, and makers in the 1940s began fitting pedals that would simultaneously alter the tunings of a complete set of strings.

PEDAL STEEL GUITAR

The pedal steel guitar, as it came to be known, had two necks as standard, with eight sets of pedals and 10 strings on each neck, though as many as 12 or 14 is not uncommon. One neck is normally tuned to a chord of E9 (a combination of the notes E–G#–B–D–F#) and the other to a chord of C6 (a combination of C–E–G–A). Both the lap steel and the pedal steel are fretless guitars; the strings are stopped using a metal bar known as the 'steel' which, like Kekuku's comb, is used to slide up and down them, creating *glissandi*.

Musical Instruments Handbook

Four legs normally support the guitar with the performer sitting on a stool. The right foot will be used to control the volume while the left leg controls the pedals using both the foot and the knee to move the pedals. The strings are plucked using finger and thumb picks – metal picks that are worn like thimbles.

RESONATOR GUITAR

The early-twentieth century also saw the development of the resonator guitar. This technology used metal discs that acted in a similar way to the skin on a banjo, amplifying the soundwaves generated by the strings. The resonator guitars were somewhat louder than their wooden siblings.

THE ARRIVAL OF THE DOBRO

In the 1920s, a refinement to the resonator guitar was designed in the United States by the Slovak instrument maker John Dopyera and his brothers. They used three spun aluminium cones as their amplification system. The new design became known as the dobro guitar, partly based on the brothers' name and partly because 'dobro' means 'good' in Slovak. It has the characteristic guitar shape with a large, decorated aluminium disc where the sound hole would normally be.

The Dobro was developed in the same period as the electric guitar; the latter's greater efficiency and lower cost meant it overtook the former in popularity. Nevertheless, the Dobro's characteristic sound became an important component of both the bluegrass and blues traditions, and remains in use today.

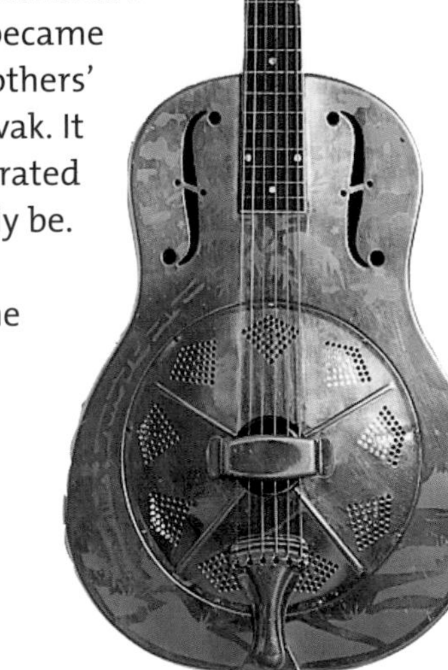

▶ *This National Style O guitar has a brass alloy body and cone resonator.*

Section One: The Instruments

ZITHER

To most people, the word 'zither' evokes *The Third Man* film theme and an image of a flat box with a lot of strings. But in organological classification it is a term covering a substantial proportion of the world's stringed instruments.

The technical definition is a little convoluted, but in effect a zither is one or more stretched strings, usually with a resonating board, box or other vessel. Those instruments with necks – such as lutes – aren't classified as zithers, neither are harps.

▼ *The* berimbau *is used in the* capoeira, *a martial-arts dance from Bahia, Brazil.*

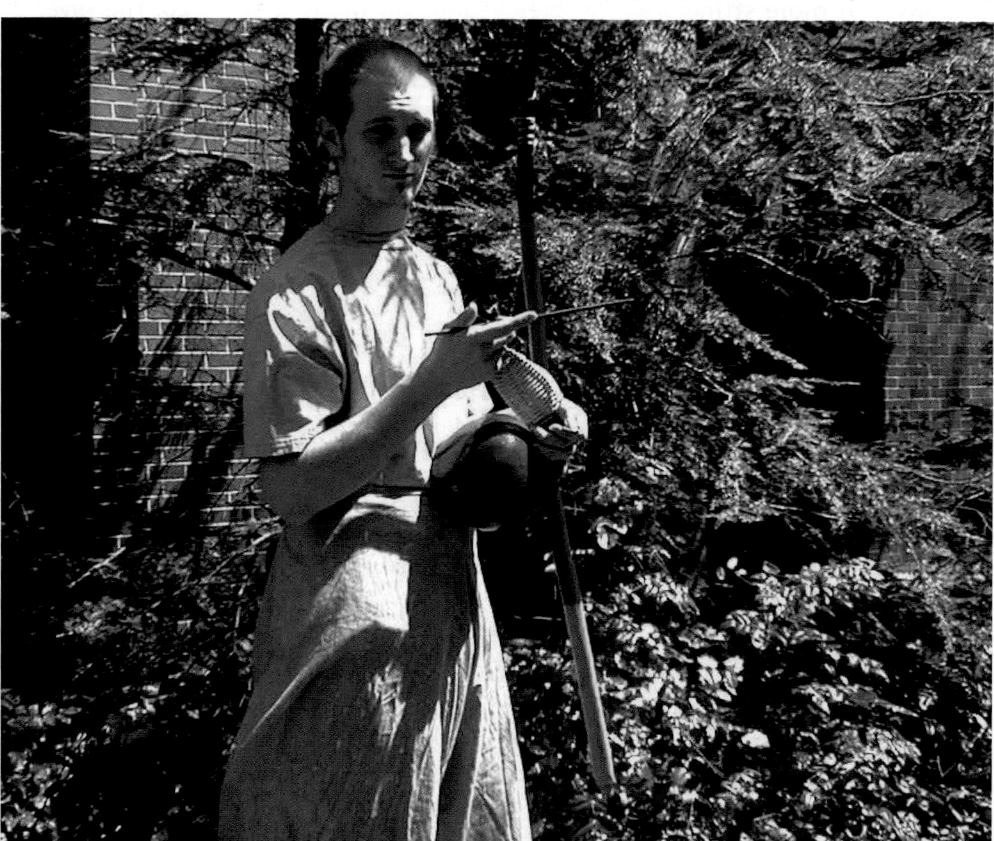

Musical Instruments Handbook

MOUTH-BOWS

A twanged hunting bow can be seen as the common ancestor of all three – zithers, lutes and harps. More developed, the limbindi of the Baka pygmies is a musical bow in which the string is tucked under the player's chin, dividing it into two parts, and then goes back across the bow, making three. It is not loud, but the player can hear through bone conduction and by holding a reflecting palm leaf. Some other bows use the mouth as a variable-volume resonant cavity that can amplify as well as change the timbre. A player of the Ivory Coast *dodo* puts its tape-like string across his mouth and hits it with a stick. Some other mouth-bows worldwide are played with the wood resting against the side of – or in – the mouth.

RESONATORS

In parts of Europe, a pig's bladder was once used as a resonator. In Africa the most common resonator is a gourd tied to the bow shaft – for example in Angola's *ungo*, the progenitor of the Brazilian *berimbau* or *urucungo*. Stiffen the bow and more strings can be stretched, as on the Malian *orozo*. The *mvet* of Equatorial Guinea has a notched stick attached to the gourd; the strings pass through the notches to make two sounding lengths each.

The bow of the Malawian *bangwe* is a flat board, along which multiple strings are stretched side by side. The resonator of the multi-stringed Afghan *waji* or *wuj* is a box with a skin soundboard, through which the bow-shaft is threaded; in it meet bow, harp and spike-lute. The Malian *dan* or *bambara* has multiple bows whose strings pass over the curved side of a hemispherical calabash.

▼ *The whammy bar of the* dan bau *is bent with the left hand; the pick (below) is held in the right.*

The single string of the Vietnamese *dan bau* runs from one end of a long rectangular wooden soundbox to near the top of a flexible stick inserted vertically into the other end. The player bends the stick back and forth with his left hand to change the string's tension and thus pitch – in effect like flexing a bow – while with his right hand he picks the string and simultaneously touches it momentarily with the edge of the same hand, producing ringing harmonics.

Section One: The Instruments

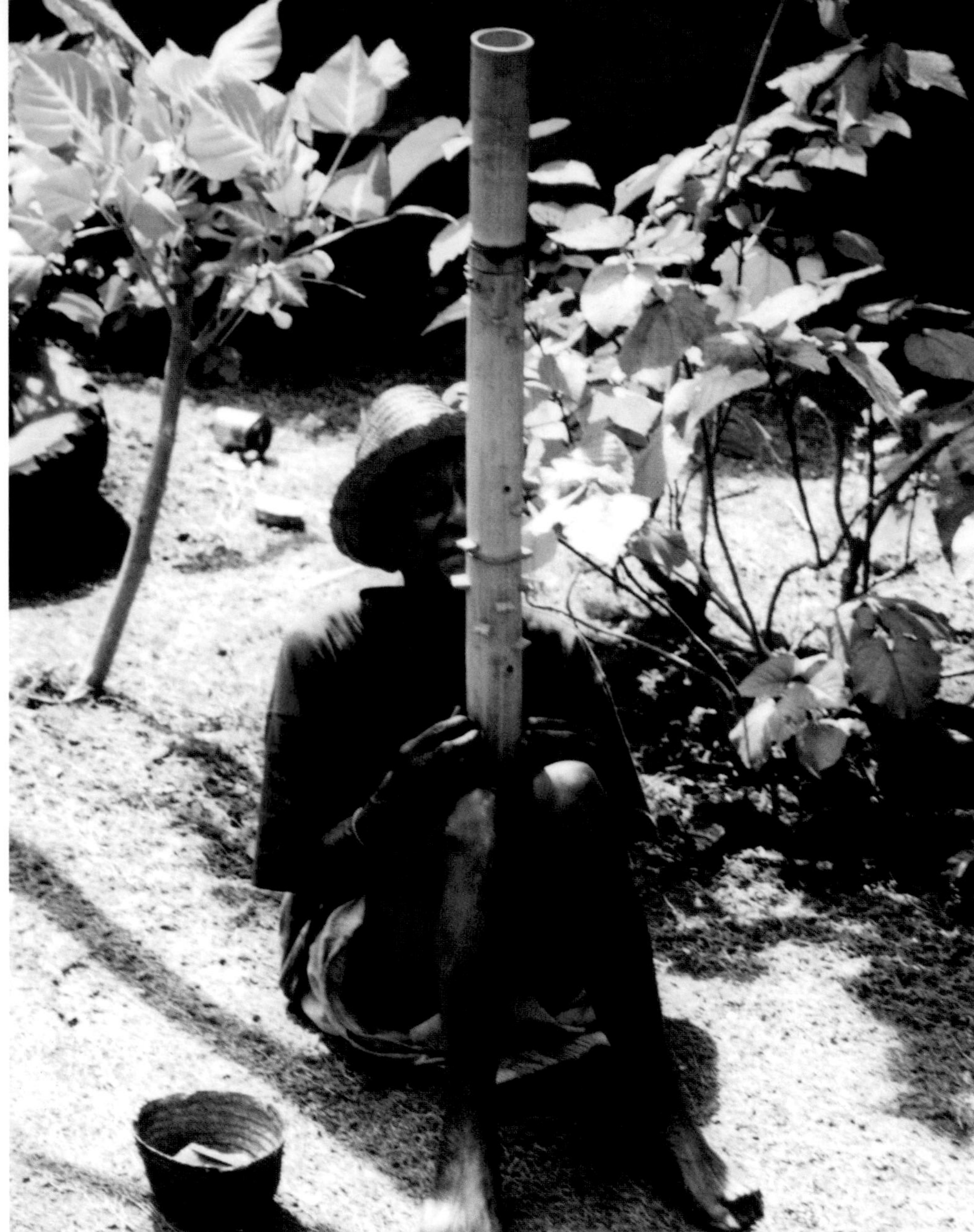

▲ *The Madagascan* valiha *is played by plucking metal or bamboo strings.*

STICK ZITHERS

Stick zithers are in effect straight bows. They consist of a string-bearing stick with a series of raised sections that function as frets, to which is attached a resonator. The *jejy voatavo* of Madagascar is typical; it has one set of strings running over the frets, another set running along the side of the stick, and one or two gourd resonators. It is normally played held horizontally in front of the

Musical Instruments Handbook

player, very much like the *jantar* of Rajasthan, which itself resembles early forms of the northern Indian *rudra vina* or *been*.

TUBE ZITHERS

The term 'tube zither' denotes a category of zithers in which strings run parallel to a tubular soundbox. Often the soundbox is made of bamboo – a material of such tensile strength that it can form the string material too. A one-string tube zither can be made by splitting out a thin strip of bamboo from the tube surface, leaving it attached at both ends, and inserting a bridge-stick at each end to lift the string from the surface.

A raft zither is a series of such one-string bamboo or reed monochords joined together. Examples include the *balambala* of the Jola people of Gambia and Guinea-Bissau and the Japanese sorghum *kokkinna*. In the *yomkwo* of the Birom people of Nigeria, strings are tuned by being bound with thread to increase their mass and thus lower their pitch.

VALIHA

The most common form of tube zither is a single tube with multiple strings. The best-known of these is the Madagascan *valiha*, which can have up to 19 strings around a wide bamboo tube. Most *valihas* now have steel strings, made from single strands untwisted from bicycle-brake cable. They are tuned, using slideable bridges, to produce a scale by alternately picking on left and right sides of the cylinder with the thumbs and fingers of both hands.

Madagascar was settled by voyagers from Indonesia, where there is a small bamboo-tube zither, the *sasandu*, which is normally surrounded by a palm leaf to focus the sound. Other *valiha*-like instruments include the *kulibit* and *saludoy* of the Philippines, the *jajuka* of the Pandonc people of northern Thailand, the kalimantan of Borneo and the *koh* of the Mnong people of Vietnam, which has tuning pegs and an additional gourd resonator.

The four strings on the raphia-palm-tube zither *ngombi na pekeh* of the Baka pygmies are each divided by a stick-bridge, giving eight notes. Some are struck rather than plucked; an example of this is the *celempung* of Sunda, Indonesia, which has sound holes that can be opened or closed with the hand to change the resonance. Some are bowed; these include the Laotian *saw-bang* and North America's *tzii'edo'a'tl* or 'Apache fiddle', a one- or two-stringed bowed zither made from a length of hollow agave stalk. Madagascar's *marovany* is a transfer of the *valiha* principle to a box with strings on two opposite sides.

Section One: The Instruments

TONKORI

The *tonkori* of the Ainu people of Hokkaido and Sakhalin is hard to categorize, but can be seen as a non-cylindrical tube zither. It has a long canoe-shaped soundbox, with five strings running the length of it across shared bridges. On some instruments these divide each string into two sounding lengths, terminating in a tuning-peg box. The tonkori had all but disappeared when Ainu roots-rock musician Oki successfully revived it.

▲ *Oki, an Ainu musician from Japan, with his* tonkori.

SEMI-TUBE ZITHERS

In East Asia there is a large family of long zithers described as 'semi-tube'. In these, the strings pass over a soundboard that is gently curved, like a segment of a cylinder.

The most typical of these – indeed the model for many – is the Chinese *zheng* or *gu-zheng* (the latter meaning 'old zheng' and traditionally with 16 strings). Each of the zheng's 21 or more strings passes over its own movable bridge, dividing it into two sections; one is plucked, the other is pressed to bend or *vibrato* the note.

The *koto* is the *zheng*'s Japanese descendant, first appearing in the eighth century. Traditionally it has 13 silk or synthetic strings, though some recently developed *kotos* have more. The Korean *kayagum* has 12 silk strings. The strings of the Vietnamese *dan tranh* run to an angled row of wooden tuning pegs set into the soundboard. Closely related to all these are the Mongolian and Tuvan *yat-kha*, the Khakassian *chadagan* and Kazakh *zhetigen*. The Chinese *yazheng* or *yaqin* and Korean *ajaeng* are bowed with a rosined forsythia stick.

◀ *The* koto *is the Japanese descendant of the Chinese* zheng.

Musical Instruments Handbook

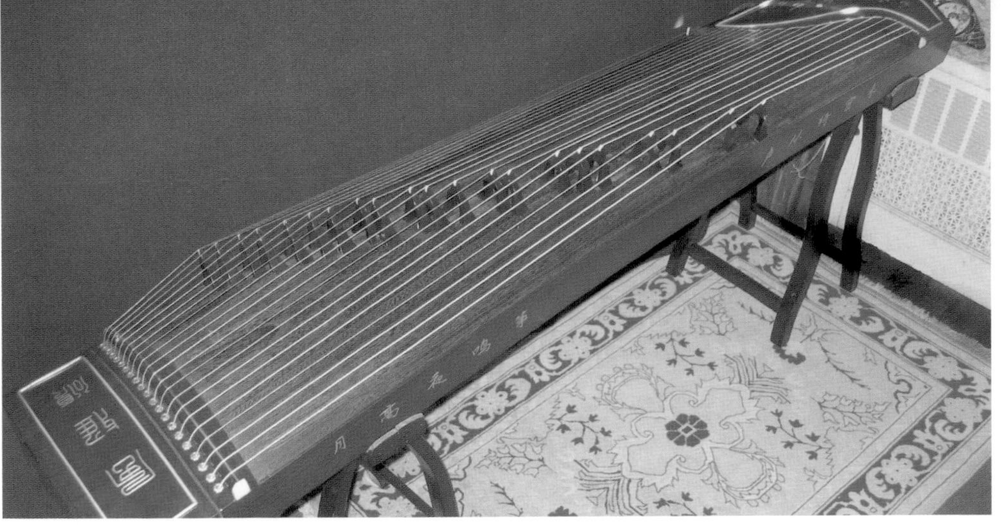

▲ *The Chinese* zheng *is plucked mainly by the right hand while the left presses the strings to bend the notes.*

QIN

The Chinese *qin* or *chin* is a revered instrument that has remained unchanged for over 1,000 years. It has no movable bridges and no soundbox. It is often played on a table to increase resonance. Seven silk strings run from end to end of a long, curved, lacquered board; these are stopped by being pressed to the board.

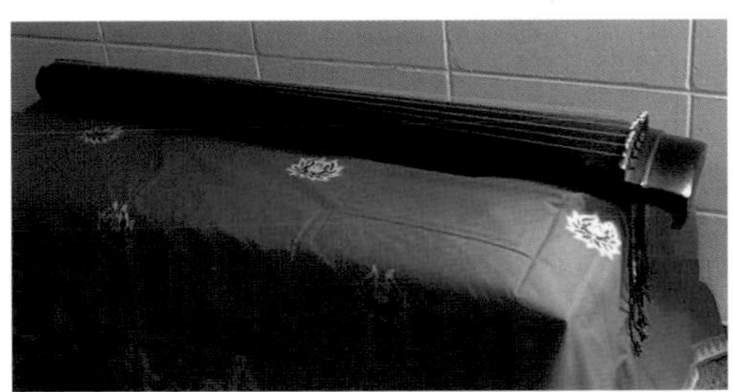

▲ *The* qin *has no bridges.*

The Japanese version is called *shichigen-qin*, meaning 'seven-stringed *qin*'. The single string of Japan's *ichigenkin* ('one-stringed qin'), and the two of the *nigenkin*, are stopped with a bone or ivory tubular slide in the manner of a bottleneck in blues guitar-playing. Korea's *komungo* is unusual among semi-tube zithers in that its soundboard bears a row of wooden frets, on which the central three of its six strings are stopped.

BOX ZITHERS

The dominant zither of the Middle East, Turkey and North Africa is the *qanun*. Trapezoidal with one end rectangular, it has around 26 triple courses of nylon strings that run from a forest of wooden tuning pegs across a bridge that rests on four skin rectangles set into the soundboard. Today's *qanuns* have tangents under the strings to facilitate tuning to microtonal scales.

The zithers of Europe are, like the *qanun*, generally box zithers which, when unfretted, are sometimes termed 'psalteries'. In Finland, the Baltic states and among some of the peoples of Russia, a family of these instruments are played.

Section One: The Instruments

KANTELE

The basic form of the Finnish *kantele* is a small tapering box, traditionally hollowed out of a single piece of wood. It bears five strings, now normally of steel, tuned to the first five notes of a diatonic scale. The strings pass directly – without bridges – from a single metal anchoring bar at the narrow end, to wooden tuning-pegs at the other.

In the nineteenth century, larger forms of *kantele* appeared, which had more strings, metal zither pins for tuning, and an individual hitch-pin for each string. In the 1920s the 'concert *kantele*' was introduced. This has a smooth-levered roller system to make it chromatic. Estonia's *kannel*, Latvia's *kokles* and Lithuania's *kankles* are close relatives of the Finnish small *kanteles*.

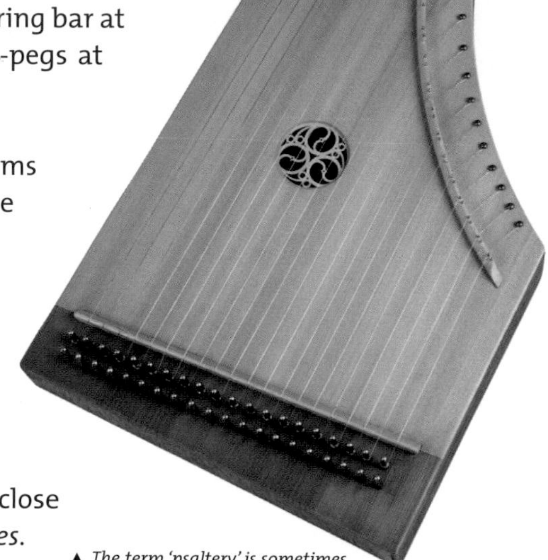

▲ *The term 'psaltery' is sometimes used to cover a wide range of unfretted box zithers.*

GUSLI

The Russian *gusli* is related too, but has a bridge-strip over which the strings pass before the pegs. The larger *guslis* developed for Soviet gusli-orchestras have a half-step turn-lever on each string for chromatic playing. The *guslis* of the Mari and Udmurt peoples are a rounded, truncated triangle in shape, with two curved string-anchoring bars. Despite its *cobza*-derived neck-like section, the Ukrainian *bandura* is a zither, too. In Indonesia, the *kechapi* of Sunda and Bali has evolved into a *gusli*-like box zither.

SANTUR

The *santur*, a widespread box zither, is trapezoidal in form, its strings passing over two or more rows of bridges resting on the soundboard, and played by striking with a pair of sticks. The design probably originated in Persia. Today's Iranian *santur* has a set of steel strings in quadruple courses, divided by one row of bridges into two lengths sounding a perfect fifth apart. It also has an interpolated set of brass strings, sounding an octave below, running to another row. Most others have all steel strings. India's *santoor* as only been accepted as a classical instrument in the past half-century as a result of the work of virtuoso Shivkumar Sharma.

Musical Instruments Handbook

▲ *The* cimbalom *is fully chromatic and has a range of four full octaves.*

CIMBALOM

A *cimbalom*, *tambal*, *cymbaly*, *tsimbl* or *cimbal* is a key instrument in the musics of many eastern and central European countries. A big table-legged *cimbalom* with pedals to control string dampers, created in Budapest in the 1870s, has been particularly taken up by Roma (Gypsy) musicians and played with astonishing skill and speed. British and American versions are called hammered dulcimer, Austrian and German hackbrett, and in eastern Asia the Chinese *yang-chin* or *yangqin* (meaning 'foreign zither', and probably introduced from Persia), Mongolian *yoochin*, Thai and Cambodian *khim chin*, Korean *yanggeum*, Vietnamese *duong cam* and Tibetan *gyümang*.

▼ *(L-R):* ruan, erhu, yang-chin, di-zi, sheng.

Section One: The Instruments

FRETTED ZITHERS

Another family of box zithers, mainly in north-western Europe, has some or all of its strings running over frets. Iceland's long, tapering *langspil* is usually bowed. The Norwegian *langeleik* is a long rectangular or swell-sided box with one or more strings running over wooden frets, plus some unfretted strings to provide accompaniment and drones.

The Flemish *hommel*, French *épinette*, Swedish *hummel* and Danish *humle* are similar, but have metal frets, and the usual technique was to fret the melody strings with a short stick. The Hungarian *citera* which, now largely fingered (as nowadays is the United States' offspring of these European zithers, the Appalachian dulcimer), has two sets of frets, one diatonic, the other providing the half steps, and drone strings of varying lengths running to a series of separate scrolls.

▲ *The Appalachian dulcimer traditionally has an hourglass, teardrop, triangular or elliptical shape.*

The Alpine form evolved during the nineteenth century to become the *konzertzither*, which has five melody strings over a chromatically fretted fingerboard and curving soundboard bearing around 37 accompaniment strings. This instrument was very popular in the early- and mid-twentieth century, its fame greatly increased by zitherist Anton Karas's playing of his theme to the film *The Third Man*.

CHORD ZITHERS

From the mid-nineteenth to mid-twentieth centuries, a dazzling range of ingenious box zithers was created and manufactured mainly in Germany and in the United States. Sold under a panoply of names, these were intended for home entertainment, and embodied devices to aid the unskilled in picking out

Musical Instruments Handbook

▲ *Autoharps are used in the United States as bluegrass and folk instruments.*

melodies and chords. The most common of these – many of which can be described as 'chord zithers' – have melody strings arranged in a chromatic scale to the player's right, and to the left groups of the strings tuned as chords. Others comprise just chord-groups or just melody strings. (One of the latter has become the *surmandel*, which provides drones in northern Indian classical vocal music).

There is considerable variation in layout and elaboration of form and decoration. On a few the chord and melody strings cross one another. Some have elaborate systems, of varying effectiveness, for plucking or striking the strings. The only one widely played today is the autoharp, in which bars with slotted felts are pressed on the strings to damp some and leave a selected chord to ring.

The problem for all of these creations was that the average buyer was not experienced in tuning a multi-stringed instrument. Latvia is a country with a zither (*kokles*) tradition, and is thus more experience in tuning. It is home to a remarkable array of homemade chord zithers, from huge to cylindrical.

Fact

Occasionally chord zithers have melody strings that are bowed in a similar way to those of the long-triangular bowed psaltery, which, though sometimes presented as being of great antiquity, is actually a twentieth-century invention.

Section One: The Instruments

VIOL

One of the most popular instruments in the sixteenth and seventeenth centuries, the viol, or viola da gamba, developed alongside the violin family. It has been central to the development of western art music.

It is thought that the viol developed from the *vihuela*, a Spanish guitar-like instrument. At some point a bow was used with the *vihuela* instead of it being plucked. This necessitated turning the instrument around so the bass rested between the player's legs and the neck rose up, parallel to the player's body. The bowed *vihuela* became known at the *vihuela da gamba* (or 'leg vihuela') and evidence from Valencian paintings made in the early 1500s suggests that the vihuela da gamba and the viola da gamba were initially very similar in design.

▲ *Renaissance consorts would include recorders, viol and voice.*

RENAISSANCE POPULARITY

The viol quickly spread from its Spanish roots to other Mediterranean countries and by the mid-sixteenth century, it had become ubiquitous in both amateur and professional circles. At its best in ensemble, the consort of viols formed a vital part of Renaissance music making; it was combined with consorts of other instruments and was also immensely popular on its own. Many households would have a 'chest of viols' containing at least one instrument of each standard size.

CONSTRUCTION

Although the viol was made in many different sizes, three were most commonly used: treble, tenor and bass. The alto viol rarely appears in music or in writings,

Musical Instruments Handbook

and the deeper contrabass viol was played mainly by professional soloists. All sizes of viol were played in the same way: they rested either on the calves or the knees and were bowed using an underhand grip with the palm facing upwards.

The viol was a fretted instrument so it was easy to play in tune. There were normally seven frets, each a half step apart, with an occasional eighth fret enabling each string to play a fully chromatic octave. Viols had six strings as standard, tuned in the sequence fourth–fourth–major third–fourth–fourth. So the treble viol was tuned *d–g–c'–e'–a'–d''*, the tenor *G–c–f–a–d'–g'* and the bass *D–G–c–e–a–d'*. The strings were made of gut, with lower-pitched strings being covered in silver or another metal to aid their tone. The bow would be like an archer's bow and ideally light and of medium tension.

▲ *Viols were popular amongst amateur players.*

FALL AND RISE

Since neither the bow nor the strings of the viol are at high tension, it is a quiet instrument. Its timbre is light and extremely colourful, perfectly suited for playing the many-voiced music for which it is famous. The development of the violin and its siblings, however, inevitably brought about the decline of the viol. In spite of the ease with which the viol could be played, the violin's strength and agility was unbeatable and interest in the viol had dwindled by the mid-1700s.

Curiously, though, it was not long before interest was revived. A series of *concerts historiques* in France in the 1830s was designed to rediscover the viol's qualities, and a number of cellists also took up the bass viol in the late-nineteenth century. The period since the Second World War has proved the most fertile time for rediscovery, and composers including George Benjamin (b. 1960), Peter Maxwell Davies (b. 1934) and David Loeb have subsequently scored for the viol specifically in new work.

Section One: The Instruments

VIOLIN

The violin family is a group of fretless bowed stringed instruments that has its roots in Italy. Four instruments make up the family: the violin, the viola, the violoncello (commonly abbreviated to cello), and the double bass.

The characteristic body shape is one of the most recognizable in music; the particular acoustic properties this shape imparts have made the violin and its siblings uniquely flexible, and they have been the most dominant instrumental family in western music for the past 400 years.

▲ *Three members of the violin family: violin, viola and cello.*

BIRTH OF THE VIOLIN FAMILY

In Europe in the fifteenth century there were two bowed stringed instruments in common use – the medieval fiddle and the rebec. The fiddle was normally a five-stringed instrument with no fixed tuning system; the rebec a three-stringed instrument tuned in perfect fifths. Both used either a flat bridge or no bridge so that the strings were generally sounded together rather than being used singly to play melody.

Although it is by no means clear that they were the inventors, two brothers, Jean and Charles Fernandes, played on three-string fiddles in the 1480s that used an arched bridge. This pushed the middle string higher than the outer ones so each string could be sounded individually.

The end of the fifteenth century saw the development of the consort principle, in which instruments of the same design but different sizes were combined to create a homogeneous ensemble. Initially this was applied to shawms, flutes and recorders, but the first decade of the sixteenth century saw the first fiddle ensembles develop: the violin family was born.

Musical Instruments Handbook

VIOLIN VERSUS VIOL

To begin with, the violin was less popular than its cousin the viol. Although similar techniques were used to perform on both instruments – and many professional musicians in the sixteenth century used both – their sound and characteristic repertoires were quite different. The viol was a soft but full-toned instrument, ideally suited to complex contrapuntal music; the violin, with its brighter tone and clearer attack was preferred for dance music.

As early as the mid-1500s, violins of all sizes were made, from small soprano violins through alto and tenor to bass violins. The family quickly spread throughout Europe, appearing in courts in France, England, Germany and Poland by the middle of the sixteenth century. Soon the violins were used not just in dance music but also in church music, in processionals and in the large antiphonal ensembles so popular during the period.

▲ *By the seventeenth century, violins and cellos were an integral part of ensembles.*

Section One: The Instruments

GROWTH IN POPULARITY

By the beginning of the seventeenth century, the violin's size and shape were well established and it had settled at four strings tuned in fifths to *g–d'–a'–e''*. It was beginning to develop its own solo repertoire and the art of violin-making was acquiring a glamorous lustre. Italy was again the focus, in particular the northern town of Cremona.

A number of great instrument makers lived and worked in Cremona during the 1600s and it was common for trade secrets to be passed down the generations. Notably successful violin makers include Andrea Amati (*c.* 1520–*c.* 1578) and his sons, whose work first gave Cremona its reputation, Andrea Guarneri (*c.* 1626–98) and his more famous grandson Giuseppe Guarneri (1698–1744, otherwise known as 'del Gesù'), and most famously of all, Antonio Stradivari (1644–1737).

ANTONIO STRADIVARI

It is thought that Stradivari was at one time a pupil of Andrea Amati's grandson, Nicolò. He began producing violins in his early twenties, although he did not acquire any great reputation until the death of Nicolò Amati in 1684. During the final decade of the seventeenth century, Stradivari began to produce violins of the quality for which he is known today but it wasn't until the first two decades of the eighteenth century – often referred to as his golden period of violin making – that he reached his peak. The violins made by Stradivari in this period are still regarded as the pre-eminent examples of the craft.

Stradivari never received anything like the adulation heaped on him today while he was alive, although he was certainly regarded as a fine craftsman. Nevertheless, his particular violin design has remained almost unchanged, and is the model to which all makers aspire.

Fact

There are believed to be just over 500 genuine Stradivari violins in existence, most of which have been discovered. Authentic examples can sell for millions of dollars; even specially commissioned copies of his violins have been known to sell for twice a maker's normal price.

Musical Instruments Handbook

CONSTRUCTION

Some 70 parts make up the violin; it is one of the most acoustically complex instruments in existence. The familiar figure-of-eight body shape is a hollow box made from spruce and maple. Protruding from the top of the body is the neck, which is covered by an ebony, unfretted fingerboard.

The neck is topped by the scroll, so-called because it resembles a scroll of paper, which is pierced laterally by four pegs, to each of which is attached a string. These strings run down the neck – above the fingerboard – and back across the body to the tailpiece. The strings are supported by the arch-shaped bridge that sits just below the two 'f'-shaped holes, out of which much of the instrument's sound is projected.

The asymmetric bridge is specifically designed to raise the middle strings slightly to different heights above the outside strings and maintain a reasonable distance between them. This means that by angling his bow, a player is able to sound one string at a time. It is also possible for the bow to be drawn across two neighbouring strings simultaneously.

▼ *Some scrolls on older instruments were carved in the shape of lion's heads.*

VIOLIN STRINGS

The strings were originally made from sheep gut that had been cleaned, soaked in a form of bleach called lye or in red wine, twisted and finally dried. Although prone to snapping if they became too dry, gut strings were relatively durable and produced excellent tone quality.

Four aspects of a string affect its pitch: length, density, diameter and tension. Gut is not a particularly dense material, so lower-pitched strings had to be either very long or very thick. On the instruments of the violin family, all four strings need to be of an equal length, so the only way to achieve a lower pitch was to have very thick strings. They are consequently slow to speak, since they require more energy to start vibrating and are difficult to control.

▲ *Some players use olive oil on gut strings to extend their life.*

Up to this point, bass violins had been rather large – as large, in fact, as the makers thought possible without rendering them unplayable. In the mid-1600s in Bologna, however, a discovery was made that would revolutionize their construction.

OVERSPINNING

Based on the work of Marin Mersenne (see p. 188), someone – it is not certain who – had the idea of wrapping a thin metal wire over the top of a gut string. This significantly increased the string's density and consequently lowered its pitch. The technique of overspinning, as it became known, enabled the length of low-pitched strings to be reduced, therefore making the bass instruments far less cumbersome.

By the beginning of the eighteenth century, all the siblings of the violin family used overspun strings. Initially they were only used on the bottom string and occasionally the bottom two strings. In the twentieth century, though, it became standard to use the technique on all four strings.

Musical Instruments Handbook

The use of metal in strings produced other benefits, including a brighter, more focused tone and better projection. There were side effects, though – the most significant of which was a hard-edged brittle quality in the sound. Other materials also developed in the 1900s that were used to make strings, most significantly synthetic materials such as nylon. The preference amongst professional players today is for strings with a gut centre overspun with metal ribbon, although there has been a revival of pure gut strings among certain players.

▲ *Pressing the bow down on the string tends to produce a harsher, more intense sound.*

THE BOW

No instrument, no matter how beautifully made, can sound great without a comparable bow. The instrument is the source of exquisite sound, but it requires a master craftsman to create a bow that will elegantly encourage that sound into being.

The bow must afford the player the best control possible. The player must be able to predict how the string will respond to the pressure of the bow in order to know what kind of sound will be made. The bow's weight must be light enough to allow for speed but heavy enough to play a strong *legato*. The tension must be high enough to allow for clear articulation, but too high a tension and the bow will break.

The quality of sound produced by a violin is strongly dependent on the materials the bow is made from. It would be simple, for instance, to create a high-tension, light bow by using carbon fibre. The resulting sound, however, would be harsh and lacking in subtlety.

◀ *Some early violin bows measured 35 cm (14 in); modern ones are usually 75 cm (29 in).*

Section One: The Instruments

BOW DEVELOPMENT

The earliest musical bows can be traced to Byzantine Empire in the tenth century. They were a convex shape, much like a hunting bow, using the desire of the wood to straighten as a means of creating tension in the hair. Experiments were carried out with different lengths of bow and different shapes of arc. Some bows were designed to allow the performer to alter the tension while playing by pulling on the bow hair.

In the mid-1700s, makers experimented with a new bow structure. Instead of a convex bow shape, craftsmen cut the wood to curve in towards the hair, allowing for higher tension. There remained, though, a kaleidoscopic range of bows, each with its own peculiar characteristics.

TOURTE'S BOW

This disparate world of bows came suddenly into focus when, in 1785, François Tourte (1747–1835) created a revolutionary new bow design. His work, which combined the best of numerous recent developments, was so good that virtually every other design quickly became obsolete.

Tourte used not a tropical hardwood – as had been typical up to that time – but pernambuco wood. By heating the straight stick and bending it while still hot, he was able to achieve a curve in towards the hair. This meant that instead of the wood pulling the hair taught, the hair itself could pull on the wood.

▲ *Illustration of Stradivarius (left) and Guanerius violins, with a Tourte bow in the foreground.*

He discovered that the ideal bow design was not one of uniform thickness, but one that tapered and was a specific length. The result was a light bow with sufficient tension to allow controlled bounce, good *legato* and power. His design meant that more pronounced sonic effects could be achieved by playing with different parts of the bow.

Tourte's design was slightly refined by subsequent bowmakers, but the essential features of his bow have remained. The whole violin family uses this bow design, although the double bass has an alternative that uses a different grip.

Musical Instruments Handbook

▲ *There are many bowing techniques that allow for every type of playing style.*

BOWING TECHNIQUES

Drawing the bow across the string generates the basic sound of all instruments in the violin family. Nearest the held end, known as the 'heel' or 'frog', the tension is highest so a powerful, hard-edged sound can be made. At the far end, known as the 'point' or 'tip', a light, delicate sound can be made. Between these two extremes exists a vast range of shades.

The downward force used by the player also affects the sound. Pushing very hard on to the string will result in a gritty, unpleasant sound. In contrast, if very little pressure is applied, then a thin, intermittent sound is heard.

FLAUTANDO

The bow's velocity is also a significant factor in the character of sound. A very slow bow, if skilfully executed, can produce a wonderfully rich, deep sound. Conversely, a fast bow will produce a light, floating sound known as *flautando* (Italian for 'fluting' since the sound resembles a flute's).

COL LEGNO

By turning the bow upside down, the wooden part can be used to generate sound. This technique, known as *col legno* ('with the wood' in Italian), creates a very short, dry sound with no sustain. It was known about as far back as the seventeenth century but only really developed in the late-nineteenth century.

Section One: The Instruments

PIZZICATO

Another technique dating from the seventeenth century is *pizzicato*. Here, the fingers pluck the strings in a similar way to the guitar or lute. Johann Sebastian Bach (1685–1750) made extensive use of *pizzicato* in his works for solo string instruments, but it was not popular in orchestral music before the Classical period. Normally, the bowing hand is used to pluck the string, but it is also possible to use the left hand, which allows for a plucked note to be sounded simultaneously with or in quick succession to a bowed note.

▲ *In jazz, the double bass's* pizzicato *provides harmony.*

Normally, a *pizzicato* note is played by gently pulling the string in parallel to the fingerboard. Béla Bartók (1881–1945), however, developed a particularly forceful pizzicato, which requires the performer to pull the string vertically so that on its release it hits the fingerboard, making a slapping sound. His love of this effect ensured it acquired the name 'Bartók *pizzicato*'. Double-bass players in jazz often use a similar effect, sometimes called 'slap bass'.

OTHER SOUNDING TECHNIQUES

The part of the instrument normally used to produce a sound is immediately below the end of the fingerboard and above the bridge. The closer the bow is to the bridge, the more brittle and glassy the sound becomes. The instruction *sul ponticello* (Italian for 'on the bridge') is used to indicate this. If the bow is drawn across the string above the fingerboard – an instruction known as *sul tasto* ('on the fingerboard') – a more veiled, ethereal sound is created.

By gently resting a finger on certain points of the string, instead of fully depressing it on to the fingerboard, a player is able to alter the way it vibrates and produce sounds called harmonics. These are gossamer-light notes, sounding far higher than the fingering would produce if the string was fully 'stopped', and have been used to great effect in solo, chamber and orchestral music.

Musical Instruments Handbook

▲ *Hungarian violinist Roby Lakatos employs myriad techniques in his sound.*

MULTIPLE STOPPING

The other important technique available to all members of the violin family is multiple stopping – the sounding of more than one string simultaneously. Sounding two together is double stopping, sounding three is triple stopping and four is quadruple stopping. This allows for one instrument to play complex sounds and even, in the hands of a skilled composer, to sound like two or more independent voices.

Multiple stopping was developed in the mid-1500s and has remained a popular technique. Bach was one of the most skilful and well-known proponents of multiple stopping, particularly in his cello suites. Double stopping has also been adopted as a drone technique in folk music.

THE VIOLIN

The violin has had an immense impact on the development of music. Its many attributes including flexibility, agility, varied colour and capacity to blend, have made it the central instrument in the development of solo, chamber and orchestral music. The qualities exhibited when the violin plays with large numbers of its siblings are unrivalled; the magical sound created when 20 violins together play *pianissimo* is one of the most extraordinary acoustic flukes in history.

Section One: The Instruments

The violin's development has been amply described above. In construction it remains almost unchanged from the developments made in seventeenth-century Cremona: four strings tuned to *g–d'–a'–e''* strung along the neck and over the body, which amplifies and projects the instrument's sound. The bow is held by the right hand (examples of left-handed violins do exist but they are rare, not least because of the physical chaos caused when played in the orchestra) and is of the same basic design Tourte created in the late 1700s.

▲ *The violin has a long history of virtuosi: Nigel Kennedy.*

The repertoire created for the violin is too vast to describe here. It started at the beginning of the seventeenth century in Italy, some time after the violin had become an accepted instrument. By the end of the Classical period, there was already a solid body of work; by the beginning of the twentieth century, the violin was the major solo instrument – a position it has yet to relinquish. Outstanding examples of the concerto repertoire include Beethoven, Edward Elgar (1857–1934), Alban Berg (1885–1935), Felix Mendelssohn (1809–47), Johannes Brahms (1833–97), Piotr Ilyich Tchaikovsky (1840–93) and Jean Sibelius (1865–1957).

THE VIOLA

The viola is the alto member of the violin family. It had become established by 1535 and at that time it was more commonly known as the *viola da braccio*, meaning 'arm viola' to distinguish it from members of the viol family, which were known as *viola da gamba* or 'leg viola'. The *viola da braccio* was supported by the player's arm in the same way as the violin.

Musical Instruments Handbook

The viola's body is larger than the violin's; consequently the sound it produces is warmer and darker. Its four strings are tuned a perfect fifth below the violin to *c–g–d'–a'* – but here there is a problem: the ideal length for viola strings would make the body too long to be held by the arm. Violas range in size from 38 cm (15 in) to 48 cm (19 in), sometimes larger. The perfect length would be 53 cm (21 in), but this would be a laptop instrument, so the choice of size is left up to the individual player.

The viola's size also means that greater stretches are required from the fingering hand and more energy is required from the bow, which is generally shorter and heavier than the violin's. Nevertheless, it is common for players to be able to play both the violin and viola, although most professionals concentrate on a single instrument.

From the beginning, the viola has been the subject of mockery: musicians learn the viola, it is said, only when they have too few teeth left to play the French horn. Although it retains the aura of a dunce instrument – dating from when its construction made it difficult to play with any virtuosity – the viola proved its immense musical worth hundreds of years ago. Georg Philipp Telemann (1681–1767), Johann Stamitz (1717–57) and Mozart provided early concerti; Beethoven, Carl Maria von Weber (1786–1826), Hector Berlioz (1803–69) and Mendelssohn soon expanded the instrument's reputation for solo playing.

▲ *Viola bows are slightly shorter and heavier than violin bows.*

The great works for viola, though, came in the twentieth century. Composers including Bartók, Walton, Paul Hindemith (1895–1963), Ralph Vaughan Williams (1872–1958), Benjamin Britten (1913–76), Dimitri Shostakovitch (1906–75) and Luciano Berio (1925–2003) all wrote excellent solo works. Not only that, but the viola took up a more prominent position in the orchestra. It is today regarded as one of the most beautiful and expressive of instruments.

Section One: The Instruments

THE VIOLONCELLO

The baritone instrument of the family, the original bass violins had three strings tuned to *F–c–g*; a fourth string was added in the mid-1500s giving a low B♭. The bass violin was often known as the *violone* and was at least 80 cm (31 in) long in order to accommodate the long gut strings. The development of overspinning meant the strings could be shortened by about 15 per cent, making the instrument much more manageable. This new size was called the violoncello, or cello for short.

Cremona was the centre for making bass violins, and once again it was Stradavari whose work established the violoncello's size and basic construction. His work in the early-eighteenth century set the cello's body size at 75–76 cm (30 in), which was ideal for a tuning system of *C–G–d–a* that by then had become standard.

The cello has a vast range: it is capable of playing up to *c'''* and even higher in some player's hands. It is also incredibly expressive and flexible, commanding a tone perhaps more like the human voice than any other instrument. Consequently it has been an immensely popular instrument among composers from its inception to the present day. The concertos of Edward Elgar (1857–1934) and Antonin Dvorák (1841–1904) are the best known, but there are great works from almost every major composer including Shostakovich, Britten, Debussy, Beethoven and of course Bach.

THE DOUBLE BASS

There is no standard double-bass design. The instruments commonly used in orchestras are around 115 cm (45 in) high and have four strings tuned to *E'–A'–D–G*. It is not tuned to the pattern of perfect fifths usually found in the violin family

Musical Instruments Handbook

because it would be too awkward to play, since the stretches between notes are large. Some instruments have a fifth string that is tuned either to *C'* or *B''*.

▲ *The German style of bow is held palm upwards.*

The history of the double bass is contentious because even today it exhibits characteristics of both the violin and the viol. Examples of double-bass-like instruments appeared in the second decade of the 1520s. These early instruments were likely to have six strings, be tuned in patterns of fourths and thirds, and have frets – all characteristics of the viol family.

During the early-seventeenth century, five-string basses were preferred in a variety of tunings. By the eighteenth century the most popular bass was a three-stringed version, most often tuned to *A'–D–G*. This bass was fretless and remained the normal instrument for orchestral work throughout the nineteenth century. Indeed, the low *E'* string did not become standard until the early-twentieth century; prior to this, passages moving below *A'* were simply transposed up an octave.

The double bass's dual nature did not deter performers. From the 1700s there have been successful double-bass virtuosos. The end of the eighteenth century saw an explosion in solo repertoire and, although the appeal of the bass is significantly less than the violin or cello, it has continued to be an instrument that attracts attention, not least in the hands of some of the jazz greats.

Section One: The Instruments

FIDDLE-TYPE INSTRUMENTS

Fiddles, generically, are bowed lutes. The term 'fiddle' denotes a stringed instrument with a neck, bearing strings that are sounded by the use of friction rather than plucking or striking.

PLAYING THE FIDDLE

In almost all fiddles the world over, friction is provided by a bow strung with rosined horsehair. The hair is tensioned by the springiness of the bow, or held in tension by the fingers of the player, or by tightening a screw mechanism.

The most common playing position for fiddles is to hold them not under the chin like a violin, but vertically, with the soundbox resting either on the knee or the ground, and bow them in a cello-like fashion (the bow-hand palm facing variously upward or downward). A few of the smaller ones are held horizontal on the arm, and a very few are played with the soundbox resting on the shoulder, the neck downward, and the strings stopped with the joints of the fingers of the left hand, held palm-inwards.

ERHU

Spike-fiddles are essentially spike-lutes that are bowed instead of plucked. These instruments are found all over China. The most common is the *erhu*, a member of the *huqin* family. It has a small soundbox, cylindrical, hexagonal, or octagonal in shape, open at the back, with a snakeskin soundboard supporting a small wooden bridge. Its thin stick-neck is cylindrical with no

▲ Erhu *(left) and* di-zi *(right).*

Musical Instruments Handbook

fingerboard, and has two large wooden friction-pegs at the top. Below this, the two strings run through a loop of silk or nylon to form an adjustable nut, then onward across the bridge to the stub of the spike. The strings are stopped with the fingers, not pressed against the neck. The bow hair runs between the two strings, which are normally tuned to a perfect fifth apart – one feature that is significantly different from western fiddles.

The *zhuihu* or *zhuiqin* is descended from the Chinese lute *sanxian*, with the strings stopped by being pressed down on a flat fingerboard on its neck. Japan's four-stringed *kokyu* is likewise a bowed version of that country's lute, the *shamisen*, with a rounded-rectangular soundbox and neck bearing a fretless fingerboard, played with an unusually long bow.

REGIONAL VARIATIONS

Other countries of East and Southeast Asia and Indonesia have spike-fiddles closely related to the *huqin* family. Korea has the *haegum*, Japan the *kokin*, Tibet the *piwang*, Tuva the four-stringed *byzaanchy*. Vietnam's equivalents are the *dan nhi* or *dan co* and the deeper-pitched *dan gao* or *dan ho*, and Cambodia's include the *tro u*, larger *tro sau* and, with bow-hair not passing between the strings, the three-stringed *tro khmer*. The Okinawan *kucho*, traditionally three-stringed, has recently gained a fourth. Thailand's *saw u* and *saw duang* are very like an *erhu*, but the three-stringed *saw sam sai* is a rather different shape, with a rounded-triangular soundbox and long lower spike.

▲ *The* saw duang *has a high, clear sound and acts as leader in string ensembles.*

Indonesia also has spike-fiddles, which include the chunky two-stringed *geso-geso* and an elegant long-spiked fiddle, rather like the *saw sam sai*, having a rounded-triangular soundbox and extremely long turned tuning-pegs, known as a *rebab* (a fiddle-name found commonly in Arabic and other Islamic countries); a similar one is also used with gamelan orchestras in Java.

Section One: The Instruments

▲ *One of many varieties of spike-fiddle.*

RABAB

The Bedouin, Syrian and Jordanian one-stringed *rabab* or *rababah* has a more-or- less rectangular skin-covered soundbox, often with extended wooden side-pieces making an 'H'-shape with the soundbox as crossbar. The Ethiopian *masenqo's* square soundbox is set diamond-wise, while many other African one-string fiddles such as the Senegalese-Gambian *riti* or *nyanyere*, Rwandan *iningiri*, Burkina Faso *duduga* and Kenyan and Ugandan *siiriri* or *orutu*, have circular, usually gourd soundboxes.

In Tunisia and Morocco the name *rabab* signifies a different kind of fiddle, with no evident spike; it has a wedge-shaped combined soundbox and neck, with skin over the wider lower half and metal or wood with incized decoration covering the neck part, and a back-angled peg-box.

The construction and the name has obvious connections with the Afghan *rubab*, which is a plucked, not bowed lute. Here, the rapid decay of notes is converted to a long ring by the addition of a number of thin steel sympathetic strings.

SARANGI

One of the foremost of its bowed relatives is the *sarangi*, which makes one of the most evocative and voice-like sounds of north India and Pakistan. It is a squat, chunky fiddle, carved from a single piece of wood, with a goatskin soundboard, a very wide neck and a hefty peg-box. From the back the soundbox appears hemi-cylindrical, but the sides of the front are scalloped to make a waist.

Musical Instruments Handbook

The gut playing strings are, as with many such fiddles, stopped without being pressed on a fingerboard – here, though, the surface of the nails and the skin immediately above them are used. Their sound is given a silvery reverberation by sympathetic strings, which on present-day 'concert' *sarangis* number about 35. The three melody strings, usually joined by a drone string, run over the bridge to the peg-box, while the sympathetic strings run under the bridge – most of them to rows of tuning pegs inserted in the side of the neck, but some to extra pegs beyond the melody peg-box via a pair of flat bridges adjusted to make the strings buzz like those of a sitar.

SETOR

In appearance like typical plucked lutes, but bowed, are the *setor, sato* or *satar* of Uzbekistan, Tajikistan and the Uighur people of western China. These have a teardrop-shaped, wood-fronted soundbox, one melody string and up to 12 sympathetic strings. The almost mandolin-like Uighur *kushtar* has sympathetic strings and a scalloped-sided front to its teardrop-shaped soundbox. The Turkish *tambur*, which has a nearly circular soundbox, wooden soundboard, and neck with fingerboard and tied frets, was usually plucked but bowing it has become common.

HORSE-HEAD FIDDLE

The cello-length Mongolian spike-fiddle *morin khuur* ('horse-head fiddle' because of the shape of its head) has a trapezoidal soundbox whose skin soundboard is now replaced by a wooden one with f-holes. Its two strings are made of parallel (not twisted) horsehair – sometimes synthetic – one with more strands than the other. The Tuvan *igil* is equivalent, but its soundbox is usually small, shallow-bowled and leaf-shaped or polygonal, with a skin soundboard. Khakassia and Altai have the closely related *yykh* or *ikili*.

▶ *The Mongolian horse-head fiddle has two strings.*

Section One: The Instruments

TARHU

A significant new development in the technology of spike-fiddles can be found in the circular-bodied instruments called *tarhu*, made by Australian luthier Peter Biffin. There is no soundboard in the usual sense – one foot of the bridge rests very lightly on the apex of a rear-facing wooden cone inside the body, while the other rests on the front of the body, taking the string pressure and acting as a pivot. The result is an extremely efficient transfer of string vibration and thus great volume and extraordinary richness of tone.

GUSLE

In the area of former Yugoslavia the instrument of the *guslars* – bardic ballad-singers – is the *gusle*, a single-stringed spike-fiddle with a skin soundboard on a teardrop shaped body, and cylindrical neck without finger-board, usually ornamented at the top by a carved goat or other animal head. Albania has a similar instrument, the lahuta.

▲ *Stringed instruments like the lute and gusle are often highly decorated.*

LIJERICA

On the Dalmatian coast a small three-stringed *lijerica* or *lirica* is played. This is flask-shaped in outline, with three gut strings running straight from pegs on a disc-shaped head to a flat bridge, and from there to an anchor-point on the bottom end. There are two 'D'-shaped sound holes in the wooden soundboard, one on each side of the bridge. The latter rests partly on the soundboard, but one end of it presses on a removable soundpost that goes through a D-hole to rest on the back of the soundbox.

The instrument is held vertically and all three strings are bowed together – two acting as drones while the melody string is stopped from the side with the fingertips; there is no fingerboard. The *lira* of Calabria, at the southern tip of mainland Italy, is similar.

Musical Instruments Handbook

The Pontic *lira* is a slim bottle-shaped lira with a fingerboard upon which its three steel strings, tuned in fourths, are stopped. Like the violin it has a nut, and its bridge rests on the face of the soundboard, over an internal sound-post.

SCANDINAVIAN FIDDLES

Norway's *hardingfele* or *hardanger* fiddle is the shape of a violin, though with a slightly shorter neck and decorated with pen-drawn acanthus patterns, mother-of-pearl inlays and figuratively carved head. What makes it different, though, are two features: the fingerboard and bridge are much flatter than a violin's, making bowing of more than one string the norm – producing a drone effect – and the fact that it is enhanced to a silvery ringing by the presence of four or five sympathetic strings that run under the bridge to extra pegs in the pegbox.

Among today's Swedish folk fiddlers there is increasing use of a larger sympathetic-strung instrument, usually called a drone-fiddle, based on the viola d'amore. Other European regional violin relatives include the three-stringed, nearly flat-bridged viola and three-stringed bass played in the fiddle music of Hungary, Romania and other parts of Eastern Europe, and the *zlóbcoki*, a slim pocket-violin used by Polish highlanders in the Tatra mountains. Transylvania's *ütögardon* is cello-shaped, but its strings are alternately hit with a stick and plucked for percussion.

The phonofiddle or Stroh violin is, for the player, just like an ordinary violin. However, it has no soundbox – the vibration of the strings passes via the bridge to resonating metal and thence to an amplifying horn pointed at the audience. There is usually a second horn directing sound pointing at the player's ear. These instruments continue to be made and played, including by fiddlers in some of Eastern Europe's Roma bands.

► *A variety of different tunings are used by players of* hardingfele.

Section One: The Instruments

BOWED LYRES

Nordic bowed lyres, known in Finland as *jouhikko*, in Estonia *hiiu-kannel* and Sweden as *stråkharpa*, comprise a more or less rectangular soundbox, across which run three or sometimes four horsehair strings.

These pass from a tailpiece across a bridge resting on the soundboard to tuning pegs on a flat extension of the body. This extended section has an aperture that allows access from behind for the player's left hand to one, two or more of the strings. The melody is played on the first string, which is stopped with the back of the fingers; some players, particularly in Estonia, also stop the second and occasionally third string.

CRWTH

The *crwth*, surviving in Wales, was once also played in England and other parts of Europe. It is related to the Nordic bowed lyres, but it also has features of a fiddle. Although it has two arms springing from the soundbox in lyre fashion it also has a neck with a violin-type fingerboard running up the middle of the space between the arms, against which four of the six gut strings are stopped. The other two run beside them, playable with the bow or left thumb as drones. All go to tuning pegs on the bar between the lyre-like arms.

As with the Bulgarian *gadulka* and *liras* of Calabria, Dalmatia and Crete, one leg of the bridge goes through one of the two soundholes beside it, and rests on the back of the soundbox, forming a sort of sound-post.

► *The bridge of the Welsh* crwth *is flat, so all the strings are bowed at the same time.*

Musical Instruments Handbook

KEYED BOWED INSTRUMENTS

Sweden's *nyckelharpa*, now experiencing a boom in skilled players and makers, is known to have existed in the fourteenth century.

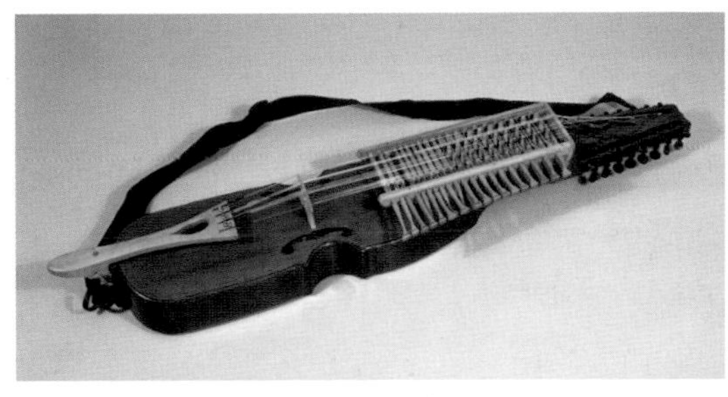

Its soundbox is a slightly waisted boat-shape, the prow extending to a short, thick neck, covered by a mechanism containing one or more rows of gravity-returned sliding wooden bars, pressed with the fingers of the left hand while the right hand wields a short bow. Each bar bears one or more wooden pegs that can be pressed against the melody strings to shorten their sounding length. Thin sympathetic strings, running in groups beside the bowed strings, add a silvery sustain to the sound.

The chromatic *nyckelharpa*, created early in the twentieth century, has three melody strings, one drone and 12 sympathetic strings. Some of today's players are developing new forms and exploring the possibilities of older, slightly simpler forms such as the *silverbasharpa*.

HURDY-GURDY

The hurdy-gurdy, or *vielle à roue*, reached its most highly developed form (until today) in seventeenth- and eighteenth-century France, and it is France – and to some extent Hungary – that has been the epicentre of its current renaissance. Its key mechanism is broadly similar to that of a *nyckelharpa*, but it is bowed by a rosined wheel, rotating within the lute or guitar-shaped soundbox, driven by a handle inserted where a guitar's endpin would be. Designs vary widely, but all have melody and drone strings, and sometimes sympathetic strings. Many have a *trompette* – an extra drone running over a loose bridge that buzzes on the soundboard to provide a rhythmic pulse when the handle is jerked.

Section One: The Instruments

INTRODUCTION

KEYBOARDS

In the history of musical instruments, the keyboard is something of a Johnny-come-lately, having first appeared some 2,250 years ago.

The earliest instrument of all is the human voice, and some form of rudimentary percussion probably came next. The plucked string – ancestor of the harpsichord family – is likely to have arrived with the firing of the first arrow, if not before; the wind family with a blade of grass clasped between the thumbs; the brass with the sounding of a conch shell, a ram's horn with the tip broken off, or something similar. What binds all these together, models and families alike, is the direct contact between the player and the source of sound – something the keyboard player entirely lacks.

▲ *The barrel organ's sound is mechanical.*

KEYBOARD CONSTRUCTION

In construction, keyboard instruments range from the relatively simple (virginals and clavichord) to the incredibly complex (the grandest organs and the most advanced electronic instruments), but the basic principle of them all can be seen in action in every children's playground containing a see-saw: a rigid bar (key) pivoted on a fulcrum. When one end goes down, the other goes up, and vice versa. The complications and greatest subtleties arise from what is attached to that hidden end of the key.

The player's end is generally covered in ivory (now rare) or a plastic imitation. Mounted on the hidden end is the mechanism through which the strings or pipes of a keyboard instrument are sounded when the key is depressed. The technical term for this device is 'action', though the same term is used to describe the whole set-up – bar, fulcrum and sound-producing mechanism as a single unit.

◀ *The harpsichord is touch sensitive: pressure on the key directly affects sound quality.*

Musical Instruments Handbook

▼ *Touching an organ key triggers a process to produce sound.*

In the harpsichord family, the name 'jack' is given to that part of the action that carries the plectrum upwards, causing it to pluck the string. In the clavichord, the plectrum is replaced by a tangent, which remains in contact with the string for as long as the key is depressed. In the piano, the sound-producer is a hammer whose head is covered in felt, some lighter fabric, or leather. The much-used term 'dampers' refers to the pads of felt or other cloth that normally rest on the strings, preventing them from vibrating unless the key is depressed or, in the piano, when the sustaining or *sostenuto* pedal is depressed, lifting all or some of the dampers as desired.

ORGAN HISTORY

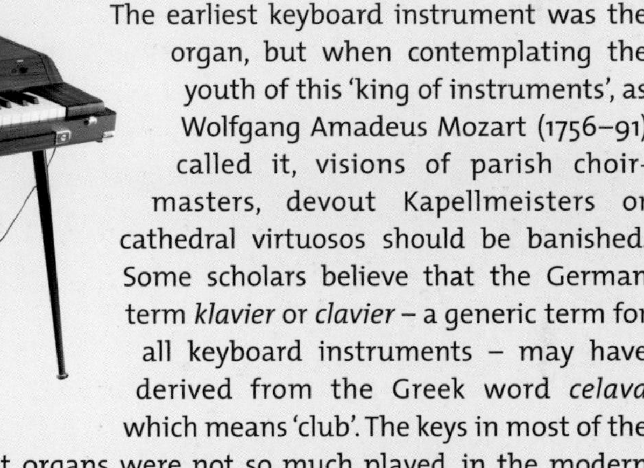

The earliest keyboard instrument was the organ, but when contemplating the youth of this 'king of instruments', as Wolfgang Amadeus Mozart (1756–91) called it, visions of parish choir-masters, devout Kapellmeisters or cathedral virtuosos should be banished. Some scholars believe that the German term *klavier* or *clavier* – a generic term for all keyboard instruments – may have derived from the Greek word *celava* which means 'club'. The keys in most of the earliest organs were not so much played, in the modern manner, as roundly thumped. Nor did they much resemble keys as we know them. In the water organs of Roman times they were a row of simple levers, requiring the full force of a man's fist to push them down. The organ, however, early parted company with simplicity, becoming one of civilization's most complicated machines. With hundreds – even thousands – of parts, it sometimes required three able-bodied men to subdue it.

Fact

Early organs were so large and complicated to use that organists were sometimes known as 'organ beaters'.

▲ *Electric pianos lack the piano's size and weight, but also their timbre.*

Section One: The Instruments

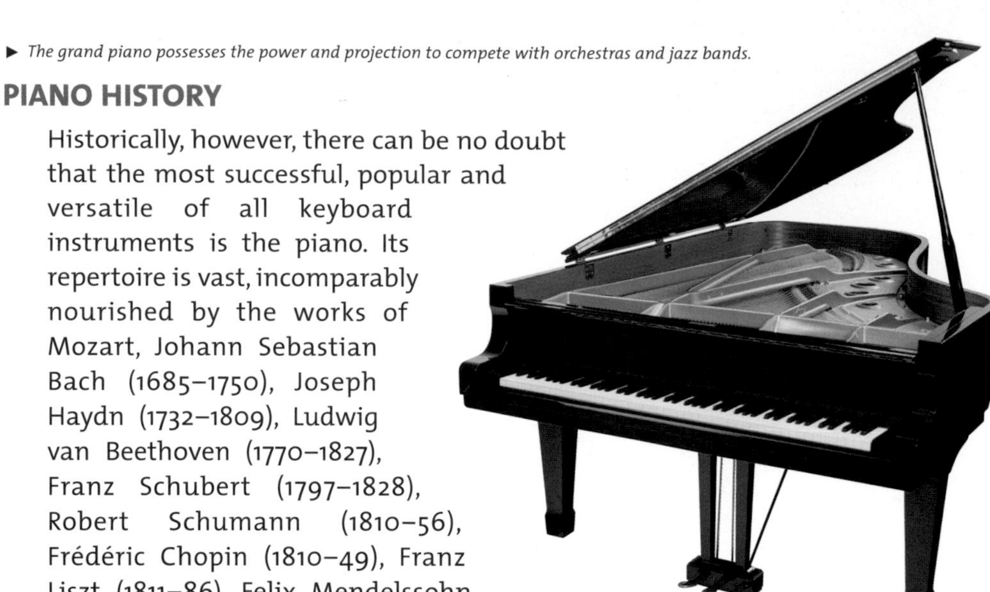

▶ *The grand piano possesses the power and projection to compete with orchestras and jazz bands.*

PIANO HISTORY

Historically, however, there can be no doubt that the most successful, popular and versatile of all keyboard instruments is the piano. Its repertoire is vast, incomparably nourished by the works of Mozart, Johann Sebastian Bach (1685–1750), Joseph Haydn (1732–1809), Ludwig van Beethoven (1770–1827), Franz Schubert (1797–1828), Robert Schumann (1810–56), Frédéric Chopin (1810–49), Franz Liszt (1811–86), Felix Mendelssohn (1809–47), Johannes Brahms (1833–97), Claude Debussy (1862–1918), Maurice Ravel (1875–1937), George Gershwin (1898–1937) and many more. Its foremost practitioners, from Liszt to Jan Paderewski (1860–1941) and beyond, were the pop stars of their day.

Great music, however, like great pianists, has played a relatively minor role in the piano's history. For nearly 150 years it scored its most resounding success as a status symbol all over the world. On top of uprights or within piano benches throughout the western world, it was common to find leather-clad volumes of collected sheet music. Just occasionally these included a sonata by Mozart or Beethoven, but far more typical of them was the century's runaway bestseller, composed by Thekla Badarzewska (1834–61), an obscure Polish woman of small talent.

◀ *The portable harmonium has brought music into countless numbers of homes.*

Musical Instruments Handbook

▲ *Due to their popularity, pianos have gained a place in the popular consciousness.*

THE MAIDEN'S PRAYER

The phenomenal success of *The Maiden's Prayer* seems attributable solely to its title and its subsequent packaging. The piece itself is of no distinction – outclassed even within its genre by literally thousands of better efforts by composers with equally undistinguished credentials. Who can wonder, then, at the American writer Ambrose Bierce's definition of the piano in his *Devil's Dictionary* (1906): 'Piano, *noun*. A parlor utensil used to subdue the impenitent visitor. It is operated by depressing the keys of the instrument, and the spirits of the audience.'

The perpetrators of this domestic misery were usually young women of marriageable age, whose doubtful prowess at the keyboard was held to be proof both of their respectability and of their father's prowess in the marketplace. Its role as an agent of seduction, by both sexes, is well documented in the literature of two centuries, as is its neglect once the ploy had worked. Its death knell, in that department anyway, was sounded with the advent of electronic instruments. Despite this, however, it seems that the piano is here to stay.

Fact

The piano was so popular in the United States at the turn of the nineteenth century that one architect designed an entire block of flats in New York's Harlem district with an upright piano built into the walls of every one.

Section One: The Instruments

VIRGINALS

The sole remaining mystery of the virginals is its name – and its singular plurality. A virginals? Nor need there be two instruments to speak of a 'pair' of virginals. This was common parlance in Tudor times.

ORIGINS OF THE VIRGINALS

As to the singular or plural form, both are acceptable these days – but why 'virginal' in the first place? Can this be an instrument conceived never to be played? A feast for the eyes alone? Of course not. Nor, despite the mythology, has the name anything to do with Elizabeth I (the 'Virgin Queen'), however accomplished her playing. The instrument was well established before she was even born. Its feminine attributes, however, are unmistakable. What may well be the most famous title page in the history of music reads: PARTHENIA OR THE MAYDENHEAD OF THE FIRST MUSICKE THAT EVER WAS PRINTED FOR THE VIRGINALLS. The date was 1613, and the collection – of works by William Byrd (1543–1623), Orlando Gibbons (1583–1625) and John Bull (1562–1628) was probably the first music ever printed from engraved plates. Adorning the cover is a picture of a demure young lady, whose chastity is all but contagious. The name 'Parthenia' derives from the Greek for 'virgin'. In fact, there is nothing notably feminine about the instrument, or the music written for it.

▲ *The virginals dates from as early as the 1460s.*

VIRGINALS CONSTRUCTION

The virginal(s) is really a small harpsichord, generally rectangular in shape, with the strings running parallel to the keyboard on the long side of the case. It has a single set of strings, normally with one string per key. The virginals lacks the colouristic variety of the harpsichord (though not necessarily its volume) but, as

Musical Instruments Handbook

many paintings of the period show, it outshone the harpsichord as the most popular of all domestic keyboard instruments. Confusingly, though, the name 'virginals' was applied throughout the sixteenth and seventeenth centuries, particularly in England, as a generic term for any keyboard instrument in which the strings are plucked rather than struck.

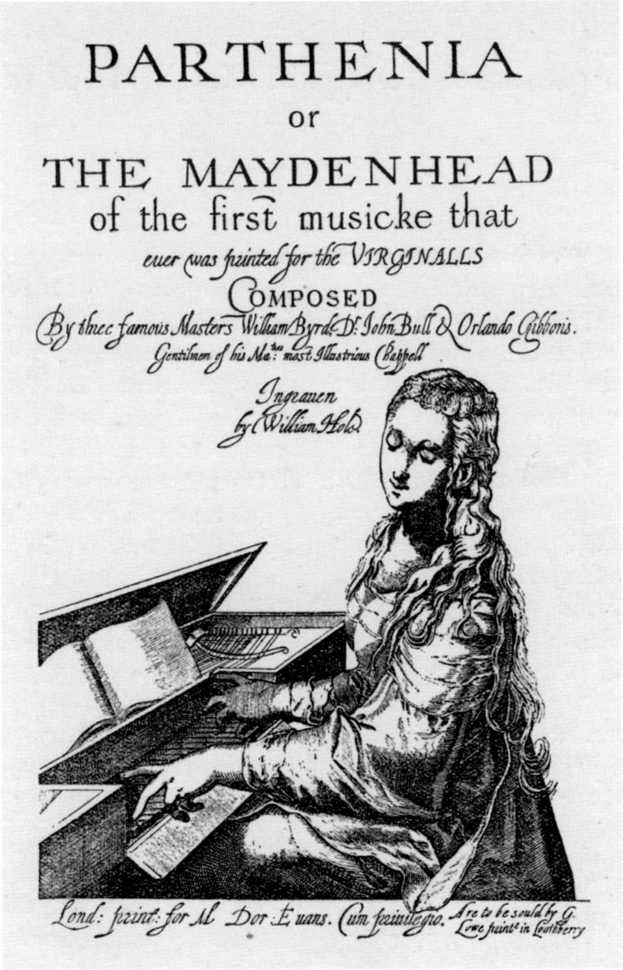

▲ *Playing the virginals was considered part of a young woman's accomplishments.*

MUSIC FOR THE VIRGINALS

Apart from its intrinsic value, the contents of *Parthenia* belong to that great body of music in which composers first wrote idiomatically for a keyboard instrument, clearly differentiating it in style from vocal or string chamber music (itself hardly distinguished at all from vocal music). It contains many passages, particularly very rapid ones, which could never be convincingly played – if played at all – on a non-keyboard instrument, with the exception of such other plucked instruments as the lute, cittarone or guitar. However, little or no stylistic distinction was made by Renaissance composers between the virginals, the spinet, the clavichord, the fully fledged harpsichord and the organ. In addition to the composers mentioned above, important composers of the English virginals school were Peter Philips (1560–1628), Giles Farnaby (1563–1640), Martin Peerson (*c.* 1571–1651), Thomas Weelkes (1576–1623), Thomas Tomkins (1572–1656) and Benjamin Cosyn (*c.* 1570–1652).

Section One: The Instruments

SPINET

The spinet is known by many names and has several definitions. Perhaps the most misleading is the American usage of the term to denote a small upright piano. The most confusing is the use of the word to describe a square piano, and a more ancient confusion arises from its use as a synonym for the virginals or, indeed, any small harpsichord.

SPINET CONSTRUCTION

The word itself derives from the Latin *spina* ('thorn'), which refers specifically to the use of quills to activate the strings. In eighteenth-century France, the word 'spinet' was applied to any quilled instrument, regardless of size or design. The true spinet is a wing-shaped instrument, with a compass ranging from four to five octaves. It has a single set of jacks, and the strings are arranged diagonally from the keyboard, as opposed to the harpsichord and the piano, where they are at right angles, or the virginals, where they lie horizontally.

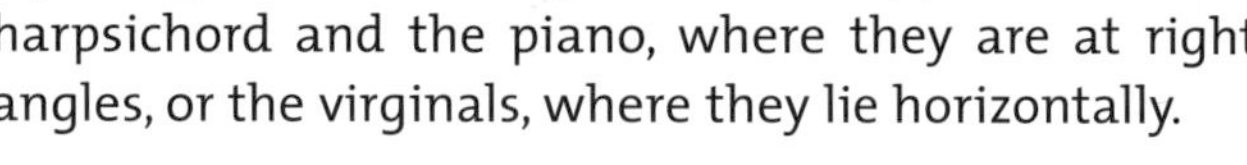

POPULARITY

Early spinets are generally small and sometimes have the decorative rose in the soundboard – which was standard issue with the older virginals. It enjoyed its greatest popularity from the mid-seventeenth century to the late-eighteenth century, when its decorative appearance made it a much-prized piece of furniture (often independently of its musical function).

SPINET MAKERS

Though apparently invented in Italy in the late-seventeenth century by Girolamo Zenti, the spinet enjoyed its greatest popularity in England, where its style and shape came characteristically to be known as 'bentside' or 'leg-of-mutton'. Its foremost makers in the seventeenth century included Keene, Player, Haward, and the family firm of Hitchcocks, and in the eighteenth, Messrs Slade, Mahoon and Baker.

▲ *The spinet's body was often wing-shaped, like a grand piano.*

Musical Instruments Handbook

HARPSICHORD

In one form or another, the harpsichord ruled the domestic keyboard roost throughout Europe – and later in America – from the late-sixteenth to the early-nineteenth centuries. Apart from the organ, it was the grandest and most versatile of all keyboard instruments until the advent of the mature fortepiano in the mid- to late-eighteenth century.

RISE AND FALL OF THE HARPSICHORD

Its prevalence may be gauged by the fact that the first 14 of Beethoven's epoch-making piano sonatas, including the famous *Moonlight Sonata* (1801), were originally published as being 'For Harpsichord or Pianoforte'. In reality, they were no such thing, but there were clearly enough harpsichords in private ownership to justify the marketing ploy on practical if not artistic grounds.

Nor was its use confined to the home. It provided a vital degree of rhythmic incisiveness and harmonic foundation in virtually every instrumental combination from the trio sonatas of the early Baroque to the earlier symphonies of Haydn two centuries later. Well before the 1820s, though, the instrument had all but disappeared, overtaken by the rapidly developing and increasingly powerful piano.

CONSTRUCTION

The definitive element in the harpsichord's mechanism is the 'jack' – a slender, upright piece of wood, mounted at the far end of a key and topped with a small artificial plectrum (comparable to the end of a quill pen and made either of hardened leather or from the wing-feathers of birds such as ravens, crows or condors). When the key is depressed, the jack at the other end is propelled upwards, plucking the string as it passes. On the downward journey, a wooden 'tongue', pivoted on the jack and originally sprung with a boar's bristle, allows the jack to pass the string without plucking it again.

▲ *Harpsichords suffered from quick decay: once a string had been plucked the note would fade.*

Slotted into the jack, next to the tongue but just above the plectrum, is a 'damper' – usually a wedge of felt or other soft cloth – which prevents the string from vibrating when the key is at rest, just as it enables the vibration when the key is depressed. The earliest and simplest harpsichords had one jack and one string for each note or key, and could thus be made very small and easily portable. Later harpsichords may have as many as five strings to each note and as many as three keyboards (as with the organ, these are generally known as 'manuals'). In instruments such as these, of course, the mechanical challenges are vastly more complex. The essential principle, however, remains the same.

The strings themselves, prior to the harpsichord revival in the late-nineteenth century, were made variously of iron, copper, brass and even steel – often in combination, with a view to achieving a wide range of tonal variety. In modern harpsichords, they generally consist of steel.

PLAYING TECHNIQUE

Among the factors affecting harpsichord timbre is the placement of the jack relative to the length of the string. A string plucked near the bridge will have a distinctly different character and 'feel' from one plucked nearer the centre. Equally, the volume (and its tonal character) will vary according to the number of strings activated at any particular moment.

Musical Instruments Handbook

The harpsichord proper (as opposed to its simpler siblings the virginals and the spinet) has two keyboards, or manuals, controlling two different sets of strings, and several 'stops', on the model of the organ, by which various combinations of jacks and strings can be brought into play at the discretion of the performer. In some of the bigger instruments, the stops can be controlled by pedals, allowing the hands to remain at the keyboard without risk of scramble. These became a standard feature of English harpsichords from the middle of the 1760s, while knee levers performed the same function in many French harpsichords from the late 1750s.

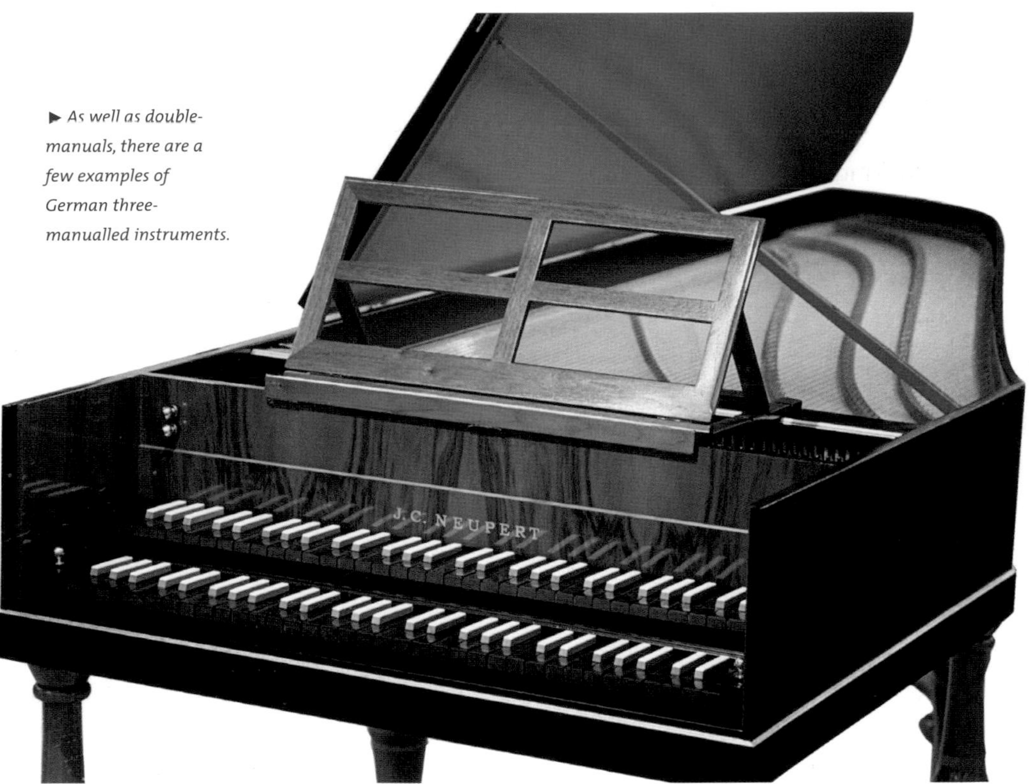

▶ *As well as double-manuals, there are a few examples of German three-manualled instruments.*

The two-manual harpsichord is effectively a pairing of two separate instruments, one on top of the other. A classic example of their juxtaposition can be heard in Bach's *Italian Concerto*, in which he contrasts the full, brilliant sound of the surrogate orchestra, with the lighter tone of the 'soloist'. On many of the bigger instruments, there is a 'coupler' mechanism, by which one keyboard can play as two, controlling 'both' instruments at once.

Section One: The Instruments

EARLY CHANGES TO HARPSICHORD DESIGN

While devices such as knee levers did much to bring an ever-wider range of sonorities to the instrument, they did not address what came increasingly to be seen as the harpsichord's most serious limitation – its inability to emulate the smooth transitions from one dynamic level to another that characterize the human voice and all wind and bowed string instruments.

To this end, there emerged a number of ingenious but ultimately rather unwieldy devices, enabling the player to raise and lower the lid, or, as in the case of Burkat Shudi's aptly named 'Venetian swell' mechanism (1769), in which a system of shutters directly above the strings could be opened and shut to whatever aperture suited the player's musical intention (just as they are in the standard Venetian blind).

▲ *Players added trills and ornamentation to compensate for the harpsichord's quick decay.*

LATER DEVELOPMENTS

Although many believe that concern for tonal and dynamic variety in the harpsichord came about in the nineteenth century, there were efforts to address this issue from earlier times. In Thomas Mace's 1676 publication *Musick's Monument*, he describes in some detail a mechanism dating from the first half of the seventeenth century comprising four pedals, which cause 'the whole Instrument to Sound, either Soft or Loud, according as he shall chuse to Tread any of them down'. Mace had one made which, in all its combinations, gave him 24 varieties of tone colour, including a hand-operated lute-stop. In the next century, C. P. E. Bach (1714–88) cited a similar invention in his *Versuch das Clavier zu spielen* (1759), by which the number of stops in operation can be increased and decreased by means of pedals without interrupting the playing, thus securing gradual changes in volume that could only otherwise be demonstrated by the clavichord and the piano.

WORKS OF ART

Well before the decline in their fortunes in the late-eighteenth century, harpsichords had been living a double life, so to speak – as musical instruments, on the one hand (often of the very highest craftsmanship), and as items of furniture on the other. Their cases were often decorated by the finest artists of their day, making them both figuratively and literally works of the highest art. Indeed, history is in the debt of these artists. Their work alone prevented many of these wonderful instruments from being broken up and incinerated once their musical sun had set. This was particularly true of those made by the Ruckers dynasty of Antwerp, which were sent to all parts of the world.

▲ *Harpsichords were often extremely graceful and elegantly decorated.*

Fact

The terms 'stop' and 'register' are used interchangeably to denote a stop proper (the mechanical device) and the particular tone colours resulting from its use.

After almost a century of neglect, the harpsichord was taken up by composers as well as performers – most notably, Ferruccio Busoni (1866–1924), Manuel de Falla (1976–1946), Henry Cowell (1897–1965), Frederick Delius (1862–1934), Jean Françaix (b. 1912), Bohuslav Martino (1890–1959), Darius Milhaud (1892–1974), Carl Orff (1895–1982), Francis Poulenc (1899–1963), Igor Stravinsky (1882–1971), and later, Luciano Berio (1925–2003), Iannis Xenakis (1922–2001), Elliott Carter (b. 1908) and György Ligeti (b. 1923).

Section One: The Instruments

CLAVICHORD

One of the oldest keyboard instruments, the clavichord has its origins in the late-fourteenth century, and was used throughout Western Europe during the Renaissance. It maintained its popularity in German lands into the first quarter of the nineteenth century, when, like its cousin the harpsichord, it was decisively superseded by the piano.

PITCH AND TIMBRE

The clavichord is the most touch-responsive keyboard instrument yet devised. The piano's range of dynamics and tone colours is vastly greater than that of the clavichord, but once the key has been depressed and the hammer has hit the string, there is little or nothing the finger can do to affect the sound.

On the clavichord, the strings are set in vibration not by a hammer but with a tangent (a small, upright wedge, originally made of brass), which remains in contact with the string or strings it has set in motion for the duration of the sound. Its tone is small, but through deft manipulation of finger pressure it can be made to swell or diminish, to achieve a true *vibrato*, even to change its pitch. The clavichord is the only instrument in which the afterlife of a tone, once struck, can be substantially affected by finger pressure alone (the slightest fluctuation in touch will clearly register a difference in loudness or pitch). It is thus the only keyboard instrument that allows *vibrato* and can thus emulate the contours of the human voice, with all its subtlety of inflection.

Musical Instruments Handbook

FRETTED AND UNFRETTED MODELS

The usual shape of the clavichord is a rectangular box, with the keyboard set into or projecting from one of the longer sides, the strings (generally in pairs – two per note) lying at 90 degrees to the keyboard. It ranges in length from four feet (common) to seven (a late-eighteenth-century development, spurred by the development of the piano).

Since the pitch is determined not by the length of the strings, as in the piano, but by the distance between the tangent and the bridge, it was frequent practice to assign two, or even three, notes to any given pair of strings. Such models are known as 'fretted' clavichords. By going for notes unlikely ever to be sounded simultaneously – C and C#, for example – makers could economize on the size and hardware of the instrument, crucial to the majority of buyers, whose rooms would not easily accommodate a harpsichord. In the mid- to late-eighteenth century, clavichords were often built unfretted, with a separate pair of strings for each key. Some instruments were built with two manuals – effectively one clavichord on top of another and a pedal keyboard, for the practice use of organists.

▲ *Clavichords were popular for solo recitals until the early-nineteenth century.*

AN INTIMATE INSTRUMENT

With all its subtleties, it is small wonder that the clavichord was so beloved of Bach (who prized 'singingness' above all other musical virtues), and of Mozart and Beethoven after him – despite their ownership and mastery of the latest pianos. Until the advent of the electronic piano, with its attendant headphones, the clavichord remained the most intimate of all instruments, its sound so small that it can be played late at night with no fear of waking any but the lightest sleeper, in the same room. This, combined with its supreme sensitivity, explains why it was dubbed by one eighteenth-century lady, 'that thrilling confidante of solitude'.

Section One: The Instruments

PIANO

In 1905, and probably for several decades before that, there were more pianos in the United States than there were bathtubs. In Europe, throughout the nineteenth century, piano sales increased at a greater rate than the population. English, French and German makers dispatched veritable armies of pianos to every corner of the Earth. It was the instrument of the age.

A ROMANTIC SYMBOL

Born around 1700, in the twilight of the traditional master craftsman, the piano grew to maturity as one of the greatest commercial and technological triumphs of the Industrial Revolution. Merely as a machine, with its hundreds of factory-made parts, combining the exotic substances of ivory and ebony (the keyboard) with iron, steel and copper (the strings, and later the frame), it was an object of reverence – not least as a bountiful source of employment. As a symbol of the Romantic era, it had extraordinary potency. Simply to own one was perceived as a badge of respectability. But the piano's ascent to the stars had been a long, slow burn.

ORIGINS AND DEVELOPMENT

The first piano was constructed in Florence by the Italian harpsichord-maker Bartolomeo Cristofori (1655–1731). From the grandiloquent title he gave it –

Musical Instruments Handbook

gravicembalo col piano e forte ('large harpsichord with soft and loud'), it seems clear that he regarded it not so much as a new instrument as the modification of an old one. Needless to say, the cumbersome name evaporated, replaced first by 'fortepiano', then by its transposition 'pianoforte', and finally, in the twentieth century, by the simpler and less pompous 'piano'. Cristofori's title was inept, since harpsichords already had the capacity to play both 'soft and loud' – albeit only in stark juxtaposition. What made his instrument unique was a mechanism by which the volume could be made to increase or decrease by finger pressure alone.

The two domestic keyboard instruments that had ruled the roost from the height of the Renaissance to the end of the Baroque (around 1450 to 1750), were beset by increasingly frustrating limitations. The clavichord, with its touch-sensitive keyboard, was capable of extraordinary nuance and tonal variety, but its sound was too small to project across a large room, let alone a concert hall. Even at the apex of its development, it remained essentially a player's instrument. The harpsichord had the requisite power but entirely lacked the clavichord's expressive, almost vocal suppleness of line. What was needed, in a world where public music-making was steadily advancing, was an instrument combining the virtues of both with none of their drawbacks. Cristofori's piano may have been only a start, but its principles remained the basis for all such developments over the next 100 years.

In Italy, strange to say – the cradle of the instrumental concerto and opera – Cristofori's invention aroused a brief flurry of interest and was then pretty much forgotten. In Germany, by contrast, the piano was an idea whose time had come.

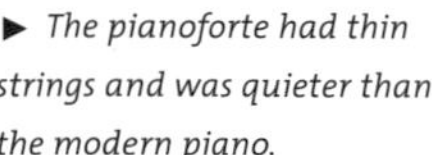

► *The pianoforte had thin strings and was quieter than the modern piano.*

Section One: The Instruments

▲ *Countless artists owe their success to the development of the piano.*

NECESSITY BREEDS INVENTION

Throughout much of the seventeenth and eighteenth centuries, Germany had been experiencing a rise in 'feeling' that led straight to the Romantic movement, as exemplified in literature by Goethe and Schiller. What had begun as a religious movement known as Pietism, dedicated to the humanizing of worship, had developed into a generalized worship of 'sensibility'. Unsurprisingly, the small-toned, touch-sensitive clavichord was much cultivated by the Pietists.

As the eighteenth century wore on, however, the thrill of solitude increasingly gave way to the thrill of exhibitionism. Emotion was celebrated above logic, song above form, humanity above doctrine. What was needed to voice the warm humanity of this strongly family-based society was an instrument combining the melodic subtlety of the clavichord with the power and grandeur of the biggest harpsichords.

Any instrument that is restricted to a very narrow dynamic range, like the clavichord, or confined to a set number of inflexible dynamic levels, like the harpsichord, is correspondingly limited in the range of emotions it can embrace. The piano, on the other hand, can move smoothly from one dynamic extreme to another, and any number of contrasts in between. The stage was thus set for a spectacular and prolonged instrumental success.

Musical Instruments Handbook

GERMAN PIANOS

In 1730, Gottfried Silbermann, already renowned for his clavichords and organs made the first German piano. He is often credited (along with a number of others from various countries) with inventing what is surely the piano's most unique feature – the sustaining pedal (often miscalled the 'loud' pedal), which raises all the dampers of the instrument *en masse*, freeing all the strings to vibrate simultaneously, regardless of what keys are depressed. Thus the right hand can execute an *arpeggio* from the lowest part of the keyboard to the highest with every note continuing to sound. The device pays dividends even with the striking of a solitary key. The sounding of a single note – for example C – in the bass, can trigger the sympathetic vibrations of every other C on the piano, greatly increasing the depth and richness of the tone by virtue of what might be described as a synchronized multiple echo. Until the late-eighteenth century, the mechanism was operated not by a pedal but by a knee-lever.

Next to this, from the 1720s onwards, was the so-called 'soft' or *una corda* pedal, which derives its Italian name from the days when the piano had two rather than the modern three strings per note. Depressing the pedal with the left foot shifts the entire keyboard, action and hammers to the right, so that the hammers strike one less string than usual – one in the case of the fortepiano (hence *una corda*, literally 'one string' – and two on the fully fledged grand. Just as the sustaining pedal is not primarily a 'loud' pedal, so the *una corda* is not primarily 'soft', but an agent of subtle tone-colouring.

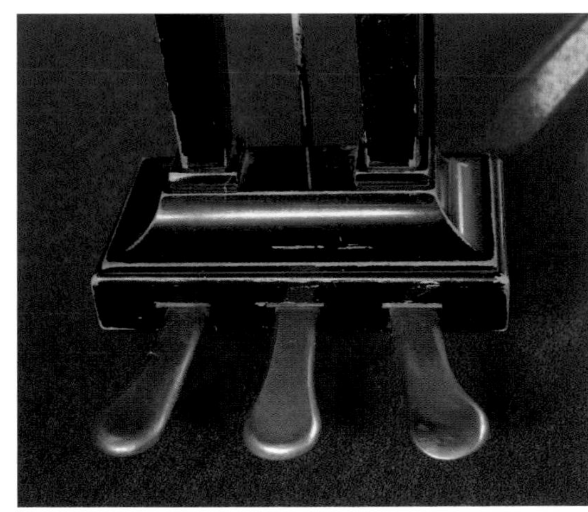

▲ *Piano pedals, left to right: mute, sostenuto and sustaining pedals.*

Even in Germany, more than half a century passed between the piano's invention and its first public airing (in Vienna, in 1763), and even then it seems to have made little impression. Not until 1768, in Dublin, was it publicly unveiled as a solo instrument. A fortnight later, on 2 June, it made its solo debut in England, played by Johann Christian Bach (1735–82). Now, at last, time, place and circumstance combined to welcome it. In a very short time, the piano took its place as the most fashionable instrument in town.

Section One: The Instruments

JOHANNES ZUMPE

▲ *The modern piano suits all genres of music – classical, pop and jazz.*

Living and working in London at that time was one Johannes Zumpe, a former apprentice to Silbermann in Germany. The rapidly evolving keyboard market in London was dominated at that time by the firms of Shudi, Broadwood and Kirkman, whose instruments, in the venerable tradition of the continental craftsman, were made exclusively for the moneyed aristocracy, and were priced accordingly. Zumpe was the first to recognize the potential custom of the rising middle classes and set out to make and market pianos at a price they could afford. To that end, he simplified Cristofori's action, which had remained essentially unaltered through five decades, and adopted the modest rectangular form of the clavichord. His success was almost instantaneous and he rapidly entered the history books as the father of the commercial piano.

▲ *A concert piano consists of over 12,000 parts.*

JOHANN ANDREAS STEIN

In Germany, Johann Andreas Stein (1728–92), an accomplished and sensitive musician, produced more than 700 pianos, which were widely copied and thus became the foundation of the Viennese tradition in piano-building. The most far-reaching of his many contributions was the invention of the 'hopper action', or 'escapement', whereby the hammer is enabled to fall away from the string while the activating key is still depressed.

Stein's enthusiastic endorsement by Mozart in 1777 set the seal on the perennially fruitful association of piano builders with the leading composers of

Musical Instruments Handbook

the day. In old age, his business was mainly carried on by his daughter Nanette (herself a pianist of genius, according to the normally unsparing Mozart, and a close friend of Beethoven). In 1794, the business was augmented by her marriage to Johann Andreas Streicher, one of the lynchpins of the Austrian piano tradition.

At the end of the eighteenth century, three basic designs were in common use: that of the 'grand', which retained the essential, wing-shaped structure of the harpsichord, the upright; and the so-called 'square', whose rectangular, box-like form grew out of the fad for reconstructed clavichords. Indeed in form and general construction they were little different from their predecessors, apart from the metal strings, a considerably strengthened frame, necessitated by the resulting increase in tension, and of course the hammer action.

▲ *The outer case of a quality piano is usually veneered maple or beech.*

Fact

The average concert grand today measures 2.74 m (9 ft) in length, weighs in at around 635 kg (1,400 lbs), and has more than 7,000 moving parts. Its minimum of 234 strings are of steel, with three strings per key, except the bottom two octaves, where there is two. The hammers are covered with densely compressed felt, and the overall string tension is well over 20 metric tons.

GRAND PIANOS

There is a significant difference between the pianos of the 1700s and the concert grands of today. Well into the eighteenth century, they were closer in sound and construction to the harpsichord than the instrument of our time. The strings were fewer and thinner, the frame was of wood and the hammers, covered in leather, were both lighter and harder. For many decades, the piano was less brilliant and less powerful in sound than the biggest harpsichords of the time.

Section One: The Instruments

SQUARE PIANOS

The first known square piano was built in Germany in 1742, almost 20 years before Zumpe produced the first English model. Later, Zumpe was overtaken by John Broadwood, whose first original square pianos date from 1780, and whose clients included some of the greatest musicians of the day – Beethoven foremost among them. In 1775, Johann Behrend had exhibited his square piano in Philadelphia, and within a year of that, Sébastien Erard in Paris produced the first French model.

▲ *Piano hammers consist of woollen felt wrapped around maple.*

Even at this time, though, the instrument left a great deal to be desired. Its tone, in particular, was weak, and was hardly to be compared with that of the grand. In the early 1780s, however, John Broadwood hit on the idea of moving the wrest plank – that part of a keyboard instrument into which the tuning pins are driven – from the right-hand side (its traditional siting in the clavichord) to the back of the case. The improvement in tone and volume exceeded his hopes and transformed the construction of square pianos. Within a short time it was universally adopted, and with it the European contribution to the instrument's evolution came unexpectedly to a halt. Thereafter, all significant improvements came from America, where the square piano enjoyed a unique popularity for the best part of a century. By 1890, however, its sun had set.

UPRIGHT PIANOS

The radical relocation of the strings, hammers and soundboard to make the upright piano involved considerable technical challenges. Even today, the best upright seldom equals the quality, versatility and resonance of a good grand, but its staying power is a matter of record.

Musical Instruments Handbook

The idea of the upright was hardly new. As early as 1480, the harpsichord had been up-ended, with its action suitably adapted, and was given the grandiloquent name of 'Clavicytherium'. In 1795, William Stodart of London applied the same idea to the grand piano, and three years later William Southwell of Dublin tried the same thing with a square piano. In each of these cases, however, the instrument rested on a stand. Not until 1800 did it occur to anyone to let the instrument rest upon the floor, and then it occurred to two men simultaneously, on opposite sides of the Atlantic: Matthias Muller in Vienna and Isaac Hawkins in Philadelphia.

COMPOSER-PIANISTS

From the 1770s, the majority of pianos were designed for and sold to the amateur market, in which the square and the upright remained the dominant models. Grands have always been costly and inimical to small rooms. Their evolution has been guided not by the requirements of the domestic pianist, but by the demands of the great virtuosos and the music they played. From the Renaissance to the first half of the nineteenth century, the great virtuosos were almost always important composers – think only of Bach, Handel, Domenico Scarlatti (1685–1757), Mozart, Muzio Clementi (1752–1832), Beethoven, Johann Hummel (1778–1837), Chopin and Liszt. Of the great composer-pianists before 1850, only Mozart, Hummel and Chopin were content to work with what they had. Beethoven and Liszt, above all, regularly wrote and played beyond what the available instruments could accommodate – and caused serious injury to many pianos in the process.

▼ *The great Romantic concertos, including Chopin's, were written for pianos different from today's.*

Section One: The Instruments

▲ *In the 1800s, careers as concert musicians were generally only open to men.*

If Hummel and his teacher Clementi may be said to have represented the transition between the Classical and Romantic styles, their younger pupils and colleagues – most notably Liszt, Carl Czerny (1791–1857), Frédéric Kalkbrenner (1785–1849), Sigismund Thalberg (1812–71) and Henri Herz (1803–88) – allied themselves firmly with the latter. They were by no means the first composer-pianists to write immensely difficult works for the instrument, but in the emphasis they placed on *bravura*, on technical innovation and virtuoso display, they were very much sons of their age.

NINETEENTH-CENTURY DEVELOPMENTS

For various reasons – among them the pervasive influence of the 'demon fiddler' Nicolò Paganini (1782–1840) and the growing interest in orchestral and operatic music – the piano music of the nineteenth century is full of figures with repeated notes in imitation of the violin *tremolando*. And here pianists and composers were at least one step ahead of the manufacturers. In order to fulfil

▲ *Piano strings are steel; bass strings have a steel core overwound in copper.*

Musical Instruments Handbook

the requirements both of the new virtuoso style and the amateur craze for transcriptions and arrangements, an action was needed where the note could sound at two different levels of the key – that is to say, where the key itself needn't rise to its full height in order to re-strike.

In 1821, Sébastien Erard in Paris achieved the breakthrough – an action combining a powerful stroke with a light flexible touch, enabling the player to re-strike any note with a rapidity beyond the capacity of the 'hopper action' devised by Stein. It was an epoch-making invention and forms the basis of virtually all 'double escapement' actions to this day. It might also be said to have provided the model on which the whole of modern piano technique was built.

FINAL STAGES OF EVOLUTION

Less subtle but perhaps more urgent was the need to build pianos to withstand the increasing force brought to bear on them by performers and composers alike. Despite a widespread belief that the introduction of iron into the piano would impair the quality of tone, it was clear by the second decade of the nineteenth century that some form of metal frame was needed to withstand the stress. Well before the complete iron frame became established, however, many manufacturers experimented with various sizes, shapes and constitutions of metallic braces, either solid bars or various lengths and diameters of tubing.

▲ *A piano's white keys used to be made from ivory, bone or even mother-of-pearl.*

Among the first pioneers of the fully integrated iron frame were Karl Röllig, who was experimenting with the idea as early as 1795, and Isaac Hawkins in Philadelphia who patented a metal frame in 1800. But it was Alpheus Babcock who made history with his patenting in 1825 of the first full, single-cast metal frame. All subsequent developments of the cast-iron frame derived from this device. In the story of its journey to perfection, a special place must be accorded to Jonas Chickering of Boston, whose single-cast grand-piano frame of 1843 represents a significant landmark in the piano's evolution.

Section One: The Instruments

The last step in the evolution of the piano was the introduction of cross-stringing – the arrangement of the higher strings in the form of a fan, spreading over the largest part of the soundboard, and with the bass strings crossing them at a higher level. Cross-stringing was invented by Babcock around 1830, but was not generally adopted until 1855, when Steinway & Sons of New York gave it its definitive form. Since then there have been numerous, relatively minor innovations that make the sound between an 1855 Steinway and a 1955 model significantly different, mainly in the area of power, but apart from the invention in 1862 of the so-called *sostenuto* pedal – which sustains the sound only of those notes held down at the time of its depression – the piano was now fully fledged.

PIANO TYPES

No survey of this instrument would be complete, however, without recognizing that the piano, like the harpsichord, clavichord and virginals before it, has always lived a double life – as a musical instrument on the one hand, and as an item of furniture on the other. Among the displays at London's Great Exhibition of 1851 was William Jenkin's 'Expanding and Collapsing Piano for Gentlemen's Yachts, the saloons of steam ships, ladies' cabins etc., only 13½ inches from front to back when collapsed.' At around the same time, Broadwood offered the potential buyer a stress-inducing choice of styles, including 'Sheraton, Jacobean, Tudor, Gothic, Louis XIII, XIV, XV and XVI, Flemish Renaissance, Elizabethan *cinquecento*, Queen Anne, Empire and Moorish'.

▲ *Different pianists are drawn to the tone, action and response of different manufacturers.*

The ingenious Henri Pape of Paris could provide instruments of almost any size and shape. Round, oval, hexagonal, pyramidic, concealed within a table or a

Musical Instruments Handbook

▲ *The piano is a crucial instrument in jazz, as well as most other western complex musical genres.*

writing desk, or brazenly displayed as a trendy conversation piece. Most spectacular of all, however, was a Victorian aberration patented by a Mr Milward. To paraphrase the inventor's own description, 'the piano is supported by a frame which rests upon a hollow base, containing a couch, which is mounted upon rollers and can be drawn out in front of the piano'. Also discreetly contained are 'a closet, designed to contain the bedclothes, a bureau with drawers, and a second closet containing a wash-basin, jug, towels, and other articles of toilet'. Another part of the invention consists of a music stool 'so arranged that it contains a work-box, a looking-glass, a writing-desk or table, and a small set of drawers.'

Section One: The Instruments

PLAYER PIANO

The name 'player piano' is a misnomer, indeed the precise opposite of the truth. In fact, this is a playerless piano – a piano that plays itself.

ORIGINS OF THE PLAYER PIANO

Though almost exclusively associated with the early-twentieth century, the idea of a self-playing piano had been around for centuries. Henry VIII's self-playing virginals and Clementi's studded-cylinder piano of 1825 were part of the same dream. The key to its fulfilment was forged with the invention of the automatic loom in 1804. In this device, a perforated card on a cylinder allowed certain needles to pass through it while rejecting others. The same principle could be applied to 'needles' of air, pumped by a bellows. In the case of the piano or the organ, this would determine the movement of the keys.

The first complete pneumatic piano-player was patented in 1863, but made no headway. By the turn of the century, though, the machinery had advanced to the stage where the left foot pedalled the bellows, leaving the right to manage the sustaining pedal while the hands manipulated the speed and volume controls as the 'player' saw fit.

PIANOLA

Two significantly different types of player piano emerged. One, popularly known as the Pianola, furnished a roll containing nothing more than the bare notes (or perforated equivalents) of whatever the piece happened to be, leaving the 'interpretation' entirely in the hands of the operator. Rolls soon appeared, however, with specific, anonymous guidelines as to how the tempo and rhythm of any given piece should be controlled. By 1905, such instructions were increasingly replaced by authorized interpretations of various world-famous pianists.

Musical Instruments Handbook

MIGNON

In 1904, in Freiburg, Germany, Edwin Welte invented a device by means of which a piano roll, properly perforated, could record with a then-unprecedented degree of fidelity performances given by living pianists. He called it *Mignon* and soon persuaded many of the greatest pianists and composers of the day to record on it. It could be fitted to any piano, and was frequently added to otherwise conventional instruments by such makers as Steinway, Chickering, Broadwood, Knabe, Weber and Steck. The Welte-Mignon mechanism alone was available at one time in 115 different makes of piano. The extent of its fidelity remains hotly debated, and in any case, the invention of electrical recording in 1926 inevitably put an end to the careers of all such systems.

While it was some decades before the gramophone could rival the actual sonority of the instrument, it could catch details and subtleties of nuance more convincingly than even the best piano rolls. An unexpected bonus of the reproducing piano, however, was its liberation of composers from the hitherto-insuperable limitations of a pianist's 10 fingers. Among noted figures who took advantage of this to write directly for the new instrument were Stravinsky, Paul Hindemith (1895–1963), Gian Francesco Malipiero (1882–1973), Herbert Howells (1892–1983), and the American Conlon Nancarrow (1912–97), who decided to devote his entire output to the medium, as it allowed him incredible precision beyond the gift of pianists to perform and control of the performance of his works impossible before the advent of the computer.

▲ *The piano rolls in player-pianos are usually no more than 30 m (100 ft) long.*

Section One: The Instruments

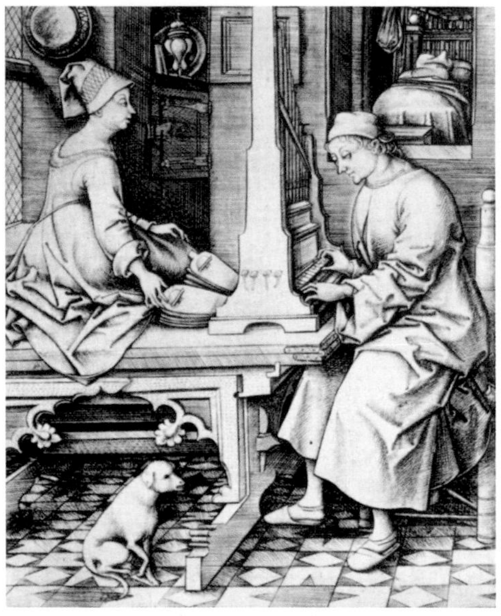

▲ *The positive organ, larger than the portative, required two people to operate it.*

ORGAN

The organ is an instrument of extremes – the biggest, the loudest, the lowest, the highest, the oldest, the newest and the most complex, it is also among the smallest, the most intimate, the most modest, and the simplest.

ORGAN EXTREMES

The aptly named portative organ – much played from the twelfth through the sixteenth centuries – rested comfortably on the player's lap, while being pumped with the left hand and played by the right. Slung from the neck by a strap, it could even be played in transit, like the bagpipes.

In Atlantic City's Convention Hall, by contrast, there is the largest organ ever built. A deaf and vibration-insensitive tenant could quite feasibly live inside it, walking the length of several city blocks each day without retracing a single step. Equipped with two giant consoles, one with seven manuals, the other with five, it has 1,225 'speaking' stops and 33,000 pipes.

Between these extremes, the variation is enormous. Such extravagances were not just typically vulgar examples of the twentieth century. In the city of Winchester, England, more than 1,000 years ago an organ was raised that had 26 bellows, worked by 70 strong men 'labouring with their arms, covered with perspiration, each inciting his companions to drive the wind up with all its strength, that the full-bosomed box might speak with its 400 pipes'. It was played by two organists on two keyboards,

Fact

In the Atlantic City organ, the wiring on the instrument, if stretched out, would encircle the Earth twice over.

Musical Instruments Handbook

▲ *Organ design varies according to geography and time.*

each with 20 'sliders' (long wooden slats with holes corresponding to those at the foot of the pipes), and its effect was such that 'everyone stops with his hands his gaping ears, being in no wise able to draw near and bear the sound'.

In 1429, more than 250 years before Bach's birth, the organ of Amiens Cathedral in France had 2,500 pipes, the lowest of which were the sequoias of their kind, fit to make the very Earth tremble.

ANCIENT INSTRUMENTS

Though among the most complex of instruments, the organ is also among the oldest, reaching back more than 2,000 years. The earliest-known example is the *hydraulus* of 250 BC, a highly refined, mechanically advanced Greek invention, in which the air column was regulated by water pressure. The first exclusively bellows-powered organ followed some 400 years later. By the eighth century, organs were being built in Europe, and by the tenth century, their association with the church had been established.

Despite its great antiquity, the underlying principles of the organ remained essentially unchanged between AD 250 and the advent of electronic instruments in the twentieth century. The usefulness of electricity has by no means put a stop to traditional methods, which are still much preferred by the majority of organists.

▶ *This organ at Alexandra Palace, London, was made by master organ builder Henry ('Father') Willis in 1875.*

Section One: The Instruments

▲ *Organ pipes are arranged in ranks: a set of pipes is tuned to a chromatic scale.*

ORGAN MECHANICS

Alone among instruments, the tone of the organ can be sustained indefinitely and unchangingly, merely by depressing a key and holding it down. The force or implement used to depress the key is irrelevant to the sound produced. Prior to the advent of certain electronic instruments, the organ, in all its many forms, was (and normally remains) the least touch-sensitive of all instruments. At its grandest, it is also the loudest.

If the basic principle of organ mechanics is essentially a simple one, its ramifications and development over two millennia are both very many and highly complex. The mechanism consists of the following:

- An unvarying supply of wind, kept under constant pressure – originally by a hand-pump operated by an assistant, later by electricity.
- One or more manuals (keyboards) and a pedal board (laid out on the model of the conventional keyboard and connected with the pipes by means of 'trackers' (a series of levers), electro-pneumatic devices, or electrical contacts).

Musical Instruments Handbook

- Pipes of various sizes, shapes and constitution, arranged in scalewise order.
- Various 'stops', which channel wind to each register or set of pipes.

▲ *The pedal board is essentially a large keyboard played with the feet.*

PIPES

The pipes are of two basic kinds:

- Flue type (modelled on the open sounds of flutes and recorders.
- Reed type, based on the more nasal sounds of oboes, bassoons, clarinets etc.

The sole determinant of pitch is the length of the pipe. A demonstration of the same phenomenon can be achieved by blowing across the tops of bottles containing different amounts of water. The mechanics of the organ take the effort out of blowing and never run out of breath.

▲ *Electronic organs were designed as low-cost, pipe-organ substitutes.*

The pipes are arranged over a 'wind chest', connected to the keys through a set of valves and supplied with air by means of bellows, mechanically or electrically controlled. Each rank, or set of pipes, is activated by a stop connected to a slider in the same manner as the keys are to the pipes. For a pipe to 'speak', the holes in the slider must be aligned with the bottom, or 'foot', of the pipes. The depression of a key opens the valve under a pipe, allowing the air to travel along a narrow channel, on through the hole in the slider, and finally up into the pipe.

Section One: The Instruments

PITCH

▲ *The organ stops (either side of the manuals) imitate different instruments.*

Each rank represents the same type of pipe (register) but at differing levels of pitch. Using the ratios of pitch to pipe-length, organists thus refer to stops as 8-foot (indicating normal pitch level, as on the piano), 16-foot (an octave below normal), 4-foot (an octave higher), and so on. Some stops (known as mutation stops) produce a different pitch altogether, for example a stop marked as '$1\frac{1}{3}$' would sound two octaves and a perfect fifth higher. Other stops – 'mixtures'– combine a number of different ranks at different pitches to produce an entire chord (comprising, usually, a number of the harmonics of the relevant note) when a single key is depressed. Excluding such aberrations as the Atlantic City organ, the pipes will tend to range from 10 m (32 ft) to less than 2.5 cm (1 in), giving the organ a wider compass than any other instrument (nine octaves, as opposed to the piano's seven).

ORGAN RANKS

The ranks are grouped into several separate sections called divisions. Each has a name and is controlled through its own manual or the pedal-board. Of the several manual divisions, the most common are: Great, Swell, and Choir or Positive. There is only one Pedal division. An organ, then, like an army, is organized, quite literally, into separate divisions, each with its own manual and comprising a number of ranks, controlled by a single stop. However, a stop may also activate more than one rank, or less.

▲ *Other manual divisions are known as Solo, Orchestral, Echo and Antiphonal.*

Two manuals and pedals are the minimum requirement for playing the bulk of the legitimate

Musical Instruments Handbook

organ repertoire. A large instrument, however, may have five, six or even seven manuals, one banked above another, each controlling its own families of tones and pitches.

TWENTIETH-CENTURY ORGANS

The greatest watershed in the 2,000-year history of the organ occurred in the twentieth century, with the advent of the electronic organ – a portmanteau term for organs whose tone is generated by electronic circuits and radiated by speakers in place of pipes. Their nearest ancestor was the American inventor Thaddeus Cahill's 200-metric-ton, 60-foot, keyboard-operated telharmonium, which used rotating, electromagnetic tone-wheels to generate the sound. Made in 1904, it soon lapsed, despite its bulk, into predictable obscurity. Its more modest successors, by contrast, were specifically designed as an economical and compact substitute for the traditional and more complex pipe organ.

▲ *In the silent film era, large theatre organs were installed in many cinemas.*

The most famous of all electronic organs is known by the name of its inventor Laurens Hammond (also American), who patented it in 1934. Unlike most other instruments of its type, it produces its sound through a complex set of rotary, motor-driven generators, and is capable of a great variety of tone colours. In the 1960s, circuits and components designed to operate television, radio receivers and stereos were adapted to generate music. The great breakthrough, however, came in the 1970s, when digital microcircuitry was used to create a computer organ in which sounds are not created internally but have been prerecorded and stored in the computer from which they can then be retrieved at will. Musical tones recorded from conventional pipe organs are coded in digital form and can be recreated by computer at the touch of the keys and stops.

Section One: The Instruments

BARREL ORGAN

On the face of it, barrels and music would seem unlikely bedfellows. Their alliance, however, goes back at least to the ninth century, when the first detailed description of a barrel organ appeared in an Arab treatise.

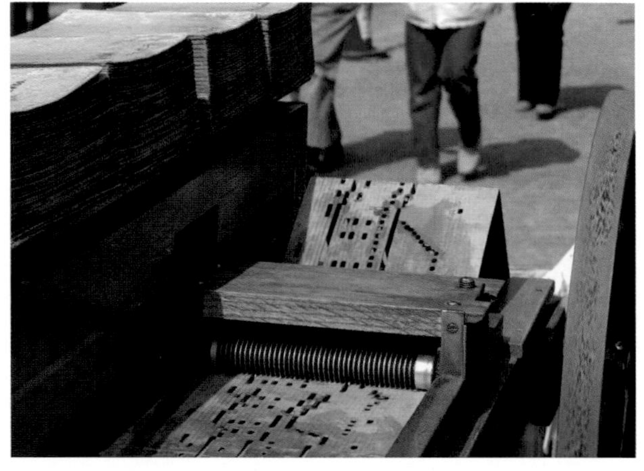

MECHANICS OF THE BARREL ORGAN

The mechanical principle underlying all such instruments, from the automated organ and piano to the spectacular mechanical orchestras of the nineteenth century, for which Beethoven composed his notorious *Battle Symphony*. At its heart is a revolving cylinder or barrel, placed horizontally and bearing brass or steel pins which open (or trigger the opening) of the required pipes or keys. These are activated by puffs or currents of air provided by bellows, which are operated by the same motion that turns the barrel. The simplest of these are the little hand-cranked 'lap' organs used in the eighteenth century to teach canaries melodies These of course produced only unaccompanied melodic lines.

From the sixteenth century onwards, barrels were widely used for mechanical organs and musical clocks, and many were powered by a waterwheel. Such instruments were often found in the more affluent gardens of Italy and Austria. Other organs were propelled by weight-driven clockwork.

EUROPEAN DEVELOPMENTS

In Tudor England there were barrel-operated virginals, and 1687 saw a combined organ-and-spinet with 16 pipes and 16 strings, all within a single clock. In 1736, George Frideric Handel (1685–1759) wrote and arranged numerous pieces

Musical Instruments Handbook

▲ *Barrel organs now generally run on piano rolls.*

for a clock that played both bells and organ pipes. In 1790 Mozart composed a great masterpiece expressly for a form of barrel organ.

Hand-cranked barrel pianos first appeared, in Italy, late in the eighteenth century. Initially small, but by the 1880s resembling an upright piano and placed on a two-wheeled cart, they were made and played almost exclusively by Italians, until Mussolini banned all street music in 1922.

COMPOSITIONS FOR BARREL ORGAN

With one important exception, barrel organs and other related instruments were used primarily for mostly domestic entertainment. In eighteenth- and nineteenth-century England, however, they served a purpose both practical and spiritual, providing psalm and hymn tunes, chants and voluntaries in churches and chapels throughout the land, effectively sidelining the parish organist for the best part of 200 years. The ordinary street organ joined the urban landscape at the beginning of the nineteenth century, flourishing in the streets of London and other English towns until the outbreak of the First World War.

Many of the grander barrel organs disgorged numerous overtures, symphonic movements, selections from operas, sets of waltzes and other music. One of these had a formative influence on the child Piotr Ilyich Tchaikovsky (1840–93).

In 1825, Clementi in London produced a machine that marked a new chapter in the story of the piano, though its full import was not perceived at the time. 'This curious instrument,' wrote one critic, 'furnished with a horizontal cylinder, and put into motion by a steel spring, performs without external force or manual operation, the most difficult and intricate compositions.' For amateur piano players, the writing was on the wall.

Section One: The Instruments

HARMONIUM

Often regarded as the country cousin (and hence the bumpkin) of the organ family, the harmonium did add a touch of warmth to many nineteenth-century rural homes, where the purchase of a piano would have been an unaffordable luxury. But the two instruments often cohabited, too.

HARMONIUM COMPOSITIONS

Today, unlike the piano, the harmonium is a rarity, ousted among other things by its electronic successors, but it was never a bumpkin. Many distinguished composers have taken it very seriously, among them Tchaikovsky, Gioacchino Rossini (1792–1868), Antonin Dvorák (1841–1904), César Franck (1822–90), Camille Saint-Saëns (1835–1921), Max Reger (1873–1916), and the lesser-known (though famous to organists) Siegfried Karg Elert (1877–1933), who not only wrote a book on the art of registration on the harmonium but toured as a recitalist on it.

▲ *The Estey harmonium was widely used in the Second World War.*

Saint-Saëns wrote a set of six pieces. Franck arranged his own *Prelude, Fugue, and Variations* and composed many other pieces specifically for the instrument. The original scoring of Rossini's *Petite Messe solenelle* was for two pianos and harmonium. The only keyboard music Hector Berlioz (1803–69) ever wrote are three pieces for harmonium (1845), and nothing in the chamber-music repertoire exceeds the charm and warmth of Dvorák's delectable *Bagatelles* (Op. 47) for two violins, cello and harmonium.

Musical Instruments Handbook

FREE REEDS

The harmonium belongs to the family of 'free-reed' instruments that includes not only the accordion and concertina but such ancient instruments as the near-universal jew's harp and the *sheng* of China, whose importation to St Petersburg in the eighteenth century is said to have directly inspired the precursors of the harmonium.

In all of these, the sound is produced by 'reeds' (generally brass in the case of the harmonium) mounted in a frame and set vibrating by gusts of air, usually activated by bellows. In the case of many early, portable harmoniums – especially in America, where they are often called melodeons – the instrument rested on the knees, the bellows being operated by one elbow while the hands attended to the keys.

▲ *The player pumps the bellows with one hand and plays with the other.*

HARMONIUM MECHANICS

At the grander end of the spectrum there is the handsome two-manual instrument, like the harpsichord and smaller organs, the reeds now encased in an impressive cabinet, while the bellows are pumped in alternation by the feet. The volume of tone, and a measure of shading too, is directly affected by the speed of the pedalling, and multiple ranks of reeds constitute stops of varying tone quality and register, analogous to those of a pipe organ. In the larger harmoniums there are two 'knee swells', one of which, by a sideways pressure of the knee on a projecting piece of wood, brings the full power of the instrument into action, while the other operates on the principle of the swell pedal of the organ. The standard repertoire consisted of many hymns and sentimental songs, offset by a soufflé of polkas, waltzes, marches and simple arrangements of operatic arias.

Section One: The Instruments

► *The harmonium is used in nearly all Indian musical genres except south Indian classical.*

INDIAN HARMONIUM

The decline of the harmonium in the west was balanced in the twentieth century by its enormous popularity in the Indian subcontinent. It reached India by means of missionaries, who took with them French, hand-pumped versions of the instrument. Its ease of use and portability quickly made it popular among the native people. In the following decades, the Indians took the basic French design of the harmonium, and further developed it, adding, among other things, drone stops and a scale-changing device.

The instrument remains an important part of Indian music to this day, particularly among Sikhs (to whom it is known as the *vaja*), who use in their prayer-songs. It is considered to be a versatile instrument. Until recently it was largely heard as an accompaniment to vocal music in India, along with the tabla. However, in the past few years, more and more Indian musicians have seen the harmonium's potential as a solo instrument. Among the pioneers of this breakthrough are Pandit Tulsidas Borkar and Arawind Thatte.

Musical Instruments Handbook

ACCORDION

Like its close relation the concertina, the accordion is a glorified mouth organ, in which the 'reeds' (now generally made of tempered steel) are set in vibration by a rectangular bellows.

The bellows are operated by the left hand, which also – as in all keyboard instruments – manipulates the so-called bass keyboard, in this case a collection of buttons, rather than keys proper, which produce both single notes and certain pre-ordained chords. The right hand operates the treble keyboard, often though not always modelled on the conventional piano keyboard, giving rise to the term 'piano accordion'. The instrument is suspended by shoulder straps, providing the hands and fingers with maximum room for manoeuvre.

HISTORY AND DEVELOPMENT

Though evidently invented by Christoph Ludwig Buschmann of Berlin in 1821, and further developed by Cyrillus Demian of Vienna in 1829, it achieved its first widespread marketing in Belgium and France, and is still most frequently identified with the popular music of those countries. This is particularly true of France, where it ranks to this day, in national stereotyping, just below bérets and louche moustaches.

Despite its association with popular music, it has quite often found its way into concert-hall compositions by, among others, Berg, Prokofiev, Mátyás Seiber, Paul Creston, Roy Harris, Virgil Thomson and many others. A music school exclusively for accordion teachers was established in Trossingen, Germany, in 1931, becoming a fully fledged state academy in 1948, and the British College of Accordionists has flourished since its inception in 1936, the American Accordionists Association since 1938. Accordions of one form or another are found in societies all over the globe.

▲ *Most modern accordions have buttons capable of producing entire chords.*

Section One: The Instruments

CONCERTINA

The affectionately nicknamed 'squeeze box' is the smallest of all conventional keyboard instruments, and the lowliest cousin of the organ (except the shirt-pocket harmonica). Strictly speaking, however, it has neither keys nor a keyboard. Nor has it a uniform shape.

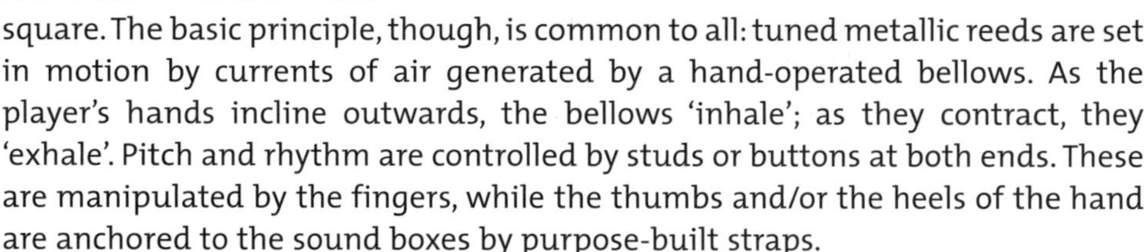

PLAYING TECHNIQUE

Whereas the standard English concertina is hexagonal, German and American models are square. The basic principle, though, is common to all: tuned metallic reeds are set in motion by currents of air generated by a hand-operated bellows. As the player's hands incline outwards, the bellows 'inhale'; as they contract, they 'exhale'. Pitch and rhythm are controlled by studs or buttons at both ends. These are manipulated by the fingers, while the thumbs and/or the heels of the hand are anchored to the sound boxes by purpose-built straps.

As on 'proper' keyboards, the left hand looks after the lower end of the pitch spectrum while the right hand attends to the upper. Considerable variety of both tone and volume can be achieved by contrasting alterations of the speed and force with which the hands control the instrument's 'breathing'. It comes in four different sizes – treble, tenor, bass and double-bass – covering between them a total range of just over six-and-a-half octaves.

ENGLISH AND EUROPEAN MODELS

One crucial difference separates the English concertina from its European cousins, namely that it sounds the same note on both extension and compression of the bellows, while the continental model sounds different degrees of the scale, each button thus producing different notes. Though widely

Musical Instruments Handbook

▲ *English Morris dancers with a concertina, accordion and fife and drum.*

associated with the so-called working classes, village dancehalls and shipboard distractions, the concertina, patented by its inventor Sir Charles Wheatstone (1802–75) in 1829, has stimulated a number of composers (albeit all of them minor) to write concertos and other concert hall works for it – among them an *Adagio For Eight Concertinas in E* and a *Quintet in D* for concertina, violin, viola, cello and piano by the Dutch composer Edouard Silas (1827–1909).

CONCERTINA COMPOSERS

Other concertina composers include Giulio Regondi (1827–72), Richard Blagrave (1826–95), George Case, Wheatstone himself, Bernhard Molique (1802–69), George Macfarren (1813–87), J. F. Barnett and Julius Benedict (1804–85). The instrument has also been drafted into the symphony orchestra, most notably by Charles Ives (1874–1954) and Percy Grainger (1882–1961). Alternative forms of it include the aeola of 1845, using an octagonal shape, and the 'Duet System' in which a full chromatic scale is provided on both keyboards. The best known variant, however, is the much larger bandoneon constructed by Heinrich Band (1821–60) and strongly favoured in South America, both in folk and popular music and in the works of Astor Piazzola (1921–92), who put the bandoneon indelibly on the musical map of the world.

Section One: The Instruments

INTRODUCTION

ELECTRIC AND ELECTRONIC

The development of electric and electronic musical instruments – as well as associated music-production systems – is one of the defining strands in the history of music over the last century. In fact, the advent of electric instruments predates even the twentieth century.

Some of the instruments discussed here – such as the electric guitar – are commonly recognizable. Others, such as the Chapman Stick or the Mellotron, are less well known, while some – such as the ill-fated Telharmonium – are nothing short of bizarre!

ELECTRIC AND ELECTRONIC

The terms 'electric' and 'electronic' are often interchanged erroneously. By convention, the term 'electric' refers to instruments that employ an electrical system to amplify and/or modify a sound that was originally produced by acoustic means. An obvious example of such an instrument is the electric guitar – an instrument in which the sound of the natural vibration of strings is amplified and modified by electrical means.

▼ *Electric keyboards were designed as portable pianos.*

On the other hand, an instrument like a synthesizer is referred to as 'electronic', because it generates its sounds entirely from electronic components – such as oscillators or microchips – with no natural, acoustic origin.

Musical Instruments Handbook

▼ *The vibes uses an electric motor to produce its breathy sound.*

A further subset of electric instruments is those that are known as 'electromechanical'. This term describes instruments in which an electric motor drives moving parts, which in turn are used to either generate or modify sound. Instruments in this category include the vibraphone and the Hammond organ.

SOUND

All sound begins as movement. A drumskin moves upon being struck; a taut string vibrates when plucked; a column of air moves across vocal chords. In turn, such movement displaces adjacent molecules of air. Each molecule then nudges and displaces its neighbour – rather like a succession of billiard balls bouncing into each other, or a 'Newton's Cradle', the familiar desktop toy. In this way, the original movement – or kinetic energy – from the sound source is transferred through air to the listener. This movement of air molecules causes the listener's eardrum to vibrate in a pattern directly related to the movement of the original sound source – the struck drum or vibrating string. The movement of the eardrum is then translated into electrical nervous energy (interpreted by the brain as sound) via a complicated system of tiny bones and a membrane suspended in the fluid of the inner ear.

▲ *Computers have revolutionized music, creating a need for controllers such as the Jazz Mutant Lemur.*

Fact

All electric and electronic instruments depend on the principle of transduction – the change of energy from one form to another. A device that changes energy from one form into another is known as a 'transducer'. Two of the most common transducers are the microphone and the loudspeaker.

Section One: The Instruments

MICROPHONE

Put simply, the job of a microphone is to turn sound into electricity. This is achieved by means of a diaphragm to which is attached a coil of wire around a magnet. As anyone who has ridden a bicycle with lamps powered by a dynamo knows, a coil of wire moved in a magnetic field produces an electrical current in the wire. Thus, acoustic energy arriving at the diaphragm of the microphone, causes the coil of wire to vibrate around the magnet. This induces an electrical signal in the wire – a signal that directly represents the characteristics of the original sound.

LOUDSPEAKER

A loudspeaker is, in fact, almost identical in construction to a microphone. It too comprises a diaphragm attached to a coil of wire around a magnet. However, the job is quite the reverse – to translate electrical energy into sound. When an electrical signal is passed through the coil of wire – in the magnet's field – the coil moves in relation to the magnet, causing the attached diaphragm to move in a pattern directly related to the original signal. This movement in turn causes the surrounding air to vibrate and thus the electrical signal has become acoustic energy – sound.

AMPLIFICATION

Once sound has been converted into an electrical signal, it can be amplified. A good high-fidelity amplifier will ensure that the resulting signal is an accurate copy of the original input – only louder. This is known as a 'linear response'. An inaccurate amplifier will introduce all sorts of distortion into the resulting sound. While it might appear to be undesirable, it is precisely this kind of effect that is sought after by, for instance, electric guitarists.

TAPE

Apart from the application of amplification and sound modification, another reason for converting sound into an electrical signal is that it can then be stored, manipulated and replayed. From the 1950s, the prime medium for

◄ *The electric guitar was the twentieth century's most defining instrument.*

Musical Instruments Handbook

recording music was magnetic tape. Sound, captured and converted into electrical signals by microphones, is stored on analogue magnetic tape as a series of varying magnetic patterns, which, when replayed, regenerate the original electrical signal and hence the original sound. However, recent years have seen the dominance of magnetic tape swept aside by the rise of digital recording and storage systems.

WHY DIGITAL?

Digital systems offer great advantages in terms of actual sound quality. While it is true that a well-set-up tape system can sound every bit as good as its digital counterpart, digital systems are, by and large, far less susceptible to hiss, noise and other unwanted artifacts. This is primarily because of the nature of digital signals which, comprising as they do a stream of binary ones and zeroes, are clear-cut and unambiguous.

In addition to this, digital signals are easily stored, manipulated and replayed on a computer. Put simply, computers – if they are good for anything – excel at saving, editing and recalling lots of numbers. This opens up countless creative opportunities for today's musicians.

Section One: The Instruments

TELHARMONIUM

The bizarre Telharmonium is widely regarded as the earliest example of a purely electronic instrument.

Patented in 1897 by Thaddeus Cahill (1867–1934), a lawyer and inventor from Washington D.C., the Telharmonium pioneered several important technologies. The sound was generated by a series of electromechanical tone wheels (rather like the Hammond organ), each of which produced a pure sine tone – one per note. Using the technique of additive synthesis, Cahill included additional tone wheels, the output of which could be used to colour the sound and produce different instrumental timbres.

The sound was controlled by multiple sets of touch-sensitive, polyphonic keyboards, each with 36 notes per octave, tuneable to frequencies between 40 Hz and 4000 Hz. The instrument was usually played by two performers (four hands) and repertoire tended to be popular classics of the day by people like Johann Sebastian Bach (1685–1750), Frédéric Chopin (1810–49) and Gioacchino Rossini (1792–1868).

TELHARMONIUM PERFORMANCES

Although a small number of performances were given in front of live audiences, Cahill's vision was to transmit music to listeners down phone lines. He achieved this by connecting paper cones to ordinary telephone receivers in order to amplify the sound sufficiently. (Cahill's work predated the invention of the amplifier by some 20 years.)

AN UNWIELDY INSTRUMENT

Although the Telharmonium contained some extraordinarily forward-thinking technologies, it was doomed to failure. For a start, it was simply enormous. In addition, telephone users complained that Telharmonium music could be heard across the network, intruding on conversations. Faced with growing competition from the new Wurlitzer organ and wireless transmissions, Cahill's company went bankrupt. Only three Telharmoniums were ever built – none survive and, sadly, no recordings of this remarkable instrument exist.

Musical Instruments Handbook

HAMMOND ORGAN

The term electric, or electromechanical, organ is used to describe instruments that produce sounds using a dynamo-like system of moving parts – as opposed to electronic organs that employ solid-state electronics.

LAURENS HAMMOND

In the same way that 'Hoover' is used instead of 'vacuum cleaner', the very name 'Hammond' has become synonymous with electric organs. The Hammond organ was developed by Laurens Hammond (1895–1973), a brilliant inventor who claimed to have no musical ability whatsoever.

Hammond graduated with an honours degree in mechanical engineering from Cornell University in 1916. Following a period of armed service in France during the First World War, he took up the position of chief engineer with the Gray Motor Company in Detroit. The invention of a silent, spring-driven clock gave Hammond enough capital to strike out on his own, and in 1928 he founded the Hammond Clock Company, which made a range of electric clocks, driven by another of his inventions – the synchronous electric motor.

However, as other clock companies went out of business during the Great Depression, Hammond's determination to remain solvent led him to develop other products, and he soon turned his attention to music. Though no musician himself, he recognized the importance of music and was keen to produce a system that could bring high-quality music-making to the domestic market.

Section One: The Instruments

DEVELOPMENT OF THE ELECTRIC ORGAN

In developing the electric organ, Hammond turned for inspiration to the underlying principles of Thaddeus Cahill's ill-fated Telharmonium. Aided by his company treasurer (and church organist) William Lahey, Hammond used his engineering skill and experience to develop an electro-mechanical system of tone-wheel generators coupled with a keyboard. The Hammond tone-wheel organ was patented in 1934 and the Model A went into production in 1935, with Henry Ford and George Gershwin among the first customers.

Fact

Hammond's legacy of remarkable inventions includes the red-and-green lenses used in 3D glasses, missile-guidance systems, and a mechanical bridge table that could shuffle and deal a deck of cards into four piles!

The now-legendary B3 was first produced in October 1955 and quickly became a lasting favourite with musicians of all genres for its distinctive sound and versatility. The B3 is housed in a large wooden cabinet on four spindle legs, with separate power amplification and speaker system. The musician is presented with a pair of 61-note keyboards and a 25-note flat radial removable pedal board. The sound generated by the instrument is controlled by a series of rocker switches and drawbars. These drawbars lie at the heart of the Hammond sound, allowing the player to build up rich timbres by combining pure tones in differing combinations – in the same way that a church organist would use stops to combine pipes of different lengths.

◀ *Influential musician Jimmy Smith was able to conjur some funky grooves from his Hammond organ.*

Musical Instruments Handbook

THE LESLIE SPEAKER

Another defining feature of the Hammond sound was not invented by Laurens Hammond but by Don Leslie (1911–2004). The Leslie speaker was developed to overcome shortcomings that Leslie felt to be inherent in the sound of the Hammond organ. Noting that the instrument sounded much more impressive in large halls, Leslie began experimenting with ways of introducing reverberation and motion into the sound. The result was the rotating speaker system that bears his name.

The Leslie speaker cabinet looks like a large chest of drawers and contains a 40-watt tube amplifier, a rotating treble horn and a rotating bass speaker. It was designed to produce two particular effects – the 'chorale' (when the speakers rotate slowly) and the 'tremolo' (when they spin quickly). However, a third effect exploited by many players was made possible by disconnecting the slow motors in order to make the change from 'chorale' to 'tremolo' much more exaggerated.

THE HAMMOND ORGAN TODAY

Hammond continued to produce different models of electric organs, all of them based on the original tone-wheel technology, until 1975. The company continued to make organs using electronics and digital technology, but it went out of business in 1986, only to be bought by the Suzuki group the following year. New instruments such as the New B3 and the XK3 use modern digital technology to emulate the vintage sound so beloved by keyboard players.

▲ *The Hammond XK3 recreates the sound of the legendary B3.*

The characteristic Hammond and Leslie combination can be heard on countless jazz, rock, gospel and blues recordings, including such classic tracks as 'A Whiter Shade of Pale' by Procol Harum and 'Gimme Some Lovin'' by the Spencer Davis Group.

Section One: The Instruments

ELECTRIC PIANO

The piano has occupied a special place in music and, since the advent of amplification, musicians have sought ways in which its expressive, versatile sound could be made louder in order to carry above the sound of other amplified instruments and also how it could be packaged into an instrument more easily transportable than the traditional acoustic piano. Electric pianos fall into three categories.

ELECTRO-ACOUSTIC PIANOS

► *The Yamaha CP-70.*

These instruments simply amplify the sound of what is, essentially, a traditional acoustic piano mechanism – hammers hitting strings. Perhaps the best-known examples of this type of piano are Yamaha's 73-note CP-70 and its bigger brother, the 88-note CP-80. Though still large and heavy, the Yamaha CP pianos were relatively portable due to the fact that they could be split into two sections – one containing the keyboard and hammer mechanism, the other containing the actual strings on the harp-like frame. Behaving like an acoustic piano, the sound of the CP-70 and CP-80 could be still be heard with the power off, albeit much quieter than a comparatively sized conventional baby grand.

▲ *The Fender Rhodes Mark I Stage 73.*

Of course, the use of a traditional piano-string mechanism meant that these instruments still needed constant tuning, more so during life on the road. The sound was amplified through a sophisticated piezo pickup and preamp system that turned the acoustic vibration of the strings into an electrical signal. Because of their imposing stage presence, responsive keyboard and bright, rich tone, the Yamaha CP-70 and CP-80 found favour with many keyboard players, including Tony Banks, Howard Jones and Vangelis.

Musical Instruments Handbook

AMPLIFIED TINES

Like the Yamaha CP-70, instruments in this category used a pickup system to amplify the acoustic sound of a mechanical action. However, instead of strings, these pianos used the percussive quality of hammers hitting metallic reeds or tines – rather like a tuning fork. Perhaps the best-known example of such instruments is the Fender Rhodes. Developed by Harold Rhodes (1910–2000), the Fender Rhodes had a distinctive bell or celeste-like sound that could be, by turns, soft and lyrical or aggressive and biting. Classic models include the Suitcase 73 (which included a tremolo system, a 50W amplifier and built-in speakers) and the Fender Rhodes 88, available in Suitcase or Stage variants. This latter version stripped the instrument of its built-in amplifier and speakers to make it lighter and less expensive. The sound of the Fender Rhodes can be heard on tracks such as Herbie Hancock's 'Chameleon', Billy Joel's 'Just the Way You Are' and Stevie Wonder's 'You Are the Sunshine of My Life'.

▲ *When played softly, the Wurlitzer has quite a sweet sound.*

Other manufacturers, such as Wurlitzer and Hohner, employed similar technology to produce their own models of electric piano. Songs featuring the Wurlitzer include Queen's 'You're My Best Friend', Supertramp's 'The Logical Song' and Ray Charles's classic 'What'd I Say'.

ELECTRONIC/DIGITAL PIANOS

These instruments do not use mechanical action or amplified acoustic sound, but generate sound by purely electronic means, usually by replaying samples of instrumental sounds stored in ROM (Read-Only Memory). For the domestic market, instruments such as the Yamaha Clavinova range come with built-in amplification, speakers, and have a full complement of different instrumental sounds, pre-programmed drum rhythms and auto-accompaniment features. Professional stage instruments, like the Kawai MP8 or the Kurzweil PC88, do not usually include built-in amplification and speaker systems.

▲ *The Kurweill PC88's keyboard has 88 keys and weighted key action that rivals a real piano.*

Section One: The Instruments

CLAVINET

The clavinet is essentially an electric version of the clavichord. Designed in the 1960s by Ernst Zacharias of the German company, Hohner, the clavinet evolved from the Cembalet, an instrument Zacharias had developed some years earlier as an electronic counterpart to the harpsichord.

CONSTRUCTION

Hohner produced several models of clavinet over the years, including the legendary D6. Most models featured a five-octave keyboard. The sound came from strings struck by small, rubber-tipped hammers, or 'tangents' and was amplified by means of pickups – like those of an electric guitar – positioned above and below the strings. Indeed, the instrument produced a guitar-level signal and was usually amplified through a guitar amp. The characteristic *staccato* sound was due to a weave of yarn through which each string passed.

SOUND

A string could vibrate as long as the key was depressed, but upon release the string was immediately damped by the yarn. A series of pickup selector rocker switches to the left of the keyboard enabled the player to alter the tone of the instrument, making it rich and full or thin and biting. Other controls include overall brightness and volume settings. The sound of the clavinet was often further modified by passing its output through guitar effects – such as a wah-wah pedal – prior to amplification.

The clavinet's distinctively bright percussive sound ensured that the instrument became a firm favourite with players of funk and rock music. John Paul Jones of Led Zeppelin used the instrument extensively on the *Physical Graffiti* album, but perhaps the clavinet's defining moment was its use in Stevie Wonder's infectious 'Superstition'.

Musical Instruments Handbook

MELLOTRON

The Mellotron and its predecessor the Chamberlain were in effect the earliest examples of a sample playback instrument.

CHAMBERLAIN

In 1949, Californian inventor Harry Chamberlain, patented the Chamberlain MusicMaster. It was the first commercially available instrument to use pre-recorded lengths of tape mounted within a keyboard in such a way that, whenever a key was depressed, a corresponding length of tape was moved across a tape play head. The resulting sound was heard through the instrument's built-in amplifier and speakers. The Chamberlain employed finite lengths of tape and required a spring mechanism to return each length to the beginning every time a key was released. The limited playback time of seven or eight seconds led players to develop a spider-like movement between chord inversions in an attempt to sustain sounds for longer. However, the system did have the advantage that the attack portion of the recorded instrument was heard with each new note sounded.

MELLOTRON MODELS

In 1962, Chamberlain's agent, Bill Fransen, in search of suppliers of tape playback heads, visited Bradmatic, a small company in Birmingham, England. Fascination with the idea of a musical instrument based on tape playback led the owners – brothers Bill and Lesley Bradley – to join forces with bandleader/broadcaster Eric Robinson and the Mellotronic company was born.

The Mellotron Mark I appeared in 1963 but, although it was technically superior to the Chamberlain, it remained temperamental and a year passed before the first truly playable instrument was produced. The Model 400, first produced in 1970, is widely regarded as the classic Mellotron. Approximately 2,000 were made. In 1976, after commercial problems and dispute over the Mellotron name, the Bradley brothers continued to produce instruments under the name Novatron. (A similar instrument, the Birotron, was an ill-fated venture by long-time Mellotron player Rick Wakeman.)

Section One: The Instruments

SYNTHESIZER

No instrument has had a more dramatic impact on contemporary music than the synthesizer. Its development opened up a whole new world of seemingly endless sonic possibilities and ushered in completely new forms of music.

HISTORY

The birth of the synthesizer dates back to the mid-1940s when Canadian physicist, composer and instrument builder, Hugh le Caine (1914–77) built the electronic sackbut, an instrument widely regarded as the first true synthesizer.

▲ *Hugh le Caine with his Electronic Sackbut.*

In the 1950s, RCA (Radio Corporation of America) built the huge Mark II Music Synthesizer, using vacuum-tube electronics and a punched-paper-tape system of programming – rather like a player piano. This cumbersome beast required hours of patching and programming before it was able to produce any musical sound.

Other developments of the time included Daphne Oram's novel technique of 'Oramics', which used drawings on 35-mm film to produce sound, a system that was employed by the BBC Radiophonic Workshop for several years.

Although American inventor Donald Buchla did create a commercially available synthesizer, most instruments of the 1950s and early 1960s were, due to their vast size and complexity, confined to academic institutions and studios. The wider explosion of interest in the synthesizer was the responsibility of the man whose name became synonymous with the instrument – Dr Robert A. Moog (1934–2005).

THE MOOG

Moog (pronounced to rhyme with 'vogue') had always been interested in electronic music, having built theremins with his father throughout the 1950s. Inspired by experimental composer Herbert Deutsch, Moog designed the circuits for his first synthesizer while studying for a PhD in Engineering Physics at Cornell University, where he was a student of Peter Mauzey, an RCA engineer who had worked on the Mark II Music Synthesizer.

Musical Instruments Handbook

Moog proudly demonstrated his first synthesizer at the AES (Audio Engineering Society) convention in 1964. Like the RCA machine, Moog's synthesizer was a flexible modular design in that the instrument comprised several different sections, or modules, each with a different function, which could be patched (connected) together in different combinations. Moog's first design still required a great deal of programming time, although it was smaller, lighter and more flexible than the Mark II Music Synthesizer.

▲ *An early, enormous Moog synthesizer.*

Interest in the new instrument was immediate and Moog began making modular synthesizers for experimental composers and the academic community. Widespread public awareness of Moog's name came when his synthesizer was featured on the Monkees' 1967 album, *Pisces, Aquarius, Capricorn & Jones Ltd.* played by Micky Dolenz. Then, in 1968, Walter (later Wendy) Carlos released the seminal, million-selling, Grammy Award-winning album, *Switched On Bach*. The synthesizer had become well and truly established. Other early synthesizer manufacturers included ARP and Peter Zinovieff's Electronic Music Studios (London) Ltd (EMS).

THE MINIMOOG

► *The Minimoog.*

In 1970, Robert Moog produced another groundbreaking instrument, the Minimoog. Unlike previous synthesizers, the Minimoog abandoned the modular design in favour of all the electronics being built into a single keyboard unit. What was sacrificed in terms of modular flexibility was gained in ease of use and portability.

POLYPHONIC SYNTHESIZERS

Until the mid-1970s most synthesizers were monophonic – that is to say they were only capable of producing one note at once. A few exceptions, including Moog's Sonic Six and the ARP Odyssey, were duophonic (able to play two notes at once). True polyphonic instruments, able to play chords, appeared in 1975 in the form of the Polymoog, with the equally classic Yamaha CS-80 and the Oberheim Four-Voice being released the following year.

Section One: The Instruments

The advent of affordable microprocessor integrated circuits enabled manufacturers to bring the advantages of digital control and memory to the synthesizer. In 1977, Sequential Circuits introduced the Prophet 5, a fully programmable, polyphonic synthesizer with digital patch memory storage, which memorized all settings – a much-needed feature.

THE DIGITAL SYNTHESIZER

The Prophet 5 paved the way for the all-digital synthesizer and in 1983 Yamaha introduced the world to FM synthesis in the form of the DX7 synthesizer. The DX7 also featured another development first seen in 1982 on the Sequential Circuits Prophet 600 – MIDI (Musical Instrument Digital Interface).

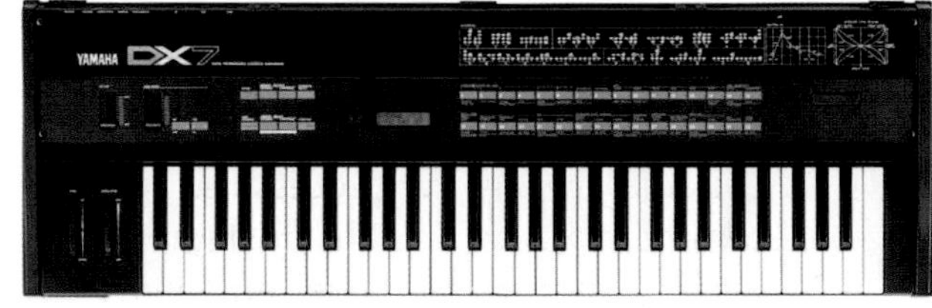

▲ *The groundbreaking Yamaha DX7, the first synth to feature MIDI.*

MIDI

MIDI is an industry standard communication protocol that enables electronic musical instruments (and computer systems) to be connected to one another to exchange musical data – such as note values or program-change information. Prior to MIDI, different manufacturers each pursued their own, proprietary standards. This meant that getting, for example, a Yamaha instrument to communicate with a Korg device was just about impossible. In 1981, Dave Smith of Sequential Circuits proposed the idea of a standard interface in a paper to the AES and the MIDI Specification 1.0 was published in 1983. The almost universal adoption of MIDI ensured that it became a key technology, central to stage and studio, with applications beyond the purely musical, such as control of lights.

DIFFERENT TYPES OF SYNTHESIS

Although most synthesizers have many fundamental principles in common, there are, in fact, several different forms of synthesis technique. These include:

- **Additive:** in which pure sine tones are combined to create different timbres according to principles discovered by French mathematician Joseph Fourier.
- **Subtractive:** in which waveforms rich in harmonics, such as a saw-tooth or square wave, produced by a VCO (voltage-controlled oscillator) are passed through filters that can strip away or accentuate certain harmonics. Most analogue synthesizers employ subtractive techniques.

Musical Instruments Handbook

- **FM (Frequency Modulation):** devised in the early 1970s by John Chowning at Stanford University, FM was licensed to Yamaha for use in their DX instruments. FM involves the frequency of one waveform being used to modulate (modify or influence) the frequency of another, resulting in a new, much more complex sound.
- **Granular:** uses multiple layers of very short (1–50 milliseconds) waveforms called 'grains' to create 'clouds' of sound.
- **Physical Modelling:** uses complex mathematical equations to simulate the physical characteristics of, for example, a plucked string or a struck drumskin. Due to the huge amount of processing involved, physical modelling has only been possible in real time with the development of extremely powerful processors. The first commercially available instrument to employ physical modelling was the Yamaha VL-1 in 1994.

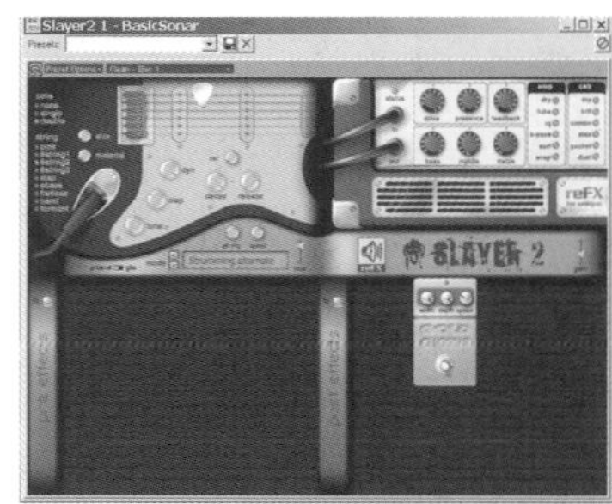

▲ *Slayer 2 emulates a plucked string.*

OTHER IMPORTANT CONCEPTS

- **Envelopes:** these refer to how aspects of a sound behave over time. For example, in terms of volume, a cymbal crash has a fast attack and a long, slow decay. Typical synthesizer envelope controls give the user control over the attack, decay, sustain and release (ADSR) portions of a sound.
- **Modulation:** modulation simply means to modify or to influence, and is a key concept in bringing expressiveness to synthesized sounds. Many different aspects of a sound can be modulated. For example, the pitch of an oscillator can be modulated to produce a *vibrato* effect or the cut-off frequency of a filter can be modulated to create a characteristic sweeping sound. Modulation can be achieved by the player operating synthesizer controls such as the modulation wheel or by increasing pressure on an after-touch-sensitive keyboard.
- **Effects:** most modern synthesizers allow the player to further modify the sound through the application of effects such as reverberation.

▲ *Sound manipulation is now an integral part of modern music.*

Section One: The Instruments

SAMPLER

Like the synthesizer, the sampler has had a huge influence on the course of electronic music.

A sampler is an instrument that can record, store and replay brief sections of audio – 'samples'. In many ways, the Mellotron might be regarded as the earliest example of a sampling instrument. However, the sampler really came into its own with the development of digital technology.

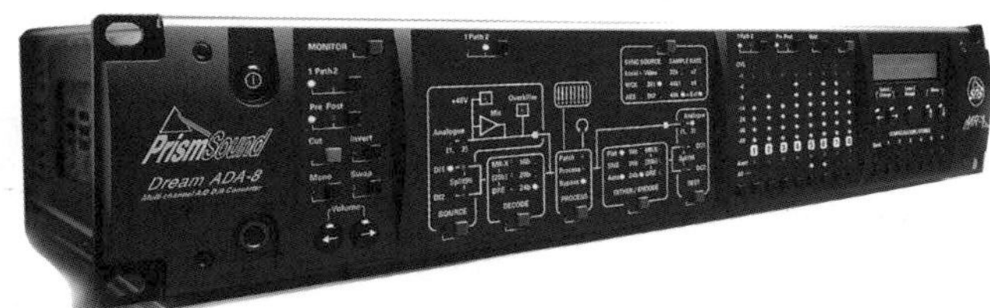

▼ *An analogue-digital/digital-analogue converter.*

DIGITAL SAMPLING

Digital sampling is the process by which a recorded analogue signal is analyzed and transformed, through an analogue-to-digital converter (ADC) into digital information that can be easily stored, manipulated and replayed. On playback, the process is reversed and the digital information is passed through a digital-to-analogue converter (DAC) to recreate the original waveform. Two factors influence the quality of the sample:

- **Sample rate:** the frequency with which the original analogue signal is measured (sampled). Obviously, if more regular readings are taken over shorter intervals, the closer the digital version will be to the original. In 1927, physicist and engineer, Harry Nyquist (1889–1974), determined that, in order to maintain fidelity, the sample rate has to be at least twice the frequency of the sound being sampled. For example, in order to accurately sample a sound that occupies a range of frequencies up to 20,000 Hz (the upper limit of human hearing), sample readings must be taken, and digital values stored, at least 40,000 times per second. (CD quality is 44.1 kHz i.e., sample readings are taken every 44,100th of a second.) Failure to do so results in 'aliasing' – the production of undesirable audio artefacts.
- **Bit depth:** having taken a sample, the bit depth of the system determines the resolution with which the digital samples are stored – the higher, the better. 16-bit (CD quality) is a very significant improvement over 8-bit. It will therefore be apparent that sampling is a very memory-hungry operation.

Musical Instruments Handbook

▼ *The Fairlight CMI.*

FAIRLIGHT CMI

The Fairlight CMI (Computer Musical Instrument) was the first commercially available digital sampler. Named after a Sydney Harbour hydrofoil service, it was developed in 1979 by Australians Peter Vogel and Kim Ryrie. The original Fairlight was capable of 10 kHz, 8-bit sampling and had an interactive VDU (video display unit) on which the user could edit, or even draw, waveforms with a light pen. Costing around $25,000, its use was restricted to academic institutions and affluent rock musicians, such as Peter Gabriel who used it extensively on his fourth album, including the single 'Shock the Monkey'.

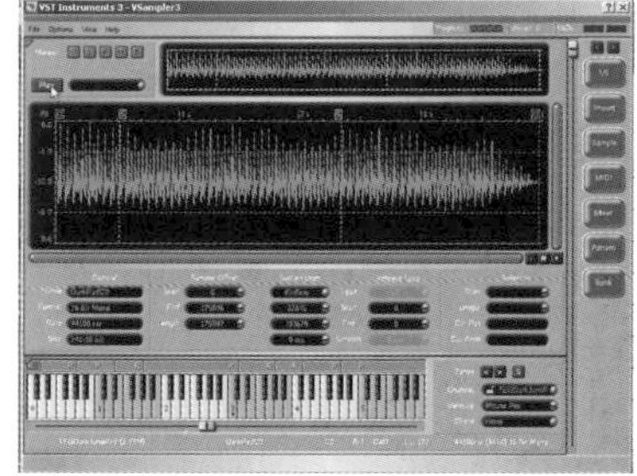

▲ *The computer-based VSampler.*

MUSICAL SAMPLING

Like its American counterpart, the NED (New England Digital) Synclavier, the Fairlight fell into disuse, unable to compete with the rising tide of affordable samplers produced by companies such as Ensoniq (Mirage), E-mu (Emulator), Sequential Circuits (Prophet 2000) and Akai (S900). Many of today's synthesizer-workstation keyboards are based on sampling technology, and vast libraries of third-party pre-recorded samples are available. However, like so many other advances in music technology, the world of sampling has come to be dominated by computer software.

▲ *The Black Eyed Peas' sound is a mix of live instruments and hip-hop samples.*

The advent of widely available, mass-market sampling instruments has given rise to numerous developments in musical styles and techniques – from the stuttering, re-triggering effect of Paul Hardcastle's '19' to the drum loops of hip-hop and the often-overt lifting of whole, recognizable musical phrases into new compositions.

VIBRAPHONE

The vibraphone (or 'vibes' or 'vibraharp' as it is sometimes known), is a percussion instrument that uses an electro-mechanical system to create its distinctive sound.

CONSTRUCTION

The vibraphone is similar in appearance to a xylophone or marimba, in that it consists of a set of bars arranged over resonating vertical tubes. However, unlike the other, wooden instruments, the vibraphone's bars are made of a metal such as aluminium. Consequently, the sound can sustain for much longer due to the vibrating properties of the metal. In order for the player to be able to control this sustain, the vibraphone is fitted with a pedal-operated system of dampers. A standard vibraphone has a three-octave range from the F below middle C, and is usually played with soft beaters to produce a mellow tone.

SOUND

What really gives the vibraphone its characteristic sound, though, is the electromechanical system of rotating discs (or 'paddles') mounted in the top of each resonator tube. Fixed to a long rotating axle driven by an electric motor, the motion of these discs continuously opens and closes the resonating tubes, giving rise to a cyclic variation in the amplitude (volume) of each note. The speed of this effect can be altered by changing the rate of rotation of the axle. The vibraphone has become a familiar sound in jazz thanks to the work of artists such as Lionel Hampton and Gary Burton.

Fact

The name 'vibraphone' is actually a misnomer, since the term *vibrato* actually refers to a variation in pitch – not volume.

Musical Instruments Handbook

ELECTRONIC DRUM KIT

The drum is perhaps the oldest instrument known to man. Drummers have always sought increasingly sophisticated ways of refining their art and gaining access to as broad a palette of sounds as possible and, in many instances, have embraced the electronic revolution as enthusiastically as their keyboard-playing counterparts.

EARLY ELECTRONIC DRUMS

Early electronic drum systems included the Electro-Harmonix Space Drum and the Pearl Syncussion of 1979, a two-channel synthesizer that could be triggered from a pair of bongo-like drums fitted with electronic transducers. This groundbreaking instrument suffered from a poor reputation due to the overuse of its synthetic, decaying-pitch tom-tom sounds in disco tracks of the era.

SIMMONS SDSV

The first full, true electronic drum kit was the Simmons SDSV (SDS5), produced in 1982. The SDSV consisted of a sound module that employed analogue circuitry to synthesize the sound of kick, snare and tom-tom drums, triggered from distinctive, visually appealing hexagonal drum pads. The player had control over various aspects of the sound – such as noise level, tone level and decay. However, many players found the playing surface of the pads too firm in comparison to conventional drums and, despite the introduction of hi-hat and cymbal sounds, most players found these inadequate and retained acoustic cymbals. The sound of the Simmons kit is one of the defining sounds of 1980s pop music and can be heard in numerous pieces of music, such as Jan Hammer's 'Miami Vice'.

In recent times electronic kits such as the Clavia ddrum4 and the Roland V-Drum system have demonstrated a high degree of sophistication, playability and convincing emulations of real drum sounds. Percussionists who have exploited the potential of electronic kits include the ex-King Crimson drummer, Bill Bruford.

Section One: The Instruments

PERCUSSION CONTROLLER

The full drum kit is not the only instrument in the percussion section to have benefited from advances in electronics and music technology. An array of different electronic percussion is available to the modern player.

Early electronic drum kits and percussion controllers used closed, proprietary systems to link the playing surfaces to the sound sources. However, most modern instruments have built-in sounds,use the industry standard MIDI protocol to communicate with sound sources such as synthesizers and samplers, or offer a combination of both approaches to afford the player access to the widest possible selection of sounds.

DRUM PADS

Instruments such as the drumKat or the Roland Octopad offer the player an array of velocity-sensitive pads mounted in a single, robust unit. Used either as an independent instrument or as a complement to an existing drum kit or percussion rig, these enable the percussionist to trigger any MIDI-compatible sound module.

While it might not immediately seem necessary to offer drum pads on a keyboard instrument, keyboard players sometimes find it easier to play and programme drum sounds using tactile pads rather than keys. The Roland Fantom X range and the Korg Kontrol 49 are examples of instruments which offer the keyboard player a four-by-four array of 16 drum pads. Standalone products such as the M-Audio Trigger Finger and the Akai MPD16 offer similar facilities.

HAND DRUMS

Nor is the hand drummer left out. Instruments like the Korg Wave Drum and the Roland HPD-15 present the player with a variety of impressive built-in sounds and surfaces responsive to the established, traditional techniques of hand-drumming.

MALLET INSTRUMENTS

Larger instruments like the xylophone, marimba or vibraphone are emulated by the malletKAT MIDI control surface.

Musical Instruments Handbook

DRUM MACHINE

A drum machine is an instrument that uses synthesized or sampled sound to emulate drums or other percussion, and allows the user to programme rhythmic patterns that can be chained together into songs.

RHYTHM MACHINES

The history of the drum machine dates back as far as the 1930s, when Leon Theremin (1896–1993) was commissioned by composer Henry Cowell (1897–1965) to produce the hugely complicated Rhythmicon rhythm machine. The rhythm machines of the 1960s tended to be built into electronic organs to provide preset accompaniment patterns such as 'Tango' or 'Bossa Nova'. The first true standalone drum machine, the Rhythm Ace, was produced in 1970 by the Ace Tone Company. Like its organ-based predecessors, the Rhythm Ace was not programmable and relied on preset patterns.

ROLAND CR-78

It was not until the Roland CR-78 of 1979 that musicians could programme in their own rhythmic patterns. Roland followed the success of the CR-78 with a range of drum machines over the following years, including the classic TR-808. This used analogue synthesis to produce its booming bass, cutting snare and piercing cowbell sounds. While no one could mistake it for the real thing, its distinctive tones ensured that it found favour among musicians.

LINN'S MACHINES

The 808's competition came in the form of a drum machine designed by guitarist Roger Linn. The LM-1, and its successor the LinnDrum, offered the musician far greater realism in the form of sampled drum sounds. Its sounds can be heard on material throughout the 1980s – notably, the Human League's *Dare* album.

Roger Linn went on to lend his expertise to the design of Akai's MPC range of sampling drum machines – instruments that are still widely thought unsurpassed in terms of their ability to impart musical feel through the subtle manipulation of nuances in timing.

Section One: The Instruments

WIND AND BRASS SYNTHESIZERS

Until the 1970s, most synthesizers were played by means of a traditional, piano-style keyboard. This tended to limit the player's ability to expressively control the sound in real time and manufacturers sought to include additional means of control, such as modulation wheels and touch-sensitive ribbon controllers.

Wind and brass players, however, realized that their experience of acoustic instruments gave them the tools and techniques – embouchure and breath control – to be able to shape and control sounds in a musical fashion. If only those skills could be applied to the control of synthesized sound...

ELECTRONIC WIND INSTRUMENT

Enter Roger Noble, William Bernardi and the Lyricon. Noble and Bernardi had patented the design for the Electronic Wind Instrument in 1971 and, in 1974, the Lyricon became the first commercially available wind synthesizer, combining a saxophone-like mouthpiece and key system with a built-in synthesizer sound source.

Subsequent developments included the Akai EWI (Electronic Wind Instrument), famously used by American saxophonist Michael Brecker, and the Yamaha WX range of instruments – WX5, WX7, WX11. These offer MIDI control of any MIDI-equipped synthesizer or sampler. The Yamaha range also includes their proprietary WX interface for connecting the control to Yamaha sound modules such as the physical modelling VL-70m.

ELECTRONIC VALVE INSTRUMENT

Brass players were not far behind. In the mid-1970s, Nyle Steiner created the Electronic Valve Instrument based on trumpet fingering. Marketed for a while by Akai as the EVI1000, this unique instrument is now still available, hand-built to order, from Nyle Steiner himself.

Musical Instruments Handbook

ELECTRO-ACOUSTIC AND SEMI-ACOUSTIC GUITARS

Broadly speaking, guitars can be divided into two categories – acoustic and electric. The term 'electric guitar' tends to be reserved for solid-body instruments. Acoustic guitars use the resonating properties of a hollow body and sound holes to produce and project their sound.

ELECTRO-ACOUSTIC GUITARS

The development of amplified music, played in increasingly larger venues, presented a challenge to the acoustic-guitar player. Though it is possible to amplify an acoustic guitar simply by playing in front of a microphone, the system can be prone to feedback and limits the player to a static position, a fixed distance from the microphone.

Guitar manufacturers produced solutions in the form of instruments that had either built-in microphones, electromagnetic or piezo-electric pickups. Such instruments can be plugged directly into amplification systems or sent via processors that can enhance the sound with effects such as delay, chorus or reverb. Modern instruments, such as Ovation's range of distinctive round-back guitars, can include sophisticated electronics, tone controls and even built-in tuners.

▲ *OP-PRO, Ovation's latest preamp design.*

SEMI-ACOUSTIC GUITARS

While electro-acoustic guitars tend to be used primarily for their natural, acoustic properties (even if amplified), semi-acoustic guitars are instruments that, even though they do have hollow, resonating bodies, are used primarily for the electric tonal qualities of the sound produced by internal pick-ups. Semi-acoustic guitars, such as the classic Gibson ES-335 of 1958 and the ES-175, have a long association with rock 'n' roll and jazz.

Section One: The Instruments

ELECTRIC GUITAR

An electric guitar usually has a solid wooden body with no acoustic resonance. All the sound is created by the vibration of strings being translated into electrical signals by pickups and then amplified.

HISTORY

The modern electric guitar has its origins in the Hawaiian or steel guitar, particularly popular in the 1920s and 1930s. These instruments were the first examples of guitars that depended on electrical amplification rather than the properties of acoustic resonance.

Three names are particularly associated with the development of the electric guitar – Rickenbacker, Fender and Gibson Les Paul. Adolphe Richenbacher (later changed to Rickenbacker) worked making components for the Dopera Brothers' National Resonator Guitars. Together with George Beauchamp and Paul Barth, he formed the Electro String Company and, in the 1930s, began building Hawaiian-style guitars using their newly developed magnetic-pickup system.

FENDER STRAT

In the late 1940s, electrician and amplifier-maker Leo Fender designed the Broadcaster guitar. After a dispute with the company Gretsch over the name 'Broadcaster', the guitar was re-christened the Telecaster. In 1954, Fender introduced an instrument that was to become the most famous, and most copied, electric guitar of all time – the Stratocaster, or 'Strat'.

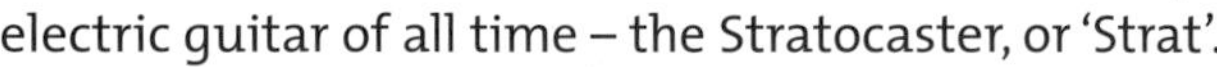

GIBSON LES PAUL

The Gibson Company's response to the huge popularity of Fender guitars was to seek out the service of jazz guitarist and inventor Les Paul. Paul had built his so-called 'log' guitar out of a simple, solid block of wood with an attached neck in the early 1940s. His association with Gibson was to produce another iconic instrument – the Gibson Les Paul of 1952.

◀ *The electric guitar has had an impact on all styles of popular music.*

Musical Instruments Handbook

ELECTRIC BASS GUITAR

The electric bass is similar in both appearance and operation to the electric guitar, but is actually a descendent of the upright acoustic double bass.

The double bass had long been an integral part of the jazz rhythm section, but the increasing need to compete with amplified instruments – not to mention the transportation problems caused by its sheer bulk – made players and manufacturers seek amplified alternatives.

ELECTRIC BASS FIDDLE

The earliest-known example of a solid-body electric bass dates back to 1935 in the form of an upright instrument designed by musician and amplifier-maker Paul H. Tutmarc, for the Audiovox Manufacturing Company of Seattle. The same company later developed a bass instrument played across the body, like a guitar. The Model #736 Electric Bass Fiddle, as it was known, was also innovative in that, unlike the double bass, it was fretted, enabling less secure players to achieve precise intonation.

This idea was also incorporated into the first mass-produced electric bass, the Fender Precision Bass of 1951. The instrument evolved into a design that has remained relatively unchanged since 1957. A similar classic instrument was the Fender Jazz Bass of 1960.

BASS MODELS

The electric bass has a slight larger body and longer neck than an electric guitar and usually has four strings – tuned in fourths, E, A, D and G. Variants include different numbers of strings – often adding a fifth, tuned to B or A below the bottom E string – and fretless models. The fretless design has a characteristic mellow tone and facilitates the technique of sliding between notes. The bass is usually plucked with the thumb or a plectrum but players, such as Mark King of Level 42, have pioneered percussive 'slap bass' styles.

▲ *Influential bassist Paul McCartney on his Hohner.*

Section One: The Instruments

CHAPMAN STICK

The Chapman Stick is a large instrument with a wide fretboard and eight, 10 or 12 strings. It is played by tapping (or 'hammering-on') a string at the desired fret with the finger and holding it down with the sustain of the note.

Since only a single finger of one hand is needed to sound each note, the accomplished player can, using three or four fingers of both hands simultaneously, produce complex passages of music comprising bass, harmony and lead lines all at once.

CHAPMAN'S VISION

The Chapman Stick was the unique vision of guitarist Emmett Chapman. Chapman recounts how, in 1969, his discovery of a novel two-handed tapping method on his guitar enabled him to play multiple, independent lines, each hand perpendicular to the fretboard and approaching the board from opposite sides. Chapman's search for an instrument that was large enough to accommodate this technique led him to design the Chapman Stick, first distributed in 1974.

There are currently six models of Chapman Stick available:

- Classic 10-string
- Grand 12-string
- Bass 8-string
- NS/Stick 8-string (co-designed by Ned Steinberger)
- Stick XG 8, 10 or 12-string with graphite-carbon-fibre body
- Alto Stick 10-string tuned to the range of a guitar

THE CHAPMAN STICK IN PERFORMANCE

The seminal 1987 album *Parallel Galaxy* by Emmett Chapman naturally makes a fine showcase for his invention. Other players who have embraced this challenging yet versatile instrument include Tony Levin, notable for his work with King Crimson and Peter Gabriel, John Paul Jones and Nick Beggs (of Kajagoogoo fame), who recently toured with John Paul Jones.

Musical Instruments Handbook

ELECTRIC STEEL GUITAR

The electric steel guitar (also known as 'Hawaiian guitar' or simply 'steel guitar') is a solid-body, steel-strung instrument that relies on pickups and amplification to produce its sound. It has its origins in the Hawaiian music of the late-nineteenth century and is similar in sound and playing technique to resonator guitars such as the Dobro or National.

PLAYING TECHNIQUE

The steel guitar has two main variants – the lap steel guitar and the pedal steel guitar. Each instrument is played horizontally – in the case of the lap steel guitar, resting on the player's lap. The instruments are, effectively, just the solid neck and head sections of a guitar (i.e., with no resonating body).

The action of the strings is raised higher above the fret-board than on a standard guitar and, rather than pressing the strings to the frets, the player alters the pitch of notes by moving a metal bar (or 'steel') along the strings with (usually) the left hand, while the right hand plucks the strings with thumb and finger picks. This produces a characteristic 'crying' *portamento* effect. Not stopping the strings with fingers limits the ability to play a diverse range of on-string chord types and the instrument's use is, therefore, primarily melodic.

PEDAL STEEL GUITAR

The pedal steel guitar is the larger relative of the lap steel, usually comprising one or two necks – each strung with 10 strings (though eight-, 12- and even 14-string models are available) – mounted on a stand. An assembly of foot pedals and knee-operated levers beneath the instrument enables the player to adjust the tensioning of the strings in performance, thereby altering the tuning of the instrument. Notable lap and pedal steel-guitar players include Jerry Byrd and B. J. Cole.

Section One: The Instruments

GUITAR SYNTHESIZER

The term 'guitar synthesizer' refers to a system consisting of a guitar controller interfaced to a synthesizer sound-module.

Such instruments afford the guitar player access to not only synthesized (or sampled) emulations of guitar sounds but also to a vast array of electronic tones and instrumental simulations. In this way, the guitarist can bring techniques, such as string bending, to the playing of synthesized sound, adding a new level of musically expressive control.

EARLY GUITAR SYNTHS

Early examples tended to be specially built instruments with proprietary electronics connecting them to analogue synthesizers, whereas modern systems offer guitar-to-MIDI pickups that can usually be retrofitted to any standard electric guitar. Adoption of the universally implemented industry-standard MIDI means that guitar players are able to connect their instrument to a wide variety of sound sources and devices.

PICKUPS

The guitar synthesizer pickup is, in fact, an array of six monophonic pickups that track the vibration of each string independently. The challenge facing the designers of guitar synthesizer pickups is to capture all the nuances of electric-guitar playing technique, while rejecting extraneous sounds such as strings buzzing or unwanted finger-scraping noise.

ROLAND'S SYNTHS

There have been many different guitar synthesizers over the years, including the ill-fated, cumbersome and extremely expensive SynthAxe – not really a true guitar but a collection of controllers, grouped around six string sensors, fashioned to look like a bizarrely angular, futuristic guitar. One company, however, is particularly associated with guitar synthesis – Roland. Their first guitar synthesizer, the GR500 appeared in 1977. Subsequent models, such as the GR300, became classic instruments – mainly due to their use by innovative jazz guitarists such as John Abercrombie, Bill Frisell and, most notably, Pat Metheny.

Musical Instruments Handbook

ELECTRIC VIOLIN

Like the guitar with its electric counterparts, other members of the stringed-instrument family have taken advantage of the opportunities offered by electronic technology – namely amplification and access to a broader palette of synthesized (or sampled) sound.

ELECTRIC STRINGED INSTRUMENTS

Stringed instruments, such as the violin, viola, cello and double bass, can all be effectively amplified through the use of built-in microphones or, more commonly, electronic pickups. Pickups are either magnetic – which translate the vibrations of metal strings into an electrical signal – or of the piezo-electric variety, which respond to vibration in the bridge or body of the instrument.

The amplification of sound in this way removes the need for a traditional, resonating body and many examples of electric stringed instruments – such as those produced by Zeta or Steinberger – are of an innovative, minimalist design.

▲ *Electric violins are often seen as 'experimental' instruments.*

AMPLIFICATION

Amplified string sounds have a tendency to sound characteristically unnatural and 'electric', a fact exploited by players using external signal processors to add effects, such as delay and reverb, in the same way that an electric guitarist would.

In addition to the amplification of acoustic sound, it is possible, with the use of specialist pick-ups, to convert the vibration of strings into MIDI information. In this way, string players can use their instruments to trigger the sounds found in all MIDI synthesizer and sampler sound sources.

Fact

Well-known electric-string players include violinist Jean-Luc Ponty and Sting, whose amplified double-bass work remains a feature of his music.

Section One: The Instruments

THEREMIN

The theremin (or 'thereminvox') is one of the earliest examples of a purely electronic instrument, and enjoys the distinction of being the first instrument designed to be played with no physical contact.

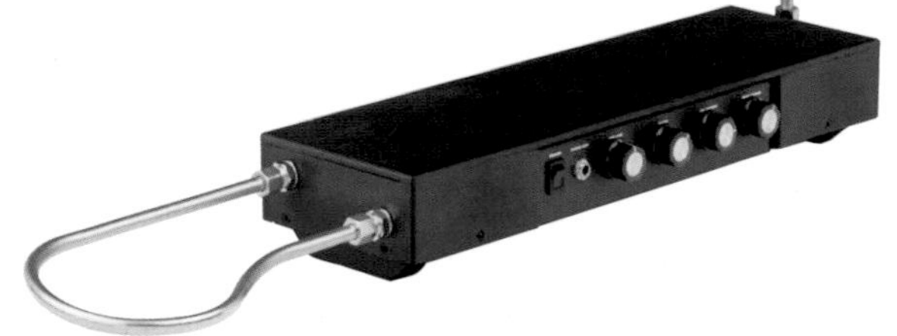

The theremin was invented in 1919 by Russian cellist and physicist Lev Sergeivitch Termen (Leon Theremin). Growing out of research into proximity sensors, the theremin exploits the capacitance properties of the human body. Movements near antennae mounted on the instrument cause changes in the audio signal. A similar phenomenon can be observed when someone moving near a radio or television aerial alters the reception.

PLAYING TECHNIQUE

The theremin is a wooden cabinet, containing a loudspeaker facing the audience, from which protrude two antennae – a horizontal loop to the left and a vertical pole to the right. Movements of the left hand around the loop alter the volume of the sound, while the right hand is used to control pitch, according to distance from the pole. A good sense of pitch and physical memory are pre-requisites for playing the theremin! The instrument emits a continuous, monophonic tone, similar in character to a violin.

THEREMIN IN PERFORMANCE

The ethereal, other-worldly sounds of this peculiar instrument can be heard on some classic recordings, including Bernard Heremann's score for the 1951 science-fiction movie *The Day the Earth Stood Still* and Led Zeppelin's live version of 'Whole Lotta Love'. Interestingly, the Beach Boys did not use a theremin on 'Good Vibrations' (a common misconception) as none was available for the session. The trademark sound of that track was created by a similar instrument, the tannerin. Though no longer in production, the theremin has a loyal following of aficionados and DIY kits are available.

Musical Instruments Handbook

ONDES MARTENOT

The ondes martenot ('martenot waves') was invented in 1928 by French inventor and cellist, Maurice Martenot.

Martenot had met his Russian counterpart, Leon Theremin, in 1923 and the two of them had discussed possible improvements to Theremin's eponymous instrument. In fact, Martenot's instrument was patented under the name *Perfectionnements aux instruments de musique électriques* ('improvements to electronic music instruments').

PLAYING TECHNIQUE

The ondes martenot has a haunting, *portamento* sound, similar to that of the theremin, but it is played by means of a finger-ring attached to a length of string, which is pulled up and down along a keyboard to determine pitch. The left hand operates volume controls, and some examples of the instrument have additional control over filters and alternative loudspeakers.

THE ONDES IN PERFORMANCE

The ondes martenot has had a diverse and illustrious career and is still called upon today for use in some orchestral repertoire. The classic ondes sound can clearly be heard in the original theme tune to the science-fiction television series *Star Trek*, and its character has lent itself to the soundtrack of countless other science-fiction and horror films. The instrument also found favour among numerous composers, including Olivier Messiaen (1908–92), who used it in his *Turangalila Symphonie*, Pierre Boulez (b. 1925) and Edgar Varèse (1885–1965).

In contemporary music, there has been a resurgence of interest in the ondes martentot – thanks to musicians like Radiohead's Jonny Greenwood, who not only used it on the band's *Kid A*, *Amenesiac* and *Hail to the Thief* albums, but also wrote the piece 'Smear' for two ondes martenot and the London Sinfonietta.

Section One: The Instruments

MUSIQUE CONCRÈTE

Musique concrète ('concrete music') was the term coined by Pierre Schaeffer (1910–95) in 1948 to describe his new approach to composition, based on tape recordings of natural and industrial sounds. The term was chosen to distinguish the new genre from pure, abstract music (_musique abstrait_).

Schaeffer was a radio engineer and broadcaster. Having gained a qualification from L'École Polytechnique in Paris, he joined Radiodiffusion Française (RF), initially as an apprentice. By 1942 he was leading research into the science of musical acoustics, using all the technological resources that RTF had to offer – turntables, and special disc-cutting recorders.

IMITATIVE WORKS

Schaeffer was interested in the way sounds behaved when recorded and manipulated. He would speed up and slow down recordings, reverse some sections of audio and repeat others. He discovered that sounds took on a different character when the initial attack of the sound was edited out. These early experiments led to the first piece of *musique concrète* in 1948, *Étude aux chemins de fer* ('Study with trains'). This work, based on the recorded sounds of train engines, wheels and whistles, was broadcast on RF, introduced by Schaeffer as a *concert de bruits* ('concert of noises').

Works in a similar vein followed – *Étude au piano* (based on the sounds of a piano), *Étude aux casseroles* (rattling pots and pans) and *Étude pour piano et orchestre* in which the sound of an orchestra tuning up was juxtaposed with an unrelated improvised piano part.

NEW MEDIUMS

Upon his return to France from a lecture tour, Schaeffer recruited a team of assistants, including Pierre Henry (b. 1927) – a young composer who had studied with Messiaen. Schaeffer and Henry soon became musical collaborators and produced a number of *concrète* works, including *Suite pour quatorze instruments* ('Suite for fourteen instruments') and *Symphonie pour un homme seul* ('Symphony for a lone man'). This latter piece made use of human sounds

Musical Instruments Handbook

▲ *Pierre Henry was a prolific composer as well as an acoustical inventor.*

such as breathing and vocal noises, as well as the sounds of percussion instruments, doors slamming, piano and orchestral textures.

In the 1950s, Schaeffer established the 'Group de Recherche du Musique Concrète', a studio equipped with the very latest invention – magnetic tape recorders. The new medium enabled Schaeffer, and the other *concrète* composers, to develop new techniques for the manipulation of sound – cutting, splicing and looping.

Other composers began combining the ideals of pure *concrète* works with other forms of electronic music. In 1958, Varèse used the found sounds of *concrète* with synthesized electronic sounds to create his *Poème électronique*, debuted at the Belgium World's Fair through a system of some 400 loudspeakers.

MUSIK ELECTRONISCHE

Musique concrète eventually fell out of favour, giving way to the school of Musik Electronische, arising from Karlheinz Stockhausen (b. 1928) and his contemporaries of the Studio für Electronische Musik in Cologne. But the genre had made its mark and remained an abiding influence on the electro-acoustic music of the latter part of the twentieth century. The use of sound recorded from non-musical sources carried through into much rock and pop work, with many examples to be heard in the music of groups such as the Beatles and Pink Floyd. Indeed, many of the techniques of sound manipulation established by Schaeffer lie at the heart of sampling technology today.

Section One: The Instruments

ALTERNATIVE CONTROLLERS

There are many different instrumental interfaces through which it is possible to control synthesized or sampled sounds – the most common being the piano-style keyboard. The electronic musician is also able to access a wide range of sounds through electric guitar, string, percussion and wind instruments.

These devices are, to a large extent, quite recognizably conventional, and owe a great deal to the heritage of acoustic-instrument design. However, there is a group of performance controllers that break the mould: instruments that challenge the idea that electronic music needs to be wrapped up in the trappings of the traditional. These are the alternative controllers.

▲ *Jean-Michel Jarre's laser harp.*

LASER HARP

The laser harp is an instrument made up of several beams of laser light, each representing a different note. When a beam is blocked (or 'plucked', to further the harp analogy) the interruption is detected by a light-sensitive cell, and a corresponding MIDI note is transmitted to a synthesizer or sampled sound source. The instrument comes in framed or non-framed varieties and is visually dramatic. The most famous exponent of the laser harp is the French musician Jean-Michel Jarre, whose spectacular live shows often feature the instrument.

SOUNDBEAM

Soundbeam was invented by composer Edward Williams 'to give dancers a new relationship with music'. It is an invisible ultrasonic beam, scalable over distances of up to 6 m (20 ft), which senses movement and converts physical gestures into MIDI. It works on a principle similar to that of bats' radar in that a

Musical Instruments Handbook

▼ *The Soundbeam translates body movement into digitally generated sound and image.*

transmitter/sensor emits a series of ultrasonic pulses. Any object moving within the path of the beam will cause these pulses to be reflected back to the sensor. Performing a quick calculation, the system is able to establish the distance of the object from the sensor and transmit the appropriate associated MIDI message.

Of course, MIDI is not limited to just the production of sounds and a suitably equipped system will enable the performer to also control lighting. Using such an instrument, the player becomes a dancer and the choreographer becomes a composer! In addition to its dance applications, the Soundbeam has proved particularly useful in enabling those with physical disabilities to take part in music-making.

▼ *Jazz Mutant Lemur's controller.*

D-BEAM

Controllers that require no physical contact have made their way into mainstream instruments, notably in the form of Roland's D-Beam system, which can be found augmenting the control panels of instruments such as the V-Synth.

BUCHLA THUNDER

The Buchla Thunder, designed by Don Buchla, is an array of 36 touch-sensitive pads mounted within a robust playing surface. The instrument is played with both hands and is highly programmable.

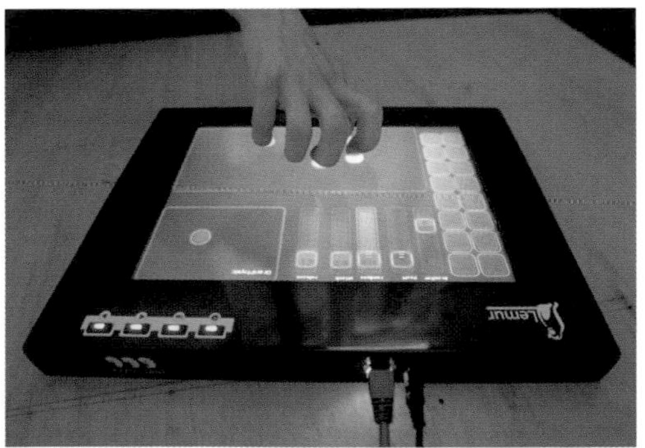

▲ *The Lemur's touchscreen technology can track multiple fingers simultaneously.*

JAZZ MUTANT LEMUR

This relatively new control surface is a touch-sensitive screen upon which the user can programme a display of graphical shapes and objects. The Lemur can be interfaced with a computer to give the player real-time control over sophisticated synthesis and performance programs such as MAX/MSP.

Section One: The Instruments

RECORDING STUDIO

There can be few environments as challenging and exciting to the musician as the recording studio. Since the post-war introduction of the magnetic tape recorder, the technology used to capture musical performance has become an increasingly important part of our culture.

The studio has long been more than simply an acoustically pleasing environment in which to capture and document a particular live performance. Under the guiding production hand of George Martin, the Beatles embraced studio technology as part of the creative process. The work of bands like Pink Floyd with Alan Parsons elevated studio engineering and production technique to an art form.

STUDIO TECHNOLOGY

Although there have been major advances in studio technology, particularly in relation to the place of computer-processing power and digital audio, the essential principles of a recording studio remain relatively unchanged.

A typical recording studio comprises two main spaces – the recording area (or 'live' room) and the control room. It is common for the control room to be adjacent to the live area, with line-of-sight communication between the spaces provided by a glass window. Commercial recording facilities will invest a good deal of money in the design and construction of the building to ensure that, as far as possible, the studio spaces are soundproofed. Triple-glazing, double doors and suspended, room-within-room construction all help to ensure that the studio environment is sonically isolated from the outside world. An ancillary space, (known as the machine room) houses items of equipment such as tape machines and computers, the noise from which might disrupt the listening environment.

Musical Instruments Handbook

THE LIVE ROOM

The live room is where the musicians perform, their sound captured by an array of microphones. The selection and placement of these is a science in its own right. Headphones or foldback speakers enable the musicians to hear themselves, each other and previously recorded material. Drums kits are often isolated behind screens and singers occupy vocal booths in order to assist the engineer capture each part as cleanly as possible and subsequently apply different treatments to each element of the arrangement.

▲ *The acoustics of a live room are crucial.*

Fashions in studio design come and go. In the 1970s there was a tendency to dampen the sound in studios with carpets and walls covered in fabric. The theory was that 'live-ness' and reverberation could be artificially – and therefore controllably – added later. Contemporary studio design favours a more natural, brighter sound, with materials like wood, stone and glass used throughout.

THE CONTROL ROOM

▲ *Although most studios are now digital, some engineers insist recording only to analogue.*

The control room is the domain of the recording engineer and the producer. The recorded sound is captured to a multitrack recording format – tape, digital tape or, more commonly now, computer hard disc.

The music is monitored and played back over high-quality loudspeakers. Everything in the control room is geared to ensuring that the listening environment is as accurate as possible. The engineer needs to be able to hear a balanced stereo or surround-sound image with very detailed sound. The shape of the room and the acoustic treatments on the walls, floor and ceiling are all designed to reduce unwanted reflections and booming bass.

The control room is centred around the mixing console, through which all signals are routed. At the mixer, the engineer can control the relative levels of different sounds; position sounds within the stereo (or surround) field and apply effects.

Racks of additional equipment house various sound processing devices, such as delays and reverb units, the creative application of which play such an important part in the recording process.

Section One: The Instruments

COMPUTER MUSIC

Computer music can be defined as music that is generated by, or composed and produced by means of, a computer. The idea that computers might have a role to play in the production of music actually goes back a lot further than one might think.

As early as 1843, Lady Ada Lovelace suggested in a published article that Babbage's 'Analytical Engine' might even be used to compose complex music, if only the correct data could be properly processed. Today, computers are an all-pervasive part of the music-production process and functions that were traditionally the preserve of hardware are now increasingly accomplished in the software domain.

▲ *Computers have opened up new avenues of musical creativity.*

THE ROLE OF COMPUTERS IN CONTEMPORARY MUSIC PRODUCTION

It is rare to come across a piece of music that has not, at some stage, benefited from the involvement of a computer system in its composition, performance, recording or distribution. Composers and producers of music use computers throughout every stage of the process and the various tasks that a computer music system performs can be broken down into a number of discrete, yet interrelated, areas.

COMPUTER-GENERATED COMPOSITIONS

Composers have long been fascinated by the idea of music generated independently by systems over which they can exert varying degrees of control. As early as 1787, Wolfgang Amadeus Mozart (1756–91) used a system known as *Musikalisches Würfelspiel* to randomly select sections of music to be played.

Musical Instruments Handbook

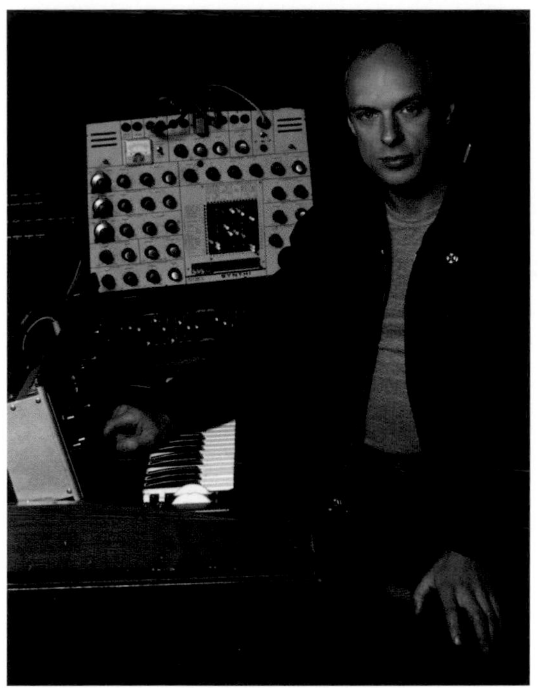

▲ *Electronic music pioneer Brian Eno is the father of ambient music.*

Algorithmic and aleatoric composition was much beloved by the *avant-garde* composers of the 1950s and 1960s, including John Cage (1912–92). In computer-generated music, the computer produces musical material within parameters determined by the composer. One of the first computer composers, Iannis Xenakis (1922–2001), wrote a computer program, in the FORTRAN programming language, to produce musical scores that could be played by live musicians.

More recent examples include the program M – originally produced in the 1980s, now revived and distributed by Cycling '74. M is capable of generating endless variations of cyclically looping material and triggers sound via MIDI control of synthesizers or samplers. Musician and producer Brian Eno used SSEYO's Koan Pro software to produce his *Generative Music* album of 1996. This algorithmic-composition package also plays a role in his 2005 release, *Another Day on Earth*.

NOTATION

Musicians, composers and publishers use sophisticated music notation software – such as Sibelius or Finale – to produce musical scores. Effectively, musical desktop-publishing systems enable the user to input music on to staff notation using a combination of MIDI keyboard, QWERTY keyboard and mouse. In this way, passages of music can be edited and laid out on the printed page in much the same way as a word processor handles language.

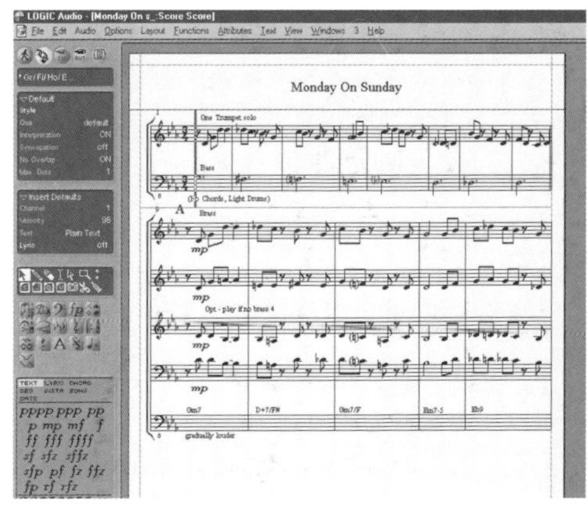

▲ *An arrangement created with a computerized score editor.*

Section One: The Instruments

The software uses MIDI sound modules or built-in software instruments to play back the score and allow the composer to hear what the music actually sounds like before it is ever printed and put before live musicians. Becoming increasingly sophisticated, software like Sibelius can even interpret written instructions such as *pizz.* and automatically switch playback to an appropriate sound, as well as introduce elements of dynamic and rhythmic expression into its simulated performances. The software is also able to instantly generate parts for all the individual musicians from a full score.

The widespread use of such programs, coupled with increased use of the Internet, has given rise to a new phenomenon – Internet music publishing. It is now possible to view, listen to and purchase musical scores online and many websites now offer composers a virtual shop window from which to sell their scores. The Pat Metheny Group made the score to the first section of their 2005 release, *The Way Up*, freely available on the Internet as a Sibelius file, which required no more than the installation of the Scorch plug-in to view and listen to.

PERFORMANCE

Programmes such as MAX/MSP enable the user to create computer-music performance environments that can generate musical events; process sounds and even interact with other live performers – all in real time. In the world of rock and pop music, computers are used to replay backing tracks to support live performances, add effects and even control video screens and lighting rigs.

▲ *Computers can coordinate lighting with music and sound.*

COMPOSITION

Computer programs known as 'sequencers' enable the musician to use MIDI to record, edit and play back musical ideas. Arrangements and compositions can be built up by layering sounds on different tracks, looping material and copying and pasting sections of music. Sequencers offer the user a number of different visual representations of the musical material. A graphical overview of the whole piece enables the musician to move around whole blocks or sections of music – such as 'verse' or 'bass line' – while other editing screens allow for fine tuning of detail.

Musical Instruments Handbook

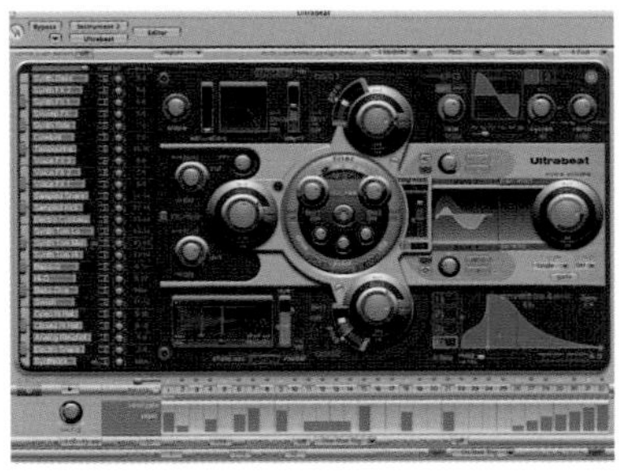

▲ *Sequencers capture sound that can be manipulated.*

Lists of numerical values give the musician precise control over every nuance of a performance. Music can be presented as a 'piano-roll' display, each note represented by a graphical block, the position of which indicates the pitch of the note and the length of which indicates its duration – analogous to the holes cut into the paper tape of player-piano systems. For those who read music, material can be presented as traditional staff notation. Well-known and widely used sequencers include Apple's Logic and Steinberg's Cubase.

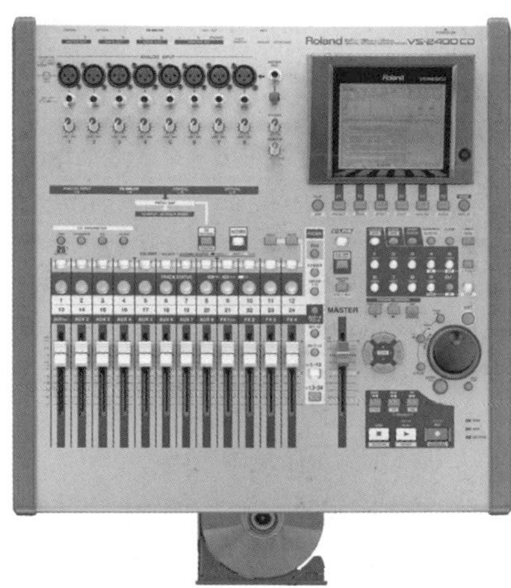

▲ *DAWs can record, mix and master.*

RECORDING

The computer has, to a large extent, replaced tape-based media in the recording studio, with most multitrack recordings now being made directly to hard disc. Digital Audio Workstations – or DAWs as they are commonly known – bring to the recording of live audio all the flexible, editing versatility of the MIDI sequencer. Non-destructive editing (the ability to undo actions) allows for creative experimentation in a way that editing tape with a razor blade never did.

▲ *Pro Tools was one of the first computer-based DAWs.*

Today, most MIDI-sequencing software also includes the ability to record and manipulate audio signals and many sound-recording systems also offer MIDI functionality – blurring the distinction between 'sequencer' and Digital Audio Workstation. DAWs include Steinberg's Nuendo and the widely adopted industry standard Digidesign's ProTools.

EFFECTS

As with so many tasks that were once handled by dedicated hardware units, the effects-processing of sound is increasingly being undertaken by software – usually by means of 'plug-ins' (small pieces of third-party software that can be installed within the DAW environment). Such software offers many imaginative ways to enhance and transform recorded material through equalization, control of dynamics or the addition of effects such as delay and reverberation.

Many software effects now emulate their classic hardware counterparts and sophisticated reverberation programmes – such as Audio Ease's Altiverb – can accurately simulate the natural sound properties of real acoustic spaces, making it possible for, say, a recording made in a London studio to sound as though the music was performed in a concert hall in Vienna.

▲ *Plug-ins enable sound to be processed futher.*

SYNTHESIS AND SAMPLING

The advent of ever-faster, more powerful microprocessor computing power has meant that it is now possible for computers to perform sound synthesis, triggered in real time from connected MIDI keyboards. Software now gives musicians access to a vast range of synthesis techniques. Some companies, like Native Instruments, specialize in producing software that emulates vintage synthesizers such as the Sequential Circuits Prophet 5 or the Yamaha DX7 – even down to the way the on-screen interfaces resemble the visual detail of the original instruments' control panels. Propellerhead's Reason effectively gives the user the software equivalent of a whole rack of synthesis, sampling, sound-processing and sequencing devices – even connected together by virtual patch cords!

▼ *Native Instruments FM7, which emulates the Yamaha DX7.*

Software is also used to perform sampling duties. In fact, recent years have seen a decline in the market for hardware samplers, unable to compete with the relatively low cost of high-speed computer processors, Random

Musical Instruments Handbook

Access Memory (RAM) and hard-disc capacity. A significant industry has grown up around sampling, creating and supplying extensive libraries of sampled musical phrases, drum loops and recordings of every conceivable instrument.

▲ *Many prefer a hands-on hardware controller.*

MIXING

Most DAWs include extensive mixing facilities, enabling the sound engineer to accomplish the task of mixing – balance of relative level, stereo (or surround) position, dynamic control and addition of effects – entirely within software, without the need for a hardware mixing desk. Such systems afford great flexibility, including the ability to instantly recall all the settings of mixes from a previous session and full automation of any changes that might be made throughout a piece, such as fade-ins or panning.

However, many musicians find that operating such a complex system with the computer QWERTY keyboard and mouse is unsatisfactory and turn to hardware control surfaces to regain a sense of physical interaction. These controllers are collections of dials and faders, resembling a traditional mixing desk, which, when connected to a DAW, control the software and, in turn, reflect the status of the on-screen virtual controls. Examples of such controllers include the Mackie Control Universal and the Digidesign ICON.

MASTERING

Mastering is the final stage of music post-production that takes place prior to the manufacture and distribution of the chosen medium (CD, vinyl, DVD). At the mastering studio, an engineer will often use a specialist software DAW to make final adjustments to the overall levels and equalization of the sound, before arranging the musical tracks into the desired order. At this stage, the gap between songs can be established and any fades accomplished. If the material is destined for CD, the mastering engineer will also 'tag' each piece of music with track IDs to enable CD players to find each track.

Section One: The Instruments

REFERENCE

CHRONOLOGICAL OVERVIEW

The history of musical instruments has always been very closely linked to the history of music itself. New musical styles often come about because new instruments become available, or improvements to existing ones are made.

▲ *Music has reinvented itself century after century.*

Improvements to the design of the piano in the 1770s, for instance, led to its adoption by composers such as Wolfgang Amadeus Mozart (1756–91), who quickly developed a new, individual style of keyboard writing. On the other hand, instrumental developments can come about because composers or performers demand them. In the 1970s, for example, polyphonic synthesizers were developed because monophonic synthesizers, which could only play one note at a time, under-used the abilities of keyboard players.

It is often obvious that a new instrument is needed when existing instruments are forced to use unusual, high-risk techniques to overcome shortcomings in their capabilities. In the eighteenth century, for example the natural horn, was asked to use awkward hand-stopping more and more frequently to provide extra notes, and it was therefore inevitable that it should be given a complete chromatic range as soon as the latest valve technology became available.

When a new instrument is introduced, there is usually quite a lot of interest on the part of musicians and composers, who are eager to find out what it can do. If it offers something unique for which there is a real need, it is fairly likely to survive. If it duplicates an instrument that exists already, it may still survive if it is easier to play, produces a better sound, costs less or is more practical than its rival. Even if it does become obsolete, it may well be resurrected for its curiosity value or for reasons of authenticity.

Musical Instruments Handbook

WESTERN INSTRUMENTS BEFORE 1600

In Western Europe, instrument-making only started to reach a high level of sophistication after about 1500, when more advanced manufacturing techniques were developed and when the impact of the Renaissance movement had raised music to a new level of importance. Before that time, prototypes of most instruments had been developed, but these lacked the refinement necessary for their long-term survival. By the beginning of the sixteenth century, instruments had been loosely categorized into two types. 'Bas', or 'soft' instruments were used indoors for background music and dancing, and were generally quiet instruments such as bowed and plucked strings, woodwind and portative organs. 'Haut', or 'loud' instruments were used outdoors, often for processions and outdoor dancing, and included shawms, trombones and slide trumpets. Beyond this loose arrangement, ensembles were formed freely, often just using whatever instruments happened to be available.

► *During the Renaissance, the recorder was a consort instrument.*

A much clearer pattern emerges from the Renaissance period (1450–1600) onwards. The Renaissance style was based on polyphony, meaning 'many voices', and was dominated by choral music. At that time choirs usually contained between three and five separate parts, each of which spanned a different range of notes. All the parts were melodic and equally important, given the same type of melody and often imitating the melodies of the other parts. Thus, the choir was an ideal ensemble for this type of music as it was well-balanced and blended smoothly into a single overall sound.

Because Renaissance instrumental music was written in the same polyphonic style, it was natural to try to imitate the perfectly blended, single tone-colour of the choir. Therefore, 'families' of instruments of similar design but different sizes were developed by instrument makers to enable them to form their own self-contained choirs, which were called consorts. An equal consort was one in which all the instruments were of the same type, and an unequal consort was a mix of instruments of different types, such as wind and stringed instruments. To take a present-day example, a saxophone quartet would have been an equal consort, whereas a rock group would have been an unequal consort.

Section Two: Reference

The upshot of this was that when a new instrument was invented, it was often swiftly followed by different-sized versions of the same design. In the sixteenth century, the viol family was developed like this, consisting of treble, tenor and bass viol, as were the violin family, the recorder family, the lute family and the crumhorn family. Cornetts, shawms, trombones and flutes also came in different sizes.

Besides consort instruments, there were a few others that could be used as self-contained solo instruments. The organ, which had existed since Greek and Roman times, was becoming much more versatile, incorporating many more stops. The virginals, the precursor to the harpsichord, was becoming popular domestically, and clavichords were steadily developing. The lute was a very popular solo instrument and also accompanied solo singing – the English composer John Dowland (1563–1626) was a notable champion of the instrument. As polyphonic music was hard to play on these instruments, music written for them tended to be more chord-based, anticipating the change of style that came with the Baroque period.

▼ *The virginals was a popular desktop instrument, largely used domestically.*

Musical Instruments Handbook

1600–1700

One of the catalysts for the change from the Renaissance style to that of the Baroque period (1600–1750) was the growth of opera, which had become particularly popular in Italy in the late-sixteenth century. In opera, solo singers were playing individual characters on stage, so it made much more sense for them to be given solo melodies against a chordal accompaniment, rather than force them to compete with parts of equal importance in a polyphonic texture. Therefore, accompanying instruments such as the harpsichord and the chamber organ became essential in opera orchestras. As their bass notes were fairly weak, other instruments such as the cittarone, the theorbo and viola da gamba, were used to reinforce the bass notes and together these instruments formed a 'continuo group'. In early opera, passages for solo singer and continuo alternated with fuller, louder music for a larger group of instruments, and it was in this way that choruses and groups of similar instruments, such as trombones, plucked instruments and stringed instruments, would participate.

Solo operatic singing was now becoming very agile and flamboyant, and melodic instruments that could imitate this sort of soloistic writing were therefore favoured. The cornett, a kind of wooden trumpet, was capable of this, as was the violin, which was rapidly replacing the viol as the preferred string instrument, because of its greater volume and expressive range. The Italian composer Claudio Monteverdi (1567–1643) wrote virtuoso music for both instruments in his 1607 opera, *Orfeo*, and Italian composers such as Giovanni Gabrieli (1557–1612) wrote for trumpets in this way within their instrumental music.

▲ *The harpsichord flourished during the Baroque period.*

Section Two: Reference

▶ *The Baroque recorder sounded sweeter than that of the Renaissance.*

▶ *The oboe was quickly accepted as a standard instrument.*

In the seventeenth century, Italian instrument makers such as Nicola Amati and later Stradivari and Guaneri developed the instruments of the violin family to such a level of perfection that they are still in professional use today. These newer instruments were also louder, easier to play, and produced a timbre that matched the emerging styles of music and audience taste better than viols, and the effect of this was that violins, violas, cellos and double basses became more favoured. Over the next 100 years, they slowly replaced other bowed stringed instruments such as the members of the viol family and the lira da bracchio. In the second half of the seventeenth century, violins were firmly established in the standard large-scale ensemble of royal courts, the Baroque orchestra, and the viola and cello were rapidly replacing the tenor and bass viola da gamba.

As the orchestra became increasingly prevalent, a uniform musical style, of a strong bass line and top line, less prominent inner parts and regular chord changes, gripped western music. The Renaissance consorts, based on equality, were unsuited to this type of music and disappeared, along with most of the instruments they contained. Wind instruments only stood a chance of surviving if they could perform solos and had a refined-enough tone to play along with the instruments of the violin family. Flutes and the higher recorders survived, but shawms, crumhorns, cornetts, viols and most lutes disappeared from professional music.

At the same time, new wind instruments were being developed, often by rethinking the design of older ones. The oboe was basically a redesigned shawm and its greater expressiveness, better tone and tuning led to it replacing the older instrument in the second half of the seventeenth century in military bands and church ensembles. It was also used as a soloist in orchestras. Similarly, the bassoon, which been around in guises such as the curtal, the bombard and the dulcian, became

Musical Instruments Handbook

a regular member of the orchestra, doubling the bass line in the continuo group.

In church music, the organ was approaching its most influential period, as organ builders in France, Germany and the Low Countries were developing and refining stops and mixtures, increasing the number of tone colours on offer. The growing practice of equipping organs with pedal-boards allowed organ music to be written in more parts and enabled more ambitious music to be written. Among domestic instruments, the virginals gave way to the louder harpsichord, and clavichords were increasingly popular. The guitar started to spread outside Spain and was particularly favoured in French and English aristocratic circles.

▲ *Due to its lack of volume, the clavichord was a suitable instrument for the home.*

Section Two: Reference

1700–50

This period marked the heyday of composers such as George Frideric Handel (1685–1759), Johann Sebastian Bach (1685–1750), Antonio Vivaldi (1678–1741) and Georg Philipp Telemann (1681–1767), and was the culmination of the Baroque era. The Baroque orchestra's core grouping of strings and harpsichord was now very firmly established, and oboes and bassoons were the favoured wind instruments. Nevertheless, variants of these core instruments still appeared from time to time, such as the viola d'amore, the baryton, the oboe di caccia, and the oboe d'amore, and were used by composers to provide occasional contrasts of tone.

Natural trumpets and kettledrums found their way into large-scale pieces, although because they could only play a handful of notes, they tended only to reinforce the rhythm, though high solo trumpet parts were occasionally written (such as in Bach's second *Brandenburg Concerto*). Natural horns were sometimes included too, as they had become more reliable and could now play in several keys thanks to the use of crooks. Both Bach and Handel used them as solo instruments and in the 1740s, German composers such as Johann Stamitz (1717–57) wrote extremely high parts for the instrument, in registers where there were more available notes. Transverse flutes were becoming more common as solo instruments and were replacing recorders in orchestras.

▲ *Organs were more than just instruments, they were a major decorative feature in a place of worship.*

Oboes of several types and bassoons were by now dominating military bands, with horns ousting tenor oboes in the 1720s. In domestic music, the clavichord and harpsichord remained popular, but the virginals was on its way out. A new instrument, the pianoforte, had been developed in 1709, but as yet had not generated much interest. The organ remained the king of church music and with the compositions of Bach reached the height of its influence.

Musical Instruments Handbook

1750–1800

The Baroque style gave way to the Classical style (1750–1830), which had developed from the Galant and Rococo styles that had spread across Europe from the 1740s. It played on features that were not part of the Baroque style, such as subtle contrasts of volume, musical 'conversations' and the use of rests within the music. Chord changes were more irregular than in Baroque music, where they tended to happen every beat or half-beat, and textures could suddenly change from four parts to one or two parts every few bars – a great change from the uniformly thick harmonies of Baroque music.

The net result of this was that the continuo group, which had formerly provided filler harmonies more or less throughout the music, now undermined the contrasts that had been carefully written into the music. So continuo instruments like the harpsichord, chamber organ, theorbo and bass viola de gamba soon disappeared from orchestras, although harpsichords struggled on into the early-nineteenth century.

The harpsichord's decline, together with that of the clavichord, was further accelerated by the dramatic rise of the piano from the 1770s. It was now a stronger instrument, with iron reinforcement, and had become much louder and more reliable. Its great advantage over the harpsichord was its sensitivity, since it could produce notes of any volume through striking the keys with a differing amount of force. It trumped the clavichord on sheer volume of sound, and could work equally well as a soloist and accompanist. Mozart particularly favoured the instrument, writing 24 piano concertos and a wealth of chamber music and solo works. The effect the piano had on keyboard music was dramatic. Markings such as dynamics and pedal markings started to appear in printed music, more sustained music was now possible and subtle, complicated textures relying on a sensitive touch could be written, allowing keyboard virtuosos to show off their talents.

► *The fortepiano was a more versatile instrument than the harpsichord.*

Section Two: Reference

► *Clarinets began to appear in music by Bach and Mozart.*

The orchestra was becoming much more uniform. The string section of violins, violas, cellos and double basses was now standard; oboes, bassoons, horns and trumpets were the favoured wind instruments and timpani the solitary percussion. Flutes were becoming permanent fixtures and towards the end of the century, clarinets were staking a claim as the fourth woodwind instrument. The basset horn was occasionally used, such as in Mozart's *La Clemenza di Tito*, and trombones frequently appeared in both church music – where they helped create a solemn feel – and in operatic music, where they typically represented Hell or the supernatural.

▼ *The triangle emulated the Turkish jingle.*

In military music, horns, trumpets and later clarinets and flutes were used in military bands, and newer wind instruments, such as serpents and basset horns, were also tried out. An influx of Turkish instruments from the Turkish Janissary bands – such as cymbals, bass drums, triangles and Turkish crescents – became increasingly common in European bands. In domestic music, pianos started to replace harpsichords and clavichords, and the mandolin was very popular in Italy. Novelty instruments from this time included the glass armonica, barrel organ and music box.

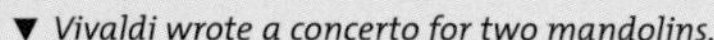

▼ *Vivaldi wrote a concerto for two mandolins.*

Musical Instruments Handbook

1800–50

This era saw the culmination of Classicism, with its orderly, balanced structures, and the rise of the Romantic period, lasting from 1830–1900. Taking its lead from literature, Romanticism was concerned with the expression of feelings and emotions. Romantic music was often based on stories rather than formal designs, and there was a great interest in supernatural subjects such as witchcraft and dreams. Composers therefore expanded their musical landscapes through exploring more instrumental colours, and wrote for larger ensembles to give their music more impact.

This dramatic musical transformation was helped by the invention, in 1815, of the valve on brass instruments and the continuing refinement of fingering systems on woodwind instruments.

► *The saxophone was a cross between single-reed woodwind and keyed brass instruments.*

Borrowed from devices controlling the air flow in blast furnaces, the valve was used on brass instruments to divert the air flow into extra lengths of tubing, thereby lowering the pitch and enabling brass instruments' 'missing notes' to be filled in. An alternative way of filling in these notes had been tried earlier using keys, resulting in the keyed bugle, the serpent and the ophicleide, which were found in wind bands and occasionally in the orchestra of the 1820s and 1830s. Valved trumpets and horns began to appear in the 1820s and entered mass production in the 1840s,

▲ *The cornet was a valved variation on the German posthorn.*

Section Two: Reference

by which time they were in common use in the orchestra. Trombones underwent a revival, losing their associations with the supernatural and entering the orchestra from Beethoven's time onwards.

New brass instruments were also invented, many of which have stayed in brass bands and wind bands ever since. The cornet, the euphonium and saxhorn families, the flugelhorn and tuba all emerged in the 1830s and 1840s, and mass production enabled brass and wind instruments to be produced at a cost that ordinary people could afford. This resulted in a huge growth in amateur music-making. In the 1840s, an entirely new family of woodwind instrument, the saxophone, was invented by the Belgian instrument maker Adolphe Sax (1814–94), who had also invented the saxhorn. It soon made its way into wind bands and was occasionally used in the orchestra, first of all by Hector Berlioz (1803–69) and the operatic composer, Giacomo Meyerbeer (1791–1864).

▲ *The piccolo replaced the flageolet in orchestras.*

Woodwind instruments were further developed and refined. The clarinet was improved and championed by composers such as Carl Maria von Weber (1786–1826), who in his Clarinet Concerto and orchestral music showed how effective it could be as a soloist. Theobald Boehm (1793–1881) brought out a simplified fingering system on the flute in 1832, and this led to similar systems on the oboe, clarinet and eventually bassoon, that made the instruments much easier to play and led composers to write more demanding parts as a result. Instrumental families were formed around the main woodwind instruments, in the same way as they had done in the Renaissance. As a result, the piccolo, cor anglais, several types of clarinet and the double bassoon soon became common in wind bands and orchestras. Berlioz was one of the first composers to use these instruments orchestrally, including a piccolo, a cor anglais, a clarinet in $E\flat$, a contrabassoon as well as a keyed bugle, an ophicleide and tubular bells in his *Symphonie fantastique* of 1827.

▲ *Tubular bells mimic church bells.*

The harp, which had been used as a folk instrument for hundreds of years, was

Musical Instruments Handbook

▶ *Berlioz's* Symphonie fantastique *was the harp's first appearance in a symphony.*

gaining a higher profile, recent improvements in the pedal mechanism by Sébastien Érard (1752–1831) now enabling it to play a full range of notes. It was in common use in the orchestra by the end of the 1840s. The percussion instruments of the Turkish Janissary bands, side drums, bass drums, tambourines, cymbals and triangles also became permanent additions to the orchestra.

The piano, meanwhile, had seen a spectacular growth in popularity. Ludwig van Beethoven's (1770–1827) music for the instrument progressively demanded more and more volume and stronger, iron-framed grand pianos were developed accordingly. These improved designs subsequently aided the rise of piano virtuosos such as Frédéric Chopin (1810–49) and Franz Liszt (1811–86), who gained celebrity status, dazzling audiences with their dexterity, power, sensitivity and stamina, and writing increasingly challenging music.

The instrument became a required accessory in middle-class homes, and upright models were developed to save space. Through transcriptions and arrangements of works such as symphonies, it provided a way for ordinary people to get to know the music of contemporary composers, and sheet-music sales rocketed as a result.

A smaller alternative to the organ, the harmonium, was developed in the early-nineteenth century, being used in small churches and for domestic music-making. The harmonica, or mouth organ, and the accordion also date from this time, and were initially popular in folk music and among amateurs.

▼ *The piano took over the harpsichord's role in domestic music-making.*

Section Two: Reference

1850–1900

▼ *Saxophones were now a staple of military bands, particularly in France.*

The Romantic period continued, and music became longer and more large-scale, as orchestras expanded to huge proportions. The growth of political nationalism across Europe encouraged countries to develop their own national styles of music, and folk elements found their way into art music. The Impressionist movement, inspired by French painters such as Claude Monet, encouraged composers like Claude Debussy (1862–1918) to take the continuing exploration of instrumental colour to a new level.

Partly to fulfil these demands, the development of new wind and brass instruments continued, but most of these later inventions did not take off. The sarrusophone family – mellophone, helicon and heckelphone – were sometimes used in orchestras and wind bands but never became standard. Richard Wagner's (1813–83) creation, the Wagner tuba, had more success thanks to its use in his operas, and it was also written for orchestrally by Richard Strauss (1864–1949) and Anton Bruckner (1824–96). The clarinet family was still expanding, mainly because of its dominant role in wind bands, and it soon contained models in C, B♭, A, E♭, D, A♭ and F as well as the bass clarinet, and towards the end of the nineteenth century, the contrabass clarinet. The saxophone family contained five members – bass, baritone, tenor, alto and soprano, and it too became central to the wind band. Two larger flutes, the alto flute and the bass flute, were developed, but were not really exploited until the twentieth century.

Other instruments were becoming obsolete. The basset horn, the natural trumpet, natural horn, keyed bugle, serpent and ophicleide were replaced by their modern equivalents and the harpsichord became virtually extinct. Although music that had been originally written for those instruments was still being played, it was assumed that composers would have preferred the modern instruments had they had the choice.

◀ *By the late Romantic, period there were two or three trumpets in an orchestra.*

Musical Instruments Handbook

▲ *The late-Romantic orchestra may have contained as many as eight horns.*

While fewer instruments were invented than in the previous 50 years, existing instruments continued to be refined, both to make them more versatile and to give them a broader tone. Improvements to the fingering systems of oboes and clarinets were made and Wilhelm Heckel (1856–1909) modernized the bassoon's fingering system in the 1880s. The bores of wind instruments were widened, and instruments such as the trumpet, horn and trombone gained a fuller sound as a result. Richard Strauss was the first composer to exploit to the full the virtuoso qualities of the French horn, with two horn concertos and spectacular orchestral horn parts.

A wider range of percussion instruments was also being used. The celesta became an occasional orchestral member after Piotr Ilyich Tchaikovsky's (1840–93) use of it in the *Nutcracker* and Camille Saint-Saëns (1835–1921) introduced the xylophone in the 1870s. The lyra-glockenspiel was becoming common in wind bands and a visit by a gamelan ensemble to the Paris Exhibition of 1889 generated a wave of interest among western composers for metallic percussion instruments such as antique cymbals, tam-tams and gongs.

In Spain, a revival of the guitar was underway, started by Francisco Tarréga. In the American Deep South, the banjo became popular among African-American workers, anticipating its adoption into early jazz groups. Nationalism was partly responsible for a surge of interest in folk instruments, such as the balalaika in Russia, the cimbalom in Hungary and the bagpipes in Scotland.

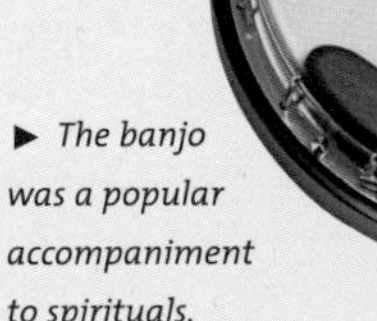

► *The banjo was a popular accompaniment to spirituals.*

Section Two: Reference

1900–50

By the time of the First World War Romanticism's hegemony was breaking down, as evidenced by a moving away from traditional harmony and rhythm in expressionistic music of Igor Stravinsky (1882–1971), Arnold Schoenberg (1874–1951) and Béla Bartók (1881–1945). The inter-war period saw the return of smaller-scale music that harked back to Classicism, while in America, jazz was fast becoming a popular phenomenon. Technological developments led to the first electronic instruments, the start of the recording industry and broadcast media – all of which had a profound effect on western music. This was the dawn of mass communication, which enabled musical styles to spread across the globe, and swing band music was the first type of music to achieve mass popularity in this way.

▲ *In the amateur market, the player piano gave the piano great competition.*

Musical Instruments Handbook

The large-scale development of new wind and brass instruments that had taken place over the previous century slowed down markedly, although one or two new instruments still came out. These included the heckelphone and the sousaphone, creations of Heckel and the American wind-band leader, John Philip Sousa (1854–1932), respectively. The orchestra, the brass band and the wind band reached their maximum size at the beginning of the century, and changing tastes and post-war austerity ensured that they never reached this size again. Their personnel had really been fixed in the late-nineteenth century.

In terms of mechanical instruments, the player piano, which could play music through holes punched in rolls of paper, appeared in the first decade, and was used as a type of jukebox, playing performances of popular piano pieces, although it was also used by Stravinsky as a compositional aid, anticipating a similar use of the sequencer by 80 years.

Early electronic instruments included the telharmonium, the theremin, the ondes martenot and the trautonium, but of these only the ondes martenot enjoyed much notoriety, thanks mainly to composers such as Olivier Messiaen (1908–92) who incorporated it into some of his orchestral pieces. Electric organs, notably the Hammond organ, were developed, too, and electronic mechanisms were now common on pipe organs. Cinema organs emerged at the beginning of the century and were usually used to play light music at leisure venues. The electric guitar was developed in the 1940s and was soon being taken up by jazz musicians such as Charlie Christian.

Percussion instruments continued to attract the interest of composers, and instruments as diverse as bull-roarers, sirens, whistles, guiros, thundersheets,

▼ *Orchestral thundersheets are made from thin metal.*

Section Two: Reference

wind machines, woodblocks, whips, tom-toms and rattles were used by composers such as Edgar Varèse (1883–1965), Stravinsky and Messiaen. In jazz, a single percussionist played several instruments in a drum kit, and to aid this, foot-operated hi-hat cymbals and bass drums became standard.

Through the immense popularity of jazz groups and swing bands, instruments such as the trumpet, trombone, saxophone, clarinet, banjo, guitar, piano, double bass and vibraphone gained a new type of appeal and helped create virtuosos such as Benny Goodman (clarinet), Louis Armstrong (trumpet), Charlie Parker (saxophone) and Lionel Hampton (vibraphone).

► *The inclusion of folk instruments in western music has enriched its harmonic language.*

► *The trombone is at the heart of the orchestral brass section.*

With recorded music now readily available through the gramophone and the radio, domestic and amateur music-making started to go into decline, although the effects were not felt until later in the century. Accordions, concertinas and mouth organs were popular among street musicians, and occasionally found their way into operas to replicate this street music.

Attempts at resurrecting certain instruments began, with the Dolmetsch family reconstructing instruments such as harpsichords, clavichords, viols, lutes and recorders in their family workshop.

Folk-music collectors, notably the Hungarian composers Bartók and Zoltán Kodály (1882–1967), travelled to rural areas of Europe and North Africa recording traditional folk music and cataloguing the instruments they came across. This stimulated a new interest in authentic folk music, and some of the instruments and instrumental techniques they discovered were incorporated into their own compositions (for example, the cimbalom). This anticipated the huge interest in world music that has sprung up in the last 20 or 30 years.

Musical Instruments Handbook

1950–PRESENT

In the last 50 years, music has branched off into hundreds of different directions. Music technology has played a large part in this, with the huge number of recordings available exposing people to many more types of music. The public's ongoing consumption of music, via the broadcast media and through the popularity of record and CD collecting, has enabled obscure music to be recorded commercially. Helped by a growth in academic study into old instruments and folk music, this has resulted in the resurrection of obsolete and rare instruments and given a new lease of life to those on their way out.

However, the flip side to this is that the ubiquity of commercial music has contributed to a decline in more traditional music. In classical music, highly experimental compositional methods have been explored, exploiting every sort of colouristic effect and instrumental combination. Movements such as integral serialism (music derived from a single series of numbers), aleatoricism (music based on chance), minimalism (the repetition of very short musical ideas) and postmodernism (music that combines modern ideas with more traditional elements) have demanded a new sort of virtuosity from performers and a consistently high quality of instrument.

Baroque instruments such as the harpsichord, recorder and theorbo, were reintroduced into performances of Baroque music in the 1950s, and were followed by Renaissance and medieval instruments. More recently, authentic classical and nineteenth-century instruments, such as natural horns and older designs of oboes, clarinets and bassoons have been used in performances of classical and romantic music.

Amplification of instruments has been a key development, enabling any sound to be made as loud as necessary. This meant there was no longer a need to develop powerful acoustic instruments, in the way that the pipe organ, grand piano and tuba had evolved, or to form vast groups of instrumentalists, such as large symphony orchestras, since a whole stadium could now be filled by, say, a singer, an electric guitar and drums.

Amplification played a crucial role in popularizing rock and pop music. Mass audiences were wowed by the sheer energy of high-decibel performances, which made acoustic performances

▶ *Necessity bred the invention of the drum kit.*

Section Two: Reference

ENSEMBLES

A musical ensemble is a group of two or more musicians who have come together to play music. In theory, an ensemble could contain any number of instruments in any combination, but in practice, certain combinations just don't work very well, either for musical reasons or because of the sheer practicality of getting particular instruments and players together in the first place.

WHY DO MUSICAL ENSEMBLES FORM?

Ensembles can develop instinctively. When someone in a group of people starts singing or sounding a rhythm, it is often a natural reaction for the others in the group to join in somehow, perhaps by singing along, tapping or clapping a rhythm, or adding an extra part of their own. The informal mass singing of football crowds, soldiers on the march or sugar-plantation workers all started this way. Jazz, pop and folk music have this spontaneity, too, with a great tradition of musicians getting together for jam sessions.

Alternatively, a composer, arranger or producer might assemble a certain combination of instruments to best serve the musical vision they have in mind. They might think of a brand-new combination of instruments, or either add or take away instruments from an existing ensemble. The Russian composer Igor Stravinsky (1882–1971) once had a dream in which he saw a flute, a clarinet, two bassoons, two trumpets and two trombones playing in a group. This then formed the instrumentation for his *Octet*. In jazz, small 'swing combos' occasionally performed in the 1930s and 1940s using three or four players from the same swing band.

An ensemble might also come into existence primarily to serve a certain function. The rise of the wind band, for instance, was closely linked to the need

Musical Instruments Handbook

for music for military parades, and other ensembles are closely linked to certain purposes, such as choirs and church services, or swing bands and dancing.

Ensembles can also be formed specifically to perform in public to an audience. This might be for artistic reasons, for commercial gain, or a combination of the two. 'Manufactured' pop groups tend to be put together for their audience appeal more than their musical originality and are dropped when they sell too few records. On the other hand, many classical, jazz and rock groups perform challenging music that audiences find difficult, and often make a financial loss as a result. They may, however, be rewarded by the artistic satisfaction of having played that music in public.

INGREDIENTS FOR A SUCCESSFUL MUSICAL ENSEMBLE

First and foremost, an ensemble must work well musically. The instruments need to form an effective team, combining their individual strengths in the most efficient way possible. For instance the string trio of violin, viola and cello tends to work better than that of three violas, as between them the violin, viola and cello possess a much wider range and a greater variety of tone colours. This allows more interesting music to be written for them. The instruments must also be able to hold their own in terms of volume. It is no accident that the more successful solo jazz instruments have proved to be more strident ones like the saxophone and trumpet rather than the oboe or recorder.

▲ *Wind and brass instruments have always domintaed military bands,*

Section Two: Reference

An ensemble also needs a supply of quality music that exploits its particular strengths and that 'sells' that particular combination of instruments to audiences and performers. The music of Joseph Haydn (1732–1809), Wolfgang Amadeus Mozart (1756–91) and Ludwig van Beethoven (1770–1827), for example. used the string quartet so well that it became one of the central mediums of classical music.

▲ *Today there are myriad music festivals catering for all tastes.*

A continuing demand for the ensemble is also important. This might be audience demand, an ongoing need for a certain sort of music for a particular event, or the desire of musicans to get together and play a certain type of music. This demand can also be dependent on people's changing tastes, their income, the sort of education they received, how they spend their leisure time and the amount of music to which they have access.

The availability of suitable performers, the right instruments and appropriate venues are all crucial to the survival of an ensemble. For instance, Karlheinz Stockhausen's (b. 1928) *Helicopter String Quartet*, which requires each member of a string quartet to play their part from a separate helicopter, is very rarely performed because of the costs involved. Orchestras on limited budgets often choose not to perform certain pieces that involve extra performers as they just cannot afford to do so. However, if an 'expensive' ensemble will draw a large audience, it can survive.

▲ *Huge audiences are vital for many musical outfits' survival.*

Finally, the survival of an ensemble also rests on the quality of the performing. All the standard ensembles have, at some point in their history, been championed by at least one group of extraordinary performers. The high level of performance of such a group inspires others to start similar groups, while public and critical enthusiasm encourages the best composers to work with them and can attract interest from concert promoters and record labels.

SMALL ENSEMBLES

Small ensembles make up the majority of standard instrumental groups, as they are easy to get together and tend to be cheaper than their larger counterparts. Their actual make-up can vary from a group of very similar instruments, such as the four clarinets of a clarinet quartet, to a group of very different ones, such as those in a standard bop-jazz quintet. Since a small ensemble does not normally have a conductor, its members need to be properly organized in order to be successful musically.

Mixed groups are often organized by each instrument taking on a specific role, such as playing a melody, sounding the rhythm or providing a harmonization. Thus in a typical rock group line-up, the singer provides the tune, the rhythm guitar the harmony, the bass guitar the bass line and the drum kit the rhythm. This way, each instrument has its own 'territory' and therefore does not conflict too much with what the other instruments are doing.

▲ *Small ensembles have formed the backbone of musical performance for centuries.*

Section Two: Reference

Groups of very similar instruments, on the other hand, usually take on comparable roles. Often the top part has a melody that is harmonized by the lower parts, which also follow more or less the same rhythm. A hymn arrangement is a good example of this. Alternatively, all the parts may have simultaneous melodies that imitate and intertwine with each other – a particular hallmark of much Renaissance music.

With composed, notated music, the composer can plan very carefully how the group will interact. This can enable the instruments to swap roles freely, to engage in musical conversations with each other, to create complicated textures and cross-rhythms and to use volume, instrumental colour and register in a very subtle way.

SOLO INSTRUMENT AND PIANO

Easy to get together, this is the most common of the classical-music ensembles. Its rise mirrors that of the piano, originating in the eighteenth century and becoming very popular from the time of Mozart – the first composer to exploit the immense flexibility of the piano. The combination of violin and piano has been written for extensively, notably in the sonatas of Mozart, Beethoven, Johannes Brahms (1833–97) and Sergei Prokofiev (1891–1953), while partnerships of piano and cello, clarinet or flute have also been very popular. Any acoustic melodic instrument will form an effective combination with a piano, as long as it uses the same tuning. Playing pieces to a piano accompaniment forms an important part of learning most western melody instruments.

VOICE AND PIANO

The combination of voice and piano really took off in the early-nineteenth century with Franz Schubert's (1797–1828) and Robert Schumann's (1810–56) highly expressive settings of German romantic poetry, often grouped together to form song cycles. They were followed by a long line of composers of songs including Brahms, Gustav Mahler (1860–1911), Claude Debussy (1862–1918) and Benjamin Britten (1913–76), who formed a highly successful partnership

Musical Instruments Handbook

with the tenor Peter Pears. The combination of voice and piano is also very popular in cabaret and comedy acts, and it has also been used in jazz, folk and pop music. Perhaps the most famous example was Elton John's performance of 'Candle in the Wind 1997' at the funeral of Diana, Princess of Wales.

STRING QUARTET

One of the most instantly recognizable classical mediums, the string quartet originated in the eighteenth century and is made up of two violins, a viola and a cello. Haydn's, Mozart's and Beethoven's sets of string quartets are among the greatest achievements of classical chamber music and, inspired by this example, classical composers, notably Béla Bartók (1881–1945), have tended to save their most complex ideas for the medium, often demanding enormous skill from the performers. The string quartet is very versatile and has a great range of colours at its disposal, including several types of *pizzicato* (plucking), *col legno* (hitting the strings with the wood of the bow), as well as many different bow strokes. String quartets are often used to provide background music at events such as wedding receptions, sometimes playing popular arrangements. They have also been used occasionally in pop music, for instance on the Beatles songs, 'Yesterday' and 'Eleanor Rigby'.

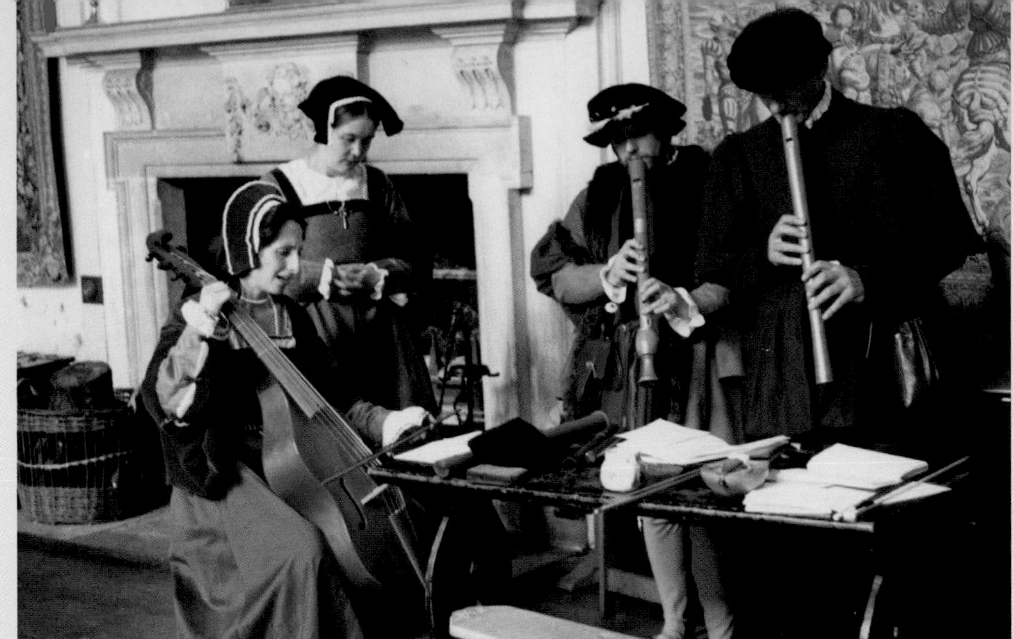

▲ *A recreation of a sixteenth-century ensemble: viol, voice and two recorders.*

CHAMBER MUSIC ON PERIOD INSTRUMENTS

A period instrument is an original instrument from a previous era, or a replica of one. Until the 1950s, music from earlier times was almost always played on modern instruments, but since then there has been a great revival of interest in authentic music-making among academics, performers and instrument makers. Nowadays, Baroque, Renaissance and medieval chamber music is almost always professionally performed on authentic instruments. Examples of reconstructed ensembles include the viol consort (usually six viols: two trebles, two tenors, two basses), the recorder consort (of four to six recorders of varying sizes) and the trio sonata, in which a continuo group (usually harpsichord plus a bass instrument such as a bass viol or baroque cello) accompanies two melodic instruments such as Baroque violins or flutes. Instruments as diverse as the shawm, tabor, fiddle, cittern, crumhorn, serpent and hurdy-gurdy have been very successfully resurrected. Current performing ensembles include the Baroque brass group, His Majestys Sagbuts and Cornetts, and the viol consort Fretwork.

OTHER CLASSICAL CHAMBER-MUSIC GROUPS

Over the years, composers have tried more or less every sensible and not-so-sensible combination of classical instruments, with varying degrees of success. Late-eighteenth and nineteenth-century chamber music is dominated by piano and stringed instruments. Ensembles such as the piano trio, piano quartet and piano quintet became firmly established then, while string duos, trios, quintets and sextets were also popular. All-wind and all-brass groups such as wind

Musical Instruments Handbook

quintet, wind octet and brass quintet developed at this time too, as a spin-off from wind band music. Mixed ensembles, such as clarinet quintet (clarinet and string quartet) and horn trio (horn, violin and piano) gave wind players the chance of more soloistic playing. In the twentieth century, composers also began to explore wackier combinations of instruments, often involving more obscure ones, in an attempt to create more unusual sounds. Performance of this music is made possible by contemporary music groups such as the London Sinfonietta, where unusual smaller groups can be formed from within the large overall pool of available players. An established twentieth-century combination is that of violin, cello, flute, clarinet, piano, percussion and singer. Ensembles of very similar instruments, such as flute duo, clarinet quartet, saxophone quartet and horn quartet are also fairly common, performing arrangements and original compositions.

SMALL UNACCOMPANIED VOCAL GROUPS

A cappella, meaning 'in church style', can refer to any type of unaccompanied vocal music. Usually there are four different parts ranging from high to low, although trios, quintets and larger groups are also common. Small groups can consist of all men (the 'barbershop' quartet is an example of this), all women, or a mixture of the two. Classical ensembles often concentrate on Renaissance vocal music (written between about 1400 and 1600) such as madrigals and motets, or on twentieth-century works, which can sometimes demand unusual techniques such as multiphonics (singing two or more notes simultaneously), very high notes, and noises such as clicks, pops, whistling and hissing. A rare example of an *a cappella* group that had chart success was the Flying Pickets, in the mid-1980s, and Jan Garbarek's saxophone improvisations with the male *a cappella* group the Hilliard Ensemble, have also proved very popular.

▼ *The Ink Spots pioneered the black vocal group-harmony genre.*

Section Two: Reference

POPULAR MUSIC GROUPS

Since the birth of rock 'n' roll, popular music groups have taken on a bewildering number of different forms. However, the choice of instruments largely follows the same general rule. There is normally at least one instrument to cover each of the four main ingredients of a typical popular-music texture: the beat (usually a drum kit), the harmonic filling material (usually one or two electric guitars or a keyboard), the melody (usually the voice) and the bass line (often an electric bass guitar).

The line-ups of early rock 'n' roll bands of the mid-1950s were often based on the jazz, blues and country-music groups from which they came. At first, a drum kit, electric guitars, double bass, saxophone, horn section and sometimes a piano might feature – the double bass was soon replaced by an electric bass. In the UK, the skiffle band – comprising guitar, double bass and washboard – was popular at the same time.

In the late 1950s and early 1960s, American groups such as the Ventures and British outfits such as the Shadows established an instrumental lineup known as the 'beat combo', comprising a drum kit, electric bass guitar and two electric guitars (lead and rhythm). A different sound was produced by keyboard-based bands such as the Doors, where the keyboard replaced the electric guitars. The development of more advanced recording techniques in the 1960s and 1970s, especially that of multitracking, meant that groups could create very rich, multi-layered textures, with the help of skilled record producers, such as Phil Spector. In styles such as rhythm and blues, funk and disco, extra musicians were often included to add richness. These included string sections (usually violins), horn sections (wind and brass instruments such as trumpet, saxophone and trombone) and groups of backing singers.

▲ *The Rolling Stones have been one of the world's most influential bands since the 1960s.*

Musical Instruments Handbook

▲ *Kraftwerk were a dominant and influential force in electronic music's development.*

Electronic instruments have always been eagerly embraced by the pop industry as soon as they have become available, and instruments such as the Minimoog synthesizer and the clavinet were incorporated in the 1960s and 1970s by groups keen to create a new 'sound', as were both the expressive use of feedback and new pedal effects on the electric guitar. The availability of programmable drum machines and synthesizers during the late 1970s meant that live musicians could be dispensed with for the first time. Bands such as Kraftwerk consisted entirely of synthesizer players, and the instrument dominated 1980s' music until the re-emergence of guitar-based line-ups with Indie music and Britpop in the 1990s.

In the late 1980s and 1990s, music technology took a further hold on popular music, as dance music took off. Sequencers enabled musical patterns to be continually 'looped' and other sounds manipulated and rhythms tightened up. This made for high-energy, hypnotic music ideal for dancing. In addition, the DJ – who selected and played the records – turned into an instrumentalist in his own right, by mixing different records together and exploiting a number of effects from the turntable. Rap and hip-hop also exploits music technology, using rhythmical speaking over drum loops and samples. As the influence of pop music has spread across the globe, countless new ensembles have been created from the fusion of world-music styles and rock influences, including Bhangra (Punjabi and Jamaican influences) and Salsa (Cuban and Puerto Rican influences).

▼ *Decks are the musical instruments of dance, requiring technical and musical know-how.*

Section Two: Reference

SMALL JAZZ GROUPS

Jazz groups, like pop groups, have a very flexible approach to instrumentation, although certain instruments are favoured for different jazz styles. Like rock music, instruments tend to be chosen to fulfil certain roles, with the rhythm section providing a beat, a bass line and harmonic filling material, and the front-line instruments playing the tunes.

The earliest forms of jazz – New Orleans and Dixieland – have a core grouping of trumpet, clarinet and trombone supplying the tune and piano and drums forming the rhythm section. Sometimes violins or banjos would be found and a double bass soon became standard. As an antidote to the larger big bands and swing bands that took over in the 1920s and 1930s, smaller breakaway groups performed occasionally, including Benny Goodman's trio of clarinet, piano and drums, to which a vibraphone was later added. From groups like this, the bop style of the 1940s and 1950s arose, which was improvised to a large extent and demanded great agility. A typical bop group might consist of a front line of between one and four players, often including a trumpet and saxophone, and a rhythm section of piano, double bass and drums. 'Cool' jazz, which was pre-composed and more restrained, tended to feature more varied combinations of instruments as tone-colour became more important. Miles Davis, the dominant

▲ *Benny Goodman's line-up ushered in the Swing Era.*

Musical Instruments Handbook

▲ *The Soviet Children's Orchestra.*

figure of cool jazz, had at various times a nonet, a quintet and a sextet.

'Free' jazz, a highly experimental type of jazz pioneered in the 1960s, often included unusual or bizarre instruments, such as the pocket-sized plastic trumpet of Don Cherry and the sirens, rattles and modified saxophones (called the stritch and the manzello) of the saxophonist Roland Kirk. Bossa nova integrated Brazilian percussion instruments such as the congas and claves, while jazz-rock fusion, which sprung up in the 1970s, combined traditional jazz instruments such as the saxophone and trumpet with electronic instruments. Here, the electric bass guitar and synthesizer tended to replace the double bass and piano in the rhythm section.

LARGE ENSEMBLES

Most large-scale ensembles originated in the last 200 years or so, and mainly comprise orchestras, military bands and large choirs. They almost all read from music and usually evolved from the expansion of smaller ensembles. The reasons for forming a large ensemble can vary, from providing more instrumental colours, and hence richer sounds, to simply producing an overwhelmingly loud noise. Volume is certainly a big factor in dictating the size of outdoor ensembles, and with military bands this size also helps convey a sense of military power. Large-scale indoor ensembles are either formed for the purpose of giving concerts in large venues to a paying audience, or as a leisure activity by groups of amateur musicians. Large groups are usually directed by conductors, choirmasters or bandleaders, who beat time and communicate their interpretation of the music to the performers, taking rehearsals and conducting in concerts and recordings. Large professional ensembles are very expensive to run and this often affects how often they can perform and the music that they play.

Section Two: Reference

STRING ORCHESTRAS

Consisting of groups of first and second violins, violas, cellos and double basses, the string orchestra is one of the oldest present-day classical ensembles. When the violin family started to expand in the sixteenth century, the string orchestra soon began to replace viol consorts for ensemble music, as it had greater projection, which made it far more effective at accompanying dancing. 'Violin bands' were favoured at the French court of the seventeenth century and as the Baroque period progressed, string orchestras became commonplace fixtures in royal courts throughout Europe, often with a violinist-composer such as Jean-Baptiste Lully (1632–87) or Arcangelo Corelli (1653–1713) as its figurehead.

Baroque string orchestras were usually directed by a harpsichord player, but these began to disappear with the change in musical styles from Baroque to Classical, in the second half of the eighteenth century. After a period of relative neglect in the nineteenth century, the string orchestra made a comeback in the twentieth century. Famous works for string orchestra include Mozart's *Eine Kleine Nachtmusik*, Bartók's *Divertimento* and Krzysztof Penderecki's (b. 1933) *Threnody for the Victims of Hiroshima*, which uses unconventional effects such as plucking behind the bridge and hitting the bodies of the instruments.

▲ *String orchestras can range from 12 to 60 players.*

Musical Instruments Handbook

SWING AND BIG BANDS

The big band developed in the late 1920s as a cut-down version of the larger New York dance bands of bandleaders such as Paul Whiteman. Early big-band pioneers, notably Fletcher Henderson, helped establish a standard instrumentation that eventually grew to three or four trumpets, three trombones, four saxophones and four rhythm-section instruments. In contrast to the small-scale jazz of the 1920s, the music, orchestrated by skilled arrangers and conducted or led by the bandleader, was written down, but still left opportunities for soloists to improvise over repeated melodic fragments, or 'riffs'. The clarinettist and bandleader Benny Goodman did much to bring swing bands to a mass audience in the mid-to-late 1930s, together with bandleaders such as Glenn Miller, Duke Ellington and Count Basie. The Swing Era lasted from around 1928 to 1945. The word 'swing' referred to the light, infectious type of rhythmic drive that is typical of the music. Many soloists of the bop era learnt their trade by performing in big bands, and vocalists such as Ella Fitzgerald and Billie Holliday gained their early solo experience with them.

CHAMBER ORCHESTRAS

The chamber orchestra emerged from the practice of occasionally adding wind instruments to the Baroque string orchestra in the seventeenth and early-eighteenth centuries. Composers such as George Frideric Handel (1685–1759) and Johann Sebastian Bach (1685–1750) might reinforce the bass line with a bassoon, give solo parts to oboes, flutes and horns, and use timpani and trumpets to flesh out *tutti* sections. By around 1770, pairs of oboes, bassoons, horns and timpani were more or less standard fixtures in the classical orchestra of Haydn and Mozart and over the next three decades, pairs of flutes, trumpets and clarinets became permanent and string sections increased. This arrangement lasted from about 1800 to 1830, and composers such as Beethoven and Schubert wrote the majority of their orchestral works for this instrumentation. After a period of dominance by symphony orchestras, financial considerations led to chamber orchestras making a comeback in the twentieth century.

▲ *Big band music is highly arranged, leaving gaps for soloists.*

Section Two: Reference

SYMPHONY ORCHESTRAS

The best-known of all classical ensembles, the symphony orchestra developed from the expansion of the chamber orchestra in the 1820s and 1830s, when composers such as Beethoven and Hector Berlioz (1803–69), and later Franz Liszt (1811–86) and Richard Wagner (1813–83), added more instruments to increase the volume of sound and the number of available tone colours. The main difference from the chamber orchestra is its use of a full brass section of three trumpets, four horns, three trombones and tuba, which was possible after valved brass instruments became commonly available in the 1840s. To match the extra volume this created, there also tend to be more string players, and usually three or more of each woodwind instrument rather than two. Extra colour is added through doublings on piccolo, cor anglais, bass clarinet and contrabassoon. One or two harps and two or more percussionists, playing instruments such as side drum, bass drum, cymbals, triangle and tam-tam, are often found in addition to the timpani.

▲ *A full-sized orchestra will consist of about 60 players.*

Towards the end of the nineteenth century, composers such as Richard Strauss (1864–1949) and Mahler expanded the orchestra even more – sometimes writing for four of each woodwind instrument, six or eight horns and very large brass and percussion sections, and sometimes extra groups of trumpets and horns to play from offstage.

In the twentieth century, further instruments were introduced, especially percussion instruments such as the piano, celeste, glockenspiel, xylophone, vibraphone, cimbalom and tubular bells and occasionally an organ, saxophone, guitar, mandolin, or ondes martenot. Since about 1950, non-western percussion instruments such as marimbas, tuned gongs, tom-toms and bu-bams have become increasingly common in orchestral music. Non-western melodic instruments occasionally appear, too, with the composers Toro Takemitsu (1930–96) and Tan Dun (b. 1957), for instance, writing for traditional Japanese and Chinese instruments in their scores. Music technology has also found its way into the orchestra, with pieces for pre-recorded tape and orchestra by Stockhausen and Luciano Berio (1925–2003) dating from the 1950s. Electronic instruments have included synthesizers, samplers and electric guitars, while amplification and occasionally live digital manipulation of sounds are sometimes employed.

Musical Instruments Handbook

▲ *New percussion instruments have added to composers' sound palettes.*

LIGHT ORCHESTRAS

While professional chamber and symphony orchestras mainly give public concerts, there are many other types of orchestra – similar in make-up – that perform other functions. In the nineteenth century, orchestras were formed specifically to accompany dancing, particularly waltzes, and often went on foreign tours. The Austrian waltz composers, Johann Strauss I and Johann Strauss II, were masters of this genre and their works are still popular today. This tradition was followed by a whole stream of 'light' orchestras, which tended to play more accessible, non-symphonic music and were associated with forms of popular entertainment such as dancing, operettas, music-hall entertainment, and, in the twentieth century, film music, musicals and, before the arrival of rock 'n' roll, the music of popular singers and crooners.

In the nineteenth century, they were roughly the same size as chamber orchestras, although freer in make-up. With the arrival of jazz and then popular music in the twentieth century, they began to incorporate many popular influences. Orchestras in American musicals, for instance, often combine features of the big-band style such as the use of the piano, saxophones, drum kit and jazz trumpet and trombone techniques with a rich string sound, often omitting instruments such as oboe and bassoon.

The huge costs involved in running orchestras, together with the growing popularity of rock music and the increased use of recorded music in live situations, meant that the number of light orchestras declined steadily from the 1960s. Today, it would be virtually unthinkable to hire an orchestra for a television show, whereas in the 1970s this was commonplace.

Section Two: Reference

CHOIRS AND CHORUSES

Originating in the plainsong singing of the early Christian Church, church, chapel and cathedral choirs tend to be small or medium-sized (between 16 and 40 singers). In many Catholic, High Anglican and Greek and Russian Orthodox churches, male-voice choirs are common, although the numbers of mixed choirs are growing. In all-male choirs, boy singers (or 'trebles') are employed to sing the highest part and male altos (men singing falsetto), supply the alto or second-highest part. Church choirs are frequently accompanied by instruments, usually by the organ in the Christian Church, occasionally by small orchestras or brass ensembles and, in some denominations, by rock-music instruments. Other choirs of this size include gospel choirs, mixed chamber choirs – which give concert performances of both sacred and secular music – and the chorus lines of shows, which perform in musical theatre.

Large-scale choirs in the West, usually known as choruses, probably originated

Musical Instruments Handbook

in Italy towards the end of the sixteenth century to accompany operas and masques, in imitation of ancient Greek choruses. This tradition has been preserved ever since, with the inclusion of choruses in operas, oratorios (religious musical works) and large-scale orchestral works such as cantatas and choral symphonies. In the nineteenth century, the amateur-choral-society tradition started, where groups of amateur singers met to rehearse works such as Handel's *Messiah*. Choral societies are still popular today and can have as many as 250 members.

Children's choirs also tend to be very large, partly because it is easy to get together large numbers of children in schools, and partly because children produce less sound than adults. Male-voice choirs are particularly associated with Wales, where groups of miners formed choirs in the nineteenth century, singing mainly hymns and folksong arrangements in close harmony.

BRASS BANDS

The brass band has strong associations with the north of England, although there are also traditions in the United States, India and parts of Europe. While some brass ensembles had existed previously using keyed bugles, trombones and serpents, brass bands only really became viable with the invention of the brass instrument valve in the early-nineteenth century, which meant that a full range of notes could be produced. By the 1840s, valved brass instruments were becoming more affordable and were

▲ *American marching band with sousaphone (centre).*

Section Two: Reference

taken up by workers in several countries, who formed colliery, factory or town bands. Soon regular brass-band contests were held. To make these fair, a standard instrumentation was agreed upon, comprising one E♭ cornet, 10 B♭ cornets divided into four parts, three E♭ tenor horns, two baritones, two euphoniums, two tenor trombones, bass trombone, two basses in E flat and two basses in B♭.

Brass bands were at their most popular in the late-nineteenth century and, despite industrial decline, many continue to this day. The Salvation Army has a strong brass-band tradition, having manufactured its own instruments until the 1960s. In the United States, military bands became all brass for a time in the middle of the nineteenth century, before reverting back to mixed wind and brass.

WIND BANDS

Wind bands – usually consisting of choirs of woodwind instruments, brass and percussion – come in many different shapes and sizes. Their most familiar public appearances are at military parades, state events such as funerals and at sporting occasions. They are suited to outdoor performance, as the instruments are loud, portable and relatively unaffected by the weather .

Wind bands have always been closely associated with the military. In Europe, small bands of instruments such as shawms, slide trumpets and drums existed from the thirteenth century, and trombones, bombards, cornetts and crumhorns were later added. As more versatile modern instruments such as oboes, bassoons, flutes, clarinets and horns, became available in the seventeeth and eighteenth centuries, they soon replaced their older counterparts. An important influence was the impact of Turkish Janissary bands in the early-nineteenth century. These military bands included instruments such as timpani, cymbals, Turkish crescents, triangles and bass drums and were eagerly copied in Europe.

Wind bands really took off in the nineteenth century with improvements to existing wind instruments, the development of new ones and the invention of the valve for brass instruments, allowing for a fully functional brass section. Professional training colleges (such as Kneller Hall in Twickenham, England) were set up and band contests organized; and by the 1880s, most military regiments and towns across Europe and America had a wind band, with groups as large as 80 being found. By this time, all the modern orchestral wind, brass and percussion instruments had made their way into the ensemble, as well as instruments such as euphoniums, saxhorns and cornets. At that time, wind bands mostly played marches and arrangements of classical pieces, though since then much original music has been composed.

Musical Instruments Handbook

Wind bands are especially popular in the USA, where almost every school has its own wind band and where marching bands have a high public profile. Other types of wind band include the Scottish pipe band, consisting of bagpipes and drums, the Northern Irish flute band (flutes and drums) and the Russian 'horn band', popular in the late-eighteenth century and comprising of hunting horns which could each only play one note.

▲ *This Bavarian marching band includes both wind and brass instruments.*

Section Two: Reference

DECIBELS

A decibel is a measurement of the ratio between two quantities, and is used as a comparator in many branches of physics.

In acoustics, decibels (or dB, for short) are used to indicate the loudness of a single sound in comparison to a fixed reference sound. This reference is the quietest sound audible to the healthy human ear – roughly equivalent to the sound of a mosquito flying 3 m (10 ft) away. This is called 0 dB.

The reason for using decibels as the measurement system for loudness is that our perception of loudness corresponds to a logarithmic curve rather than a simple straight line. Increased loudness is caused by increased air pressure, the consequence of which is that sounds approaching 125 dB will begin to cause pain and sounds over 180 dB will cause damage to the hearing tissue. Because changes in air pressure alter our perception of loudness, the term dB (SPL) is normally used, meaning 'decibel sound pressure level', in order to distinguish it from other dB measurements.

The human ear, however, is more sensitive to high frequencies. Noises above *a'* have a greater impact on the ear than those below. An additional method of dB measurement takes this into account, altering higher-pitched sounds slightly upwards to giver a truer indication of the effect they have on the ear. This measurement is known as dB (A-weighted).

Decibel level alters dramatically with distance and if there is interference from other noises. A string section in a symphony orchestra, for example, is not 45 times louder than a solo violin. It should also be remembered that any instrument can be played so quietly that it is inaudible – it is only in the upper levels of loudness that a limit is reached.

The figures reproduced opposite are provided by Marshall Chasin, Associate Professor at the University of Western Ontario in Audiology and Adjunct Professor at the University of Toronto in Linguistics. They stem from research conducted over the past 20 years into the effect of music on both auditors and practitioners.

Most of the measurements were taken at a distance of 3 m (10 ft). Some, however, were taken next to the ear of the musician, which is particularly significant in terms of instruments such as the piccolo and flute. It should be noted that different styles of playing and different instruments will give different results; these figures should be regarded as a general guide only.

Musical Instruments Handbook

Instrument measured (at a distance of 3 m/10 ft unless otherwise indicated)	dB (A-weighted)	dB SPL (peak)
Normal piano practice	60–90	105
Loud piano	70–105	110
Keyboards (electric)	60–110	118
Vocalist	70–85	94
Chamber music (classical)	70–92	99
Violin/viola (at left ear of player)	85–105	116
Violin/viola	80–90	104
Cello	80–104	112
Acoustic bass	70–94	98
Clarinet	68–82	112
Oboe	74–102	116
Saxophone	75–110	113
Flute	92–105	109
Flute (near right ear)	98–114	118
Piccolo	96–112	120
Piccolo (near right ear)	102–118	126
French horn	92–104	107
Trombone	90–106	109
Trumpet	88–108	113
Timpani and bass drum	74–94	106
Percussion (hi-hat near left ear)	68–94	125
Amplified guitar (on stage using ear monitors)	100–106	118
Amplified guitar (on stage with wedge monitors)	105–112	124
Full symphonic orchestra	86–102	120–137
Amplified rock music	102–108	140+
Portable music (e.g., iPod) in ear canal (50% volume)	94	110–-130*
iPod in ear canal (full volume)	105	110–142*

** Depends on earphone used. Measured with a probe tube microphone situated near the eardrum.*

Comparison of loud to quiet sounds	dB (SPL) peak
Damage caused to hearing tissue	180
Jet engine	155
Trumpet played as loudly as possible from 5 ft	150
Full symphonic orchestra	120–137
Piccolo (near right ear)	126
Threshold of pain	125
Cymbal clash	125
Planes on airport runway	120
Timpani and bass drum	106
Singer singing *fortissimo*	70
Conversational speech at 1 ft away	60
Average office noise	50
Quiet conversation	40
Quiet office	30
Quiet living room	20
Threshold of hearing	0

Section Two: Reference

PITCH RANGES

STRINGS

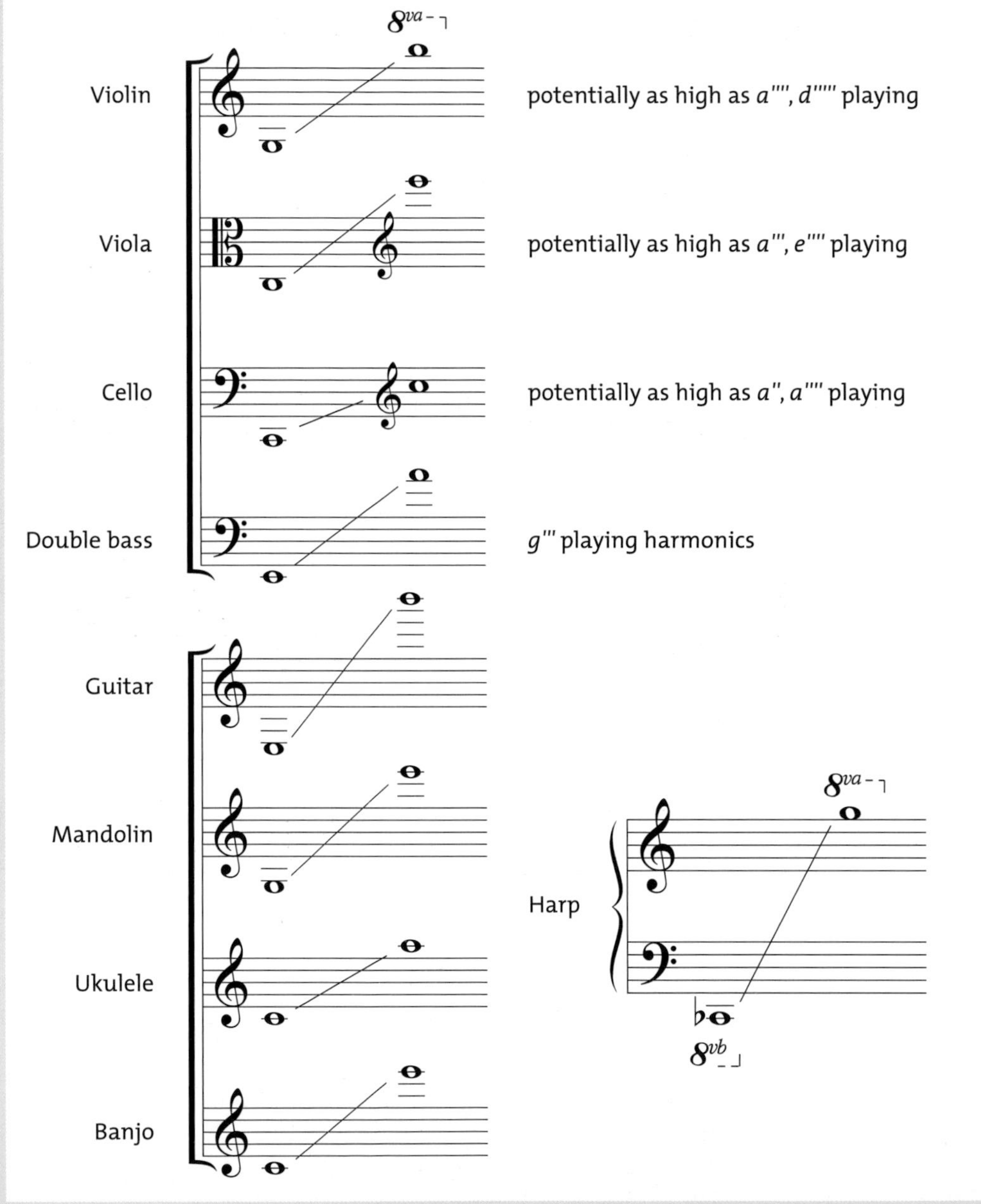

Musical Instruments Handbook

FLUTE

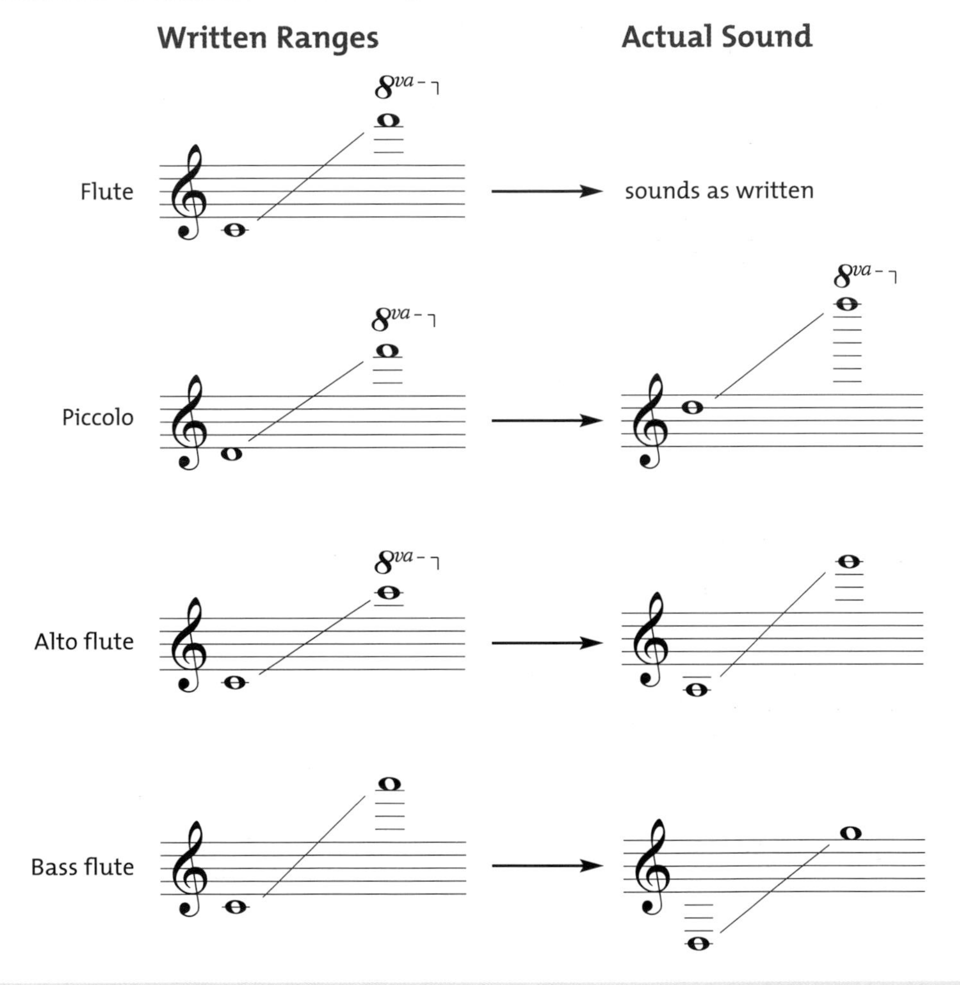
Written Ranges
Actual Sound
8va
Flute
sounds as written
8va
8va
Piccolo
8va
Alto flute
Bass flute

CLARINET

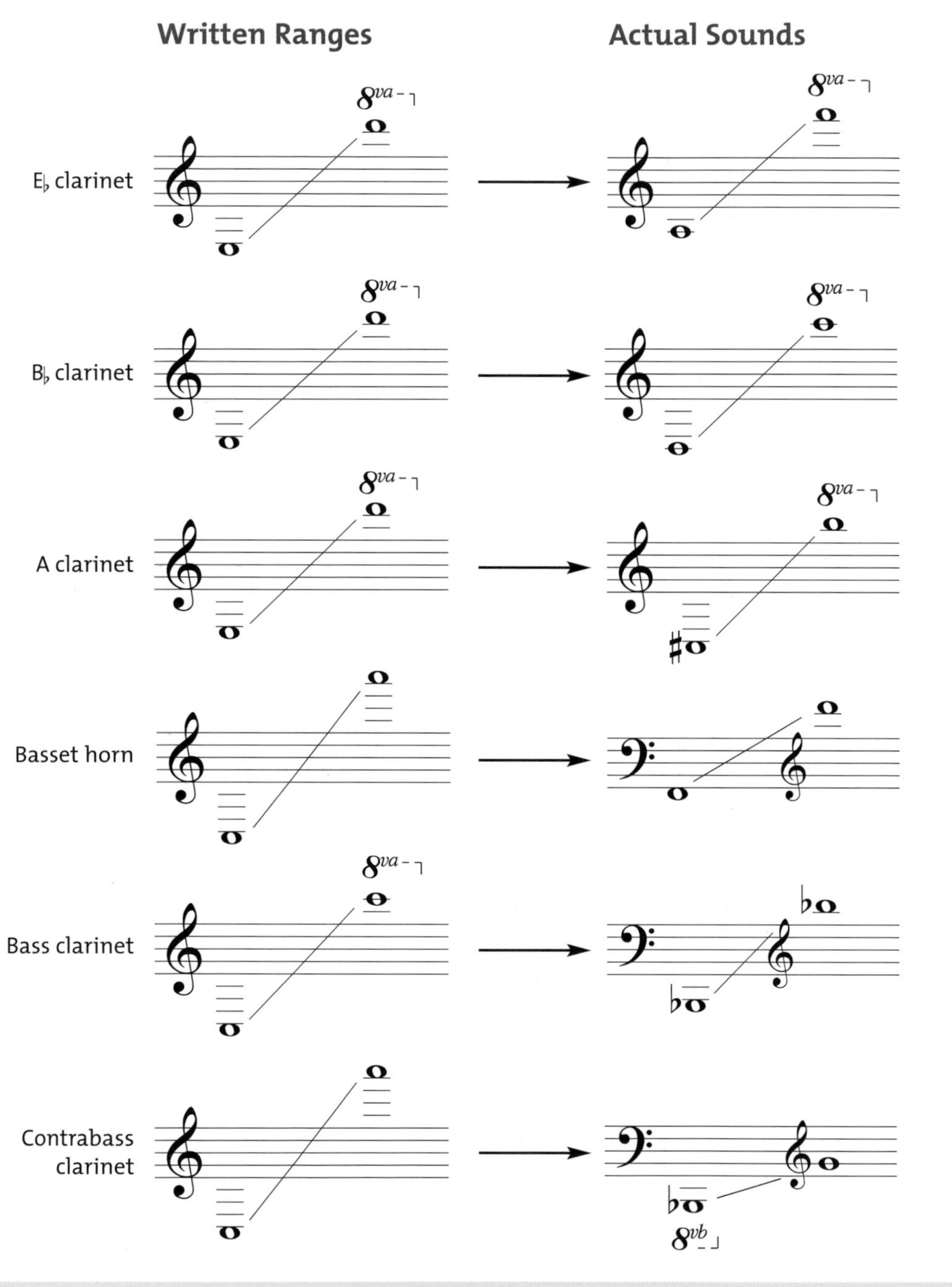

Musical Instruments Handbook

SAXOPHONE

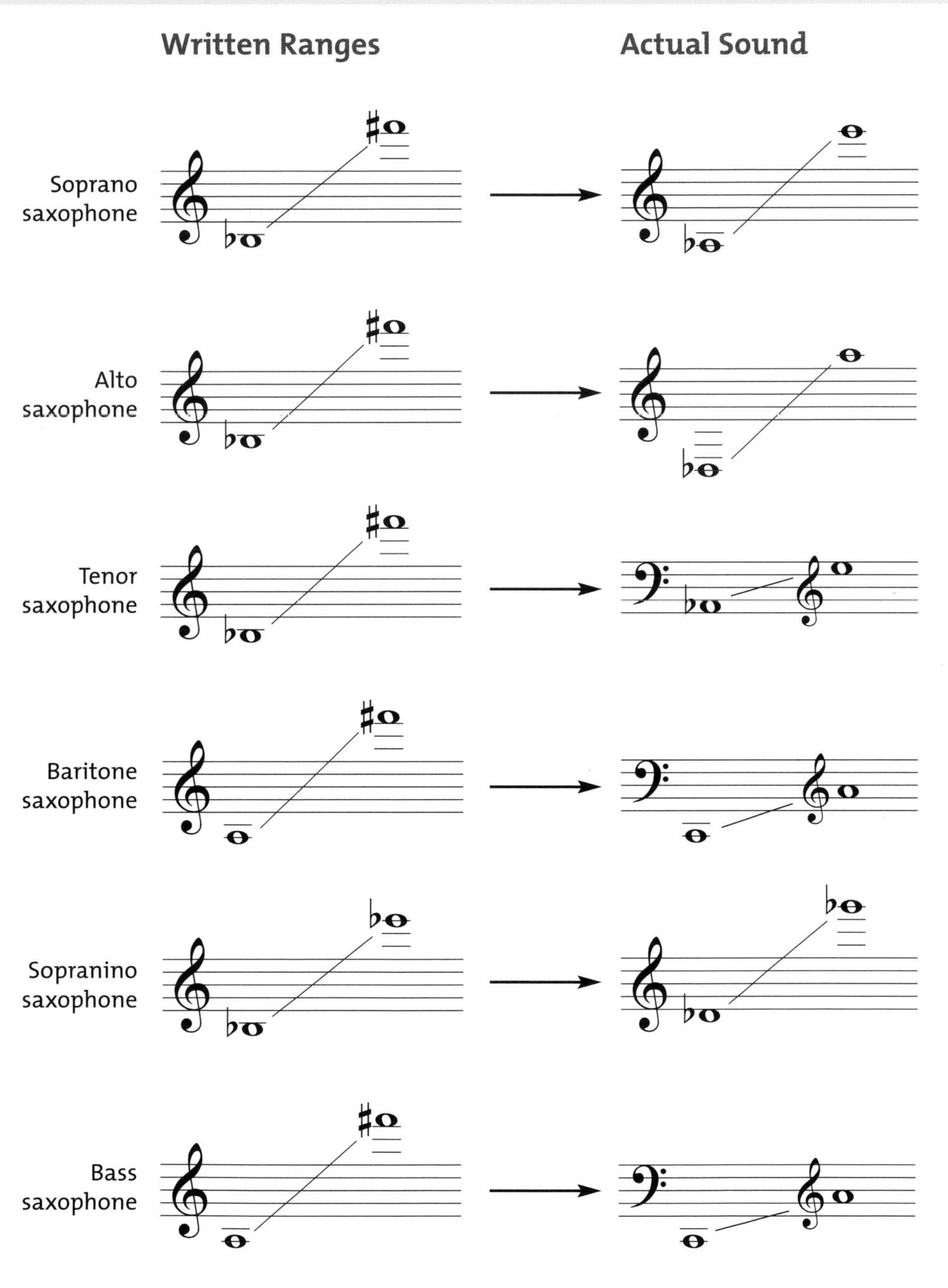

REFERENCE

Section Two: Reference

OBOE

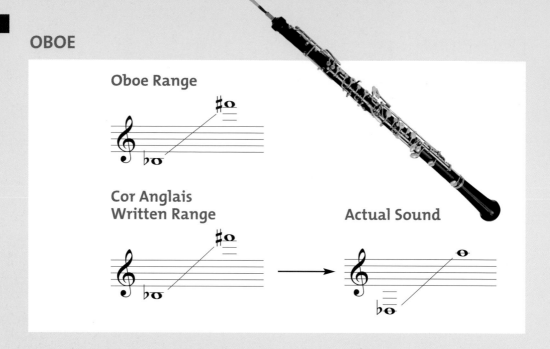

Oboe Range

Cor Anglais Written Range

Actual Sound

BASSOON

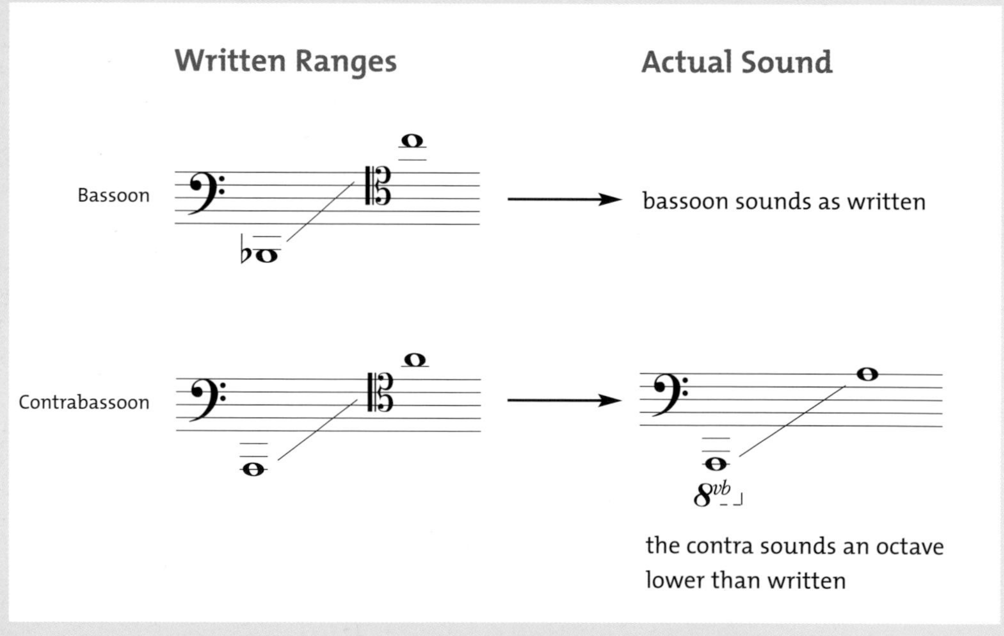

Musical Instruments Handbook

HORN IN F/B♭

The horn sounds a perfect fifth lower than written

TRUMPET

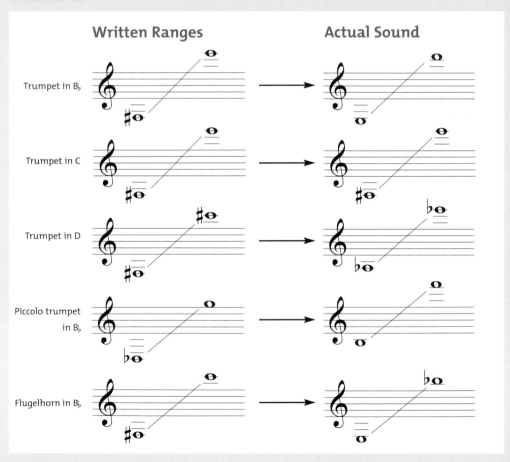

Written Ranges

Actual Sound

Trumpet in B♭

Trumpet in C

Trumpet in D

Piccolo trumpet in B♭

Flugelhorn in B♭

REFERENCE

Section Two: Reference

TROMBONE

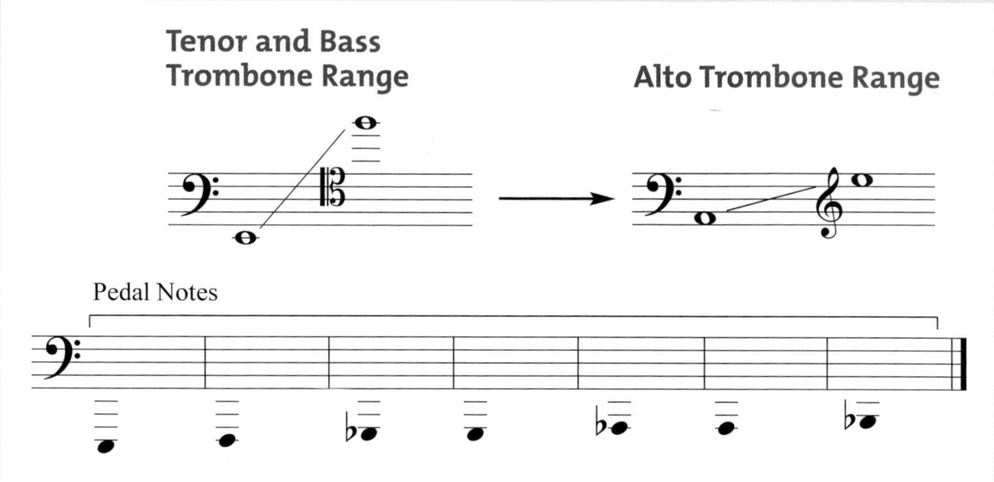

TUBA

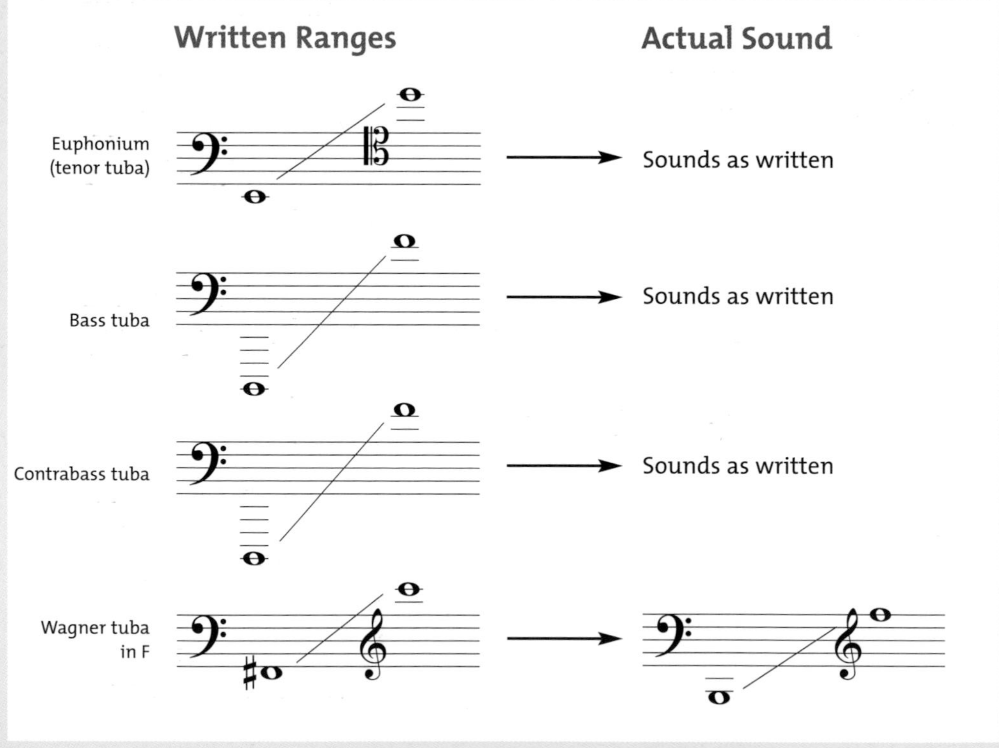

Musical Instruments Handbook

PERCUSSION

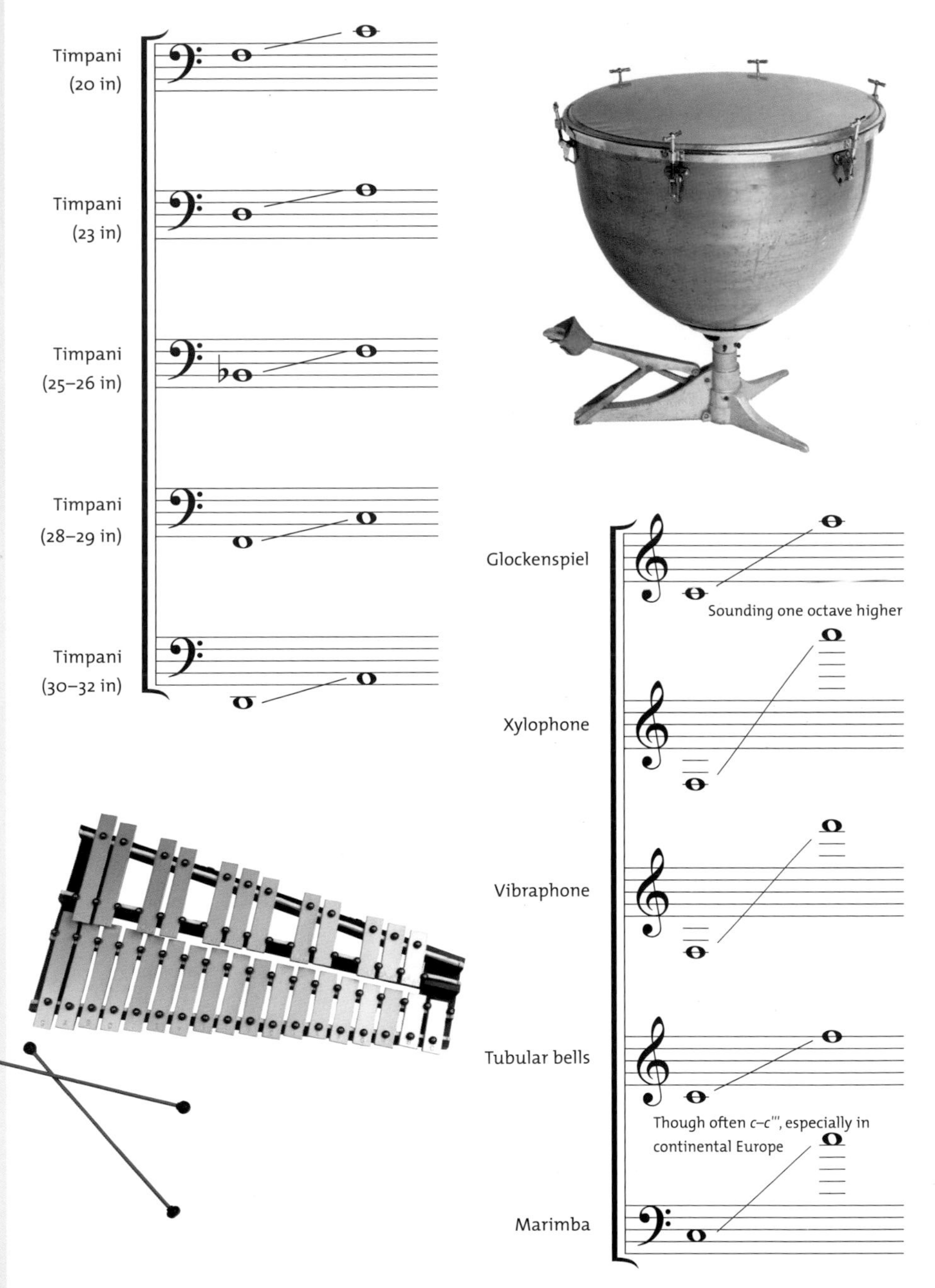
Timpani
(20 in)
Timpani
(23 in)
Timpani
(25–26 in)
Timpani
(28–29 in)
Timpani
(30–32 in)
Glockenspiel
Sounding one octave higher
Xylophone
Vibraphone
Tubular bells
Though often c–c''', especially in continental Europe
Marimba

PIANO

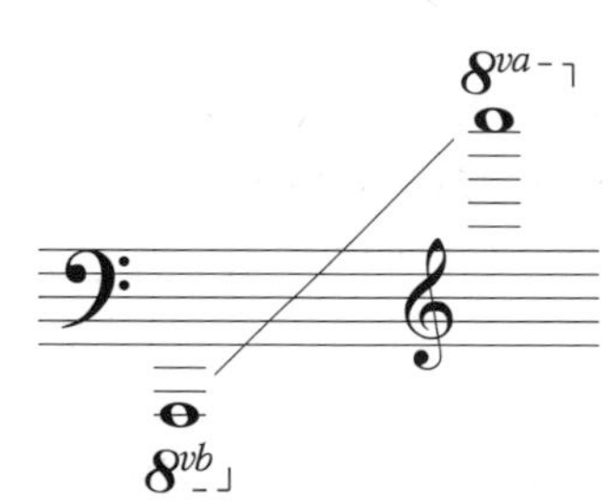

Piano ranges differ according to the maker and instrument type. Grand pianos typically have a larger *tessitura* than an upright piano. However, the exact pitch range is dependent on the manufacturer though will be close to the range here.

CELESTA

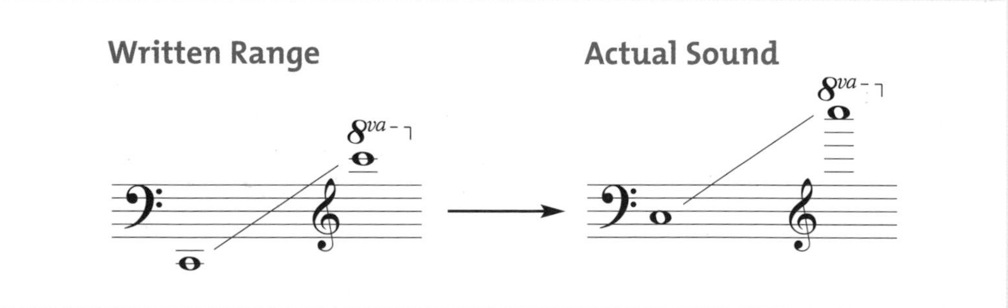

Musical Instruments Handbook

ACCORDION

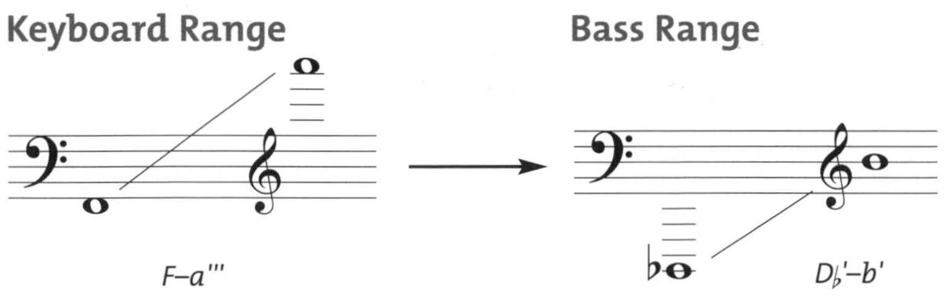

HARPSICHORD

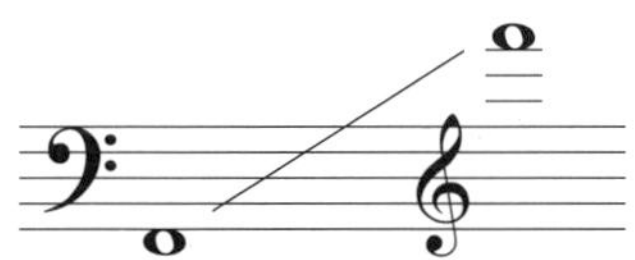

Range is dependent on country of origin, manufacturer and period but is likely to be within the four octave span *F–f'''*

PIPE ORGAN

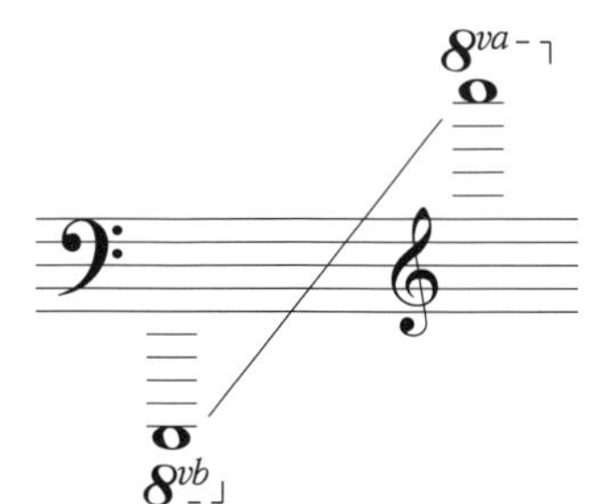

The pipe organ varies enormously in range since each instrument is tailored to its setting. The potential range is vast, however, capable of stretching from *C''–c'''''*

Section Two: Reference

VOICES

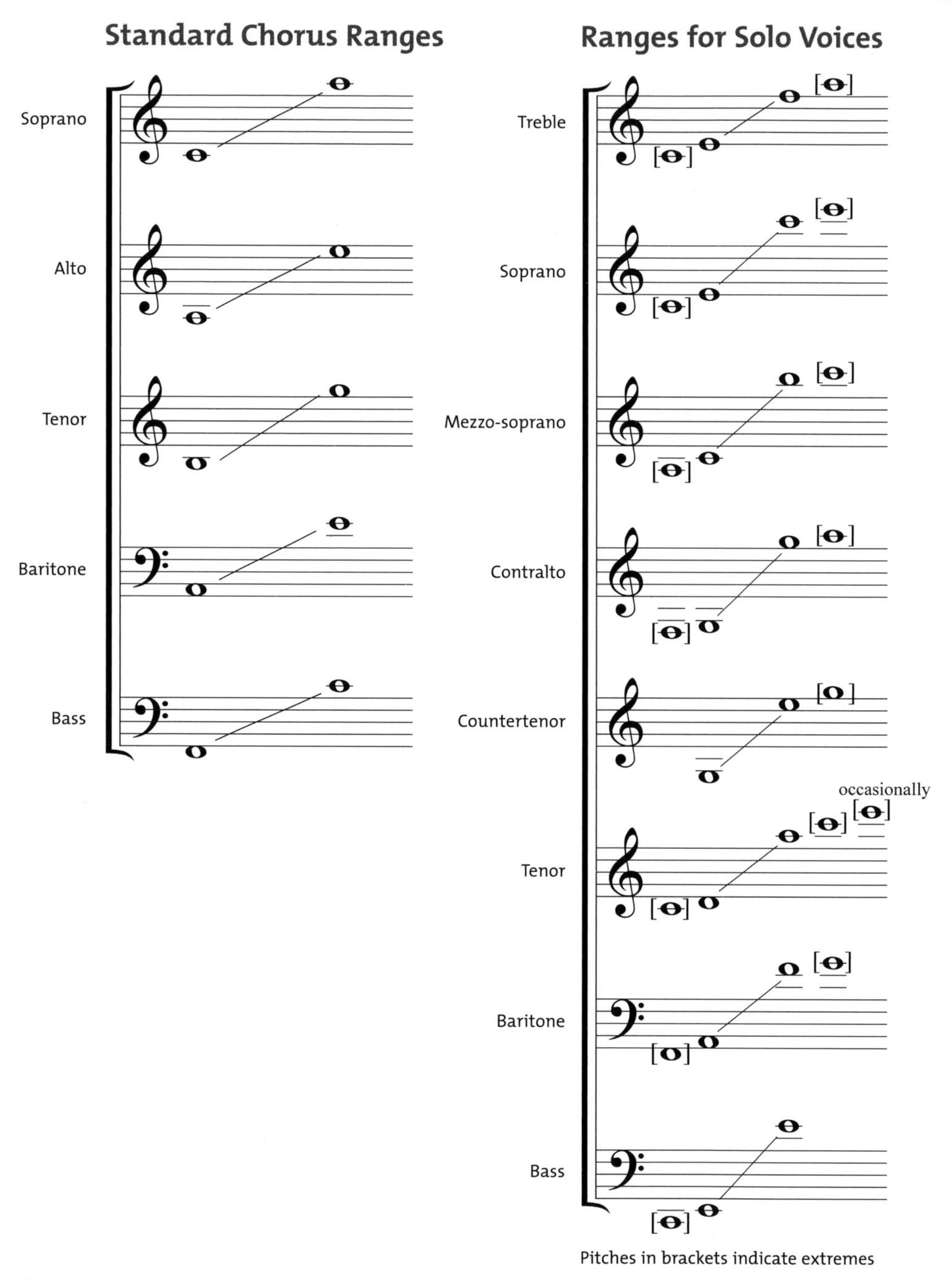
Standard Chorus Ranges
Soprano
Alto
Tenor
Baritone
Bass
Ranges for Solo Voices
Treble
Soprano
Mezzo-soprano
Contralto
Countertenor
occasionally
Tenor
Baritone
Bass
Pitches in brackets indicate extremes

RECORDER

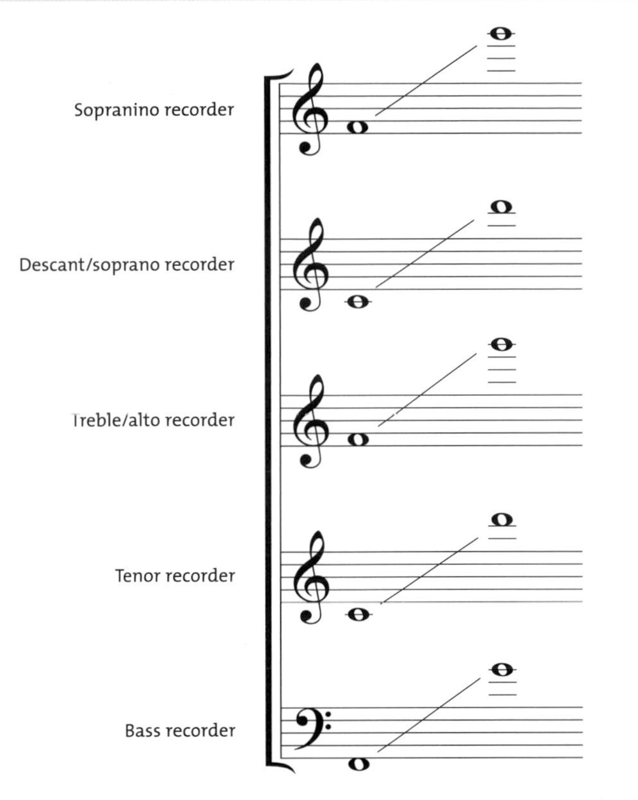

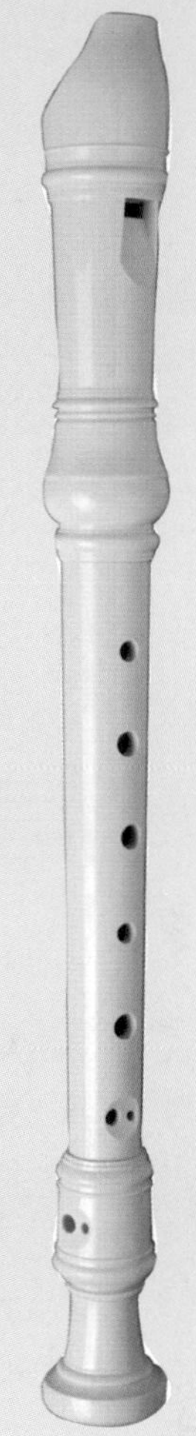

PITCH NOMENCLATURE

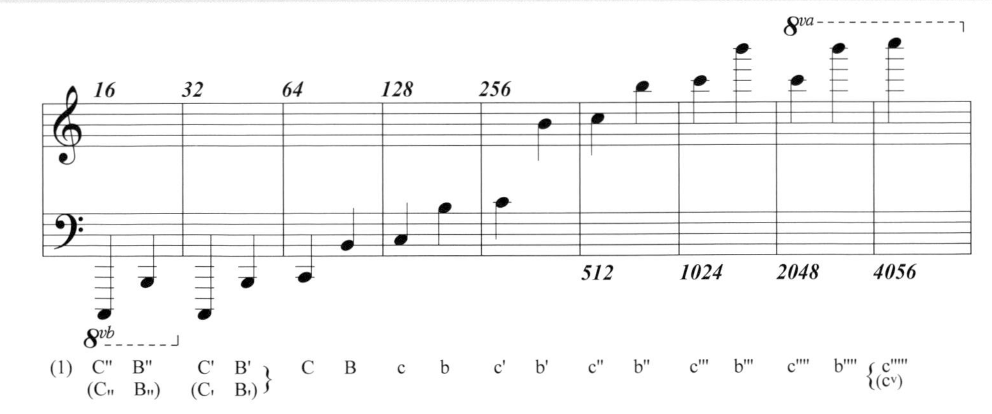

Section Two: Reference

GLOSSARY

Accent i) Giving a note greater prominence than its neighbours by slight alteration of volume or length, or by slightly delaying the point of attack. ii) The symbols used in notation to indicate this.

Adagio It. 'easy, leisurely'. A tempo direction normally taken to mean 'slow'. Its meaning has changed considerably since first used in the early 1600s.

Allegro It. 'cheerful, merry'. A tempo direction that when first used in the 1500s indicated that a piece should be performed in a joyous manner.

Alto Term used to refer to the voice lying above the tenor. Often used in an instrumental context, the term is generally taken to mean the lowest of the female voices more properly referred to as contralto.

Andante It. 'at a walking pace'. A tempo direction indicating a gentle pace; its exact meaning differs considerably between eras and even composers.

Antiphony Describes music in which the instrumental or choral ensemble is divided into groups that are physically separated. Antiphonal music is characterized by call-and-response effects.

Arco It. 'bow'. Indication that the bow should be used; most often seen reversing the indication *pizzicato*.

Atonal Refers to music that is not organized using key or tone centres.

Avant garde Fr. 'advance guard'. Referring originally to a group of soldiers who cleared the way for the main body of troops, the term describes those artists who are radical or experimental.

Ballet A style of theatrical dancing developed in France during the seventeenth century and closely associated with opera.

Bar see *Measure*.

Baroque A style in the arts in Europe prevalent from 1600 to 1750, characterized by drama, detail and grandeur.

Bass The lowest male voice; also the lowest part in an instrumental ensemble.

Beat The underlying pulse of a piece of music.

Bel canto It. 'beautiful singing'. A style of singing particularly associated with early-nineteenth century Italy that emphasizes *legato*, agility and drama. Also the work of the composers associated with that style, including Bellini, Donizetti and Rossini.

Bitonal Describes music that uses two distinct tonalities simultaneously.

Bow A flexible stick, normally wooden, that is held in tension by hairs, usually horsehair, and drawn across strings to generate sound.

Breve see *Double whole note*.

Musical Instruments Handbook

Cadence A chord progression that establishes or undermines the key of a passage; the capacity of cadences to sound in varying degrees final or interrupted means that they function as musical punctuation.

Chamber music Music intended for performance in intimate circumstances for voices or instruments, normally one to a part. The term often implies music written to be played for pleasure.

Chamber orchestra A small orchestra of variable instrumentation, generally with one instrument per part.

Chant The rhythmic speaking or singing of words on a single note or to a simple melody; often considered a form of heightened speech. See also *plainchant*.

Choir A group of singers generally divided into soprano, alto, tenor, bass, or combinations thereof.

Chorus i) A term used interchangeably with choir when referring to a group of singers; ii) a work written for a group of singers that can also involve instrumentalists; iii) also known as the *refrain*, the section of a strophic composition that is repeated after each verse.

Chromatic Derived from the Greek word for 'coloured', the term refers to music based on an octave divided into 12 half steps, in contrast to diatonic music, which is based on the octave divided into seven whole steps and half steps.

Classical Most commonly used in music to refer to the Viennese Classical period from the late-eighteenth to early-nineteenth centuries, in particular the Viennese classics composed by Haydn, Mozart and Beethoven.

Clef A sign placed at the beginning of a line of music that defines which pitches are represented by which lines and spaces.

Col legno It. 'with the wood'. A technique for playing bowed stringed instruments in which the wood of the bow rather than the hair is used to agitate the string into action.

Compass The scope or range of pitches available to a voice or instrument; can refer to both the instrument or voice itself and the range used in a specific composition.

Concerto From the Latin *concertare* meaning 'to contend or debate', the term describes music that contrasts an orchestra with an instrumental group, or more usually a solo instrument.

Consonance Refers in acoustics to soundwaves of differing but closely related frequencies that sound pleasing. In musical terms this translates into intervals in relation to a fundamental; therefore the octave is the most consonant interval, followed in decreasing consonance by the fifth, the fourth, the third, the second and then microtones.

Consort Refers to a small instrumental or vocal ensemble used during the period 1575 to 1700.

Continuo A bass line running throughout a piece from which harmonies are extemporized by a keyboard player; it is often supported by a bass instrument, especially violoncello or bassoon.

Section Two: Reference

Counterpoint From the Latin *contra punctum* meaning 'against the note'. The technique of combining two independent melody lines so they sound consonant.

Crotchet see *Quarter note*.

Demisemiquaver see *32nd note*.

Diatonic Music using pitches derived from the division of the octave into seven notes; the intervals separating these notes consist of five whole notes and two half notes. The most common arrangement of these intervals is the major scale: whole-whole-half-whole-whole-whole-half. Other diatonic arrangements include the natural minor scale and the church modes.

Dissonance The converse of consonance. Mathematical definitions of consonance, and by association dissonance, go back to Pythagoras in the fifth century BC. Consonance and dissonance are also used in relation to perceived tension and release and, as such, are relative terms.

Dominant Refers in the tonal system to the perfect fifth degree of the diatonic scale and the triad that it is built on.

Double whole note In western notation, a note eight times as long as a quarter note; also known as a breve.

Drone A sustained pitch or pitches that sound throughout a piece or section of music.

Duet A composition or section of a composition for two performers with or without accompaniment.

Duo Name given to the two performers playing a duet.

Dynamics Refers to the volume at which a note is played. Instructions are normally in Italian and stem from two terms: *forte* or *f* (loud) and *piano* or *p* (quiet). More subtle distinctions are indicated by reiterations, *fortissimo* or *ff* (louder than *f*) or *pianissimo* or *pp* (quieter than *p*), or by combination with *mezzo* or *m* (half), *mezzoforte* or *mf* (less loud than *f*) or *mezzopiano* or *mp* (more loud than *p*).

8th note In western notation, a note half as long as a quarter note; also known as a quaver.

Ensemble Fr. 'together'. A group of instrumentalists or singers; also used to refer to part of an opera that uses two or more singers.

Equal temperament see *Temperament*.

Étude Fr. 'study'. A piece written to develop or show off a particular performing technique.

Expressionism In music a term normally applied to atonal works written near the beginning of the twentieth century, characterized by large orchestras, extreme *tessitura* and avoidance of repetition.

Fifth describes an interval between two pitches that are five degrees of the diatonic scale apart: C-G, D-A, E-B etc. A perfect fifth consists of three whole steps and a half step (C-G), a diminished fifth consists of a perfect fifth minus a half step (C-F#), an augmented fifth consists of a perfect fifth plus a half step (C-G#).

Musical Instruments Handbook

Figuration Loosely applied to sections of music consisting of continuous, normally changing, patterns of short notes.

Flat i) The sign ♭, placed before a note or in a key signature, indicating that the note should be lowered by a half step; ii) also used to describe a note that is too low in pitch.

Flautando It. 'fluting'. Instructs the performer to produce a flute-like tone.

Forte loud. see *Dynamics*.

Fourth Describes an interval between two pitches that are four degrees of the diatonic scale apart: C-F, D-G, E-A etc. A perfect fourth consists of two whole steps and a half step (C-F), a diminished fourth consists of a perfect fourth minus a half step (C-E), an augmented fourth consists of a perfect fourth plus a half step (C-F#).

Fret A strip normally of metal, bone or wood placed across the fingerboard of a stringed instrument to stop the string while perfectly in tune and creating a clear sound.

Fundamental The lowest note of a harmonic series.

Glissando From French *glisser* 'to slide'. Literally implies moving from one pitch to another by slide, i.e. not sounding individual intervening pitches. Rapid scales on the harp or piano are also referred to as *glissandi*.

Half note In western notation, a note twice as long as a quarter note; also known as a minim.

Half step An interval half the size of a tone; in equal temperament it is equal to $1/12$ of an octave. Generally used as the smallest interval, though experiments have been made with smaller divisions. Also known as a semitone. See also *Quarter tone* and *Microtone*.

Harmonic series A vibrating string or air column simultaneously generates a number of pitches – also known as partials or overtones. These pitches have a precise mathematical relationship to the fundamental of $1/2$, $1/3$, $1/4$, $1/5$ etc. In musical terms, the first partial sounds an octave above the fundamental, the second another perfect fifth higher, the third a perfect fourth above that (or two octaves above the fundamental) and so on.

Harmonics i) Another term for partials or overtones; ii) gossamer-light notes that are sounded on stringed instruments by lightly stopping the string in order to prevent lower harmonic frequencies from sounding.

Harmony The practice of sounding two or more notes simultaneously to produce chords.

Impressionism Refers to the predominantly French style of music from the 1880s to the early 1900s in which clear musical forms are jettisoned in favour of sensual evocation, particularly of nature, through the use of instrumental colour and fragmented melodies.

Instrumentation see *Orchestration*.

Interval The distance between two pitches measured using the diatonic scale. It is an inclusive measurement, so the interval between C and E is a third counting C as 1, D as 2 and E as 3; similarly the interval between G and C is a

Section Two: Reference

fourth counting G as 1, A as 2, B as 3 and C as 4. These intervals are further distinguished by the use of qualifying adjectives to describe chromatic alterations: see *Second, Third, Fourth, Fifth, Sixth, Seventh, Octave*. Intervals wider than an octave are treated in the same way, e.g., a ninth like a second, a tenth like a third etc.

Intonation To intone is to produce a tone, thus the term was used in plainchant to indicate the initial melodic statement sung before all the voices enter. Intonation is also used to refer to the use of pitch in music.

Key Tonal music is organized around a pitch or set of pitches to which all others refer and seem to belong. The roots of this system can be heard in the harmonic series in which all frequencies, however close together, are related to the fundamental. The system of keys can be seen as an artificial rationalization of the harmonic series, in which pitches are arranged in such a way as to give a sense of rootedness. As an organizing principle, this allows composers to create and release tension by moving away from and back to the home key; this in turn enables the creation of longer structures, which are understood aurally by distance from or proximity to the home key.

Keyboard A set of levers used to remotely operate a sound-producer; instruments using a keyboard include piano, organ, harpsichord and accordion. It can also refer to a series of percussion instruments, including the xylophone, glockenspiel and marimba.

Legato It. 'bound'. The technique of playing or singing notes without intervening silences; this does not imply, as is often supposed, a lack of articulation, accent or colouration. The opposite effect is *staccato*.

Major The name given to a diatonic scale whose pitches conform to the following pattern: whole step–whole step–half step–whole step–whole step–whole step–half step, e.g., C-D-E-F-G-A-B-c.

Masque An elaborate form of courtly entertainment developed in England but popular throughout Europe during the sixteenth and seventeenth centuries. It involved instrumental music, singing, dancing, acting and poetry often based on mythological themes and staged on ornate sets.

Mass The celebration of the Eucharist in the Roman Catholic Church carried out in Latin. The setting of the Mass to music, initially to medieval plainchant and subsequently in polyphonic style, has been vital to the development of western art music.

Measure Also known as a bar, this divides music into metrical units from which patterns of stress and inflection can be inferred.

Melody A succession of single notes of differing rhythm and pitch that is perceived as a single entity.

Microtone Refers to an interval smaller than a half step.

Minim see *Half note*.

Minimalism A style of music developed during the 1960s and 1970s, commonly described as

Musical Instruments Handbook

demonstrating highly repetitive harmony, melody and rhythm.

Minor The name given to a diatonic scale whose pitches conform to the following pattern: whole step–half step–whole step–whole step–half step–whole step–whole step, e.g. C-D-Eb-F-G-Ab-Bb-c. This is more properly known as the natural minor scale. It has two other forms: the melodic, in which the sixth and seventh degrees are raised by a half step in its ascending form and remains as the natural minor in the descending form, and the harmonic, in which the seventh degree is raised both ascending and descending.

Mode Term derived from the Latin *modus* meaning 'measurement'. It has three meanings: the first related to the notation of note values in medieval music; the second a system that describes intervals developed in the ninth century; and the third a system that describes scalic arrangements of whole steps and half steps. The system of modes defines not only which pitches are used but also their relationship to each other, in particular the predominance in a melodic and harmonic sense of one or more pitches over the others.

Modulation The technique in tonal music of shifting from one tonal area to another using a recognizable harmonic progression.

Monophony From the Greek for 'single voice'. Music for a single part such as plainchant; most often used in contrast with polyphony.

Multiple stopping The technique on bowed stringed instruments of sounding more than one string simultaneously: sounding two strings together is known as double stopping, three strings, triple stopping; and four quadruple stopping.

Musical A form of musical theatre involving music, songs, dance and spoken dialogue all tied together in a dramatic structure. Initially distinguished from opera through its use of popular-music styles and discrete musical events as opposed to a through-composed dramatic structure, the boundaries between the two have become increasingly blurred.

Mute A device designed to alter an instrument's timbre.

Neoclassicism A style of composition prevalent in the early-twentieth century reflecting a renewed interest in the pure, clean characteristics of Viennese Classicism that developed as a reaction against the perceived excesses of late-nineteenth century Romanticism and Expressionism.

Ninth Describes an interval between two pitches that are nine degrees of the diatonic scale apart: C-d, E-f, A-b etc. A major ninth consists of seven whole steps, a minor ninth consists of six whole steps and a half step.

Nonet Chamber music scored for nine solo players; the ensemble that performs such music.

Notation A set of visual instructions designed represent musical sound. It can take many forms but the method most familiar to western art music has been in a process of continuous development since plainchant was written down in the ninth century. As a language, all

Section Two: Reference

notation is necessarily inaccurate since there is no direct visual analogue for sound. As a result, performers have to interpret the notation in order to produce the most accurate possible recreation of the composer's intentions.

Octave Describes an interval between two pitches that are eight degrees of the diatonic scale apart: C-c, E-e, A-a etc. The term is generally taken to mean a perfect octave consisting of six whole steps; a diminished octave is one half step less than a perfect octave; an augmented octave is one half step higher than a perfect octave. The octave is the simplest interval, occurring at the first overtone; the two notes sound remarkably similar, differing only in register and blending almost into a single note.

Octet Chamber music scored for eight solo players; the ensemble that performs such music.

Opera From the Latin for 'works'. Opera in the broadest sense is a theatrical form in which music, text and spectacle all combine in the service of an overarching drama. It is the most flexible of all musical forms and has been subject to an immense range of styles.

Oratorio A large-scale dramatic composition using orchestra, chorus and vocal soloists, normally on a sacred subject. Oratorios were simply concert works and were not intended to be staged.

Orchestra Refers to a large group of instruments. The term is usually used as a shortened form of symphony orchestra, but can equally refer to a mandolin orchestra or gamelan orchestra.

Orchestration Also known as instrumentation. The practice of arranging music for performance by large group of instruments.

Overtone A frequency component of a sound other than the fundamental. See *Harmonic series*.

Partial A frequency component of a sound other than the fundamental. See *Harmonic series*.

Pedal note Derived from the pedal notes of the organ. Refers to a note that is sustained while harmonies alter above it; pedal notes are also used in the middle and at the top of textures.

Pentatonic Refers to a scale using only five separate pitches.

Pizzicato From the Italian *pizzicare* 'to pinch'. Direction to pluck a string with the fingers; normally used in relation to bowed instruments and countermanded by the direction *arco*.

Plainchant The body of monophonic chant officially used in the liturgies of the Catholic Church.

Polyphony From the Greek for 'many voiced'. Refers to music in which there are two or more clearly individual and independent parts or voices.

Polytonal Describes music that uses three or more tonalities simultaneously.

Portamento From the Italian *portare* 'to carry'. Instruction used normally in singing to indicate the connection of two notes by passing through all intervening pitches; also used instrumentally, particularly in unfretted stringed instruments.

Musical Instruments Handbook

Postmodernism Term used in reference to both a historical period and to a musical style but in each instance resisting clear definition. Most easily understood as a reaction against Modernism rather than something self-contained.

Quarter note In western notation a note half as long as a half note; also known as a crotchet.

Quartet A composition or section of a composition for four performers, with or without accompaniment; the group that performs such a composition.

Quaver see *8th note.*

Quintet A composition or section of a composition for five performers, with or without accompaniment; the group that performs such a composition.

Reed A thin strip of material over which air is passed to cause vibrations and generate sound. Normally made from *arundo donax* grass, reeds are also constructed from metal, plastic or even wood.

Register Used to describe a particular part of the range of an instrument or voice, e.g., 'his voice sounds beautiful in this register.' Also refers to an organ stop.

Renaissance Used in music history to refer to the period between 1430 and 1600.

Rococo Term used particularly in connection with French music of the eighteenth century, characterized by grace, playfulness and opulence.

Romanticism Aesthetic prevalent during the nineteenth century that placed emphasis on the individual, on expression of emotion, on the idea that a work of art should be a complete entity and on the pre-eminence of the artist as genius.

Scale A set of notes ordered by pitch, either ascending or descending.

Second Describes an interval between two pitches that are two degrees of the diatonic scale apart: C-D, E-F, A-B etc. A major second consists of one whole step (C-D), a minor second consists of one half step (C-C#).

Semibreve see *Whole note.*

Semitone see *Half step.*

Semiquaver see *16th note.*

Septet A composition or section of a composition for seven performers, with or without accompaniment; the group that performs such a composition.

Serialism System designed most famously by Arnold Schoenberg to lend logic to a composition through the use of a fixed series of notes that must always appear sequentially whether in melody or harmony. Though most often associated with music that uses all 12 half steps in a series (known as 12-note music), it can also be used with fewer notes. A branch known as 'total serialism' used in the 1950s by Pierre Boulez and Karlheinz Stockhausen also fixed the order of other musical events such as dynamics, rhythms, tempo and even attack.

Section Two: Reference

Seventh Describes an interval between two pitches that are seven degrees of the diatonic scale apart: C-B, E-d, A-g etc. A major seventh consists of six whole steps and a half step (C-B), a minor seventh consists of six whole steps (C-B♭).

Sextet A composition or section of a composition for six performers, with or without accompaniment; the group that performs such a composition.

Sharp i) The sign #, placed before a note or in a key signature, indicating that the note should be raised by a half step; ii) also used to describe a note that is too high in pitch.

Sixteenth note In western notation a note a quarter as long as a quarter note; also known as a semiquaver.

Sixth Describes an interval between two pitches that are six degrees of the diatonic scale apart: C-A, E-c, A-f# etc. A major sixth consists of four whole steps and a half step (C-A), a minor sixth consists of four whole steps (C-Ab).

Sonata From the Italian *suonare* 'to sound'. Initially used to indicate a piece that was to be played instead of sung, by the classical period the sonata had become the pre-eminent instrumental form, a position it retains today.

Soprano The highest female voice; also used to describe a high form of an instrument e.g. soprano saxophone.

Staccato It. 'detached'. Indicates that notes should be separated by a silence; it is often wrongly understood to imply that notes should be played short.

Sul ponticello It. 'on the bridge'. Instruction for stringed instruments to be sounded close to, or even on, the bridge, producing a brittle, glassy sound.

Sul tasto It. 'on the fingerboard'. Instruction for stringed instruments to be sounded over the fingerboard, producing a light, flute-like sound.

Symphony From the Greek for 'sounding together'. Initially referred to a work for a large group of instruments. By the classical period, it had acquired a specific form that continued to develop through the nineteenth and twentieth centuries. Regarded by many to be the ultimate musical form.

Tablature System of notation showing where the fingers should be placed on an instrument.

Temperament Tuning of the scale. It is impossible to tune the 12 half steps of the chromatic scale so that all the intervals are mathematically perfect, so compromises have to be made to achieve the best fit. The system used today is known as 'equal temperament', in which all half steps are equal. This results in all intervals being slightly out of tune but enables total access to all keys. Earlier systems of temperament include Pythagorean tuning, in which the perfect fifths were made pure; this resulted in sharp-key intervals being good (e.g. D-F#-A) but flat-key intervals being out of tune (e.g. D♭-F-A♭).

Tempo It. 'time'. Refers to the speed or pacing of a piece of music.

Tenor The highest contemporary male voice; also refers to instruments covering roughly the same range (*c to a'*).

Musical Instruments Handbook

Tenth Describes an interval between two pitches that are ten degrees of the diatonic scale apart: C-e, E-g, A-c' etc. A major tenth consists of eight whole steps (C-e), a minor tenth consists of seven whole steps and a half step (C-e♭).

Tessitura It. 'texture'. Used to describe the part of a voice's or instrument's compass in which a piece or section of music lies.

Third Describes an interval between two pitches that are three degrees of the diatonic scale apart: C-E, E-G, A-G etc. A major third consists of two whole steps, a minor third consists of a whole and a half step.

32nd note In western notation a note an eighth as long as a crotchet; also known as a demisemiquaver.

Timbre Refers to the colouristic and tonal qualities of an instrument or voice.

Time signature A sign placed at the beginning of a composition or the start of a new section that indicates the pulse and stress pattern of the music that follows.

Tonality Refers to a system of musical organization in which pitches and chords have a hierarchical relationship based around a central pitch or chord. Most often used in association with the diatonic tonal system.

Tonic In the diatonic tonal system, refers to the first degree of the scale and the triad that is built on it.

Treble A high, unbroken boy's voice; also used to refer to instruments whose compass is similar, e.g., treble recorder.

Tremolo It. 'quivering'. The rapid re-articulation of a single pitch without regard for measured time values.

Triad A chord of three notes consisting of two superimposed thirds, e.g. C-E-G. A major triad consists of a major third plus a minor third (C-E-G), a minor triad consists of a minor third plus a major third (C-E♭-G), a diminished triad consists of two minor thirds (C-E♭-G♭), an augmented third consists of two major thirds (C-E-G#).

Trio A composition or section of a composition for three performers, with or without accompaniment; the group that performs such a composition.

Tuning The adjustment of pitch to ensure that an instrument is in tune with itself and with others.

Vibrato From Latin *vibrare* 'to shake'. A subtle fluctuation of pitch and intensity while remaining on the same pitch.

Virtuoso From Latin *virtus* 'excellence'. A performer or composer of outstanding skill; often used in a more limited way to refer to performers who demonstrate great technical ability.

Whole note In western notation, a note four times as long as a quarter note; also known as a semibreve.

Whole step An interval twice the size of a half step; in equal temperament it is equal to 1/6 of an octave.

Section Two: Reference

CONTRIBUTOR BIOGRAPHIES

Evelyn Glennie (Foreword)
Evelyn Glennie is one of the world's foremost percussionists,. An eclectic and innovative musician, she is the first person to sustain a full-time career as a solo percsussionist. She performs globally with the greatest conductors, orchestras and artists, and has commissioned more than 100 new works for solo percussion from the most eminent composers.

Lucien Jenkins (General Editor)
Lucien Jenkins is the author of *Laying out the Body* (Seren) and co-author of *Classical Music Encyclopedia* (Collins). He edited the *Collected Poems of George Eliot* (Skoob), *Dictionary of Music in Sound* (Rhinegold), and numerous books for secondary-school pupils. He was formerly editor of *Music Teacher* and *Early Music Today* magazines, governor of the Poetry Society and writer-in-residence for the Open University. He has academic status at Bristol University and writes for the *Guardian* on ICT.

Leon Botstein (Consultant)
Leon Botstein has been president of Bard College since 1975. He is music director of the American Symphony Orchestra, founder and co-artistic director of the Bard Music Festival, and music director of the American Russian Young Artists Orchestra. He has been a frequent guest conductor with numerous orchestras around the world and has been the featured conductor on many classical recordings. He is also editor of *The Musical Quarterly*.

Richard Buskin (Consultant)
Richard Buskin is the *New York Times* best-selling author of more than a dozen books. His articles have appeared in music and film magazines around the world, as well as newspapers, and he has also co-authored the *Billboard Illustrated Encyclopedia of Music* and several showbusiness autobiographies.

Rusty Cutchin (Consultant)
Rusty Cutchin has been a musician, recording engineer, producer, and journalist for over 25 years. He has been Technical Editor of and a columnist for *Guitar One* magazine, Editor in Chief of *Home Recording* magazine and most recently an associate editor of *Electronic Musician*, the leading US magazine for the home-studio musician. He has also served as consulting editor on four books, including volumes about guitar, home recording, and building a personal computer.

Rebecca Berkley (Percussion)
Rebecca Berkley is a freelance writer and musician. She has taught percussion to students of all ages, as a private teacher and as a workshop leader, and has published percussion music. She also runs a community choir and directs music festivals with her husband.

Andrew Cleaton (Electric and Electronic)
Since gaining his masters degree in Music Technology from the University of York in 1990, Andrew Cleaton has enjoyed a varied career, spanning the fields of community music, higher education and the arts funding system. An accomplished composer and producer, Andrew is a founding co-director of Epiphany Music Ltd, offering creative music-technology solutions in production, education and consultancy.

Alan Charlton (Reference)
A music writer and international award-winning composer, Alan Charlton studied with Raymond Warren, Sir Peter Maxwell Davies and Robert Saxton. The recipient of Bristol University's first-ever PhD in Composition, he was subsequently the first Eileen Norris Fellow in Composition at Bedford School. Performers of his music include The Lindsays and Birmingham Contemporary Music Group. His music can be heard at www.alancharlton.com

Andrew Cronshaw (World Instruments)
Andrew Cronshaw is a multi-instrumentalist, playing instruments from the shelf marked 'What is that?', including zithers, *fujara*, *ba-wu* and other stringed and wind instruments. He is a record producer and writer on world musics, particularly those of Europe, for publications including *fRoots* magazine and the *Rough Guide to World Music*.

Robin Newton (Brass, Woodwind, Stringed)
Robin Newton is active as a conductor, specializing in contemporary music. In 1997 he formed his own ensemble, e2k, with which he gives regular concerts in London. He has worked on several high-profile academic publications as writer and editor, chiefly for the *New Grove Dictionary of Music and Musicians* and the *Northern Arts* magazine *Artscene*.

Jeremy Siepmann (Keyboards)
Jeremy Siepmann is a writer, musician, teacher, broadcaster, and editor of *Piano* magazine. He is former Head of Music at the BBC World Service and the teacher of many concert pianists. His books include biographies of Chopin, Brahms, Mozart and Beethoven and two volumes on the history and literature of the piano. He is also Professor of Musical Aesthetics and the History of Piano Performance at the International Piano Academy, Lake Como, in Italy.

Musical Instruments Handbook

PICTURE CREDITS

Alpha Rhythm Roots: 189, 199 (t)

Apple Computers Inc.: 338

Arbiter Group plc: 50 (t), 217 (l); Akai Professional M.I. Corp: 320; Arbiter Music Technology: 342 (b), 363; Millennium Products: 59 (t)

ArenaPal.com: Jak Kilby: 175 (b)

Barinya: 153 (t)

Beloplatno: 136 (l), 202 (b)

K. Billett: 308 (b), 309 (b)

Bjornredtail: 354 (t)

Bournemouth Orchestras: Mark Hill: 29 (b)

Mike Braithwaite: 308 (t)

Stefan Bremer: 10, 154 (b)

Bells & Motley Consort: John Bromka: 47 (b), 142; Sondra Bromka: 178, 179 (t), 180 (t), 182, 229 (t)

J. D. Chapman: 287 (t), 290 (t), 350,

Chikar Studio: 228 (t)

Christie's Images: 238, 269, 272, 283 (b), 345, 347, 348 (c), 351, 355 (b)

William Crozes: 301 (b), 335 (c, b)

ddrum.com: 319

ERP Music: 205 (b)

Fender Musical Instruments Corporation: 302 (b), 324 (t), 325 (t)

Foundry Arts: 27, 58 (b), 63 (t), 315 (t), 317 (c), 339 (b), 341 (t, b), 342 (t), 343 (b), 386, 387, 388, 389, 390, 391, 392, 393, 394 (c & b), 395, 396, 397

Hammond Suziki: 11 (l), 305, 307 (all)

Dr Kuo Huang Han: 35 (b), 47 (t), 50 (b), 53 (t), 56 (all), 78 (t), 96 (t), 99 (b), 125 (b), 127 (t), 133, 135, 137 (t), 140, 141 (t), 152, 153 (b), 173 (all), 174 (all), 179 (b), 186, 206, 207, 224, 225, 229 (b), 251, 360 (t)

Mark David Hill/hammond-organ.com: 12, 306

Hobgoblin Music: 92 (b), 189 (b), 213 (t)

istock: 4 (all), 5 (r), 6, 8 (r), 11 (r), 13, 20 (t), 22, 23 (t), 24 (b), 25, 30, 37, 40 (t), 43 (t), 45 (b), 46 (t), 51 (all), 54 (all), 60, 63 (b), 64 (b), 69, 70 (all), 74 (all), 83 (l), 84 (t), 86 (all), 92 (t), 94 (b), 95 (b), 96 (b), 97 (t), 102 (t), 104 (b), 109 (b), 111 (t), 112 (t), 115 (t), 123 (t), 124 (b), 125 (t), 126 (t), 127 (b), 134 (b), 138, 141 (b), 143, 145 (b), 146, 148, 158 (b), 160 (t), 177, 188 (r), 190 (t), 191 (b), 195, 220 (b), 233, 239 (all), 240, 241 (t), 243, 249 (t), 258 (t), 261, 273 (b), 275, 276 (b), 278 (t), 280 (all), 282, 288, 289 (t), 290 (b), 291, 292, 296, 297 (b), 303, 336, 343 (t), 348 (t), 353 (b), 357 (t), 365, 368, 381, 394 (t)

Lebrecht: 26 (all), 29 (t), 31, 32 (b), 34 (b), 41 (b), 43 (b), 44, 46 (b), 52, 55, 58 (t), 62, 64 (t), 67, 68 (b), 71 (t), 72 (t), 75, 79 (b), 80 (b), 82 (all), 83 (r), 84 (b), 85 (b), 88, 89 (t), 90, 91, 97 (b), 98, 99 (t), 100, 101, 102 (b), 103, 105, 106, 107 (all), 109 (t), 110, 112 (b), 113, 114, 115 (b), 117, 118, 119, 120 (b), 121, 122, 123 (b), 128 (b), 130 (b), 137 (b), 139, 144, 147 (all), 149 (all), 150, 151, 154 (t), 156 (b), 158 (t), 159, 160 (b), 162 (all), 163 (t), 164, 165, 166, 167, 168, 169 (b), 175 (t), 181, 183, 184 (b), 187 (b), 192, 193, 197, 199 (b), 200 (all), 201, 202 (t), 208 (b), 211 (all), 212, 216, 218, 219 (all), 226, 231 (all), 234, 235, 236 (t), 237 (all), 242, 244, 245 (t), 246 (t), 247, 252, 253, 255, 256, 257 (t), 263, 264 (t), 266, 267, 268, 271, 273 (t), 274, 276 (t), 279, 281, 283 (t), 285, 286, 287 (b), 289 (b), 293, 295, 299, 304, 331, 333, 352 (r), 366 (all), 369 (all), 370, 372, 374, 375, 376, 377, 378, 379, 380, 383

Mark Lee: 7 (l), 326 (all)

Line 6: 7 (r), 328

MoogArchives.com: 313 (t)

Moog Music Inc.: 313 (b)

Museum of Art and Archeology of the University of Antananarivo, Madagascar: 136 (r)

National Library of Canada: 312

Ordongos: 48, 155

photodisc/Getty Images: 5 (l), 8 (l), 9, 14 (all), 20 (b), 21 (all), 23 (b), 24 (t), 28, 32, 33 (t), 34 (t), 35 (t), 36, 38, 40 (b), 42 (all), 45 (t), 49 (c, b), 53 (b), 57, 65 (all), 66 (b), 68 (t), 71 (b), 73, 76 (all), 77 (b), 78 (c), 79 (t, c), 80 (t), 81, 87 (b), 89 (b), 93 (all), 94 (t), 95 (t), 104 (t), 108, 111 (b), 116, 120 (t), 126 (b), 128 (t), 130 (t), 134 (t), 141 (b), 145 (t), 156 (t), 157, 161 (all), 169 (t), 170, 171 (all), 172, 176, 180 (b), 184 (t), 187 (t), 188 (l), 190 (b), 191 (t), 194 (all), 196 (top), 204 (t), 210, 214 (t), 215, 220 (t), 221, 222, 223 (t), 228 (b), 230, 241 (b), 245 (b), 246 (b), 248, 249 (b), 257 (b), 258 (b), 259 (all), 260 (t), 265, 277, 278 (b), 284, 297 (t), 298, 300 (all), 301 (t), 302, 318, 327, 330, 352 (t), 352 (bl), 353 (t), 354 (b), 355 (t), 356 (all), 357 (b), 358, 360 (b), 361, 390 (tr), 393 (t), 393 (b), 397 (r)

Adrian Pingstone: 185

Sylvia Pitcher Photo Library: 364

Prism Media Products Ltd: 316

D. H. Ramsey Library: 232

Redferns: Richard E. Aaron: 309 (t); Michael Ochs Archives: 77 (l); Paul Bergen: 324 (b); Ian Dickson: 61; David Warner Ellis: 129; Ron Howard: 310; Mick Hutson: 99 (c), 131; Simon King: 337 (b); Elliott Landy: 204 (b); Hayley Madden: 213 (b), 217 (r), 329; Leon Morris: 78 (b); Bernd Muller: 317 (b); Odile Noel: 334, 340; David Redfern: 39, 85 (t), 325 (b); Ebet Roberts: 59 (b), 214 (b), 337 (t), 339 (t)

Jan Redmood: 264 (b)

Roland Corporation: 341 (c)

Saxpix: 163 (b)

John Hornby Skewes & Co. Ltd.: 323 (all)

S.I.N.: Melanie Cox: 373 (b); Martyn Goodacre: 315 (b); Anna Meuer: 373 (t)

Soundbeam Project: 335 (t)

Chris Stock: 41 (t), 87 (t), 359

Topfoto: 367, 371

Yamaha Corporation of Japan: 314 (t), 322

Yamaha-Kemble Music (UK) Ltd: 124 (t)

Zamburu: 49 (t), 66 (t)

Musical Instruments Handbook

FURTHER READING

Abrahev, Bozhidar, *The Illustrated Encyclopedia of Musical Instruments*, Konemann, 2000

Aikin, Jim, *Software Synthesizers: The Definitive Guide to Virtual Musical Instruments*, Backbeat Books, 2003

Baines, Anthony, *Woodwind Instruments and their History*, Dover Publications, 1991

Burgess, Geoffrey and Bruce D. Haynes, *The Oboe*, Yale University Press, 2004

Campbell, Murray et al., *Musical Instruments: History, Technology, and Performance of Instruments in Western Music*, Oxford University Press, 2004

Coombes, Clyde F., *Electronic Instrument Handbook*, McGraw-Hill Professional, 1999

Dearling, Robert (Ed.), *The Illustrated Encyclopedia of Musical Instruments*, Macmillan Publishing, 1996

Dearling, Robert, *Keyboard Instruments and Ensembles*, Chelsea House Publications, 2000

Dearling, Robert, *Stringed Instruments*, Chelsea House Publications, 2000

Faber, Tony, *Stradivari's Genius: Five Violins, One Cello, and Three Centuries of Enduring Perfection*, Random House, 2005

Herbert, Trevor (Ed.), *The Cambridge Companion to Brass Instruments*, Cambridge University Press, 1997

Kipnis, Igor, *The Harpsichord and Clavichord: An Encyclopedia*, Routledge, 2006

Kolneder, Walter, *The Amadeus Book of the Violin: Construction, History and Music*, Amadeus Press, 2003

Maffit, Rocky, *Rhythm and Beauty: The Art of Percussion*, Watson-Guptill Publications, 1999

Nelson, Sheila M., *The Violin and Viola: History, Structure, Techniques*, Dover Publications, 2003

Oling, Bert and Heinz Wallisch, *The Complete Musical Instruments Encyclopedia*, Book Sales, 2003

Rault, Lucie, *Musical Instruments: Traditions and Craftsmanship from Prehistory to the Present*, Harry N. Abrams, 2000

Musical Instruments Handbook

Segell, Michael, *The Devil's Horn: The Story of the Saxophone, from Noise Novelty to King of Cool*, Farrar, Straus and Giroux, 2005

Siepmann, Jeremy, *The Piano: The Complete Illustrated Guide to the World's Most Popular Musical Instrument*, Carlton Books, 2001

Silvela, Zdenko, *A New History of Violin Playing: The Vibrato and Lambert Massart's Revolutionary Discovery*, Universal Publishers, 2001

Thrasher, Alan R., *Chinese Musical Instruments*, Oxford University Press, 2001

Wade-Matthews, Max, *Musical Instruments*, Lorenz Books, 2003

Wade-Matthews, Max, *The World Encyclopedia of Musical Instruments*, Lorenz Books, 2000

Waitzman, Mimi S. and Terence R. Charlston, *Early Keyboard Instruments*, National Trust, 2003

USEFUL WEBSITES

www.si.umich.edu/CHICO/instrument This site is based on the Stearns Collection at the University of Michigan, which, although not exhaustive, features instruments from around the world.

www.windworld.com Site dedicated to unusual musical instruments, including how to make some world instruments.

www.music.ed.ac.uk/euchmi/cimcim Homepage of the International Committee of Musical Instrument Museums and Collections.

www.playmusic.org A good site for kids that provides information about playing techniques, created by the American Symphony Orchestra League.

www.imit.org.uk Homepage of the Institute of Musical Instrument Technology, an organization designed to advance musical instrument technology through the exchange of ideas and information.

www.amis.org The American Musical Instrument Society website contains information about all aspects of the history, design, construction and restoration of instruments from many periods and cultures.

Musical Instruments Handbook

INDEX

Musical Instruments Handbook

Musical Instruments Handbook

Musical Instruments Handbook

Musical Instruments Handbook

INDEX

Musical Instruments Handbook